Contents

Business Education and Training:
A Value-Laden Process

Volume III:
Instilling Values in the
Educational Process

Editor
Samuel M. Natale

Assistant Editor
Mark B. Fenton

University P
Lanham • Ne

Oxford University Centre
ilues
Business

Copyright © 1997 by
University Press of America,® Inc.
4720 Boston Way
Lanham, Maryland 20706

3 Henrietta Street
London, WC2E 8LU England

Copublished by arrangement with Oxford Centre for the Study of
Values in Education and Business

Library of Congress Cataloging-in-Publication Data

Business education and training : a value-laden process / editor, Samuel
M. Natale, assistant editor, Mark B. Fenton.
p.   cm.
Includes bibliographical references.
Contents: v. 1. Education and value conflict--v. 2. The developing
professional : maintaining values in "practical" training--v. 3.
Instilling values in the educational process.
1. Professional education--Moral and ethical aspects. 2. Professional
employees--Training of. 3. Moral education. I. Natale, Samuel M. II.
Fenton, Mark B.
LC1059.B87 1996   378'.013--dc20   96-41779 CIP

ISBN 0-7618-0572-9 (v.3: cloth: alk. ppr.)
ISBN 0-7618-0573-7 (v.3: pbk: alk. ppr.)

Chapter One

Ethics and the Development of Work: The Central Maintenance Computer Case

Harry Hummels

Introduction

Some years ago I started doing research in business ethics — to be more specific in organizational ethics — and soon found out that (ethical) reflection was of some concern to managers when making policies, but not when implementing them. 'Bottom line mentality' was prevailing. In 1991 KLM Royal Dutch Airlines gave me the opportunity to look deeper into this matter. I was able to study a process of technological change — the introduction of an onboard maintenance computer in the newest version of Boeing's successful 747, the 747-400. Compared to its predecessors this was a totally different aircraft from a technological point of view. Instead of using analogic technology, Boeing chose to digitalize it. Introducing the Central Maintenance Computer System (CMCS) was one of the major innovations. The questions that came to mind were not so much related to the development of the 747-400, or 744 as it is usually indicated. The process of development was executed fairly autonomous by the constructor. What sprang to mind, however, were questions concerning the notions of — distributive and procedural — justice that could be detected during the process of introduction of the CMCS and in the preparation phase:

- Did management anticipate the introduction of the technological innovation?

- How did it prepare the ground engineers (e.g., training, discussing the changes in the profile of the profession, etc.)?
- What consequences does the new technology have for aviation engineering?
- What kind of problems did occur during the introduction?
- How did management respond to these?

In this paper I will go into the activities of a ground engineer and into the conflicts that resulted from the process of the technological change. I will address the following aspects:

1) First I will shortly introduce the organization: KLM Royal Dutch Airlines' Business Unit Line Maintenance.
2) Second I will characterize the maintenance process, that is the process which starts just before the airplane arrives and ends with the following dispatch or with the completion of the necessary and planned maintenance. I will also deal with the changes in the work process as a result of the recent introduction of a new technological means: the Central Maintenance Computer System.
3) And third, I will address an ethical issue that receives very little attention in the process of technological and organizational development.

But first a short outline of the organization.

Organization and Goals

KLM Royal Dutch Airlines is very well known for its quality and — more over — for the way it is communicating this message. In its commercials the company presents itself as a beautiful swan with an aura of grace, of strength, of pride and of dignity. And above all: of survival in a world where many species are endangered. The swan is landing safely.

Commercials do tend, however, to show a better world than the one that is experienced in real life. KLM still has a good reputation when it comes to quality in general and technical quality in particular, but — at present — it takes a lot of everyone concerned to uphold the image. Especially within the Business Unit Line Maintenance management and workers are confronted with serious challenges.

Line Maintenance deals with technical deficiencies during the turnaround and the process takes place at Schiphol Center. It is a fault-clearing organization. A few month ago the business unit decided that her performance had to meet the following criteria:

- the technical operational control over and preparing of KLM aircraft world-wide, with a punctuality and service level previously agreed on at a competitive cost level,
- the technical preparing of non-KLM aircraft at Schiphol with a punctuality and service level previously agreed on at a competitive cost level.

These goals have to be met by the operational units such as the Production Unit Line Maintenance.

As a side-step I like to remark that these goals are not widely accepted in the organization. Although nobody really obstructs the execution of the goals it is interesting to see that the manager of the Production Unit Line Maintenance has amended the goals fundamentally.[1] I now turn to the work process within this Production Unit.

Maintenance: The Work Process

The maintenance process starts just before the airplane comes in and ends with the following dispatch. It represents the necessary steps the ground engineers have to take during the turnaround. These steps are:

1) preparation,
2) inspection of the aircraft,
3) if necessary, troubleshooting,
4) final check,
5) release of the aircraft, and
6) administration.

This however is a limited definition of the maintenance process. The management of the business unit uses a much more comprehensive definition. In its view the process already starts during the previous cycle with the planning of and the preparation for the next turnaround. Or even better: it is a process that starts after the aircraft has been delivered by the constructor and stops when the plane is no longer operational (either because it is being inspected in the hangars or it is no longer used by Flight Operations).

At the moment I am only concerned with the process that starts with the delivery of the Bill of Work and the necessary work preparations by the ground engineer. After his preparations the mechanical ground engineer takes care of the arriving aircraft. The wheel blocks have to be placed in position and with his head-set he welcomes the crew. This procedure gives the engineer also the opportunity to hear about serious problems during the flight leg. When all this is set, the engineer and a colleague execute the Platform-inspection.

Having finished their work on the platform the engineers proceed by inspecting the logbooks and consulting the Central Maintenance Computer System. Then the trouble-shooting procedure starts. The most important steps in this process are:

- the analysis of the problem,
- the reporting of the technical status to the Line Maintenance Officer,
- the actual repair of the broken-down system, and
- the testing of this system.

The engineers finish their trouble-shooting 30 minutes before departure. That's the beginning of the stand-by period. During this period an engineer does not take up any new maintenance activity unless it concerns a NO-GO. That is, unless it concerns a fault that prohibits the captain to fly. After the final check the ground engineer gives his technical clearance and the aircraft can be pushed to the runway. The maintenance process ends with the completion of the necessary administrative work.

The Central Maintenance Computer System has had a vast impact on the transformation and meaning of labour. In the following I would like to discuss:

- the definition of the system,
- its introduction,
- the way it works, and
- its consequences.

Central Maintenance Computer System

Definition and Introduction

- The central maintenance computer system encompasses all major avionics, electrical and electro-mechanical systems.
- The cmcs is responsible for monitoring the integrity of input systems as well as performing tests on the input systems.
- The cmcs collects and displays information on failed components, stores the information in a fault history, and provides a centralized location for access to maintenance data.

The Boeing 744 is a fairly new aircraft. It was delivered to KLM as the first user on this continent in the spring of 1989. To maintain the aircraft properly all engineers — ground engineers, maintenance engineers, central engineers — had to be instructed. So that is why the constructor started with a special course in 1988. The course didn't meet the expectations. 'It was a complete disaster', as one ground engineer said, whereas another remarked: 'That course turned out to be a complete howl. In five weeks we had to master the aircraft, which was of course impossible.' Boeing also sent experienced engineers to Schiphol to instruct and train the KLM engineers. It was soon felt, however, that this training on the job was ineffective. 'The American engineers didn't train us, they more or less took over', one could regularly hear engineers complain.

After the introduction other problems became manifest. In the first place there was this alarming amount of nuisance messages — or high-frequency messages as they are called nowadays. Nuisance messages do not refer to aircraft system faults but to software-errors. Since the management was not willing to lessen the punctuality rate, engineers felt they had no other choice then to give their own interpretation of the rules and procedures. What this meant for the use of the computer I will discuss after I have explained the way the Central Maintenance Computer works and the way the engineers have to go about using the computer.

Working Procedures

The first step in the procedure is to look for flight deck effects. To put it simple, flight deck effects are anomalies, irregularities. The irregularities are identified and recorded either by the crew — in the logbooks — or by the CMCS. These messages are input to a trouble-shooting procedure. To find the message in the CMCS the ground engineer selects *Present Leg Faults* in the CMCS-menu. Present leg faults shows the flight deck effects that have occurred during the previous flight. Here a flight deck effect is indicated and subsequently elaborated on the following pages. What the engineer has to do is to record the (eight digit) fault code and also — if present — the (five digit) CMCS message number and ATA-chapter[2] numbers. He then turns to the *Fault Code Index*. Here the engineer finds which fault might have caused the flight deck effect, but usually he does not find a work around procedure. So the next thing he does is to find the CMCS message in the *CMCS Message Index*. The engineer finally finds the corrective action to take. Having finished this time consuming procedure the engineer can start with the actual maintenance — at last. In most cases this implies a careful analysis of the aircraft system itself, tinkering, repairing the system or installing spares, testing it to ensure that the flight deck effect is gone, and closing the system — and the aircraft.

During the first year after the introduction of the B 744 and its CMCS nobody worked according to the procedure I just described. In the first place, because no one ever told them properly. It took two years before (another) special Boeing-delegation — which consisted of a couple of smooth talking coaches who were going to tell the engineers how to do maintenance — came to Schiphol. It was a meeting which would rank high on the hallelujah-scale.

These guys had seen the light, and so would the engineers if they just did what they were told.

In the second place — as I already mentioned above — the maintenance process was totally disrupted by the enormous amount of nuisance messages: more than 400 fault messages — out of a total of 7000 — did not refer to real system-faults. In the first years no one really trusted the CMCS, because of this large number of nuisance messages. What they did was the following:

1) First the engineer erased the message from the CMCS screen. If the message did not return it was probably not correlated to a fault so the engineer figured. He would do nothing. The matter was settled.

2) Second, if the message did return the engineer would pull the circuit-breaker. A circuit-breaker can be compared to a fuse. When disconnected it shuts down the system. If a fault reappeared — having turned the system on again — it became more likely that the message would correspond to a real fault. If it didn't, again the matter was settled.

By introducing these two steps the engineers have prevented a total breakdown of KLM flight operations. Had they worked according to the official procedures, no 747-400 would have departed just in time, or even just to late. They all would have been dispatched much to late, if they would have left the airport at all.[3] Having made these critical remarks I will now pay attention to the consequences of the CMCS-introduction.

Consequences

Compared to other aircrafts — like the Boeing 747-300 — the flight crew has been reduced: the flight engineer has been replaced by the CMCS. This very tangible result is not the only alteration the computer has caused. Other changes are:

- much of the experience and the knowledge of the ground engineer is being ignored by the new fault detection procedure,
- a shift in dependency has occurred: the engineer has become more dependent on the computer an less on his colleagues,
- a shift in orientation has come to the fore: the engineer has to safeguard a timely dispatch. This means that work has to be deferred because there is not enough time to do the job.
- there is a growing need for avionics-based knowledge and experience at the expense of mechanical knowledge and experience.

In the remaining part of this paper I will reflect on the process of labor and the changes ground engineers are confronted with.

Work

Hannah Arendt has characterized the job an engineer does as labour. Labour has two functions she says. The first is to produce the necessary goods for life, or in her own words: labour produces life. The other function refers to the job ground engineers do, that is: the fight against deterioration. Aircrafts are commodities that are not being consumed instantly. But aircrafts are affected by nature — for instance rust — and by the use that passengers and personnel make of it. Its condition has to be monitored carefully and defects have to be repaired. So maintenance is a necessary task, although it is not a heroic one. More and more it is becoming just a job. In the recent past this was different. A ground engineer was a technician with narrowly defined skills and with a recognized body of knowledge. He had his professional pride and was very keen on delivering high standard technical quality. Most of the engineers were driven by 'a kind of lunacy', as one of them explained their motivation. They really want to know the smallest technical detail.

But it's not only technicality that came. With it came — and to some extent still comes — automatically the autonomy of the professional. When the engineer is on the platform he is the ruler of the game. The CMCS however makes them more dependent. The following quotations do illustrate the shift within the core of their profession:

> We don't need a lot of technical thinking anymore.

> In the beginning the computer is some kind of toy. However, routine takes over very quickly.

> Work has become just a matter of routine. We only push buttons and it is hardly necessary anymore to know a lot about some details.

> The computer tells you which system broke down. Therefore you become less dependent on others but more dependent on the computer.

For some engineers the opposite is also true: you become more independent because you and your computer are responsible for doing a good job. You are no longer dependent anymore on the flight engineer, your colleagues, and your boss.[4] But it's not only this kind of independency that makes the computer attractive:

The computer means a challenge and an adequate tool. You get to know much more information about aircraft systems and faults.

The opportunity and necessity to know a little about a lot of technical aspects is increased.

Running a ground test is possible. You instantly know if the system works.

Nowadays, as the manager of the Production Unit Line Maintenance expressed it recently, the organization is going through a major shift toward maintenance activities:

We do not deal in technics, he said. Our business is to deliver a service to our customers and we do that in time.

This means that, in the view of the technicians, the unit no longer is a technical fault-clearing organization. For its operations it is not important that a technical system as such is broken down. It is the severity of the fault — is the captain permitted to fly with it? — which decides wether or not an engineer will take action. This change is also reflected in the values of the various actors in the organization. The next figure shows the differences between managerial values — as I would like to call them — and engineering values

Figure 1   *Values*

Managerial Values	Engineering Values
* quality	* technical quality
* effectivity	* problem-solving
* efficiency	* tinkering
* dispatch and customer orientation	* maintenance and dispatch orientation
* team responsibility	* responsible autonomy

First of all, and most important, there is cost-reduction. This has become, as I see it, an international sport. But other values are also very popular. So engineers have to improve their effectivity, their flexibility and the quality of their performance. This means that they have to be more receptive to the desires of a client. Then there is team responsibility. The engineers are responsible as a team for the timely dispatch of aircraft. Technical quality is not a goal in itself, although a law-based minimum is maintained in order to safeguard a safe and reliable flight. Ground engineers however value different aspects of their work.

In the first place they are technically interested. If things break down they all like to know what caused the trouble. Second, as I mentioned before, the mind of the engineer is set to solve technical problems on the spot. This leads to the third value: tinkering. Tinkering means: repairing systems. It is the core of the profession. This is especially rewarding when the engineer completes a process of trouble-shooting just before departure. This does not mean that he wants serious things to come up just before departure or that he waits until the last minute to start repairing systems. Certainly not. But they find it very satisfying to put things right when the passengers are already on board and the aircraft takes off in time, because of their maintenance. So they do have an orientation toward the customer but it is a mixed one. According to the engineers this implies that management — when deciding — should consider the whole of reality and not only a part of it (that of the customer). It also means that the maintenance process should be organized in a way that leaves the engineers maximum autonomy and maximum responsibility for their own actions.

In the first paragraph I stated five questions:

- Did management anticipate the introduction of the technological innovation?
- How did it prepare the ground engineers (e.g., training, discussing the changes in the profile of the profession, etc.)?
- What consequences does the new technology have for aviation engineering?
- What kind of problems did occur during the introduction?
- How did management respond to these?

In the rest of this paper I have tried to show what it means to be a ground engineer from two different angles: that of the engineer and that of management. I have tried to show the meaning of a major technological innovation in terms of the autonomy of the engineer, his technical knowledge and capacity, his responsibilities, the orientation toward dispatch, etcetera. Also I have pointed out that the consequences of this major innovation are unevenly distributed. The tendency toward delivering just a service to some far away customer goes to the heart of the profession. If this tendency continues or — what is to be expected enhances — the engineer is no longer a technician. His profession is on the edge of being transformed by managers who don't have the slightest idea what it means to be a ground engineer. In being forced to act according to managerial values with instruments that guide his actions — instead of he using it for his own purposes — a lot of engineers feel they have lost autonomy and respectability. They have become technical gigolo's.

Notes

1. After finishing my research I was asked to become a consultant on a temporary basis. In my capacity as consultant the manager of the production unit and I developed a long term vision for the business unit — and the production unit in particular — as well as a mission statement. Vision and statement are both distinct from the goals stated above.
2. ATA is the abbreviation of Air Transport Association and is the international organization that takes care of worldwide standardization of (the registration) of aircraft systems and parts.
3. Of course it was not only the CMCS that caused trouble. Some aircraft systems were (re)new(ed) and still had growing pains. But it was also due to the inaptitude of the management to cope with the situation. It took for instance two years before the special Boeing-delegation came to Schiphol to explain the work around procedure.
4. Elsewhere (Hummels, 1994) I have indicated that the organization is going through a process of organizational change. Regaining control by management is what this development is all about. In other words, it is through organizational change — and not through technological change — that the 'autonomous engineer' is likely to disappear in the near future.

Chapter Two

Too Many Cooks Spoil the Stew — Ethical Preparation of Interdisciplinary Professionals

Vincent F. Maher

This chapter investigates didactic issues attendant to the seemingly unitary professional education of students from a variety of disciplines. Specifically, it discusses the postgraduate preparation of health services administrators who have diverse clinical and non-clinical preparation and the fiduciary conflicts which can result therefore. Can a unitary system of ethics be taught to non-clinical administrators who do not understand the reality of a clinical medical disaster, or, conversely to clinical administrators who deprecate the need to receive payment for medical services rendered from a patient whose insurance carrier is refusing further inpatient or procedural reimbursement? These pressing issues and conflicts are the reality of the contemporary American health care environment and present untold challenges to educators whose responsibility it is to fine tune or in cases, return, individual and professional ethical paradigms. The issues and conflicts are identified and discussed from policy, educational, ethical and contemporary legal (American) perspectives.

The American health care system has been known the world over for its love of bricks and mortar, the high quality of technological applications from the researcher's workbench to the patient's bedside, and its unfettered indulgence of individual needs —perceived or real— and preferences. The wonder of this system in the latter part of this century, particularly since the 1950s and 1960s, has also been the broad availability of these services to all sectors of the population. Coupled with tax supported Federal and State government financial assistance programs including Social Security Disability Insurance, Medicare, Medicaid, the Veterans Administration and others, few people would fall through the cracks of the health care system, at least theoretically. As time went by, particularly in the past ten to fifteen years, it became evident to health care providers that this construct had some significantly sized rents in the bandages. Specifically, as more and more health care facilities turned to governmental agencies to obtain reimbursement of uncompensated medical care services to the tune of millions of dollars per facility per year, it dawned upon governmental bureaucracies that there just might be a problem "out there" somewhere.

In 1991, Bill Clinton successfully ran a campaign for the presidency of the United States predicated upon the reality that 37 million Americans, of a total of 260 million, were chronically "medically indigent" Further, if acute figures were added, e.g., the short term unemployed, this number could reach as many as 65 million people. To be medically indigent means that one can span a spectrum from having no insurance whatsoever to having some but not enough— for example having sufficient insurance to cover "routine" health procedures but no coverage for catastrophic (expensive) medical disasters such as an episode of spectic shock requiring a prolonged hospitalization or a significant myocardial infarction which requires medical intervention in the nature of coronary artery bypass graft surgery or transcutaneaus coronary balloon angioplasty, or a cancer which requires expensive treatment in order to prolong or to save a life. Disturbingly, the American population was also hit square in the face that many of its children were unimmunized, hungry, homeless, abused, and illiterate.

As most people are aware, Mr. Clinton, and other individuals seeking elected office also bearing the banner of health care reform, were swept into office in significant victories throughout the country. Ironically, that very same tidal wave that carried Messers. Clinton et al to office, also refused for a second, unanticipated hit eighteen months later as evidenced both by the resounding failure of the Clinton administration sponsored Health Security Act of 1993 to pass Congressional muster, and the return of a Republican party majority to the Congress for the first time in forty years.

The most pressing issue which evidences itself to those familiar with the American health care system is that it is huge. It serves a multinational multiethnic and multicultural population unlike any other in the world. It has also developed into an unwieldy administrative right. Did this occur overnight? No. The only thing that seems to occur overnight on a corporate level is express mail. What has occurred is a broadened perception by the American public, fueled by personal and corporate economic strain that the system is severely stressed and unable to meet the demands placed upon it. In order to solve this dilemma, the industry relies upon the services of health care administrators. These are people who have or not as the case may be, a clinical background coupled, or not, with formal business skills acquired at the post graduate level in a university. The problem for post graduate educators at this level is trying to balance the experience of individuals who lack either the clinical or business skills with the need to impart these same skills.

Until recent years there was little conflict regarding the postgraduate preparation of health care professionals. Specifically, clinicians were taught that they could do essentially whatever they wanted for a patient and then some in order to effect a desired therapeutic goal or outcome. The bills would be paid by third party payers on a cost basis. Administrators were taught that the secret to running a successful health care organization was this: keep your clinicians happy and the rest will follow. The economy was essentially healthy, the cost of medical interventions was indemnified by unquestioned direct or third party payment and the government would, on an annual basis, close hospital operating deficits fueled by the provision of care to the medically indigent through the direct infusion of CASH.

Medical education flourished. Research programs strode unchecked into the unknown. Technology enabled patients to be prodded, probed and pushed to limits never before dreamed of outside the parameters of scientific fiction novels. Bricks and mortar evolved into glass and steel, high technology temples to which the public flocked seeking immortality or at least a few more years. Incomes of providers spawned a class of the nouveau riche which the public tolerated and at times even revered. Administrators and policy pundits looked upon all of this and saw that it was good. Occasional calls to fiscal responsibility and spending restraints by political and economic analysts were dismissed as the politicized ratings of the newspapers. Yes, life was good.

In the late 1960s, a group of California businessmen began creating private for profit health care delivery systems which promised low cost premiums for members who would be assured in return of protocol driven primary, no frills, medical care. These entities known as health maintenance organizations, gained ground slowly but steadily. Federal law, signed by Richard Nixon in 1972 encouraged the development of such entities in an effort both to bring spiraling health care costs under control easily and gradually and to improve access to the system without popping the bubble of the existing system.

Favorable economic climates coupled with little regulatory control spurred the growth of these entities until the time actually came that there were dozens of HMOs which enrolled hundreds to thousands of people. These people, formerly known as patients or clients, were now referred to as "covered" or "captured" lives. Private practice physicians began to see long term patients leaving their practices for those of other physicians who were panel members (individuals who agreed to be paid by negotiated and predetermined fixed fee structures usually lower than market rates, in return for volume) of the HMO. Most providers, administrators and organizations saw this trend but reacted in a surprising (or not so surprising) way, after a fashion. Rather than sensing a change of the regional financial climate, they took turns sticking their heads into the sand. "After all," they reasoned, "if we can't see this then it wouldn't happen." While buried, the upstart HMOs kept up the advance and leapt beyond the retaining walls of the California Rockies to major US cities where they sold their wares and took control of market share formerly controlled by large indemnity based concerns and only one or two HMOs.

By the time the providers emerged from the sand, the HMOs had made significant inroads and, unlike the HUNS turned from the gates of Rome, there was no one champion to ride forth in an effort to preserve the status quo. Unbeknownst to the old guard, life would never be the same again.

The first health care officials to recognize this were those responsible for facility financial affairs when they saw that invoices for uncompensated care were left by the government as due and owing. Further they saw that bills for medical tests, procedures and interventions were being paid only in part at the behest of utilization review specialists, employed by the insurers, who deemed interventions to be necessary, excessive or even unnecessary. At this juncture the COOs were apprised of the problem. The COOs declared, "We need to make it better. Do something." Life went on as it always had because the providers refused to be told what to do by "those guys." (Those guys being the HMOs, the insurers, and the suits.) Result operating deficits once manageable and recouped from alternate sources such as pass through costs, endowments and charitable bequests, corporate money and the like, began to climb to unheard of levels. Hospitals became bankrupt and either recovered or closed. Elsewhere, facilities with teeming, full service staffs looked at the empty beds and then at the market and declared "What we need to lure back patients are more amenities, more specialists and boutique medicine such as headache, low back or executive health care centers. The people need this and will be only too happy to pay for it." Indeed the people did like it and tried it as long as the insurers paid the bills. That didn't last long. The response of the health care industry, once again, was to dig a hole and bury its corporate head in the sand. The HMOs, now reorganized, larger and stronger through mergers and acquisitions and well past the point of no return, were here to stay.

Those who bothered to peek from their sandy lairs, however, posited that this couldn't be so bad. After all they had survived Medicaid, Medicare and DRGs (fees paid upon a diagnostic related groups paradigm). "Managed care is simply a new reimbursement or financing scheme we have to get used to" they thought. Close enough but not quite so in its entirety.

Insightful health care providers realized that managed care portended not only an economic revolution in the health care industry but also ultimately of American society. Positioning themselves as best they could they either joined multiple HMOs as panel members, built large volume private practices, joined forces with similarly minded clinicians, formed multiprovider and often multi-specialty large group/large volume practices, hired a business manager and garnered market share. Their colleagues of the uninsightful old guard said,

"This'll pass and besides, my patients are loyal. I've nothing to worry about." Meanwhile, their self-paying and insured patients of many years were departing one by one for HMO providers who accepted full payment for services rendered with or without a minimal copayment from the patient. Time passed and the physicians who said "this'll pass" found themselves in a professional and financial bind and thereupon lined up in droves to join provider networks of HMOs only to find not infrequently that the specialist panels were closed and the general practice panels were virtually full. It dawned upon the non-panel members that they were in deep trouble and, worse, there was and is little that they can do to rectify the situation.

Meanwhile, administrators were learning that the new financial conditions came loaded with regulations, conditions and a new cadre of professionals— utilization review experts. These individuals exist within HMOs for the sole purpose of ascertaining appropriateness of medical therapeutics in a given situation. For example, is the GP handling as much of any given problem as possible? Are only essential specific and least costly diagnostic procedures being used? Are patients being kept out of hospitals wherever and whenever possible? Are generic instead of name brand drugs being prescribed and, if a less expensive drug will do the job, is it being used instead of a more expensive agent? A business person looking at this can only agree that this makes strong business sense. Providers are less enthusiastic because data gleaned from medical records by these utilization experts are tallied provider by provider and are scored to ascertain conformity with HMO practice guidelines which may in fact differ from guidelines, not standards, of practice proffered by medical specialty boards, and/or the professional literature, and/or local professional practices.

Should the provider find him/herself with a low score in this regard, s/he receives a warning in the form of a performance evaluation in which his/her practice is compared to 1) HMO guidelines and 2) the practice utilization of his/ her colleagues. Continued overutilization of resources leads to disempanelling, or termination, of the provider from the HMO. This leaves the provider in a position which s/he never envisioned. At worst s/he's unemployed, at best s/ he's traded in the current model upscale vehicle for a used popular sedan. As this occurs more frequently, empanelled physicians become even more scrupulous in their practice and those who are left out become a vocal source of unrest. Further, the once friendly or tolerant relations between the providers and "the suits" has been destroyed as each group views the other as the constant source of personal and professional disquietude or chaos. What makes this scenario worse yet is information which is becoming readily available to all. "The suits" are earning phenomenal salaries, the HMOs are posting incredible fiscal year end profits in the millions and even billions of dollars, and patients are feeling short changed and disempowered. The valid perception that these profits are also at the expense of provider salaries and of complete patient services is contributing to the already boiling pot.

The classrooms, where professors also once narrowly specialized, are mandated by industry and student demand, to provide insight, guidance, theory, breadth and most importantly, professional applications for this new milieu. This is one in which high cost outright hostile takeover M & A (mergers and acquisitions) have given way to economically conservative and managerially radical R & R (re-engineering and redistribution) and network cooptition. (Cooptition is a word coined by our Weintraub of the Northern Metropolitan Health Association (NY), is any activity in which various interests compete on the one hand and cooperate on the other hand to achieve a desired goal. An example is to cooperate by non-repetition of specialty services or purchasing efforts, and to compete in efforts to gain or retain market share through the development of centers of excellence.)

The professor's task is to explain the new market conditions to clinical and nonclinical providers alike and to provide both a theory and application base which can be brought into practice. The goal, simple or not, is to help the warring factions to identify and to hopefully understand the others' needs and professional perspectives, including areas in which there is little likelihood for compromise.

This is accomplished in a variety of ways utilized by this writer. First and foremost, the tension must be recognized, identified, and articulated from the very first introductory course until the point of degree termination. In class, various views must be put forth on any given issue at all times.

Reading assignments must reflect this diversity whenever possible. Essential reading materials must be analyzed by the student first in a fashion that acknowledges their own professional bias and then in a fashion which is diametrically opposed to their "natural" position. This exercise can be done in a written point/counterpoint or as a simulation, oral or written, in which a case is presented by the professor, roles which reflect the panoply of players and interests are randomly assigned to the students by the professor, and the case is then analyzed in accord with the assigned role. Findings are presented in the form of a roundtable or a mock committee or board meeting. The professor must be a facile interrogator and polemicist at ease both with Socratic method and with rapidly shifting positions initiated either by the students or by the professor—which prompt issue identification, critical thinking, argument problem solving, and resolution. The professors agenda, in addition to providing the theoretical constructs and fundamental principles involved in a particular topic, must include the means to enable the students to not only hear a differing opinion but to interiorize and formulate responses to that position through the simulation process.

In a particular exercise involving financial reimbursement of institutions for services rendered, the situation is presented that the organization must downsize through staff cuts which can be made in any area. In the exercise, clinicians are assigned non-clinical roles and vice versa. The end point of the exercise is essentially moot. What is of greatest import is the ability of the various parties and interests to understand the issue from a perspective which is not naturally theirs, and to understand that there are unifying variables through which decisions can be made at an organizational level; of course information can enter the discussions at any point. For example, in this situation wherein staff are to be identified for layoffs due to budget cuts and institutional operating losses, a variable can be introduced in which disclosure is made of executive level salary and benefit increases for recent and current years when the remainder of the institutional employees have had their salaries frozen and benefits reduced or restructured and positions eliminated through attrition or through active layoffs.

When ethical paradigms are analyzed, the professor often encounters a nose to nose conflict between clinically oriented clinicians versus normatively based nonclinicians. The conflict which arises is relatively easy to anticipate simply because clinical professionals operate from a perspective in which the patient is entitled to the entire menu of services and goods in an effort to preserve or prolong life and the quality thereof, whereas normatively based nonclinicians function under an agenda of externally imposed and monitored rules in which parameters are neither permeable nor negotiable. Specifically, a failure on the part of a non-clinician to demonstrate compliance with a predetermined clinical protocol or pathway means that the institution will not be compensated at all or will be compensated at a lesser level for services rendered.

A second example of this is as follows. Recently the American College of Obstetricians and Gynecologists has recommended that a pregnant individual be given two routine sonograms during the course of the pregnancy: one at the beginning and the other at or around the 28th week. Managed care companies will pay for only one (usually the first) unless the second is absolutely indicated: Note that this does not prevent the patient from having one, rather it means that the managed care entity will pay for only one. A clinician cannot say that a patient needs it (even at a stretch) in order to save the patient some money because a utilization review expert is assessing and monitoring the patient's records and thereby the clinician's practice. The fallout of such practices is that the previously ignored but rampant classism in American medicine in becoming even more pronounced. The provision of clinical services will be menu and prepayment based rather than empirically or qualitatively or idemnity based.

A third and final example of this difficulty is illustrated by the conflict between operating room personnel and central sterile services over the issue of expensive medical supplies. Not infrequently, medical supplies which are expensive, single use, sterile, disposable items are opened for use by the operating room or special procedure staff for the Physician who then decides for whatever reason not to use the item entirely or to use one of a different size, calibre or configuration. These items, which have never entered a body cavity, must be disposed of because they cannot be resterilized and reused. The reason for this is one of manufacturers' design wherein the product is specifically engineered to be built, packaged, sterilized, and used once. Cleaning and resterilizing weaken the tensile strength of the product, thereby altering its fitness for designated use and in so doing voids any manufacturer's original warranties for the product. Administrators who must pay the bills for these items traditionally shrug their shoulders and mumble "what are we gonna do?" Physicians, when confronted with inappropriate use data, become angry and defensive of their practices and usually rejoinder about how much money they bring to the facility (monies which are now lost through payment for non-usuable equipment). The task of the educator is to provide an environment in which students can analyze the difficult issues involved in this situation, separate the personalities, isolate the turf issues, brainstorm solutions in class, and then take these ideas back to the workplace where they can be implemented.

The reason such discussion has become of paramount importance has been recently underscored in a US Supreme Court decision commonly known as US vs. Alfonso Lopez (115 S. Ct. 1624; 4/26/95). In this non health care related decision, a criminal questioned the "reach" of the federal government into areas arguably reserved to the states' jurisdiction.

In a narrow 5-4 decision, the Rehnquist majority ruled that in the particular situation (carrying a weapon near a school), that the federal agencies, citing the commerce clause, could properly intervene. Legal commentators see this narrow win as an erosion of the unanimous decisions of this nature which prevailed during the administration of FD Roosevelt during which time the federal government's powers were bolstered to unheard of and constitutionally unenvisioned depths. The political airwaves, soon to be supported apparently by the judiciary when the correct case surfaces, will return more power to the individual states as the federal government seeks to simplify itself, to downsize, and to reduce costs.

What this means is that there will be potential shifts in the delivery of essential services, including health care, from a federal to regional and state levels. It is conceivable that in such an environment, the drive to cost containment will cause an alteration in the manner in which health services are rendered, and that there will also be significant state to state variability such as is seen currently with social entitlement programs. If this environment is the direct result of the political, judicial, and economic changes which are at play in the USA, it is the opinion of this writer that post graduate educators will have their hands full for years to come attempting to attenuate the professionally polarizing forces which are likely to occur as a result thereof.

Chapter Three

Value Conflict in "Competence-Based" Training Initiatives

John Halliday

Value conflicts often appear to be unresolvable as if the values that inform the conflict were incommensurable. For example in a recently published paper, Tasker and Packham (1994:150) argue that industrial and educational values are incommensurable and they warn:

> if industrial values are implanted in Universities, they will destroy the academic values on which open intellectual enquiry and the disinterested pursuit of knowledge depend.

I dare say that many of us working in educational institutions of all kinds are sympathetic to this line of argument. It seems as if there is an unresolvable conflict between educators and those managerialistically inclined policy-makers who seek to render educational institutions more 'business-like'. I argue elsewhere (Halliday 1994) that much use of the term 'quality' in educational institutions world-wide is predicated upon what I call the 'factory' or 'service' model of education but that it is hard to see just what the 'products' or 'services' of educational organisation might be. Certainly well-qualified students might be regarded as a kind of product but students are also interested in the experience that they have on the way to qualification. The balance between product and experience is based on a series of value-judgements that cannot be justified by appealing to the ideas of consumer choice, managerial efficiency or effectiveness. The notion of the disinterested pursuit of knowledge is even more problematic for proponents of the 'factory' or 'service' model of education

So it is easy to sympathise with the 'incommensurability of values' thesis put forward by Tasker and Packham. Nevertheless along with Pring (1994:112), I do not believe that there are **necessarily** two distinct sets of values to consider in the cases of industry and education. I suggest that Tasker and Packham's argument may be seen to be the result more of a dissatisfaction with elitism in policy-formation than as a logical feature of evaluative discourse. The excesses of what might be termed the 'commercialisation' of the Education System in the 1980's may be seen as an over-reaction to a naiveté on the part of some liberal educationalists of the 1960's. The idea that increasing public funds would continue to be available without some check on how those funds were spent was as foolish as the idea that all educational funding can be accounted for on the basis of short-term measures of output. Instead it seems to me that there will always be a balance between short term accountability and long term vision in education policy. Moreover I suspect that a similar balance between long and short term considerations informs better industrial policies.

It is not only unhelpful therefore to suggest that industrial and educational values are incommensurable but it may also be incoherent. The point is that business people are also parents, school governors and taxpayers. Some teachers are also business people and all teachers have some idea of how to manage a budget. As Pring (1994:112) points out, there would be no Universities without business and it is hoped that business prospers as a result of the intelligence and skills of the workforce, part of which we might expect to have been developed in Universities and other formally constituted educational institutions.

There is a further reason however why we must reject the 'incommensurability of values' thesis. I argue that the thesis may be seen to be based on a mistaken epistemology known as logical empiricism (Halliday 1990). According to this epistemology there is a world external to us that can be known through our senses, the better we know this world the more efficiently we can move around within it. What we can never know, according to this epistemology is what we ought to do in the world. Thus we get the idea that values are essentially subjective preferences and that policies amount to the collective preferences of an elite. Deconstructionists of various kinds may be seen to trade on this feature of logical empiricism by seeking to unmask the power relations that lead to the formation of policy-making elites. The deconstructionist project is however often open to the charge that it too is just another attempt to manipulate power relations in its favour and no different in epistemological status to the policy-making elite that it seeks to unmask. (Windschuttle 1994)

Since for logical empiricists values are merely expressions of personal preference then there will always be value conflicts which logically are unresolvable according to epistemic criteria and the 'incommensurability' thesis will follow. Practically however conflicts of value might be resolved in two ways although I argue that the second way is in fact dependent on the first. An elite might be appointed that is supposed to have superior insight into what others prefer and that elite might be given sufficient power to enforce its decisions. The second way that logical empiricists might attempt to settle value conflicts is by instituting the idea of an educational market. The 'market' provides the ultimate test for empiricists in that observable preferences are used to 'settle' conflicts of value.

In order to institute a market however it is necessary to have similar items for sale arranged alongside each other. The notion of an occupational competence may be seen to provide the conceptual framework necessary to support the idea of a market in the provision of training (Hyland 1994:30). If it is possible to specify what is to count as competent performance in each occupational area then different 'providers' can compete to determine who can 'deliver' the 'competencies' at the cheapest rate. It would be wrong however to imagine that what has been called 'the competence revolution' (Hyland 1994:1) is driven by consumerism and managerialism alone. Markets in training or education always depend upon some selection of what is to count as education and training. This dependence leads us straight back to elitism in the resolution of value conflict in order to control entry to the training and education market place.

The 'competence revolution' may also be seen to have been driven by egalitarian values such as those that are evident in the attempt to facilitate mobility of labour between states (OECD 1994) and to make professional activities more accessible to public scrutiny (Eraut 1994:5). In addition some Union Leaders have seen the 'revolution' as a means of fixing their members conditions of service and salaries to national and internationally recognised criteria. (Marginson 1993:153) Finally the revolution may be seen as a useful way of evaluating and monitoring training programmes and organisations by providing some notion of training 'output' (E.D. 1992).

In the UK 'competence-based' approaches to training have gained currency in the last few years as a result of the work of the NCVQ. The NCVQ was established in 1986 with a remit to develop a framework of vocational qualifications for each occupational area (NCVQ 1986). The result of this establishment has been a burgeoning list of so-called 'competencies' or more correctly 'elements of competence' which are supposed to represent desired outcomes of training in the form of desirable features of workers of different sorts. The Australian system of VET is not dissimilar to that of the U.K. but in the case of Australia eight levels of competence are specified in contrast to five levels in the U.K. (Marginson 1993:154)

In both countries the notion of competence is broken down into 'elements of competence' which are supposed to be 'evidenced' in terms of performance criteria and range statements. It seems reasonable to assume that in order to satisfy the demand for professional accountability elements, criteria and statements should be understandable by non-professionals and judgments about whether those criteria have been met should be relatively uncontestable. Without the first requirement, there would hardly be any point in trying to set out what professionals are supposed to be doing since we must assume that professionals know what they are doing without the aid of written guidance. Without the second requirement curriculum designers of an empiricist persuasion might imagine that assessment of competence would lead to endless debate since for them values are often 'incommensurable'. The notion of competence has been tied in therefore with some sort of inter-subjective observation of performance that is supposed to avoid the evaluative nature of interpretation. It is not hard to see that the 'competence revolution' is underpinned by the fact/value distinction which is a feature of logical empiricism.

Now of course everyone wants workers who are competent. There is a large gap however between the normal ascription of the term 'competent' to someone and a completed checklist of prescribed 'elements of competence'. D.Carr is one of those who has pointed out that there are important differences between the uses of the terms 'competencies', 'competence' and 'competent'. A competent worker is not necessarily the same worker who has attained a minimum degree of competence, let alone a worker who has attained a number of set competencies. As Carr (1993:18) points out:

> to speak of a given person or performance as competent can be to say *either* that they conform to certain established standards *or* that the performance was executed in an efficient and effective way. ... the second major source of confusion about competence and competencies ... makes the mistake of construing the moral evaluative and motivational aspects of education as separable from or additional to the technical and craft dimensions in a way that wholly distorts the logical, normative and psychological relations between them.

We should remember that someone's personal values may be the most important determinant of their competence. For example it is hard to imagine a competent teacher who was not also enthusiastic, honest and fair. We should also remember that ethical considerations are essential in all occupational areas. This point was recently acknowledged by the ED in the commissioning of research into 'ethics and occupational standards' (ED 1994). While the authors of this report make several suggestions as to how ethical issues should be 'embedded' (E.D.1994:27) within occupational standards it is not clear how such a procedure is going to work out in practice. I am reminded of the so-called 'values base unit' which forms part of the Scottish Vocational Qualification in the occupational area of care (SCOTVEC 1994). This unit could be described as a 'bolt-on extra' (E.D. 1994:43) and the authors of the above-mentioned report warn of the dangers associated with such a description.

Detailed prescription of performance criteria seem to imply that the outcomes and processes of learning are independent of the preferences of individual trainees. The development of trainees' ability imaginatively to think for themselves, to criticise options they are offered and to argue for their own preferences seems to be denied importance by such prescription. I dare say that much of the criticism that has been directed against the framework for vocational qualifications (Smithers 1993) and the low rates of participation in this framework (C.B.I. 1994) might well be related to the conceptual difficulties that arise out of the way that 'competence' is specified within that framework (Hyland 1994).

'Competence' is not a term that somehow 'floats free' of the everyday contexts in which that term is used. The essence of this term cannot be 'captured' in some timeless statement of behavioural performance that is supposed to describe a competent worker. To try to do this seriously distorts and devalues the work that many people do as if their work were somehow equivalent to the most basic movement of materials or the most basic utterance of mimicry. It is true that building, for example, might be described as the movement of materials from one place to another. It matters greatly however just how those materials are moved and just how they are 'stacked' together in the final form. The notion of building as the movement of materials conceals a multitude of distinctions that partly constitute the practice of building. The notion that competence is equivalent to prescribed behaviour conceals a range of contextual subtleties that are embedded within a 'form of life'.

We do not normally describe a person as skillful or competent in a particular practice unless we have some grasp of the practice ourselves and we have observed the person at work over some period of time. Usually we like to see how the person copes with unexpected difficulties, how satisfactory their work is in the longer term. We take into account the opinion of others, the person's ability to justify their actions and so on before we describe them as 'competent'. If curriculum designers and assessment authorities insist that terms such as 'competent' should be applied to people who have interpreted a statement of competence in an approved way then it seems that one of two consequences follow: either those jobs whose entry is controlled in this way are devalued or that form of curriculum design and assessment authority is devalued. Both consequences are undesirable.

Recently there have been moves to take a more holistic view of competencies and to argue that difficulties such as the ones outlined above can be overcome. It is argued by Hager and Beckett (1995:34) for example that performance criteria need not be behavioural in a narrow sense but that:

> valid assessment of attitudinal factors will also be assisted by longitudinal and multiple assessments that gather evidence of attitudes and values from a variety of sources.

Leicester (1994:113) too argues against Hyland that:

> a "Wittgensteinian" approach to mental acts provides one that does emphasise publicly observable behaviour but without a simplistic identification of mental acts with *particular* physical behaviours.

Attractive though these arguments might be and there is much in what Leicester in particular argues, the problem of the unpredictability of particular physical behaviour remains for those charged with the formal assessment of skills and knowledge. We cannot have a highly detailed set of competencies which somehow renders transparent and predictable the behaviour of practitioners. All such 'competencies' will need a set of guidelines for interpretation and further guidelines for the guidelines and so on until we arrive at a form of language that is so abstracted from everyday experience that it is meaningless to most people. When we get to such a state we end up with appointing people to control the interpretation essentially by giving them the power to penalise those who do not accept their sometimes arbitrary view. It is only by working with someone and watching them as a sort of apprentice that one comes to internalise the values that guide an appropriate interpretation of behaviour. The idea that interpretation can somehow be prescribed independently from the practice in question is mistaken.

In my view these problems arise because of the difficulty of trying to equate **prescribed** performances with the ascription 'competent'. It is the observation of people in **unforeseen** circumstances that lead to our description of them as competent. No one believes that a newly trained doctor for example is fully competent or that all older doctors are fully competent. Competent and competence are words that are used in particular cases and the attempt to generalise their use leads to their conflation. In the end all the 'competence' movement does is to push the problem of values back to an assessor and assessee who settle conflicts of value in the particular context that is so often provided by a checklist and box.

Let us consider the oft-quoted example of a driving test to try to illustrate this last point. Such a test is widely believed to be the paradigmatic example of the suitability of 'competence-based' assessment. The examiner is faced with the central question (and it is a moral question) of whether someone should be licensed to drive. This moral question is reduced to or translated into a series of technical questions for the examiner to answer. The examiner may be worried that through informal conversation with the candidate, the candidate appears to have little concern for anyone but himself. Nevertheless let us assume that technically the candidate performed well on all criteria other than the execution of a three point turn. The candidate wants the license urgently in order to pursue his life plans. The point of conflict between them then is on the face of it concerned with the interpretation of the execution of a particular type of turn. At a deeper level however the conflict relates to the primacy of certain values and the difficulty of predicting future behaviour on the basis of selective observation of performance.

No doubt if the examiner were to spend more time with the candidate he would be better placed to resolve his dilemma. Perhaps the candidate was nervous or 'off form' and his informal responses were not typical. The point of this example is that the driving test provides a context for the interpretation of observation of performance but that that context is not necessarily helpful to a resolution of a conflict of value at a deeper level. We have responsibilities to one another that go beyond the superficiality of technique towards moral concerns such as safety on the roads, licensing doctors who have little concern for patients or teachers who are unenthusiastic and so on. Logical empiricism may appear to help us to retreat from our moral responsibilities into the technique of the assessment of performance but that appearance is illusory.

In contrast to logical empiricism many of those who engage in theoretical discourse within the area of philosophy and educational theory are now beginning to work with an alternative epistemology. For such people, researchers working in the post-empiricist tradition (and I am thinking especially of the work of Quine (1971), Popper (1969) and Lakatos (1978)) have shown that there is no once and for all distinction to be drawn between facts and values. Context is all-important in determining whether it is appropriate to claim that a combination of words should be taken more as a fact or a value.

According to this view there is no such thing as a purely technical practice. All practices involve different considerations that nevertheless relate to moral and aesthetic concerns. Following the later Wittgenstein (1953: PI 67) I argue that while all practices do not share one thing in common they share none the less a set of overlapping similarities. This degree of overlap enables people to learn by extending the range of practices in which they are able to engage. The degree of overlap also enables them to communicate with other practitioners and to agree on ways of developing their communal institutions such as schools, colleges and workplaces. Recently Rawls (1993) has developed the idea of an 'overlapping consensus' to explain how we may agree on many things without agreeing on all things. He uses this idea to defend his (1972) theory of justice and to explain the idea of political liberalism in which there is an interplay between individual freedom and mutual dependence.

The notion of family resemblance also allows us to understand how people can be a parent, industrialist and teacher and how an example taken from the world of business may be a useful example in teaching. Moreover the notion also allows us to explain how the incommensurability of values thesis is mistaken and how the thesis leads to the idea that values are imposed or that practices are deformed (MacIntyre 1981:23). In this paper I use the terms training and education interchangeably to mean an induction into practices that are widely believed to be desirable. (Dewey 1916:301) That use is in contrast to the more common use of education as something liberalising and training as something that is purely utilitarian in nature. Dewey of course, sought to break down what he saw as a damaging distinction between the liberal and the vocational.

In common with Taylor (1985:281) and other hermeneutic theorists I hold that the need for interpretation arises out of difficulties in achieving understanding in dialogue between different people. In dialogue evaluative commitments are modified. A kind of 'fusion of horizons' (Gadamer 1975) has to take place for agreement to be achieved. That understanding is achieved not simply by reaffirming either of the participants' prior evaluative commitments, but in a kind of limited consensus negotiated between them. The negotiated consensus is not however unrelated to other attempts to come to agreement. Instead negotiation takes place against a background of some stability in practical attempts to understand.

Gadamer (1975) uses the term 'prejudice' to refer to the values that are embedded within a person's 'horizon of expectation'. For him 'prejudice' is not a pejorative term. Instead the term is meant to indicate the effect of tradition which is manifest in ordinary linguistic use. According to Gadamer, linguistic development takes place as a result of the risking of prejudice in hermeneutic encounters between different interpreters or between interpreter and text. Instead of there being one final interpretation, understanding consists of a series of 'fusions of horizons' in which 'prejudice' is continually being transformed.

The concept of understanding as a fusion of horizons emphasises the temporal nature of conflicts of value. The more that prejudices are risked, the more likely it is that understanding takes place and conflicts of value are resolved. Thus it makes no sense to Gadamer to argue that competence for example, can be decided once and for all in an overwhelmingly important hermeneutic encounter. Instead our understanding of 'competence' is itself located in the stream of an on-going series of fusions of horizons and 'competent' has no more special significance than any other word that we might use to describe someone.

One of the most persistent criticisms of hermeneutic accounts of linguistic development such as the above is that there are no clear grounds for determining which interpretation is to be preferred. After all, it might be claimed, according to the above account the resolutions of value-conflict depends simply on the empirical matter of providing opportunities for one group to talk to another. Examiners and candidates should have the opportunity to meet with equal opportunity to contribute to a discussion and with a symmetry in power relations so that the prejudices of examiners and candidates might both be modified.

This criticism may be met by pointing out that a discussion between candidate and examiner is also guided by the authority of a text, which is provided in this case by the description of the driving test and the criteria for success within it. Moreover examiners have authority in judging whether the criteria have been met by virtue of their superior knowledge. That is not to say however that the interpretation of the text is unproblematic or that conversation between examiner and candidate is inappropriate. As Gadamer (1975:327) points out in connection with legal interpretation the judge ... has to take into account the change in circumstances and hence define afresh the normative function of the law.

Instead it is to note along with R.J. Bernstein (1983) that a shift to an alleged hermeneutic approach to epistemology helps us to move beyond the objectivism of representations of an external reality as described earlier. The move beyond relativism however does not mean that we have to develop some other timeless criterion for demarcating once and for all between preferred and other interpretations. Instead we may encounter narratives against which we are prepared to risk our prejudices in something like the kind of ongoing conversation that Rorty (1980) describes.

Let us return to the example of the driving test to try to illustrate this point. The examiner and candidate are in conflict over the interpretation of the execution of the three point turn. As described above the conflict appears to be based on the execution of a particular technique but at a deeper level the conflict is about the primacy of certain values and the difficulty of predicting future behaviour on the basis of limited observation of prescribed performance. Examiner and candidate meet with their 'prejudices' embedded within 'horizons of expectation'. In the candidate's case the horizon is dominated by future life plans. In the examiner's case the horizon is embedded within some overall idea of the kind of candidate who is likely to be a safe driver. The three point turn is only relevant to a possible fusion of horizons in so far as it provides a means for the examiner to justify his moral decision on grounds that appear merely technical and that avoid what might become endless debate about the moral consequences of failure.

As a practical basis for assessment of driving ability, logical empiricism might seem to have much to commend it though it is not clear that anyone would employ somebody as a driver **only** on the basis of an assessment of technical ability. However in other cases of assessment it is precisely the ability to justify actions which were not prescribed, that might serve as the best form of assessment of suitability for employment. I suggest that the occupational areas of teaching and caring would be paradigmatic examples of this latter sort of occupation and that there are rather more of this latter sort of occupations than the former (if indeed there are any occupations of the former sort).

It might be objected that if we were to give up the empiricist presuppositions upon which the 'competence revolution' is based that we would then have no basis on which to assess how well actions have been justified. Gadamer draws out attention to the appraisal of a musical performance: we have no difficulty judging a musical performance so why asks Gadamer rhetorically should we have difficulty with the idea of judgement generally. The fact that there is some indeterminism about this does not mean that we cannot appeal to the authority that comes about as a result of membership of a tradition and demonstration of superior performance within that tradition. Those who are recognised within a tradition as having superior knowledge and insight are more likely to be able to support their claims than those who are not. It is the consensual norms and intersubjective meanings of the communities of which the conversational partners are members that sustains authority and helps us to avoid the relativistic conclusion.

We have already considered and dismissed the idea that there might be an elite to which we might appeal to adjudicate between competing solutions to moral dilemmas. Instead we have considered the idea that there is a variety of groups with a variety of different interests that nevertheless share what might be called an overlapping consensus about what is valuable. Of course the degree and nature of that consensus changes over time. For example changing one's mind about something depends upon their being a possibility of understanding an alternative and coming to accept that alternative while at the same time coming to reject a previous commitment. If this were not the case then there would simply be groups of people unable to see beyond their prior evaluative commitments and ultimately unable to communicate with the members of other groups. They would have no means of interpreting each other's actions in a common language.

So while individuals and groups may value different things there is sufficient overlap between their values to enable them to interpret each other's actions in ways that are mutually understandable. The 'incommensurability of values' thesis arises out of logical empiricism. Post-empiricists recognise that enthusiasm for and commitment to particular activities are not the result of trying to meet performance criteria. Instead these values are realised more when practitioners devise their own programme paying attention to what they perceive to be 'needs' in particular contexts.

Let us consider the example of a 'competence-based' programme of teacher education (Strathclyde University 1994) to illustrate this point. The course descriptor lists elements of competence such as the following:

- operate within given specifications
- determine individual and group needs
- plan discrete teaching and learning experiences
- select teaching and learning resources
- modify and reproduce teaching and learning materials
- establish positive learning environments

In turn these elements are broken down into performance criteria such as the following:

- appropriate learning outcomes are pursued
- appropriate administrative arrangements are complied with
- planned experiences are structured within given time allocations

Presumably no-one would deny that criteria such as these are necessary though perhaps not sufficient criteria for good teaching practice. There is more than a hint for example in recent *Guidelines for Teacher Training Courses* (SOED 1993) to suggest that reflection, critical appraisal, theorising and understanding might also be important abilities for teachers to acquire. (McPherson 1995:115)

Now even if these latter abilities were included in a list of performance criteria, under current arrangements for 'competence-based training' in the U.K., some form of evidence would need to be compiled to show that criteria such as these had been met. The problem then arises as to what sort of things could count as evidence of, for example, a reflective ability. Certainly we may recognise such an ability in others but not as the result of asking them to provide evidence for us. The ability may be seen to be based more on an appropriate set of personal values than on an ability to perform in a certain way. There are many other instances where the specification of what amounts to a set of values destroys all chance of seeing whether or not someone genuinely holds those values. Yet 'competence-based training' leads teacher educators into the same reduction of the moral into the technical that characterised the driving test example. While teacher educators are busy ticking boxes whenever prescribed behaviour is observed, the notion of teaching as a moral activity (Halliday 1996) is being denied.

We might therefore come to reject the current fashion to talk about the acquisition of knowledge, skills and attitudes as if such acquisition were value-free and disinterested. As the previous argument was meant to show, training is a value-laden activity and some conflict of value is inevitable when the results of training programmes are assessed. The way that people speak, live their lives, their activities interests and so on provide clues about those things that they value. It is rare however that in conversation two conflicting values are expressed directly. It is in the course of working with people that we become aware of differences and that awareness does not necessarily lead to a direct expression of those differences.

There is no one way of separating facts from values or of providing a method for resolving conflicts of value. Instead these problems may be treated as practical problems, the solutions to which are based on the best accounts of the way things are at any particular instance. It is foolish therefore to assume that aim, method and assessment can be distinguished once and for all and that the means may always be justified on the basis of the end. Instead both means and ends are modified in an ongoing way in which the notion of individual practical judgement is central. Hence method, aim and assessment necessarily merge in training.

We need to take far more seriously the idea that people are attracted to and enthusiastic about those things that interest them at a particular time. Such interest and enthusiasm is not prescribable nor controllable by systems of inspection and appraisal which may be circumvented by getting to know the criteria of inspection and appraisal and learning to 'play the game' as it were. People are persuaded to do things differently when they are shown a better way of doing something and their evaluative assumptions are successfully challenged. Yet the language of persuasion and the ethics of cooperation are not generally included in 'competence-based' training policy and practice. Instead performance criteria are presented as if they were definitive statements of the way things must turn out and as if it were obvious how to meet the criteria.

As we have seen values cannot be assessed in this way. Instead there seems no alternative to examining our own evaluative assumptions and engaging in the kind of open debate and persuasion that characterise the best training. Of course such examination and engagement is not easy. Open argument and persuasion are often associated with personal rancour. Therefore the kind of changes that I have advocated in this paper depend upon disagreements not being interpreted as personal dislikes. In public and in private clarity, scepticism, criticism and disagreement may come to be viewed as indications of a genuine concern and liking for someone rather than as indications of hostility or threat. In this way we may argue passionately in favour of our point of view but at the same time recognise the contingency of our passion. The ensuing discussion is informed by a genuine respect for the views of others and a discursive ethos. Empiricism leads us not to value argument and persuasion but instead to value hierarchy and elitism as substitutes for the authority that was supposed to be supplied by the idea of an objective reality.

In this chapter I have argued that logical empiricism pervades the British and Australian systems of 'competence based' training. That epistemology supports the idea that there is an objective reality even though the nature of that reality is elusive. Clinging to the ideal of objectivism some people tend to substitute a written description of behaviour in place of the elusive notion of objective reality. Thus they seek definite answers to their dilemmas and look to the unproblematic interpretation of texts to supply those answers. Objectivism in educational assessment leads to a seemingly endless series of guidelines for others to follow in the implementation of assessment. Objectivism also leads to a proliferation of managerial controls and inspectoral devices to monitor the implementation. In turn those controls and inspections are supported by a proliferation of bureaucratic procedures designed to prove that assessments are valid.

The more detailed the performance criterion is, the more resources are consumed in interpreting the what the criterion means. More guidelines are needed to interpret the first set of guidelines. More groups or managers are needed to check the various phases of implementation and so on. Hence for empiricists elitism in education policy leads to elitism throughout the system as an attempt is made to objectify interpretation in the language that a particular group or groups use. In other words an empiricist ethos within the education system tends to lead to the establishment of permanent groups, the members of which can be relied upon to agree upon a preferred interpretation of educational practice. When necessary those groups can also be relied upon to issue the appropriate bureaucratic endorsement of policy or practice.

It is important to recognise that there is nothing particularly conspiratorial in this thesis. The present state of affairs arises not as the result of a conspiracy on behalf of a powerful elite but as the result of a mistaken view of objectivity as that which corresponds to an external reality. Empiricists imagine that all forms of educational knowledge can be somehow independent of human desires and interests. A fear of evaluation in the real sense of the **value** of educational activities leads empiricists to narrow evaluation down to a consideration of the efficiency, effectiveness or 'quality' of those activities designed to achieve some predetermined 'element of competence'. If the arguments against logical empiricism are correct then it is only a matter of time before current conceptions of occupational competence will need to be rethought.

References

Bernstein R.J. (1983) *Beyond Objectivism and Relativism* Oxford: Blackwell

Carr D. (1993) 'Guidelines for Teacher Training: the Competency Model' *Scottish Educational Review* 25:1 pp 17-25.

Confederation of British Industry (1994) *Quality Assessed — The CBE Review of NVQ's and SVQ's* C.B.I.

Employment Department (1992) *National Standards for Training and Development* E.D.: Sheffield.

Employment Department (1994) *Ethics in Occupational Standards* Report by Steadman S.D. Eraut M.R. Cole G. Marquand J., E.D.: Sheffield.

Dewey J (1916) *Democracy and Education* cited as the 1966 edition New York: Free Press.

Eraut M. (1994) *Developing Professional Knowledge and Competence* Falmer.

Gadamer H.G. (1975) *Truth and Method* Sheed and Ward.

Hager P.and Beckett D. (1995) 'The Integrated Model of Professional Competence' *Educational Philosophy and Theory* 27:2 pp 30-42.

Halliday J.S. (1990) *Markets Managers and Theory in Education* Falmer

Halliday J.S. (1994) 'Quality in Education: meaning and prospects' *Educational Philosophy and Theory* 26:2 pp25-41.

Halliday J.S. (1996) *Back to Good Teaching: diversity within tradition* Cassell. Forthcoming.

Hyland T. (1994) *Competence, Education and NVQs: dissenting perspectives* Cassell.

Lakatos I. (1978) *The Methodology of Scientific Research Programmes* Cambridge University Press.

Leicester M. (1994) 'Competence, Knowledge and Education: reply to Hyland' *Journal of Philosophy of Education* 28:1 113-118.

MacIntyre A. (1981) *After Virtue* Duckworth.

McPherson I. (1995) 'Competence, Competencies and Rational Equilibrium' *Papers of the Philosophy of Education Society of Great Britain Annual Conference, Oxford.* pp 113-120.

Marginson S. (1993) *Education and Public Policy in Australia* Cambridge University Press.

O.E.C.D. (1994) *Jobs Study: Facts, Analysis, Strategies* OECD: Paris.

Packham D. and Tasker M. (1994) 'Changing Cultures? Government Intervention in Higher Education' *British Journal of Education Studies* 42:2.

Popper K.R. (1969) *Conjectures and Refutations* R.K.P.

Pring R. (1994) 'Editorial' *British Journal of Education Studies* 42:2.

Quine W.V.O. (1971) *From a Logical Point of View* Harvard University Press: Cambridge Mass..

Rawls J. (1972) *A Theory of Justice* Oxford University Press: Oxford.

Rawls J. (1993) *Political Liberalism* Columbia University Press, New York.

Rorty R. (1980) *Philosophy and the Mirror of Nature* Blackwell: Oxford.

Scottish Office Education Department (1993) *Guidelines for Teacher Training Courses* SOED: Edinburgh.

Scottish Vocational Education Council (1994) *The Values Base Unit* SCOTVEC: Glasgow.

Smithers A. (1993) *All our Futures: Britain's Education Revolution* Channel 4 Television.

Strathclyde University (1994) *Certificate in Education: further education module descriptors* Scottish School of F.E.: Glasgow.

Windschuttle K. (1994) *The Killing of History: How a Discipline is being Murdered by Literary Critics and Social Theorists* Macleay Press: Sydney.

Wittgenstein L. (1953) trans. G.E.M. Anscome *Philosophical Investigations* Blackwell: Oxford.

Chapter Four

Knowing One's Place:
The Professional's Need for an
Education in the Ecology of Practice

Mike Bottery

This paper argues that professionals must pay particular attention to issues of a societal, 'ecological' dimension if a full conception of their practice is to be achieved. It also reports on an ongoing research project which, through investigating the reactions of professionals in education and health to UK legislation over the last decade, is beginning to suggest that this is a neglected area in the education and training of such professionals.

Issues at a societal level are important because excellent practice, does not take place in a social vacuum. It takes place within certain societal parameters, assumptions, and values. These affect the manner in which professional practice is initially conceived, both by lay people, and, as importantly, by the profession itself. This dimension of practice, which in this paper will be called the 'ecological' dimension, has at least three aspects to it:

(a) an understanding of how a profession arrived at its present position vis-a-vis its practice and values;

(b) a firmly argued base for claiming its present territory and expertise, which is capable of transcending pure historical accident;

(c)   an understanding of present changes in society which may affect this value base, and a clear conception of how a profession will respond to these challenges.

This ecological area lies beyond that of an appreciation of excellence in the mechanics of practice. Whilst a grounding in practical excellence is clearly vital, such practice may be conducted within the kind of 'paradigm' which Thomas Kuhn (1970) described vis-a-vis scientific theories : within an accepted set of conventions and values which are rarely questioned. The adoption of such a mindset can lead to issues being excluded from consideration, issues which may be crucial to a fuller understanding of practice.

This paper then will argue that such 'ecological' considerations are important, and that there is evidence to suggest that they are not adequately addressed. It will discuss the reasons for lack of such provision, and makes suggestions for remediation. Evidence will be taken mainly from that of the practice of teaching in the U.K., but will also consider evidence from medicine, nursing and the police.

Definitions

A paper on professional practice should probably begin by defining what is meant by the term 'professional'. A central problem here is that at least 17 different criteria have been claimed as defining professionalism (see Bottery 1994 Ch.6). However, much of the debate centres around three concepts: those of *expertise* (possessing an exclusive body of knowledge and practice) of *altruism* (an ethical concern for clients), and of *autonomy* (the professional's need and right to exercise control over entry into, and subsequent practice within, that particular occupation). More recently, others (e.g. Collins, 1990) have been inclined to suggest something they believe more fundamental. It is suggested that one must look beyond such characteristics to concentrate upon the power which these give occupations. Such power then allows them to exercise 'occupational closure' , thereby increasing their ability to influence matters in society with regard to their practice, and, not unimportantly, to increase their financial remuneration for their practice.

There seems no a priori reason why the two orientations are incompatible. An occupation may have something unique to offer others, it may want to do the best for its client, and to do this properly, its practitioners may feel that they should be given considerable autonomy in its implementation. Yet members of that same occupation are also likely to want to ensure that their practice has influence on others, and that they are well paid for it as well. It would seem then that whilst the term 'professionals' encompasses more occupations than the traditional set of medicine, law, and the clergy, nevertheless, at the margins, there will be continued debates on the inclusion of specific occupations.

Within this paper, the term will be used fairly liberally. This is firstly because of the different views regarding the *characteristics* which are needed for an occupation to qualify as 'a profession'. However, it is also used in this manner because there are also different opinions concerning whether particular *occupations* qualify for the proposed 'professional' characteristics. In making particular reference to four occupations — nursing, medicine, teaching and the police — the possible objections which the use of some of these occupations as examples may raise are recognised, but they are included because they illustrate the range of jobs which may claim professional status. Moreover, if as this paper argues, changes in what constitutes professional practice are occurring, these particular occupations may well be at the vanguard of such redefinitions.

Professionals and Their Practice

Such changes to, and re-conceptions of, what professions do seem to stem from two different sources. The first is from economic, political and ethical questions about ailing economies, and the predominance of producer concerns in welfare provision, questions which derive predominantly, though not exclusively from free-market orientations. These go back at least fifty years (Hayek, 1944, Friedman 1962), but have gathered in strength and number over the last ten to fifteen years on both sides of the Atlantic (Graham and Clarke (1986), Chubb and Moe (1990), Osborne and Gaebler (1992)). The upshot of such literature is that, increasingly, professional claims to such things as expertise, altruism, autonomy, or necessary influence, are challenged directly, and their actual practice has been subject to increasing scepticism and scrutiny, which has meant an increasing need by such occupations to justify their practices and privileges. This issue will be returned to later.

The second source for the re-conception of professional practice stems from studies of what professionals actually do. These suggest that a major undergirding assumption of most professions — that they have a solid, objective bank of scientifically researched solutions which they can rely upon to give them the remedies to problems presented by clients — is either not true, or insufficient for dealing with many of the situations with which they are confronted. It is perhaps best summed up by Schon (1983, p.43) when he talks of two kinds of professionals:

> There are those who choose the swampy lowlands. They deliberately involve themselves in messy but crucially important problems, and when asked to describe their methods of inquiry, they speak of experience, trial and error, intuition and muddling through. Other professionals opt for the high ground. Hungry for technical rigour, devoted to an image of solid professional competence, or fearful of entering a world in which they feel they do not know what they are doing, they choose to confine themselves to a narrowly technical practice.'

Schon's own work (1982, 1987) suggests that much of the practice of the professionals he investigated — architects, psychoanalysts, town planners, and counsellors — did not operate in the manner described above. This view — the 'technical rationality view' is not supported by Schon's work, which suggests that in many cases this high ground of technical rigour is either not completely available, or simply irrelevant to the professional's practice.

His work is supported by other literature. Bittner (1974, p.35) describes police work as 'a solution to an unknown problem arrived at by unknown means'. In the medical world, Payer (1990) has described how culture influences the identification of disease. For example, blood pressure considered high in the USA might well be considered normal in the UK, leading to considerable variation in treatment. Finally, much of the work on the hidden curriculum of schools (e.g. Whitty and Young 1976) illustrates very clearly that many learning problems are socially or culturally constructed by teachers and society rather than being simply 'facts' to be treated.

Practitioners then bring to bear previous expertise, previous knowledge, previous understandings, some of which may be highly debatable as to their veracity. At the same time they necessarily utilise conceptions, intuitions, and paradigms, which owe as much to artistic as to scientific endeavour. The standard model of professional practice, then, which assumes that problems are previously defined, and that professionals search through a bank of expertise and apply the appropriate solution, in fact misdescribes what professionals do. In so doing, the necessary and valuable place of practice in a full understanding of professional expertise is then reasserted. Further, in invoking the place of practice in explaining what constitutes professional expertise, it may then be that, on its own, the professionals' perspectives may be defective, their banks of technical expertise may be of limited help, and they may need to supplement their understanding with the understandings of others to define the problem correctly. Much professional practice, then, may belong to the swampy lowlands.

The recognition of this, Schon suggests, means that professionals need to move beyond an initial level of 'technical rationality' , beyond a further level of 'thinking like a...', where individuals are inducted into the practices, thoughts and habits of that particular occupation, to a further level which is considerably more flexible and personal than either of the others, and which increasingly includes the perspectives and contributions of other interested parties into the definition of the problem within situations, and therefore to its probable resolution.

It has to be recognised that 'reflection' has become something of an 'in' word in professional development literature, such that at times it has had a tendency to guarantee a writer approbation by its simple invocation. Yet, as writers like and Van Manen (1977), Zeichner (1986) Adler (1991) and Jarvis (1992) have all pointed out, the term can mean different things to different people. For Schon it remains wedded to an improvement of individual professional practice: it rarely transcends this level to one which examines the institutional, cultural and societal constraints of practice. Yet an appreciation of best practice at a personal level must be extended to an appreciation of the profession's moral and political commitments, not only because this provides a fuller understanding of what practice entails, but also because this is, as argued above, increasingly being challenged by governmental legislation, particularly that of a free market orientation.

Reflection Inward

Reflection at this level, then, upon this ecological area, has both an inward-looking and an outward-looking component. An *inward looking component* examines the nature of the profession itself. It asks such questions as

- what was perceived to be the profession's original purpose upon inception?
- do such inheritances affect its practice, and laypeople's reaction to that practice?
- which aspects of occupational closure are defined and justified in terms of exclusive expertise or simply in terms of historical privilege?
- what historically have been the primary motivations of its representative body vis-a-vis legislation? Would other bodies agree with the profession's assessment of itself?
- in what major respects does their situation differ from other similar groups, and why?
- how does the situation of the profession in this country differ from that of the same profession in other countries? Why does it differ?

Such self-examination enables professionals to assess themselves more objectively, to see that some justifications for professional practices are valid, others little more than the rationalisation of historical accident. It allows them to move from a 'Ptolemaic' view of themselves, as being at the centre of some occupational universe, to a much more accurate understanding as a 'Copernican' occupation, moving and interacting in an ecology of professions, pressure groups, and social forces. It allows for greater honesty, better communication with clients, and a more rational analysis of those forces acting upon their practice. In looking inward more accurately, it enables a profession to develop the outward component of this level as well: the ability to understand how societal changes affect a professional's value base, and how it should respond to such challenges.

Reflection Outward — Professionals and the Market

Perhaps the most direct challenge to professional practice throughout the western world over the last twenty years has been, as argued above, from legislation intended to facilitate the development of free market circumstances. This legislation has resulted partly from economic desires to curb inefficiencies and increase effectiveness; and partly from moral and political considerations, with particular emphasis upon the over-bureaucratisation of welfare states, and the exploitation of services by producers within them. When allied to increasing scepticism by laypeople with the abilities of scientists to alleviate many of the worlds most pressing problems — indeed with increasing belief in their complicity in exacerbating them — it is perhaps not surprising that the central tenets of professionals described above — their claim to expertise, their altruism, and their need for autonomy — have all been increasingly questioned. A minimum response by professionals would seem to be an awareness of the nature of these challenges, and of a satisfactory professional response. Where there is increasing pressure on professionals to practice within competitive market situations, this cannot merely amount to developing ways of competing more effectively. Before such strategies are even considered, there needs to be debate and consciousness-raising at both pre-and in-service levels regarding the following kinds of questions:

- is the service the profession offers a public good or a market commodity?
- is competition the best way of providing this service?
- should there be a balance between the public and private provision of this service, and what should it be?
- does the use of commercial language affect the way that professionals think and speak? Is this helpful or unhelpful?
- if the profession comes to believe that there is excessive use of a market situation, resulting in an impairment of practice, how can it contribute to redressing the balance?

This is clearly not the same agenda as one which discusses the practicalities or problems in developing strategies for the implementation of legislation. So, for example, discussions by teachers in schools regarding how best to cope with formula funding, whereby the funding for a school is dependent upon the number of children within a school, will almost inevitably be directed at questions of how to maintain present intakes, or to increase them. This may include discussion of better relationships with parents, of putting on new, attractive courses, of designing brochures or leaflets advertising the school. What it does not question is whether the road which formula funding takes a school down is a desirable one for the school, its pupils, and society in general.

Arguments Against Professional Involvement

It may still be argued that discussion of professional issues at the sociopolitical level is rarefied, distanced from day-to-day practice, and therefore has little actual effect: it doesn't get children taught, patients cured, or villains caught, and therefore must be given a much lower priority than technical issues. Against this one may put forward a number of arguments:

(a) The questions posed in this paper are those which policy makers pose. If professionals are prepared to allow others to dictate policy, then they invite other parties to set their agendas. If they wait for policy to be decided elsewhere, and then react to it, they act too late. If they wish to preserve professional practice, they must be proactive, and actively engage in discussions about the nature of legislation before it is enacted.

(b) Professionals may argue that they have central executive bodies which deal with these matters, leaving them to get on with the problems of practice. Their representatives, then, consult with governments, and make their position clear. They, therefore, have no need to become involved. However, when a central tenet of much free market thinking is that the providers have been the primary creators of problems, there is little likelihood that their representatives will be given serious consideration by a government wedded to such free market ideals. This has certainly been the case in the U.K., where, for example, consultation documents on legislation have generally been remarkable for the limited time they have been sent out for consultation, their timing (apparently to coincide with major holiday periods), and for the lack of interest ministers have shown in professional response to them. A professional strategy of leaving such issues to an elite few places responsibility on those who may be in no position to exercise influence, because a government does not wish to listen to them.

(c) Corporatist notions of select members of professional bodies dealing exclusively with government bodies are untenable, for the reason given in (b), but also because such an approach misdescribes much of what was said earlier about reflective practice, and the need to incorporate others' views of that practice. Thus, if a profession is intent on defending itself, it should do this from a position of strength. This comes from being able to defend practice, and criticise unwelcome legislative developments, not to governments, but to clients. This , firstly, improves professional practice because if professionals can't justify practice to their clients, they won't be practising for long ; secondly, it provides professionals with a large body of support, namely all those who they treat effectively; and lastly, it has a major effect upon the public's understanding of societal issues, and provides them with an opportunity to become increasingly articulate on such issues. Put bluntly, it increases participation in the running of society, and therefore strengthens the running of a democracy. All three reasons cohere into a very powerful argument for increasing professional education at this level.

If these, then, are issues with which professionals must wrestle, the question is: do professionals address them?

Professional Awareness, Professional Education

There appear to be two ways of deciding on the degree to which professionals address such questions. The first is to assess the extent of their understanding and interest in such matters. The second is to enquire about whether these kinds of issues are addressed in professionals' training at both the pre-service and inservice levels.

The first area — that of professional interest and awareness — has been the author's major area of research over the past year and a half. This research has involved a reading of literature upon the intentions and effects of legislative change in the areas of Health and Education, as well as the investigation of the reactions of professionals in these areas in the U.K. to changes in their practice due to legislation over the last ten to fifteen years.

A number of things can be said about the findings so far.

Firstly, a reading of literature in the Health and Education fields, depicting the legislative changes, suggested that not only was there a similarity of effects upon teachers, doctors, and nurses, which came out at the interviews, but that there was also a pattern to the thrust of the legislation which suggested a general policy for the public sector, rather than individual policies pursued by individual ministers. This suspicion led to informal talks with members of another profession, the police service, to see whether the similarities could be extended beyond two public institutions. This seems to be the case (see Figs.1, 2, and 3 on this, and, more fully, Bottery (1995)). It was also strongly supported by writers such as Hood (1991) who suggested that there has been a culture change in the public administration of much of the western world, which has seen the rise of what he called the 'New Public Management' (NPM). He suggested (p.4-5) that this has seven distinct elements:

- 'hands-on' professional management in the public sector;
- the use of explicit standards in the measurement of performance;
- greater emphasis on control via measures of output ;
- the development of smaller manageable units;
- a movement to increased public sector competition;
- a stress on private-sector styles of management;
- greater discipline and parsimony in the use of resources.

An initial conclusion, then, was that part of the similarity of the issues which professionals in the pubic domain face stems from the nature and effects of their management and supervision.

Secondly, the investigation of the effects of legislation upon professionals working in the public sector in the UK over the last decade has taken the form of a series of case studies of schools and hospitals, in which semi-structured qualitative interviews with professionals have been conducted regarding their work and concerns. Whilst numbers interviewed have been relatively small (between 150 and 200 individuals), there appear to be a similarity in response which merits further quantitative investigation. To be put these findings briefly, there appears to be:

- a devolution of responsibility to all levels;
- more paperwork, less time for the 'real' job;
- more stress at all levels;
- a degree of entrepreneurial enjoyment of the job by those at the more senior levels; little of apparent benefit to those at lower levels;
- an increasing concern about job security.
- a general preoccupation with the mechanics of legislative implementation.

This fieldwork has also provided the opportunity to investigate the level of awareness of professionals to macrosociological issues. The interviews conducted suggest that the level of awareness of practising professionals regarding both internal and external 'ecological' issues is patchy at best. Specifically, those in more senior positions in schools and hospitals appear to have a better understanding of the reasons behind legislation, and of its long-term implications. This might be expected from those whose work necessarily calls for the management of the interface between the institution and the outside world. However, in most cases this appreciation did not appear to be communicated in any formal manner to those lower in the hierarchy. This is in spite of the fact that a fairly constant element of the management strategies of the institutions visited was to increase the involvement of staff in decisions which had previously been the exclusive remit of management — such as in decisions in the allocation of finance. This lack of formal communication about macrosocial issues may be one reason why, for the majority of professional individuals interviewed who were low in institutional hierarchies, their appreciation of such issues was fairly rudimentary. In some cases this lack of awareness appeared to be due to indifference to such issues ('my job is to teach my subject/ cure patients/ care for patients/ deal with criminals'). However, in many other cases it seemed that this was due more to a lack of time: more immediate problems of policy implementation were, not surprisingly, given priority. Curiously enough, even the initiatives to involve professionals more in managerial issues, in many cases seemed to be a constraining rather than a liberating factor in the development of an ecological perspective. Involvement in management meant, for many interviewed, nothing more than increased responsibility and paperwork, which consumed what little extra time they may have had for such ecological issues. A second conclusion is then that professional awareness of this ecological area is limited, and that, because awareness is so limited, this area is not given the importance it is due.

Professionals' Inservice Education

If awareness is limited, is this situation redressed by education of professionals at pre-service or inservice levels? An initial enquiry into this took place by an investigation into schools' inservice priorities. A questionnaire was designed and sent out to 40 secondary and 48 primary schools concerning their inservice priorities. The results (see tables 1 and 2 in this article, but more fully reported in Bottery and Wright (1995)) are, I believe, disturbing. These suggest that virtually no direct attention has been paid over the last two years, nor will it be paid in the coming two years, to the kinds of ecological issues raised in this paper. Perhaps even more worrying, when these schools were asked what their Inset priorities would be 'in an ideal world', the picture, apart from catering more to individual teachers' preferences, was little different. A conclusion drawn from this research was that the teaching profession in the UK may be consciously or unconsciously collaborating in its own deprofessionalisation by failing to substantively address the issues raised.

The limited research on inservice priorities conducted in the health service, and with police trainers is not much more encouraging. The situation in the police force appears to follow the same pattern. Interviews with police trainers at the 'junior' of the two police training colleges at Harrogate in North Yorkshire, which trains constables, sergeants, and inspectors, indicated that whilst an approach which pays acknowledgment to 'reflective practice' has been an important part of police training and thinking since the early 1980s (see Southgate (ed) (1988)), extended reflection at the ecological level is hampered by the time scale of the courses (12 weeks of extremely intensive coursework), and by the fact that the level of reflection is very much in keeping with a Schon-type perspective, where little of the actual courses go beyond reflection upon specific situations which police officers may encounter during the working day. Interviews with trainers at the senior police training establishment in the UK — Bramshill in Hampshire — suggest that such issues are given rather more time, the implication being that such issues are generally left until later in training, and then to an elite.

Professionals' Preservice Education

Whilst the current research does not specifically investigate the preservice level of professional education, there are strong indications that the situation is no better than at the inservice level, and is probably worse. One reason for this claim is the very general conviction encountered whilst talking to trainers in education, medicine, nursing and the police, that such issues can be left until later, and that pre-service education should be more concerned with the acquisition of practical skills. This is despite the kind of critical literature stemming from writers like Kemmis and Carr (1988), which suggests that a more 'critical' approach to inducting recruits in education is essential to more professional bodies, and to a fairer, more just, and more participative society. Other literature which describes attempts to develop this more critical approach within teacher education courses in both the UK and the USA (see Zeichner and Liston (1987), Adler and Goodman (1986) Furlong, Hirst, Pocklington and Miles (1988)) also admits that there is strong evidence that this is difficult to achieve because of initial value orientations by students and staff, and by communication difficulties between universities and schools. Further, Dart and Drake (1993) describe how current legislation in the UK is exacerbating such situations because it increasingly limits the time for the discussion of such issues.

In the Health service, my discussions with Junior doctors suggest that their training is largely devoted to the anatomy and physiology of the human body, and to abnormalities of function: little time appears to given to issues of ward practices or interpersonal skills such as counselling the bereaved. Practically none is given to internal ecological issues such as the development of medicine as a discipline, the challenges to it in the past, or its role in the future. Similarly, external ecological issues, such as the challenges to clinicians' practice and ethics from working in an Internal Market, or the implications of Trust Hospital status upon hospital functioning, finance, or care rationing are similarly given little attention. Again, discussions with police trainers suggests the same kind of concentration upon the mechanics of practice at the preservice level.

An overall definitive conclusion is difficult to draw at the present time. Nevertheless, a picture is emerging that in a number of key occupations within the public sector in the UK there is a distinct lack of awareness of both the inward and outward looking components of an ecological dimension of practice. This, if it is corroborated by further research within these professions, and even more so if the picture is replicated elsewhere, is a worrying aspect of professional awareness and training.

Conclusions

The argument of this paper, then, has been that professional development needs to include much more centrally an education in an ecology of practice. This involves an understanding of the profession in an historical perspective, a clearly and rationally argued base for present practice, and a complementary understanding of present changes in society which may affect practice, and how a profession will respond to these. This, it has been suggested, should be predicated much more on the notion of reflection, but reflection which enables the ordinary practitioner — not just the elite of a profession — to be able to articulate to clients reasons for not only resistance to legislative change, but also the need for changes in practice. In so doing, professionals participate more fully in policy decisions, they defend their own best practice, and they educate their clients to participate in such decision making. In so doing, they not only improve their own practice, they also increase the degree of genuine democracy within society.

Table 1
Inservice Priorities Identified by Secondary Staff Development Officers
(n = 29)

Ranking	Key areas during the last two years (% of schools indicating)	Likely priorities for the next two years (% of schools indicating)	Priorities in an ideal world (% of schools indicating)
1.	Management (59%)	National Curriculum Post Dearing (52%)	Classroom Based Work (76%)
2.	Information Technology (45%)	Management (45%)	Management (48%)
3.	Assessment (41%)	Assessment (38%)	Personal Development (31%)
4.	Subject related Work (38%)	SEN Technology (27%)	Information (6%)
5.	Differentiation (34%)	Information Technology (24%)	
6.	National Curriculum (31%)	Vocational Education (20%)	
7.	Teaching & Learning Styles (24%)	Differentiation (20%)	
8.	Pastoral Care (24%)	Teaching & Learning Styles (20%)	
9.	SEN (20%)	Pastoral Care (20%)	
10.	Counseling (17%)	Evaluation (13%)	

Table 2
Inservice Priorities Identified by Primary Staff Development Officers
(n = 34)

Ranking	Key areas during the last two years (% of schools indicating)	Likely priorities for the next two (% of schools indicating)	Priorities in an ideal world (% of schools indicating)
1.	National Curriculum Work (79%)	National Curriculum Work (91%)	National Curriculum Work (48%)
2.	Special Educational Needs (27%)	SENs (24%)	Staff Development (45%)
3.	Other subject areas (21%)	Management (15%)	Other subject areas (7%)
4.	Assessment I.T. (18%)	OFSTED I.T. (11.%)	Management Class Man. (4%)
6.	Staff Differentiation LMS (12%)	Staff Development Other Subject	I.T. Development, Assessment Areas (9%)
7.	Class man. OFSTED (12%)	Learning Styles (3%)	
8.	Differentiation Assessment (6%)		
9.	Differentiation (6%)	No reply = 5	
10.	Management LMS Appraisal (3%)	Class Management Appraisal (3%)	

References

Adler S. The Reflective Practitioner and the Curriculum of Teacher Education' *Journal of Education for Teaching* Vol. 17, no. 2 (1991) pp. 139-150.

Adler S. and Goodman J. 'Critical Theory as a Foundation for Methods courses' *Journal of Teacher Education* Vol. 37, no. 4. (1986) pp. 2-8.

Bittner E. 'Florence Nightingale in pursuit of Willie Sutton: a theory of the police' in Jacob J. (ed.) *The Potential for Reform of Criminal Justice* pp. 11-44 (Beverly Hills: Sage, 1974)

Bottery M. *Lessons for Schools: A comparison of business and education management.* (London: Cassell., 1994)

Bottery M.) 'The Challenge to Professionals in State Bureaucracies by the New Public Management: Implications for the Teaching Profession' *with Oxford Review of Education.*

Bottery and Wright 'Cooperating in their deprofessionalisation? The need for an appreciation of the 'public' and 'ecological' natures of teaching within inservice education and training.' *with British Journal of Educational Studies*

Chubb J. and Moe T. *Politics, Markets and America's Schools* (Washington: Brookings Institute, 1994)

Collins R. 'Market closure and the conflict theory of the professions' in Burrage M. and Torstendahl R. *Professions in Theory and History* pp. 24-43. (London:Sage, 1990)

Dart L. and Drake P. 'School-based Teacher Training: a conservative practice?' *Journal of Education for Teaching* Vol. 19 no. 2. (1993) pp. 175-189.

Freidson E. 'Are professions necessary?' in Haskell T. (ed.) *The Authority of Experts: Studies in History and Theory* pp. 3-27. (Bloomington: Indiana University Press., 1984)

Furlong V.J., Hirst P.H., Pocklington K. , and Miles S. *Initial Teacher Training and the Role of the School* (Milton Keynes: Open University Press, 1988)

Graham D. and Clarke P. *The New Enlightenment: the Rebirth of Liberalism* (London: Macmillan, 1986)

Hayek F. *The Road to Serfdom* (London: Routledge, 1944)

Hood C. A. Public Management for all Seasons?' *Public Administration* Vol. 69 (1991) p.3-19.

Jarvis P. 'Reflective practice and nursing' *Nurse Education Today* Vol. 12 (1992) pp. 174-181.

Kemmis S. and Carr W. *Becoming Critical* (Lewes: Falmer, 1988)

Kuhn T. *The Structure of Scientific Revolutions* (Chicago: Chicago University Press, 1970)

Osborne D. and Gaebler T. *Reinventing Government* (New York: Addison-Wesley, 1992)

Payer L. *Medicine and Culture* (London: Gollancz, 1990).

Schon D. *The Reflective Practitioner* (New York: Basic Books, 1982)

Schon D. *Educating the Reflective Practitioner* (San Francisco: Jossey Bass, 1987)

Southgate P. *New Directions in Police Training* (London: HMSO, 1988)

Van Manen M. 'Linking ways of knowing with ways of being practical' *Curriculum Enquiry* Vol. 6 no. 3, (1977) pp. 205-228.

Whitty G. and Young M.F.D. *Explorations in the Politics of School Knowledge* (Driffield: Nafferton, (1976)

Zeichner K. 'Content and contexts: neglected elements in studies of student teaching as an occasion for learning to teach' *Journal of Education for Teaching* Vol.12 no. 1, (1986) pp. 5-24.

Zeichner K. and Liston D. 'Teaching Student Teachers to Reflect' *Harvard Educational Review* vol. 57 no. 1. (1987) pp. 23-48.

Chapter Five

Integrating Ethics into Technical Courses: An Experiment in Its Fifth Year

Michael Davis

In 1990, IIT's Center for the Study of Ethics in the Professions received a four-year grant from the National Science Foundation (#DIR 914220) to introduce ethics into technical courses. During the summers of 1991, 1992, and 1993, the Center offered 30-hour workshops to prepare IIT faculty, fifteen at a time. Each fall our "graduates" introduced into their courses ethics material they had prepared during the workshop, asked students to assess it, and reported back the results.[1] During the summer of 1994, we held a similar workshop for faculty from twenty other universities. Most of their reports are now in, making possible for the first time a relatively firm assessment of the entire effort. I shall offer that assessment here. But before I do, I must explain what we mean by integrating ethics into technical courses, why it should be done, how it can be done, and with what effect. Explaining all that will put us in position both to appreciate how much has been accomplished and to consider what it has to tell us, especially philosophers, about who should do ethics education and how it can be done.

Integrating Ethics into Technical Courses

I must begin with an esoteric but important distinction, that between morality and ethics. People generally use "ethics" in one of two senses, that is, as a synonym for morality or as the name of a specifically philosophical discipline (the attempt to understand morality as a rational enterprise). I shall use "ethics" in a third sense.

"Morality", as I use that term, refers to those standards of conduct everyone (every rational person) wants every other to follow even if everyone else's following them would mean he had to do the same. Morality is the same for everyone. We were all quite young when we learned the basic moral rules: don't lie; don't kill; don't cheat; keep your promises; don't steal; and so on. We were still quite young when we learned that these rules have exceptions (for example, "except in self-defense" for "Don't kill"). Now and then, we may change our view on how to interpret a particular rule or exception—for example, we may come to think that speaking the truth, knowing it will be misunderstood, is (or is not) a form of lying. But, since we entered our teens, such changes have been few and relatively minor. Our students are much like us. They arrive in class more or less morally mature. We have little to teach them about ordinary morality.

Not so with ethics. "Ethics" (as I shall use that term) refers to those special morally permissible standards of conduct every member of a group wants every other member of that group to follow even if that would mean having to do the same. Ethics applies to members of a group simply because they are members of that group. Medical ethics applies to people in medicine (and no one else); business ethics applies to people in business (and no one else); and Hopi ethics applies to Hopis (and no one else).

Ethics is both a higher standard and a moral standard. Ethics is a higher standard because ethics demands more than (ordinary) morality. Ethics is nonetheless a moral standard, not just a standard consistent with morality, because (and only when) members of the relevant group have reasons to set themselves a higher standard, reasons beyond what law or market would impose whatever the group in question did. Such reasons turn maintenance of that higher standard into a cooperative enterprise, that is, an undertaking the benefits of which depend in part at least on others doing their share of carrying the burden of maintaining the special standards. That is as true of a profession as of any other group with its own ethics. For example, one's status as a CPA is worth more if other CPA's generally do a better job than morality, law, and market demand, less if they do not. Professionals never practice alone.[2]

The higher standard that constitutes a profession's ethics are formulated in codes of ethics, in formal interpretations of those codes, and in the less formal practices by which older members pass on the special ways they do things to new members. So, except for those students following a parent into a profession, no one is likely to learn much about a profession's ethics except at a professional school or while practicing the profession. Professional ethics is as much a part of what members of a profession know as ordinary "technical" knowledge. Professional ethics is part of thinking like a member of the profession in question. Teaching professional ethics is part of teaching how to practice the profession.

"Profession" is a large category, but even it is not large enough for my purpose. Business, for example, is not a profession (though many professionals are in business and many businesses have codes of ethics); many "humanists" resist describing the humanities generally, or their particular discipline, as a profession; indeed, many scientists take the same attitude with respect to science generally or their particular field.[3] Nonetheless, in this paper, when I use "profession", I should be understood to include business, the humanities, and the sciences. I do this in part simply for convenience. Our workshops included faculty in "non-professions"—humanities (literature, technical writing, and philosophy), mathematics, biology, sociology, and business—as well as in law, architecture, computer science, engineering, chemistry, veterinary medicine, and so on. I need some short-hand for this unconventional mix of occupations. But, in part, I shall call all these occupations "professions" on principle. Whatever the differences between them, all shared enough to allow us to talk about teaching their respective ethics (as well as about their teaching the ethics of other professions in their classrooms). Like engineering, accounting, architecture, and other traditional professions, the humanities and sciences had special standards of conduct they wanted students to know. While business faculty (or, rather, faculty in departments of management) did not have a similar set of standards to teach, they did want their students to recognize the moral problems that arise in business, to be prepared to understand the professionals with whom they would have to deal (including their ethics), and to be prepared to work with the code of ethics of an employer (if the employer has one).

This use of "profession" means that, when I refer to "technical courses", "technical" must be understood to include much more than math, science, and the like. In fact, "technical course" is my short-hand for any course the subject matter of which is generally not explicitly ethical. So, for example, a first-year course in composition or a third-year course in French would be technical (in my sense).

What Can Teaching Ethics Accomplish?

Teaching ethics (in my third sense of "ethics") can achieve at least four desirable outcomes: 1) increase the ethical sensitivity of students; 2) increase their knowledge of relevant standards of conduct; 3) improve their ethical judgment; and 4) improve their ethical will-power (that is, their ability to act ethically when they want to). How can teaching ethics accomplish all this—indeed, any of this?

Teaching ethics can increase student sensitivity simply by making students aware that they, as members of a certain profession (or otherwise engaged in a certain business), will have to resolve certain ethical problems. Generally, pointing out an ethical problem will mean pointing out the consequences of a seemingly inconsequential act ("a mere technical decision"). Just being exposed to a few examples of a particular problem (for example, how using this method here will have such-and-such harmful effects) will make it more likely than otherwise that the students will see a problem of that sort when it arises on the job. Why teaching ethics might have this effect is not hard to understand. The mechanism is precisely the same as for learning to see technical problems. Both knowledge and practice sharpen perception, make it easier to see a particular decision in context, and make it easier to imagine what the context might contribute.

How can teaching ethics increase student knowledge of relevant standards? Again, the answer is much the same as for any technical standard. For example, a marketing student who reads the Better Business Bureau's Advertising Code of American Business is more likely to know what is in it than a student who has not read it. A student who has had to answer questions about the code is more likely to recall the relevant provisions than one who has not. And so on.

"Knowledge of standards" includes more than just knowing what is written in codes or handbooks. Part of knowing standards is understanding the rationale for them (especially the consequences of departing from them). So, for example, part of teaching engineering students to take operating (and disposal) costs into account when designing something is pointing out how uneconomical a product can turn out if they don't. Only then are they likely to appreciate that a standard requiring them to act as a "faithful agent and trustee of their client or employer" might require them routinely to take operating costs into account when designing something. There is no sharp line between raising sensitivity and teaching standards.

How can teaching professional (or business) ethics improve ethical judgment? Ethical judgment, like technical judgment, tends to improve with use (as well, of course, as with relevant knowledge and sensitivity). If a professor of finance gives a student a chance to make ethical judgments, explain them, and compare them with those other students make, the student is more likely to judge well than if she gets no such experience. The classroom and laboratory provide a safe place to make mistakes and learn from them—ethical mistakes as well as purely technical ones.

But how can teaching professional (or business) ethics increase a student's ethical will-power? Easily. Isn't an accountant who knows that he shares a commitment to a particular standard of conduct with other accountants more likely to follow it than one who believes himself alone in that commitment? One benefit of discussing ethics in the classroom is that it shows students how much consensus there is (among members of their profession) on most of their profession's standards of conduct. There is power in numbers. That is one source of will-power. Another is a sense of the standard's reasonableness. A student who believes he understands what makes the standard reasonable is more likely to try to explain its reasonableness to others (and so, more likely to win their support and act accordingly). While there are other ways classroom discussion can enhance will-power, these two examples are enough for now. We must get to what professors can actually do to teach ethics.

Finding Room for Ethics in Technical Classes

There are at least eight ways to teach ethics in an academic environment. They are more or less consistent with each other, indeed potentially mutually supportive.

Two ways are outside the curriculum. One is independent study, for example, giving students the appropriate code of ethics and telling them to read it. The other outside way is by special event, for example, a public speech on professional ethics or a movie like *China Syndrome* or *The Firm*, with a discussion afterward of the ethical issues it raises.[4]

One of the eight ways of teaching students professional ethics is supracurricular (operating inside the curriculum as well as outside): hold students to their profession's code while they are still students. I am not talking about an "honor code". Honor codes are codes of student ethics, not of professional ethics. A student will learn more about her profession's code by living it than by living by an honor code.[5] A university, college, or department can hold its students to the professional code corresponding to the student's major. Professional codes are sufficiently alike to preserve reasonable order across disciplines, but sufficiently different to be worth a student's effort to learn the particulars.

The other methods of teaching students professional ethics are all internal to the curriculum. The easiest is the guest lecture. (If the guest stays all semester, the course is "team taught".) By itself, the guest lecture makes professional ethics look optional: "If all members of my profession are supposed to know this stuff, why doesn't my Prof. know enough to teach it?" The same question arises for the sort of course I routinely teach, that is, a free-standing course in a profession's ethics taught outside the department, whether optional or required. A different question arises when the course in the profession's ethics is, while optional, taught by a member of the profession: "If this stuff is important, why isn't it required?"

The free-standing required in-house course answers all these question, but only at the cost of raising another: "How do we fit this into the curriculum?" The last of my eight methods, the pervasive, provides an answer to that question: "You don't have to because you can do something better. You can teach the ethics of your profession in a way that brings home how integral it is to the practice of your profession. You can make ethics pervade the curriculum."

But how can you make room for ethics in technical courses, courses notorious for being both too full already and too technical for ethics? I propose to answer this question—for our purposes, at least — by giving a few examples of what can be done. These are not alternatives among which one must choose, but options which one can mix and match in a course (with the understanding that, all else equal, the more the better).

To make my answer convincing, I shall avoid easy examples. I shall not, for example, talk about including a question of professional ethics in a first-year composition course (where instructors are always in need of topics to interest students) or of including some discussion of research ethics in an advanced course in philosophy of science (where many of the usual topics discussed, especially early in the term, are too technical for students to know what to write about). I shall also not draw my examples from a field (such as medicine or management) where the ethical issues seem relatively obvious; or from courses (such as engineering's introduction to the profession) where technical content seems to have left room for practical considerations; or from labs, where issues of safety, honesty, and care cry out for discussion. Instead, I shall take my examples from second- and third-year lecture courses in electrical engineering, hoping that you will agree that if there is room for ethics in those courses, there should be room for ethics in any technical course in any curriculum.[6]

One way to integrate ethics into a course is simply to enhance student awareness of ethical issues. For example, in a course on electric circuits, the instructor might take a moment now and then to point out the practical effect of getting a problem wrong:

> These circuits are typically used in aircraft navigation systems; a small error here, combined with two common errors of pilots, could cause a crash. In practice, your calculations will be checked many times, but some errors slip through. The easiest way to prevent disaster is to get the problem right the first time. Next problem.

Even a few such comments in the course of a semester can help engineering students see the practical context of highly abstract calculations, both the relation of those calculations to such ethical concerns as safety and the relation of their education to what they want to do after graduation.

An easy way to provide information about ethical standards is to pass out a code of ethics at the beginning of the term and refer to it often enough during the term so that students get the idea it would be good to read it. For example, a professor of electrical engineering could mention that such-and-such a provision makes engineers responsible for the safety of what they help to make. I am still surprised at how many engineering faculty have not read a code of engineering ethics (and at how many science faculty don't even know that their field has a code of ethics). Needless to say, their students are likely to have read even less. Just exposing students to a code is therefore a significant contribution to ethics education. Asking students questions on problems or exams requiring them to look through the code would, of course, be a further significant contribution.

That, however, is not all a professor teaching an advanced course in electrical engineering can do. Like most engineering courses, much of a course in electrical circuits consists of solving problems. Often several problems assigned on a given night differ little. They can in fact be interpreted as several solutions to the same design problem (for example, three ways of designing the same turn signal for an automobile). An instructor could, then, provide a little "background information" about the design problem, including not only the use to which these solutions will be put but also some factors relevant to cost, safety, reliability, and even manufacturability, and then ask the student (as a fourth step) to recommend one of the solutions and briefly state her reasons (as she might in a memo to a supervisor). The student then has an opportunity to exercise her engineering judgment—including her ethical judgment (and to practice writing too).

The last example I shall give, though not the last I could give, would require a larger commitment of class time, say, fifteen minutes now and then, to let students discuss their recommendations. Such discussion would not only improve their public speaking but also help them see how much agreement there is among students in their class—and, by extension, engineers generally— about what the code demands (and also how many different ways there may be to satisfy the code). It would, in other words, provide an opportunity to enhance their ethical will-power.

These examples share an overall strategy. Abstract principles, both technical and ethical, are put in the context of practice. The context then brings them to life, allows students both to see their point and to use them. Education becomes practical (while remaining academic).

Why Integrate Ethics into Technical Courses?

I have already touched on two reason why professional ethics should be integrated into the technical curriculum. Such integration both reinforces what is taught about the profession's ethics elsewhere and helps students develop habits of thinking about ethics while thinking about technical questions. A third reason to integrate ethics into the technical curriculum is that, as a matter of fact, many students will get no ethics training except as part of the technical curriculum. Required ethics courses are unlikely to become universal any time soon; and other methods tend to miss most students. There are two more reasons why professional ethics should be integrated into technical courses: one you may have guessed from the examples I have given; the other may surprise you, though I have substantial empirical evidence to support what I shall claim.

The reason you may have guessed is that integrating professional ethics into technical courses can remind students of what attracted them to their profession. So, for example, the analytic courses of the second and third year of engineering are a perpetual problem in engineering education, tending to weed out students who went into engineering because they wanted to make things, leaving behind those who think engineering is only "problem solving" (in the narrowest sense of that ambiguous term). Integrating ethics into a course like circuits puts analysis in context, making clear its instrumental importance and thereby livening up the problems (and the course).

My last reason for integrating ethics into technical courses, the one you probably did not guess even though I now have lots of empirical evidence for it, is that students like it. We have required graduates of our seminar to have their students evaluate the ethics component. Class after class, year after year, both at IIT and now at all seventeen of the other schools that have so far reported, the great majority of students—often, over ninety percent—expressed appreciation for the concern shown ethics, some because they thought ethics important, some because it helped them to understand what they would be doing after graduation. Few wanted less ethics; many wanted more. This last reason seems to me as good as any for doing as much professional ethics as we can. We are always looking for ways to make our classes more enjoyable (without pandering to the urge merely to entertain). Here is one more (respectable) way to make class more enjoyable.[7]

Assessment (and Speculations)

Our fourth workshop differed in one important way from the other three (aside from the origin of participants). Participants in the last workshop were supposed to leave the workshop able to teach their own faculty what we had taught them; they came with the understanding that they would have to go back and help colleagues (in their department and outside) to integrate ethics into technical courses. The fourth workshop thus involved a double transfer of "technology". First, there was, as in the other three workshops, the transfer of what we at IIT knew about integrating ethics into technical courses; and second, there was a new element, the transfer of what we knew about transferring that technology.

At IIT, philosophers always taught the workshops. In the first year, I teamed with Pat Werhane; in subsequent years, with Vivian Weil. All three of us had had many years of teaching professional or business ethics. The workshop was, however, not simply the work of philosophers. We developed the workshop at sack lunches with self-selected faculty from psychology, engineering, various sciences, business, public administration, and so on. After an initial period of considerable misunderstanding, we learned a great deal from each other.

The result was a workshop that differed from others philosophers have offered over the years. Ours was not a workshop in "remedial ethical theory". (We gave only three out of thirty hours to ethical theory and our message was,

"This is something you may want to know, but it's not something you need to know.") Nor was our emphasis on special substantive topics ("recent developments in _____"). Our emphasis was overwhelmingly pedagogical. We provided participants with a framework for teaching ethics and then gave them an opportunity to try it out. While we always spoke as philosophers, as well as teachers of professional or business ethics, the contribution of philosophy to what we did was generally oblique. I shall now try to explain what it was because that explanation will help us to assess the place philosophers should have in professional and business ethics even as its teaching and the teaching of its teachers pass (as I believe they will) to other disciplines.

We made, I think, three distinct contributions as philosophers to ethics across the curriculum: legitimacy, experience, and philosophical insight. Let me explain these contributions in turn.

Philosophers routinely teach courses with "ethics" in the title. Other departments do not. Hence, for academics worried about "turf battles", philosophers have a clear claim to "ethics". Anyone not in philosophy who wants to teach "ethics" has to explain why he or she is competent (and why the philosophers do not have prior claim). Many disciplines have developed ways to finesse questions concerning the legitimacy of their teaching ethics. For example, engineers like to talk about courses in "professionalism"; lawyers, about courses in "professional responsibility"; business professors, about courses in "business environment". But the problem of legitimacy will remain until other fields have established their own recognized tradition of ethics teaching. That day is far off for most fields.

Philosophers, of course, have a similar problem of legitimacy. Most professionals quickly recognize how little a philosopher knows about their field, including the ethical problems that arise, what standards apply, and what responses are appropriate. Philosophers with an expertise in ethics do not, as a matter of fact, generally have an expertise in professional ethics. The fields are largely distinct. Yet, even when philosophers make that clear at every possible opportunity, non-philosophers generally continue to feel illegitimate using the term "ethics"; and, even when they don't, their colleagues think they should.

For this reason alone, those of our graduates who have begun to try to get their colleagues to follow their lead have tried to find a philosopher on campus with whom to work. So far, they have succeeded, though some of the philosophers seem initially to have been dubious. (Those of us who work in practical ethics can be surprised at how suspicious of our philosophical credentials philosophers who do not work in our field can still be.) The most effective technique for reducing doubts has been handing such philosophers something— for example, one of my articles—published in a philosophy journal. The place of publication, as much as the helpful instructions and philosophical content, provide a dubious philosopher with what she needs to overcome her doubts. With a philosopher present, our graduate can legitimately talk about "ethics" to other non-philosophers.

The second contribution philosophers can make, even philosophers who have no experience teaching professional ethics, is experience. Philosophers routinely teach through guided discussion. Though we take this method for granted, many disciplines, especially engineering, mathematics, and the physical sciences do not. Their standard teaching method is lecture rather than guided discussion. They are therefore naturally worried about leading a discussion until they do it successfully a few times. And they usually need a few tips (though far fewer than I originally supposed). Philosophers can be quite helpful here, often more helpful than law or business professors who, though they too are used to guiding discussion, tend to guide it in ways less suitable for a discussion of ethics. This difference is, I think, worth a paper of its own.[8]

Philosophers are also used to assigning open-ended essay questions, whether for homework or exams, and grading the answers. Many non-philosophers are not. Here is another place where philosophers can be helpful in ways they might not expect. They can be especially helpful by making clear how little there is to know.

This second contribution, like the first, is clearly temporary. Non-philosophers can learn in a few hours most of what there is to know about leading discussion, writing essay exams, and grading them. After that, a few months experience is generally enough to bring them even with the philosophers. That, anyway, has been our experience. The third contribution is another matter. Philosophers seem to bring to professional ethics a systematic approach, and a depth of experience with argument, that non-philosophers do not have and are unlikely to develop (without becoming philosophers).

I'm not sure why that is. In part, no doubt, it is a matter of self-selection. People become philosophers because they are different from people who become scientists, engineers, physicians, lawyers, mathematicians, or the like. Philosophers take an interest in arguments, in distinctions, in definitions, and so on where most people simply become impatient. Philosophers also have a love of abstraction of a sort many disciplines tend to discourage (and a dislike of factual detail many disciplines find unbelievable).

To whatever self-selection may initially distinguish philosophers from practitioners of other disciplines must be added another cause of distinction, years of exercising certain skills while others exercised others. For better or worse, philosophers devote their lives to arguments, arguments aimed at winning over reason, not just arguments aimed at persuading. Where a philosopher can use her discipline, she is likely to see questions others do not, to make moves in argument others do not, or at least to do such things with more facility than others do. Philosophy is a distinct discipline (even if it is hard to say exactly what distinguishes it from others).[9]

If I am right about this, then, it seems to me, philosophers will always have a distinct role in professional ethics, even after every profession has experts of its own. Whether this role will be valuable enough to sustain much participation is another question. My guess is that it will be. Philosophers seem to be useful insofar as change has created puzzling new ethics problems for a profession or made relatively routine responses to traditional ethics problems seem unsatisfactory. Indeed, it seems to me, the reason professional ethics has moved from a marginal field in a few professions to an important field both in most professions and in philosophy is precisely that traditional arrangements have broken down under the impact of a rapidly changing society. Since change seems to be continuing at a pace making unlikely the reemergence of a new stable tradition, I think it safe to predict that philosophy will continue to have a role in professional ethics.[10] But that role will, I think, come to resemble the critical but marginal role that philosophers have in science more than the central (and practical) role that they now have in, say, medical ethics. We will do "philosophy of professional ethics" (a subdivision of my second sense of "ethics") rather then (as now) professional ethics (in my third sense of "ethics").

Notes

1. For a report of early results, see Michael Davis, "Ethics Across the Curriculum: Teaching Professional Responsibility in Technical Courses", *Teaching Philosophy* 16 (September 1993): 205-235.
2. For a more extended defense of this distinction generally (including subtleties ignored here), see Michael Davis, "The Moral Authority of a Professional Code", *NOMOS* 29 (1987): 302-337. For its application to various professions, see "The Use of Professions", *Business Economics* 22 (October 1987): 5-10; "Vocational Teachers, Confidentiality, and Professional Ethics", *International Journal of Applied Philosophy* 4 (Spring 1988): 11-20; "Professionalism Means Putting Your Profession First", *Georgetown Journal of Legal Ethics* (Summer 1988): 352-366; "The Special Role of Professionals in Business Ethics", *Business and Professional Ethics Journal* 7 (Summer 1988): 51-62; "The Discipline of Science: Law or Profession?", *Accountability in Research* 1 (1990): 137-145; "Thinking Like an Engineer: The Place of a Code of Ethics in the Practice of a Profession", *Philosophy and Public Affairs* 20 (Spring 1991): 150-167; "Do Cops Need a Code of Ethics?", *Criminal Justice Ethics* 10 (Summer/Fall 1991): 14-28; "Codes of Ethics, Professions, and Conflict of Interest: A Case of an Emerging Profession, Clinical Engineering", *Professional Ethics* 1 (Spring/Summer 1992): 179-195; "Wild Professors and Sensitive Students: A Preface to Academic Ethics", *Social Theory and Practice* 18 (Summer 1992): 117-141; "Treating Patients with Infectious Diseases: An Essay in the Ethics of Dentistry", *Professional Ethics* 2 (Spring/Summer 1993): 51-65; and "The State's Dr. Death: What's Unethical about Physicians Helping at Executions?" *Social Theory and Practice* 21 (Spring 1995): 31-60.
3. See, for example, William M. Evan, "Role Strain and the Norm of Reciprocity in Research Organizations," *American Journal of sociology* 68 (1962): 346-54, in which it is suggested that *industrial* scientists stand to their employers as artist to patron rather than as professional to client.
4. One of my colleagues, Robert Ladenson, has been experimenting with another device, an "ethics bowl". Students form teams of four each to compete, much as on Public Television's College Bowl, except that they must answer questions concerning how to respond to ethics problems (presented in the form of a situation requiring a decision); the responses are evaluated by a panel of practitioners (as in a diving contest), and (unlike a diving contest) the teams have the right to criticize the "official answer" if they believe their own is better. After two years of experiment with this format at IIT, the ethics bowl went intercollegiate this spring (with DePaul, Loyola, and Western Michigan holding a joint ethics bowl (after each held an internal ethics bowls to choose a team to represent the school). Students enjoy the competition while appreciating the opportunity the ethics bowls gives them to practice making decisions.
5. For a good critique of the honor system, see the entire *Perspectives on the Professions* 14 (January 1995).
6. For other examples, see the entire issue of *Perspectives on the Professions* 13 (February 1994), as well as Davis, "Ethics Across the Curriculum".
7. In preparation for this conference, I had my research assistant, Victor Kabuye, do a follow-up survey of IIT faculty who had participated in the work during 1991-93.

Of the 45 faculty we began with, seven had left IIT (and we were not able to find them). Of the remaining 38, 34 returned questionnaires (some in response to our mailing, some in response to a follow up mailing, and a few only after Victor had phoned them). Four remain officially unaccounted for. I do not believe their absence is significant a) because I could see no difference in responses between those who responded early and those who responded later and b) because in one case of "no response" I know from a student that he continues to do a substantial amount of ethics in at least one of his courses. I collated the questionnaires. For the question, "Are you integrating more, less, or about the same as you did the first semester (or the first time) after taking the workshop?", the results were: 1991 (7 more, 1 "a little bit" less, and 2 commented in ways not easily categorized), 1992 (3 more, 2 less, and 6 same), and 1993 (4 more, 2 less, 5 same, 2 not easily categories). For the question, "What is your present opinion of integrating ethics into technical courses?", the results were: 1991 (6 favorable, 1 neutral, 3 hard to categorize), 1992 (9 favorable, 1 neutral) and 1993 (all 13 favorable). To the question, "What effect, if any, has your integrating ethics had on colleagues in your department? None? Some? Lots? Details?", the results were: 1991 (2 lots, 4 some, 2 none, and 2 not sure), 1992 (0 lots, 6 some, 4 none, and 1 not sure), and 1993 (1 lots, 5 some, 3 none, and 3 not sure).

8. For some idea what such a paper might look like, see Bruce A. Kimball, *The Emergence of Case Method Teaching, 1870s-1990s: A Search for Legitimate Pedagogy* (Poynter Center for the Study of Ethics and American Institutions, Indiana University: Bloomington, April 1995), an interest contrast between case method in law and in business teaching. While philosopher's use of the case method resembles that of law faculty than business faculty, I believe there may be an important difference. While law faculty seek to identify convincing arguments (not just to raise sensitivity), philosophers seek good arguments.

9. Compare Adam Smith's discussion of the division of labor, *The Wealth of Nations* (New York: Modern Library, 1937), pp. 13-16.

10. For more on this claim, see my "The Ethics Boom: What and Why", *Centennial Review* 34 (Spring 1990): 163-186.

Chapter Six

Management as a Vocation: Towards a People Centered Profession of Management

Peter Davis

Introduction

In this chapter I want to consider the problem of finding an effective management philosophy and culture for an organization of work that has people as its subject (rather than as the object or resource for the process of capital enhancement) in line with what I take to be the Catholic social teaching on work.

In my paper *The Co-operative Association of Labor and the Community of Work* [1] I put forward among other things the proposition that the Co-operative form of business organization contained in principle at least the most appropriate structure for the realization of Catholic Social Doctrine on Work. The latter I suggested could be distilled into three fundamental principles:

1. The right to private ownership of capital (the means to work)
2. The right to access to the means of subsistence for all in need.
3. Labors priority over capital—the view that humankind is the subject not the object of work. [2]

I also suggested that, whatever structure we identified, without individuals motivated by the values inherent in the constitution of those structures the organization would inevitably fail to realize its potential. I acknowledged that through member indifference and poorly directed or motivated management such failure was often the reality within the Co-operative Association of Labor.[3] It is generally recognized in Co-operative circles today that with the increase in size and complexity of business organization the content of membership involvement is often weak and control vested in the senior management team.[4] There is also a growing realization that existing provisions in management development are themselves inappropriate to the needs of membership based organizations.[5] This interest has led me firstly to explore the value base within the Co-operative tradition for a definition of the values and principles from which a distinct Co-operative Management practice may be established.[6] I arrived at certain conclusions concerning the basis for the definition of Co-operative Management as a principle of Co-operation i.e., as an ethical practice rather than a neutral technique by making an analytic distinction between process and purpose in the Co-operative enterprise.

I want here to tentatively extend this approach to the wider question of how we may see this idea of people as the subject rather than the object of work translating into a theory of general management. I will draw on the model of professionalism as my starting point because; a) such an approach has informed much of one strand of thinking (in the UK at least) concerned to construct a coherent strategy for management development;[7] and b) the concept of professionalism as I understand it meets the concept of work that has humankind as its subject. My paper will proceed, therefore, to give a brief outline of a) the characteristics that differentiate work as a profession; b) what are the impediments that I see preventing some approaches to management being characterized as professional in the sense that I have defined the term (here I shall also discuss in particular the controversy of what constitutes the alternative practices covered by the terms Personnel Management and Human Resource Management), c) why I believe that Co-operative Management can be identified as a potential prototype for a management practice that can be fairly characterized as "professional", and d) how we might go on to develop a new approach to the management of capital based organizations that can be seen as constituting a genuine profession of management consistent with the Catholic doctrine of labors priority over capital or people as the subject rather than the object of work.

What Constitutes a Profession?

All true "professions" exhibit six characteristics that distinguish them from other forms of work. Firstly, they contain within their practice a clearly defined body of knowledge applying to a given area of application over which the profession exerts a monopoly control. Secondly, there is an established and recognized independent body of members that define and police standards of practice and conduct. Thirdly, there exists a clearly stated code of ethical conduct which governs the relationships between fellow professionals and between the professionals and their clients. Fourthly, the professionals conduct their affairs through an independent body that controls who may practice and has the power to debar individuals from practicing within the profession. This ensures ultimate autonomy from the organizational or market context for the professional practice. Fifthly, all professional conduct is underpinned by a value set that places the client as the subject not the object of the professional practice. By subject I mean that the responsibility and primary purpose of the professional is to benefit the client and to work in the clients interest. The professional always acts in the clients best interests even if that may mean turning away business. Finally the individual professional is marked out from other workers by the sense of vocation or calling that brings him or her to practice their particular profession. This sense of vocation we may recognize as connecting centrally with the individuals sense of self identity and purpose in life. Believers would recognize this calling as coming ultimately from God. Even non-believers would, I suspect, recognize in the expression of calling or vocation the commitment of the individual to a good that is perceived to be greater then merely the self interest of the professional and his or her career.

I am not arguing that all professionals motivation is necessarily altruistic or that their behavior is always ethical or professional. Clearly there are, for example, corrupt accountants and lawyers as well as doctors and dentists who encourage unnecessary treatments etc. The point, however, is that when professional practitioners are caught in this kind of action it is clearly recognizable as "unprofessional" and as such generally will merit punishment of some kind.

The professional identity is based in the occupation from which the practitioners derive their role and status in society and within the organizations that may employ or hire their services. Not all professions have the same status, of course, and in different cultures some professions are more highly regarded than in others. Teachers for example have a much lower occupational status in the United Kingdom than in India.

Status is also to some extent linked to the extent of exclusivity in monopoly control that the professional body can exercise over who and how persons become recognized as practitioners. Not all professional bodies have the same degree of control although they all aspire to it.

The dividing line between a craft and a profession on this definition I accept is not a very strong one. Both have humanistic values and distinct bodies of knowledge. Both may be said to have an occupational based status that transcends any particular organizational context. Both have autonomous associations which exert control over who may practice and the determination of their standards of practice. In the case of the craft worker the human good focuses in the skill and satisfaction of the craft workers creativity and in the utility and aesthetic appreciation of others in the craft workers product. In the case of the professional worker the human good is focused both in the skill and knowledge the professional brings to their practice and in the benefit enjoyed by the human subject that the professional serves. The distinction beyond that is mainly determined by the **location** of the former in the processes of production rather than in the provision of services and by the relative difference in expense involved in the process of accreditation which itself has a bearing on the relative scarcity of the provider of the required skills.

To a much greater extent professionals employ themselves and control the practice of their employment. The further distinction between the two is that the latter work may be for or on behalf of management but it is not supervised and controlled by management to anything like the same extent as the craft worker which has led to the process of de-skilling and the deconstruction of traditional crafts and their replacement by "skills' that are more organizationally specific. The growing management of health professionals and the increasing size of law and accountancy firms can be seen as evidence for the increasing break-down of the above model of the profession. These developments give credence to the Larson hypothesis that the professions themselves are becoming bureaucratized (Larson 1979 cited in Reed and Anthony 1992) or put another way coming increasingly under the subordination of specific organizational interests that weaken the professions value base, its corporate control and identity.[8]

From the standpoint of *Laborum Exercens* this bureaucratization of professions and craft labor is to be viewed with concern as it represents the further separation of the ownership of work from the individual who performs it. This separation leads to the subordination of the intrinsic good inherent in both professional and craft practice to that of being an instrument in the furtherance of an agenda established by organizations whose primary rationale is the enhancement of Capital.[9]

Laborum Exercens rightly insists that **all** work (not just craftworkers and professionals) has intrinsic dignity where it can be seen that humanity is its subject. "In fact, in the final analysis it is always man who is *the purpose of work*, whatever work it is that is done by man—even if the common scale of values rates it as the merest "service", as the most monotonous, even the most alienating work".[10]

This aspiration, however, can only become a reality to the extent that the management including self management) of work has humankind as its subject or purpose. Thus the development of management as a profession it can be argued is central to the realization of the aspiration expressed in *Laborum Exercens* for all work. This follows because as a result of the growth in bureaucratic control of work management is the practice that mostly determines the shape and content of employment in organizations. The problem first, however , is to discover how the shape and content of management's work is itself determined?

Can We Speak of Management as a Profession?

It is self evident that the status of managers is organizationally based. It depends critically on where in the hierarchy the manager is positioned. This determines the extent of the managers prerogatives, power, remuneration and prestige. Often senior management will not involve middle and junior levels of management in its decision making let alone the shop floor workers. Such a hierarchically based status system does not lend itself to the development of a strong sense of corporate cohesion between managers as a group **within** their organization let alone any corporate identity outside the organization. Team building, culture management, and leadership are all essential aspects of the practice of management because the theory(s) of management precisely lack a coherent statement of values and knowledge that is the hallmark of the profession. These techniques compensate for the lack of professional occupational purpose and identity and subtly enable managers to internalize and accept as legitimate the requirement of allegiance to the employing organization. The less subtle carrot of substantial rewards for senior executives creates a culture where the hallmark of individual achievement is marked by the acquisition of wealth and power. The interests of the particular business organization to increase its relative rate of capital growth faster than its competitors thus determines management behavior and priorities even if in the real world individual managers values and loyalties often generate tensions that may sometimes subvert in practice these organizational goals.

In the 1980s Prof. Charles Handy one of the leading management writers and educators in the UK reported in *The Making of Managers* (1987) that the deficiencies in British management required a national system based on collaboration between Industry, Government and Education.[11] The underlying concept of professionalism provided Handy with a framework with which the educational providers of management development could base their provision for the training and development of managers.[12] This approach which had as its flagship the *Management Charter Initiative* has been generally accepted to have failed largely because of the hostility of employers to any dilution of their control over management development[13] and the lack of a coherent community of interest from which to exert occupational control.[14] Management has been seen to occupy too disparate a range of skills and knowledge that cannot easily be codified and established in the same terms as a professional practice.[15] Read and Anthony sum up the occupational structure of management thus; "...socially fragmented, economically polarized and culturally stratified."[16]

So far the efforts of British management themselves to develop a profession of management has produced little of substance. The British Institute of Management's' *Code of Conduct and Guides to Professional Management Practice* produced in November 1992 must represent one of the blandest and least demanding Codes of Conduct ever produced even though it has been given the status of a by-law of the Institute.[17] The most glaring absence in the Code is its total failure to address or demand mangers have any responsibility for establishing or maintaining Distributive Justice in the determination of the employing organizations purpose. Indeed neither the purpose of business organizations nor there management is ever really addressed in the Institutes' Code or Guidance Notes. I would argue that the **professional** management of economic resources for the generation of wealth must be based on a value statement that includes a Human-centered and Creation-centered statement of the **use** (including distribution) of wealth not merely one that is concerned with the sustainability of resources, which itself says nothing about their correct use. It is hard in practical terms to separate use from distribution or access. A human-centered value base for the profession of management would need to spell out as one key purpose of the profession the objective of human development through the provision of conditions for creative employment leading to distributive or social justice.

If one reflects on the principle theories of management: Scientific Management; Human Relations; and Structural Analysis[18] we can note that the problem of the clash of interests between Labor and Capital has been recognized in one way or another as one of the central issues (problems) that management had to reconcile or resolve in order to be successful in two out of the three models. In the Scientific Management approach it was characterized as disorder, lack of control and "soldiering"; in the Human Relations approach as low moral, wrong attitudes absenteeism and conflict. All three have tended to focus on the processes of management either in terms of the techniques (or lack of them) being applied. In the case of Scientific Management arbitrary management and greed were identified; and in Human Relations Theory a failure to recognize the social dimension of work and apply the necessary techniques of industrial, social and individual psychology. The Structural Analysis approach is more concerned with the complex environmental and organizational constraints within which management has to function.[19] The clash of interests, real or perceived, between Labor and Capital is not understood to be a critical element determining the complexity of modern organizations and their environments by the proponents of Structural Analysis.[20]

None of the three models discuss the purpose of management outside of its service to the organization in their analysis and all three adopt an instrumental view of labor from the "close supervision" approach (Scientific Management); exercise of "leadership" and "gaining their confidence" (Human Relations); to decentralization, helping to "develop their initiative and responsibility while unobtrusively controlling them" strategy (Structural Analysis).[21]

It is difficult to construct a professional management practice out of what amounts in the case of Scientific Management and Human Relations Management to an array of ideological justifications and techniques based on very thin if any empirical research[22] and in the case of Structural Analysis a contingency framework that is silent as to the ultimate purpose of business organization or management.

A further explanation for the resistance if not hostility to the accreditation based Management Charter approach may be that it leads almost automatically to issues of human relationships and notions of justice (both natural and distributive) that are recognized as contradicting the ideological context of the Thatcher/Reagan years with its emphasis on the market as the mechanism for the control of standards and practice for business management. This approach with its focus on the individual consumer, its attempt to marginalise society, and to base an economic determinism on the outcomes of individual consumption decisions in the market may be said to represent the furthest development of the rational bureaucratic view of modern society and organization. Such a view presents human ends in terms of involvement in consumption, with production being merely a means. It contradicts much of the analysis of *Laborum Exercens* with its emphasis on the importance of humankind's involvement in and ownership of the process of production as a participation in Gods Creation.[23]

It is certainly the case that one management function in the United Kingdom, namely Personnel Management, can claim to have the welfare of people (employees) at the center of its practice and has a developed professional association and systematic and generally recognized accreditation. Yet the Personnel "profession" (as many IPD members refer to it) has found itself under considerable pressure since 1979 from within the organization. The much publicized attack on the role of Personnel Management by one of the then leading U.K. industrialists Michael Edward's in 1985 gave expression to the frustration felt by the more aggressive of the British Thatcherite managers. The development of Personnel Management's professional association, the Institute of Personnel and Development, (IPD) and the controversies concerning the role of personnel reflect the tensions and ambiguities that abound in the area of management development and the relationship of managers to the organizations that employ them.

The British personnel function began to develop during the first quarter of the 20th century based upon an emphasis on employee welfare pioneered by non-conformist and paternalistic industrialists like Jessie Boot. The Institute started its existence as the Institute of Welfare Workers most of whom were women concerned with the welfare in employment of mainly female workers By the inter-war years the emphasis had shifted towards collective bargaining amongst larger firms and with this shift came the rise of the Industrial Relations specialist. In the 1950s and 60s the need to radically improve Britain's labor productivity led the personnel function to incorporate, through techniques such as manpower planning, more of the ethos and focus of the Scientific Management approach without abandoning its commitment to employee welfare or industrial relations. The tight labor markets of these years and the growth of trade union membership led to increasing specialization within the personnel function, with the development of recruitment and selection, training and development and the continuing or even increasing importance of industrial relations. By the 1970s the increasing legal controls on employment and the tougher industrial relations climate often meant industrial relations becoming a board level appointment.

This background to the development of personnel management in the UK might help explain why it has been out of step with the rest of management thinking over such issues as the closed shop, which the IPM (now IPD) supported. Personnel as an "ideal type" may be summed up as being a view of management that held that welfare of the employees was a priority and that saw collective bargaining as a legitimate expression of the right of interest groups within the organization to contest those interests (within certain bounds at least.)

Many of the "new" ideas attributed to the Human Resource Management approach in the literature can be found to have been incorporated within the personnel function. For example the IPD had come in the 1980s and 1990s to lay greater stress on individual performance, training and development, and the integration of personnel objectives with those of the overall organization, often within the context of the management of change. Legge, (1990) has argued, for example, that both the Personnel model and the HRM model have much in common in their emphasis on the devolution of personnel work to line management; the need to integrate organizational goals and personnel management goals; and the encouragement of personal development as a means of ensuring the best contribution to organizational success.[24] These trends may reflect the growth in influence of the Structural Analysis approach to organizations and their management as much as to the influence of HRM. The emerging picture in the UK appears to be one of corporate Personnel departments facing both ways—implementing traditional collective bargaining strategies were appropriate whilst introducing new HRM oriented policies in various other areas of the organization.[25] This may, however be seen as no more than the expression of the growing dependency of Personnel Management on a general management that is unsympathetic towards the old style mix of paternalism and pluralism and who no longer fear the Trade Unions.

Guest, (1987) suggests that the HRM approach is clearly distinct from that of personnel management.[26] The adversarial and pluralist perspective of industrial relations is replaced with the unitarist perspective of employee commitment and involvement. Alternative Personnel and HRM strategies can be analyzed from within the framework of the polarity of occupation versus organization or put another way the polarity between a pluralistic value based collective regulation and the unitary and positivistic organization based market regulation of standards, processes and purposes. In HRM the occupational or functional specialist PM emphasis on employment policy is replaced by the idea of integration, with general management taking a much greater responsibility for employee relations and employment policy and ensuring its general integration the organizations strategic planning process. Guest, (1987) proposes that it is appropriate to view HRM and Personnel Management as two alternative practices both of which will, under different circumstances, be more relevant and successful than the other.[27]

The contradiction that some observers have felt to exist within the HRM framework between its concern with individual development and its emphasis on the determination of organizational need as the criteria for managing the organizations employment has led to alternative versions of HRM being identified. In the UK "Hard" and "Soft" Models of Human Resource Management have been identified by a number of writers e.g., Storey, (1987). They suggest that the soft HRM's commitment to the development of the individual employee is replaced in the hard version of HRM with a more instrumental emphasis on human resource utilization. It is here that issues of normative values in respect of the treatment of individuals comes through just as it does in terms of the HRM emphasis on the individual rather than the collective in its Employee Relations policies. Whilst HRM emphasizes the individual, with greater concern for individual development and autonomy at the same time Guest (1990) notes that it denies the individual any collective security?[28] Is a Unitary perspective a sufficient justification for this approach whilst concepts like "no compulsory redundancy" have been jettisoned by even the most dedicated HRM based organizations? Guest (1995) in his most recent reflections on union management relations under HRM has moved towards the view that there may still be space for a reduced Union role in partnership with management. Guest is extremely pessimistic that the Unions can survive without the adoption of the more enlightened HRM framework.[29] Guests' approach to Trade Union involvement within the HRM framework is reminiscent of the approach Gompers and the AFL took in response to Scientific Management where, "Gompers began appearing as a star speaker at management meetings where he stressed the humanizing effects of union objections to the contributions of scientific management, which were otherwise necessary and useful."[30]

This approach by Guest is, however, clearly to be preferred to what Sissons (1994) has described as the absence of any management policy or philosophy on employment at all. Referring to published survey results Sissons claims "In only a small number of cases, however, is this transformation in the direction of the HRM organization which so many pundits proclaimed. Rather it appears to be taking the form of substitution of individualism for collectivism, a reduction in standards and an assertion of management freedom from constraints."[31] This statement may sum up the particular British context for Personnel, but it may be argued that the post war consensus in Europe has led to a partnership between Capital and Labor. The extension of collective bargaining and industrial participation through works councils that is a variation or even a development of the old style British paternalism with its incorporated adversarial approach towards the unions remains a very strong feature of European Employment Policy.

Sparrow and Hiltrop (1994) in their historical review of the development of HRM trace its origins back to 1974 and the work of Flamholtz on human capital theory, i.e., that employees should be seen as an asset rather than as a cost.[32] The definitions of HRM all assume that there is no conflict of interest between Labor and Capital and they also assume managerial integrity and knowledge. They are totally silent on the impact of the organizations employment policies in terms of society, the labor market or the economy. The split found in American models of HRM is very similar to the Hard-Soft Models of HRM suggested by Storey (1987) and may also be said to give us an American version to the controversy between Personnel and HRM in the UK.[33]

In the Michigan School people are seen as needing to be managed just like any other organizational resource. Resources are matched to meet the changing needs of the business. This means in a word "flexibility" for the engagement (not simply employment) of labor to make the best possible fit with the organizations needs. There is an understanding in the Michigan School approach of the need to match worker behavior to ensure the realization of the strategic goals of the organization.[34] This "hard" HRM can be seen as providing the clearest expression in the field of employment of the organizational rather than the professional led approach to the management of people. Within the Michigan framework the worker is just a disposable instrument in the process of capital accumulation.

An alternative American approach to is to be found in the Harvard School of HRM.[35] The Harvard schools roots are in the Human Relations model rather than in the case of the Michigan School where it could be argued the latter are drawn more from the Scientific Management School where Taylor emphasized the need to select (match) the most appropriate worker for the task and to effect the most appropriate behavior through rewards based on individual performance and on training workers in the best way to do the task required. The Harvard model on the other hand centers on the view that HRM decisions are those that impact on the employment relationships between the organization and its employees. Employment problems cannot be resolved the model argues without management's clear commitment to identification of appropriate forms of employee development and involvement within the organization.[36] Business strategy is only one (important) consideration in the Harvard model. Cultural and social contexts as well as labor relations with Trade Unions and the particular national legal frameworks are also important in arriving at a very broad based range of matching strategies in the enterprise. In the Harvard approach, however, there is the recognition that management is not simply reacting to external pressures in the environment but is also in a position to make its own unique contribution to the situation and to some extent to even shape it.[37]

The Harvard stakeholder model of HRM implies like its UK counterpart Personnel Management a dependency on an external regulation of the market to ensure stakeholders rights are upheld. Otherwise it is difficult to see what is the basis upon which some at least of the stakeholders are to be allowed to exercise any involvement. In the political terrain it is precisely this external regulation that is under attack.

Neither Harvard nor the IPD claim for the employee more than the status of one interest among many. These two models may attempt to achieve fairness through negotiation in a pluralist framework but the wider role of general management is as problematic as ever because neither attempt to evaluate the overarching purpose of the organization and its management.

To sum up the discussion so far I have suggested that capital based models of organization and management have not addressed the issue of purpose when conducting their analysis. Rather the organization has been raised to the status of the subject whose needs all other factors of production or stakeholders must be concerned to meet. The organizations purpose is assumed rather than discussed in all models of organization and their management. The traditional management problems such as how to get the right product at the right price in the right time to the right people with the minimum of conflict and the maximum of profit ignore the central issue of the role of Human Labor in delivering the answers. The questions of ownership, access to resources, distributive justice and personal fulfillment are hardly addressed accept as subsidiary issues forced upon the organizations due to environmental constraints. Management is there to serve the organization whose needs have become the ends rather than being seen as means. Management cannot hope to develop a practice that can be characterized as professional under these circumstances because it has no human centered purpose to reflect against its standards and methodologies.

I shall argue in the next section that the strength of the Co-operative model for business organization is that as a membership based community business it has a clear objective purpose that has at its' heart the benefit of individual members (owners). It can become efficient both in its response to markets as a provider of goods and services and in ethical terms as a people centered organization led by a professional management based upon clearly under stood people centered values and purposes. I shall in this discussion present the value statement and organizational context that I have argued elsewhere may enable a fully professional co-operative management practice to evolve. I shall then return to the broader question of the establishment of a genuine profession of management in the context of a capital or share based organization. I have not the space to discuss the implications for management in public service and voluntary not for profit organizations here beyond stating that I believe the Co-operative model of professional management has very promising prospects for transfer into these areas of management practice.

The Co-operative Manager as the Prototype for the Professional Manager

The growth in power and influence of management and the withering of democratic content in many of the larger Co-operative Societies was one of the key issues that prompted the review of Co-operative Identity by the International Co-operative Alliance (ICA). Another was the question of why bother to be a Co-operative at all? Whatever may be said in public many managers, unsure as to the answer to this question, have in the past ignored falling membership participation in the process of concentrating on their responsibility for the "business" which is viewed very much in the light of capital based organizations that are seen as more successful and where management is free to manage.

The ICA draft document on Co-operative Identity (at the time of writing the final statement has not yet been approved by the ICA Congress) unfortunately fails to address let alone resolve these problems. It is not an affirmation of the "promise" of co-operation as a democratic movement but a definition of its social and economic purpose that we require.[38] To pretend as the background paper does that key decisions are taken by ordinary members through the democratic process is merely to perpetuate a myth that ignores management and creates cynicism in the latter rather than the commitment that the movement so urgently needs. Politically-correct statements using the language of European Social Policy and Business Ethics have been adopted and presented as a formula for addressing this crisis in co-operative identity.

This approach, however, just will not do. Honesty, Social Responsibility, and Equal Opportunities are important criteria upon which the performance of **all** organizations should be judged not just Co-operatives. Democracy is a distinctive feature of the Co-operative form but one that without the recognition of the role and importance of management in the decision-making process remains singularly hollow given the complexities of the modern marketplace.

Co-operatives need Co-operative Managers—people they can trust, committed to the values and purposes of the Co-operative Membership. If we are to provide such people we must first provide a clear statement of their role and their specifically Co-operative identity in terms of the Co-operative Purpose or Mission. Such a statement is not an attempt to define a "perfect co-operative" but to provide a working criteria for the direction, purpose and management of all co-operative organizations irrespective of their function.[39] *Whilst co-operative management has no recognition and no sense of its distinctive co-operative purpose democracy will continue to be undermined and the development of the strategic management of co-operative organizations will remain problematic and random.* Yet the re-drafted statement of Co-operative Identity and Principles circulated at the May 1995 British Co-operative Wholesale Society AGM simply reiterates the old formula of "common economic interests"[40]

Nor does the following statement of principles in the document concerning Democratic Control (principle 2) and Autonomy and Independence (principle 4) address how a well informed and powerful management with little understanding or sympathy for the Co-operative Movement can be prevented from mobilizing a majority of normally un-involved co-operative members to sell off the assets accumulated by past generations for immediate short term gain.[41] Indeed "common economic interest" could well be the justification for the sell off or transfer of the co-operative organizations' assets to a capital based organization. Co-operative Managers need a clear statement of the unifying purpose of co-operation that can cover the wide diversity of co-operative activities across the globe. This is not provided by the 6th principle which asserts rather than persuades that Co-operation between Co-operatives is best.[42] Unfortunately, it is **not** always in Co-operatives "common economic interest" to trade together. And as we have no other statement of co-operative purpose what else does this sixth principle refer to?

Co-operative associations today need more than ever to hold two primary over-arching common *co-operative* purposes in addition to their functional business based immediate purposes as providers of products and services. All co-operators have in common their individual vulnerability and powerlessness in the marketplace and the inadequacy of their personal wealth to meet their needs for subsistence and welfare. Secondly, for association or co-operation to be practiced by economically vulnerable people they must act together (this requires a strong sense of their community of interests). Thus we can say that; *The first co-operative purpose is therefore to redress imbalances in market power. Secondly, all co-operative associations should exist to strengthen the idea and practice of community amongst their membership both as an intrinsic good and because it is this acting together in unity that is key to successful association.*[43]

An amended definition of the co-operative identity should, therefore, read as follows.

Definition

"A co-operative is a voluntary, democratic, autonomous association of persons, whose purpose is to encourage members to grow in community and to act collectively both for the intrinsic value of being part of a living community and to overcome their problems of economic dependency and need by providing access to, and ownership of the means of subsistence and welfare.

Co-operatives as they grow develop managerial strategies, structures and policies that enhance their ability to meet these co-operative purposes."[44]

These amendments to the draft definition of Co-operative Identity in terms of the Co-operative Purpose enables a much sharper evaluation of the effectiveness of co-operative management. It implies three clear co-operative criteria upon which management performance can be judged in the co-operative context.

a) The first criteria being the strengthening of unity, involvement and community within co-operative membership.
b) The second being the accumulation of collective and individual economic resources by members.
c) The third and criteria being the extent of democratic involvement exercised by members.[45]

These three criteria are in addition to not in place of existing functional business criteria. Only when Co-operative management is directed by a clear statement of co-operative purpose, upon which appropriate values and principles have been constructed can they begin to differentiate a professional co-operative management practice. For this reason we need a statement of co-operative values that emphasizes the purpose as well as process of co-operation.

The statement of Co-operative values should read;

"Co-operatives are based on the values of community, people before capital, self-help, mutual responsibility, democracy, quality, equity, service and stewardship."[46]

These additional values of community, people before capital, quality, stewardship and service to others can hardly be said to be new. Their re-emphasis now, however, is particularly important and relevant. It enables us to define the principles governing a professional co-operative management practice and culture and suggests the inclusion of a further key principle addressing this question into the existing draft statement on Co-operative Identity.

I have urged that a new 7th principle that can help the movement address the problems we face should be under the heading of;

"Co-operative Management"

"Co-operative management is conducted by men and women responsible for the stewardship of the co-operative community, values and assets. They provide leadership and policy development options for the co-operative association based upon professional training and co-operative vocation and service. Co-operative management is that part of the co-operative community professionally engaged to support the whole membership in the achievement of the co-operative purpose."[47]

It is by the incorporation of co-operative management as part of the co-operative community and as representing an important principle of co-operation itself that we can work out the tension produced through increasing scale between management and democracy within the co-operative enterprise.

A clear, membership focused, statement of co-operative purpose underpinning a strong statement of the principles of co-operative management can empower the professional co-operative managers and at the same time improve the ability of lay members to assess management performance and ensure the integrity of the co-operative identity. The commitment by top managers to the Co-operative Purpose and their adherence to a short statement of Co-operative Management Principles will provide a succinct criteria for appraising management's co-operative performance and enable lay members to better understand and defend if necessary the integrity of their co-operative society.

The establishment of a principle of co-operative management enables the co-operative enterprise to be managed professionally and co-operatively in such a way that democracy and involvement will remain key aspects of co-operative practice. The clear definition of co-operative purpose (see above) gives the Co-operative Society of whatever type the strategic direction within which co-operative management must work and against which their performance can then be appraised.

The point of this detour into the issues facing the Co-operative Organization and its Management is that they precisely parallel the need in capital based organizations to clarify the role of management and the human centered purpose of the organization beyond its function as a supplier of goods and services.

We must define organizational purpose and management purpose if we are to break out of a straight jacket in theoretical terms within modern management thinking and move in the direction of a human centered management and organization. The co-operative model of management serving a people centered purpose gives co-operative management its legitimization and a people centered criteria upon which it may be judged. The value basis expounded by *Laborum Exercens* (which I have argued the Co-operative association already meets) may be able to direct us towards a definition of purpose for share based organizations in terms that will enable the evolution of their management into an autonomous professional vocation.

Towards a Catholic Concept of Management and Organizational Purpose?

How are we to formulate a clear statement of the over arching **purpose** of business organization that enables management practice to be developed within the context of a human centered value set?

From the perspective of *Laborum Exercens* any company or friendly society operating in the marketplace has the following purposes to;

- facilitate the growth of individual ownership of property,
- facilitate Labors priority over capital ,
- facilitate peoples access to the means of subsistence and welfare,
- facilitate individual human development , and to,
- facilitate the development of community and family life.

There is, in the terms of *Laborum Exercens* , no contradiction between private ownership of capital and labors priority over capital because it is precisely through the **widespread** individual ownership of the means of production and distribution that the priority of Labor over Capital can be established. This idea is developed in the section dealing with the "personalize" argument in *Laborum Exercens*.[48] The focus on the economic needs of the individual member remains one of the great advantages of a membership based organization over one with traded shares because shares can and do end up being held and controlled by smaller and smaller concentrations of people whose economic interest are often best served by actions that deny many other people access to these means of subsistence and welfare. Generally membership based organizations admit those whom they employ into membership thus further developing the sense of ownership of work by the worker in equality with other share based members.

One problem for the share based context blocking the development of a professional management is, as we have seen, the hostility of the present owners of these companies to such an independent management. In the case of the co-operative society the average member lacks the resources to effectively challenge co-operative management. Thus of necessity Co-operatives require the highest standards of ethical or professional behavior on the part of Co-operative Managers.

They require managers that are not merely civil servants but members providing the leadership within the same community of interest The Co-operative Manager must have a co-operative people centered vocation in order to rise to the task.

I shall leave to one side just for the moment the issue of power in the share based company and consider what sort of statement of management role, purpose and values would be helpful for the identification of a professional management practice in the context of the organizational purpose as expressed in *Laborum Exercens*.

The work of Managers is the organization of economic resources to facilitate the creation, growth and distribution of wealth (as opposed to the generally understood narrower purpose of profitability and the protection of shareholders interests) in order to enable;

- the growth of individual ownership of property,
- labors priority over capital,
- peoples access to the means of subsistence and welfare,
- individual human development , and,
- the development of community and family life. (*Laborum Exercens*)

The achievement of a widespread acceptance of this organizational and management purpose will require a professional association of managers committed to the achievement of the human centered values and principles and the establishment of high standards of professional knowledge, skills and conduct required to carry through the purpose of facilitating the individuals access, ownership, and enjoyment of the means for their subsistence and welfare. The determination of wealth creation , growth and distribution under these new conditions will require that managers rethink the techniques and practices through which they arrive at their decisions. The impact could be substantial on complex issues concerning the determination of such questions as:

1. The mix of technology and labor and training and development.
2. The establishment of remuneration and compensation policies.
3. The statutory and market led requirement to ensure a competitive rate of return to shareholders.
4. The terms of trade offered to suppliers.
5. The pricing policy to customers.
6. The location and focus of long term investment and disengagement in and out of products and services.
7. The management of information.
8. The management of environmental impact and health and safety policy.

These two purposes of management as facilitators of wealth creation and wealth distribution once situated in terms of the requirements of *Laborum Exercens* generate an ethical basis for the identification of a professional practice that could regulate management behavior and standards.

Although complex issues are raised in terms of the decision making managers must undertake under this new statement of purpose, nevertheless, there are perhaps no more that five key principles upon which the professional practice and purpose of general management need to be founded. Namely, commitment to: Expertise : Quality : Involvement : Distributive Justice : The Unity of Labor .

Expertise

Clearly managers must in order to succeed provide the analysis, vision, co-ordination and leadership acquire a wide range of knowledge and skills to a high order of development. All professionals are recognized through the expertise they bring to their chosen field.

Quality

This is important because we must recognize the ethical value basis for the professional which informs all their conduct, motivates their actions, and establishes the standards of quality in their service to others.

Involvement

Without the involvement of people, employers, customers, investors, suppliers and all those affected by the organizations operations, the commitment to being a people centered practice cannot be realized and the necessary information to guide management decision-making would be absent. Most important of all there would be inadequate scrutiny or accountability for the management's actions.

Distributive Justice

Without this central principle by which to judge management actions we have no grounds to ensure the proper growth in private ownership of capital. Nor would we be able to be assured of the priority of Labor over capital across all those sections of the society whose economic welfare and/or work experience depends on the outcomes of management decision making.

The Unity of Labor

Managers do not work alone in organizations. Ownership must be personalized even in the biggest organization whether it be share based or membership based. Work however is for most of us today a social practice where the interdependence and goodwill of each towards all is essential for the efficient achievement of organizational purposes and the sense of community and identity that comes through a shared sense of responsibility and the recognition that none of the parts is greater than the whole. The principle of the unity of labor is the foundation for job satisfaction and trust within organizations. It informs the remuneration policies as much as does the principle of distributive justice because it helps us to recognize the importance and dignity of all contributions to the organization and the necessity of restraining the top and raising the bottom to keep differential ratios within organizations within just bounds. The unity of labor thus encourages the upgrading of skills, the development of the flexibility of labor, and the sense of solidarity and community at all levels in the organization. At a another level the unity of labor enables us to recognize that whilst there will necessarily be a professional grouping of managers within large and complex organizations, nevertheless, even here a key part of their task will be to devolve the function of management as far as possible to both increase the satisfaction and enjoyment of work as well as the improvement of efficiency.

In view of the reality of failure that I briefly reviewed in the sections above, concerned with why management has not yet been able to constitute itself as a professional practice, the identification of what should or might constitute management as a profession seems rather academic. I must now identify, therefore, those forces that I believe could contradict the current trend towards the hegemony of the organization in the market that has for all practical and theoretical purposes become treated as an end in itself whose ultimate benefit to humankind is assumed in theory but rarely demonstrated in practice.

Firstly, there is public opinion. The outrage felt by consumers, small shareholders and organized labor concerning the savage cuts in employment, price rises, and cuts in service quality that have accompanied often huge salary increases for top executives has been extensively reported in the UK. The concern about environmental issues, poor health and safety records in some industries, and the financial scandals that have rocked the business community over the last decade or more are leading to a sense of cynicism and distrust concerning management's motives and values. The responsibility carried by senior management today and the social impact of their actions needs to be directed and sometimes judged by an ethically based professional body whose responsibility is to uphold professional standards not organizationally based interests.

Secondly, there are the managers themselves. All managers that is. Not just the top handful of senior executives with enormous share-options to protect. The average manager knows that management in general is dis-empowered not empowered by the current hierarchy based on power, skill and knowledge tempered by no more than the most bland and general statements of ethical standards or human centered objectives. The criteria of bottom line and market valuation of share capital is just to simplistic a statement to realistically judge the performance of organizations bigger in size than the average government exchequer and whose decisions often effects millions who can exert no influence on how or why those decisions are made. State regulation and even international regulation through trade agreements and other conventions have done little to alleviate the growth in insecurity, intensity, and meaninglessness felt by those in work. The loss of access to work with the increase in poverty and meaninglessness that comes with unemployment and forced migration has intensified along with every extension of regulation and/or deregulation alike in the last thirty years.

It is time to start on the inside. There will never be socially responsible organizations without socially responsible managers. You cannot expect managers to guess what it is that constitutes socially responsible behavior. They must have guidance, standards and the discipline that only a professional body can provide. I believe that the more senior middle managers have the position in organizations from which to organize such an association.

Thirdly, the soft or Harvard stakeholder model of HRM and UK based PM (IPD) counterpart does enable us to delineate a framework through which an alliance may be formed between a growing association of professional managers together with other sections of organized labor and with small shareholders and consumer groups to gain recognition for a Management Charter that committed the professional manager to a human centered model of management. Indeed without professional mangers and in absence of external regulation it is hard to see how to manage fairly the various stakeholders in any organization. A professional association of general managers would best be developed on the basis a trade or industry in order to maintain links between the technical conditions and the professional practice of management in a given sector whilst not allowing any particular organization to become judge and jury in its own case. The existence of functional based and general management associations may give rise to the hope that they could have the momentum to reform and develop into professions although the experience with the (British) Institute of Management does not give us grounds for confidence.

Finally, that the Church has a mission in this area cannot be disputed following the tradition and teaching which has cumulated in *Laborum Exercens.* There are already many associations of Christian Managers and Management Consultants whom the Church needs to engage in dialogue and who need the Churches encouragement. The encouragement of the human centered management of organizations is central to the realization of the Churches teaching in *Laborum Exercens.*

Notes

1. Davis Peter, Ch. 12 "The Co-operative Association of Labor and the Community of Work" in *Values, Work, Education. The Meanings of Work*, Value Inquiry Series No. 22, Eds. Samuel M. Natale and Brian M. Rothschild, Rodopi, Amsterdam, 1995, pp241-258.
2. ibid. pp241-242.
3. ibid. pp253-254.
4. Davis, Peter, *Co-operative Management and Organizational Development for the Global Economy*, Discussion Papers in Management Series, No 7 /94, 1994, p5.
5. Volk, Reimer, *Review of International Co-operation*, ICA, Geneva, 1994, p48.
6. Davis, Peter , *Co-operative Management and Co-operative Purpose*. Discussion Papers in Management Series , University of Leicester, No. 1/ 95, 1995.
7. Reed. M. and Anthony P. "Professionalizing Management and Managing Professionalization: British Management in the 1980s." *Journal of Management Studies* 29: September 1992 pp 591-613.
8. ibid. p 599.
9. The assumption I am making here will have to stand without further defense because of lack of space. Let it suffice that the surprised or skeptical reader should understand that the author does not accept that market forces are representative of the majority of individuals needs and aspirations. Rather I see the Global Market today as being essentially oligopolistic in nature and serving interests that are inimical to human development and to Creation. The oligopolistic control of the Labor Market and the separation of individual ownership from the means of their employment I have suggested in a previous paper has led to that division between Labor and Capital leading to what a Papal Encyclical refers to as "...the opposition between capital and labor ..." (*Laborem Exercens* , Catholic Truth Society Ed., London, 1981, p45) which has itself become exacerbated by the growing dependence of Labor on Capital for employment.
10. *Laborem Exercens* , Catholic Truth Society Ed., London, 1981, p23.
11. Reed and Anthony op cit. p594.
12. ibid. p594.
13. ibid. p595.
14. ibid. p593.
15. ibid. p596.
16. ibid. p 598.
17. Articles 10,11, and 12 of the Articles of Association of The Institute of Management. Reg. Office, 3rd Floor ,2 Savoy Court, The Strand , London, WC2R OEZ.
18. Guillen, Mario F., *Models of Management. Work, Authority, and Organization in a Comparative Perspective*, University of Chicago Press, 1994, Table 1.1 pp10-11.
19. ibid.
20. ibid.
21. ibid.
22. Rose Michael, (See Parts 1 &2)*Industrial Behavior. Theoretical Development Since Taylor*, Penguin, Hammondsworth, 1975.
23. *Laborum Exercens*, op cit., See in particular sections 9 and 10, pp31 to 36.

24. Legge, Karen, "Human Resource Management. A critical analysis", in *New Perspectives on Human Resource Management,* ed John Story, Routledge, London, 1990, pp19-40.
25. Storey, John, *Developments in the Management of Human Resources,* Blackwells, 1992.
26. Guest, David, E., "Human Resource Management and Industrial Relations", in *Journal of Management Studies,* 24 (5), 1987, pp 503-521.
27. ibid.
28. Guest , David, E., " Human Resource management: its implications for industrial relations and trades unions." in *New Perspectives on Human Resource Management* 1990. Ed. John Story, pp41-55.
29. Guest, David, E., Ch.5, "Human Resource Management, Trade Unions and Industrial relations", in *Human Resource Management. A Critical Text.* ed. John Storey, Routledge, London, 1995, pp110-141.
30. Rose Michael, op cit. p60.
31. Sission, Keith ed. *Personnel Management. A Comprehensive Guide to Theory and Practice in Britain*, Blackwell, Oxford, 1994, p41.
32. Sparrow, Paul, R. and Hiltrop, Jean-M., *European Human Resource Management in Transition,* Prentice Hall, London, 1994, p5.
33. ibid. Table 1.1, and pp7 to 22.
34. ibid. p8.
35. ibid. p12.
36. ibid. p12.
37. ibid. p13.
38. *Into the 21st Century: Co-operatives Yesterday, Today and Tomorrow*, Background Paper, ICA, Geneva, 1995.
39. *Statement of Co-operative Identity.* A Background Paper, ICA, 1995.
40. ibid., see clause 1 Definition.
42. ibid.
43. ibid.
44. Davis Peter, op cit. *Co-operative Management and Co-operative Purpose, 1995,* pp9-10.
45. ibid. p13.
46. ibid. p14.
47. ibid. p16.
48. *Laborum Exercens,* op cit. pp55-57.

Chapter Seven

A Theory of Business Development

Robert F. Dischner

Artical Precis

The following summarizes the argument made in this chapter. (1) There are two primary areas where structured learning interventions take place — in schools and in business. (2) The development process valued in education is different from the process valued in business, although we frequently, and unwittingly, interchange the two models. (3) It would be useful for businesses to examine the models they use, and engage in productive dialogue about the aims of their learning interventions and the best methods for achieving those aims.

Section 1 will introduce critical issues, how I became interested in them, and discuss similarities and differences in the way we seek to develop individuals in schools and business.

Section 2 will look to the literature of educational theory to establish a model of development. This model is based upon the work of Thomas Green[1] and others. It will be used to explain differences among the various means of development (conditioning, training, teaching, indoctrinating).

Section 3 will assess selected works and theoretical models in the field of business development. These works/models will be investigated in terms of the model of development established in the first section.

Section 4 will conclude by drawing out the practical implications of this investigation for business development. It is my opinion that the field of business development has much to learn from the existing literature in the field of professional education.

It is my hope that the ideas contained herein will help to incite a response from human resource professionals. It is my belief that the position described in this paper has much to contribute toward a philosophy of development for business. I seek to bring attention to this area, so that others might construct a business development model that values knowledge acquisition, the art of teaching, and respect for persons.

Section 1

Introduction

> *There are obviously two educations. One should teach us how to make a living and the other how to live.*

James Adams

One of the most significant things that I learned as a graduate student at the University of Buffalo in the late 1970s was that studying the worth and purpose of education is both very easy and very difficult.[2]

It is easy because almost everyone has been exposed to schooling. This experience, obtained through many years of direct participation as students,[3] has enabled us to contribute to debate about schooling issues in a meaningful way.

It is difficult for at least three reasons. First, when we consider the breadth of concepts we need to control, including political, psychological, pedagogical, and philosophical, it is no wonder that these issues have eluded resolution for millennia, challenging our greatest intellectual artisans — Plato, Rousseau, and Dewey, to name a few.

The second reason it is difficult, ironically, is because contributions are so easy to make. Our exposure to schools makes us feel comfortable about our ability to contribute to decision making, formulating policy, and generally in voicing our opinions about schooling issues. Sometimes it is difficult to discern the considered, thoughtful contribution from the wistful, politically expedient contribution.

The third reason it is difficult is the critical role that conceptions, or views about education, play in the evaluation of individual ideas. These conceptions differ from one another in significant ways — ways that make the same idea useful in one theory, but a conundrum in another. The power of these conceptions is so dramatic that they can make the same action plausible under some conceptions, and folly under others.

For example, those who argue, in the American Progressive tradition, that schools are the engines for social changes see the schools as places to initiate social policy. Others, arguing under a different conception of education, see schools as reflections of the society they serve. Therefore, they see initiatives to implement social changes through the schools as folly. They would argue that the schools are not engines of change in this critical sense, but rather more like cabooses, reflections of the society they serve. Under this conception, schools can be seen, perhaps, as a means of community expression, but not as a way to bring about social change.

As a graduate student, this learning demonstrated me the importance of conceptions, and also made me value the importance of discussion and debate about development issues. It helps us to understand who we are, and what we wish to become.

Some fifteen years later, as a practicing professional in human resource development, I have come to the realization that there is yet another, similar, layer of simplicity, and complexity, to address when we consider the area of business development.

That is, the challenge of conceptual consistency and clarity described above becomes even more complex when we transfer our understanding, piecemeal or otherwise, from our thinking about schools to our ideas regarding business development. We often use schools as a model, or metaphor, for our thinking about business development.[4] The difficulty of understanding educational issues becomes even more confounding when we attempt to transfer this understanding from one setting to another — from schooling to business development.

For example, the model above regarding the Progressive conception of schools as the engine of social change is also played out in the business setting. Those who believe training initiatives can cause "culture change" in corporations frequently seek to identify what has worked in other corporations and import those models. The hope is that these programs will cause the desired change — here training is seen as the engine, or cause, of "cultural" change.

However, if training is conceived of differently, as a reflection of, or expression of a corporation's values, like those who argue that education is a means of community expression, training will be seen as an effect, not a cause. And, under this conception, efforts to bring about change through training alone could be seen as wasteful.

It is easy to see how comparing business and schools can assist us in investigating these important questions, although it does not provide us with answers. Is the model of education as an engine for change useful for schools and for business? If it is not useful for schools, does this mean that it would be likewise inappropriate for business? Or, is business development, and its environment, different enough that it can be a powerful agent for change?

In order to begin to answer these questions, we need to investigate business development, and to ask how it is similar and different from schooling. It is startling that it is difficult, if not impossible, to find meaningful dialogue around these issues. While debates along these lines will rage in professional schools of education for years, similar questions may never surface in the business environment.

The beginning of such a discussion would look to the ways that the two models of development are similar and different. The similarities are striking, most notably the reliance upon the tools of schools – the classroom, instructional media, instructors, etc. Similarities also include: the belief that learning is a desirable way to change the self and, perhaps, the society/business; that the development of individuals is a worthwhile effort and is an important part of personal and organizational success; and, that there is a great deal of political expediency to be gained in the support of education or training.

The differences are many, and they are significant. For example: the ends of the development process are likely to be different in many ways; the way we describe the means of achieving the ends also differs (i.e., we "train" in business, "teach" in schools); the political context is also different (i.e., schools serve a democratic order, businesses a more autocratic order); the schools are greatly influenced by local control, tradition, and professional schools of education, while businesses are more likely to be influenced by consultants/vendors and a style of pedagogy that suits business; the amount and quality of debate about development issues differs considerably in these two areas.

Given these similarities and differences, and given the points made earlier regarding the ease and difficulty of contributing to debates about development, it is clear that there is much at stake, and much to learn. It is also clear that with the strong emotions and political aspects that attend educational issues in society, and training and development issues in corporations, the battlefield is drawn, and everyone is armed. In an intellectual sense, the battlefield has much to do with the limits and appropriateness of a metaphor, *viz.*, the appropriateness of educational/schooling models to the field of business development.

In order to more systematically compare these two areas of development I will next establish an architecture that describes the various means through which development is achieved in schools, and which are most highly valued.

A Model of Development for Education

If a man's actions are not guided by thoughtful conclusions, then they are guided by inconsiderate impulse, unbalanced appetite, caprice, or the circumstances of the moment. To cultivate unhindered, unreflective external activity is to foster enslavement, for it leaves the person at the mercy of appetite, sense, and circumstance.

John Dewey

While critical distinctions have always been a part of educational theory, it is in the latter half of this century that individuals interested in education have worked to develop a large body of work devoted to the analysis of educational concepts. This is in large part due to the work of Ludwig Wittgenstein, Gilbert Ryle, and others, who demonstrated that the analysis of concepts is an activity that is valuable both in refining present practices and enhancing future decisions. Their work is testimony to the complexity of language generally and specifically to the concepts that guide our understanding.

Practitioners of educational theory have worked extensively to clarify concepts that play a role in the educational process. The extent of these analyses, the precision of the results, and the response they incite is striking. Ryle's analysis of "knowledge" in *The Concept of Mind*[5] stands as an apposite example to demonstrate this point. In the context of analysis on a range of concepts, Ryle points to a critical ambiguity in the concept of knowledge by demonstrating the breadth of predicates that the concept can logically receive.

His purpose in this analysis was to discredit the Cartesian dualism, or what he calls "the ghost in the machine." Ryle works extensively with two kinds of knowledge: knowing that something is the case ("knowing that") and knowing how to do something ("knowing how"). Each of Ryle's two types of knowledge shares syntactical similarities, e.g., each can be used readily with concepts such as "teach" and "learn." However, there are syntactical differences, and these syntactical differences suggest conceptual, or logical differences. Ryle's distinction and his attending arguments have been the subject of considerable debate among those who study educational theory, as hundreds of works have been written in response to Ryle.

Many of these works have subsequently generated responses, which, in turn, have generated further response. These analyses have led to subsequent investigation into related concepts, *e.g.*, practicing, disposition, drill, capacities, tendencies, etc.

This phenomenon of intense debate is characteristic of intellectual inquiry and is predicated upon the idea that these issues are: worth discussing; can be resolved, or at least advanced, by such debate; and that there are standards or ways for those involved in the debate to achieve this resolution. It is a critical feature of this proposal that the value of such debates and the interest in conducting them, while common in education, is almost absent in business development.

One of the fruits of this continuing debate is the differentiation type analysis by Thomas Green to distinguish among four different concepts that are related to learning. Green analyzes the differences and similarities of conditioning, training, teaching and indoctrinating, and places them on Ryle's continuum. Green's analysis helps us to understand how these different development tools can be employed to shape behavior ("knowing how") or knowledge and belief ("knowing that"). Green's architecture looks something like this:[6]

KNOWING HOW ....KNOWING THAT

Conditioning — Training — Teaching — Indoctrinating

SHAPING BEHAVIOR   SHAPING KNOWLEDGE & BELIEF

Green uses a single axis, based on Ryle's distinction, to place the four concepts along a continuum. This organizing principle is only one way that can be used to differentiate among these concepts. This point will receive greater attention later in this section. The remainder of this section will be devoted primarily to pointing out critical features of each of the concepts.

The Concept of Conditioning

The concept of conditioning stands at the end of Green's topology, on the end of the continuum of "knowing how." As such, it stretches the concept of learning to its behavioral limits. The concept usually enters educational literature as a near relative to other, more critical concepts, such as "training" and "teaching."[7] It serves our discussion by providing a horizon that puts the field of play into perspective.

The literature of educational theory dwells on several aspects of the concept of conditioning. These are: whether it counts as learning, its relationship to intelligence, and whether it is a morally justified way to change behavior. I will address each of these issues.

The concept of conditioning stretches the concept of learning by associating it with a response, an automatic and uncontrolled reaction.[8] Since the reaction is invariable and out of control of the subject, it is questionable whether this should count as learning, as the concept of learning implies that a person has learned only what they can do at will.[9] Certain forms of conditioning are more closely associated with learning than others and are successful at bringing about behavioral learning. Though seen earlier in this century as "the basic unit of all learning,"[10] the enthusiasm for conditioning as a development tool in the schools is all but absent today. There has been some challenge to the alleged conservative social orientation embedded in the perspective and its relationship to learning.[11]

The lack of a relationship between conditioning and the manifestation of intelligent behavior is one of the reasons for its decline in support from educators. It is worth noting that the concept of thinking itself is antithetical to the behaviorist movement generally. Like training, conditioning is associated with "knowing how," shaping behavior, and relies heavily on drill. Unlike training, conditioning is more closely associated with "reflex" and therefore, mindless action. As such, it is clear that conditioning does not manifest intelligent behavior. If a response to a stimulus is conditioned, the same stimulus would produce the same response, whether or not the subject wanted otherwise. As the manifestation of intelligence aimed at in training diminishes, conditioning becomes more and more clearly exemplified. In this way, conditioning can be seen as a "stamping in" of behavior.

This "stamping in" aspect of conditioning and the potential for the target to be manipulated has brought out moral objections to the concept of conditioning.

In this way, conditioning has similarities to indoctrination, even though it stands at the opposite end of Green's topology. It is a "stamping in" of behavior, just as indoctrination is a "stamping in" of belief. Both are seen to be morally objectionable in most cases,[12] though both can be tolerated as an expedient. That is, some would argue that conditioning or indoctrinating are defensible strategy when, for example, dealing with small children.[13] Conditioning, like indoctrination, stands at the end of the topology, and, as such, brings critical issues to the forefront.

We can hypothesize that conditioning is taking place where one or more of the following are evident: 1) where there is an emphasis on consequences and reinforcement; 2) where there is an avoidance of giving reasons to bring about a desired behavior; 3) where there is an emphasis on drill as a means to learn, and 4) where other behaviorist concepts and tendencies are at work.

The Concept of Training

When we train a dog, say, to sit, we give an order and then push or pull and give reward or punishment. We do so precisely because we cannot explain the order. We cannot elaborate its meaning. The dog does not ask "Why?"... It is this elimination of intelligence or communication which disposes us to speak of training rather than teaching.

Thomas Green

The concept of training is closely associated with that of teaching. We know this because we can use the terms interchangeably in many circumstances. We know also that the they are different because there are times that we cannot use them interchangeably. Green points out that we can usually substitute "training" for "teaching" in any context where "knowing how" is concerned but not in contexts where "knowing that" is the concern.[14]

Perhaps the most seminal event in the history of training in the modern business world can be traced to the turn of this century. At this time, many aspects of life were set against the new standards of scientific inquiry. Both general education and business education were affected, and still feel the influences. At a steel plant in the United States, Frederick Taylor, operating under the influence of the newly established principles of scientific management, sought to prove that by dividing work tasks into measurable events and training people to perform these events within a specified time, productivity could be enhanced.

Taylor, using an individual by the name of Schmidt as an exemplar, trained Schmidt how to perform at a highly increased rate. Taylor accomplished this by breaking Schmidt's work into parts, analyzing the number of seconds each part took, and accounting for physiological factors. This example, aside from stressing the clear emphasis on shaping behavior, points to other salient features of training. These include: that the behavioral change is relatively immediate; that the behavior to be learned is capable of being routinized,[15] thereby requiring drill and practice; and, that while there is always at least a minimal understanding on the part of the learner, it is usually the case that little justification for the given intervention is required.

R.S. Peters sees similar conditions for application of the concept:

> The concept of training has application when (i) there is some specifiable type of performance that has to be mastered, (ii) practice is required for the mastery of it, (iii) little emphasis is placed on the underlying rationale.[16]

These aspects of training have long been a subject of controversy among educators. Most educators see a limited role for training in education, while others have defended skill training as the "only kind of teaching that is non-authoritarian."[17]

John Dewey, in *Democracy and Education,* pointed to a difference between training and "educative teaching" that relies on "mental and emotional" dispositions of behavior. Dewey saw training as something that is the beginning step of modifying behavior, "A burnt child dreads the fire; if a parent arranges the conditions so that every time a child touched a certain toy he got burned, the child would learn to avoid that toy. " So too, a person trained to dodge blows will "dodge automatically with no corresponding thought or emotion."[18]

Dewey sees this kind of training as having its place in modifying behavior, but "in too many cases the activity of the immature human being is simply played upon to secure habits which are useful. " The role of educative teaching would be to go beyond this training and secure in the individual the emotion and knowledge of the group. "Making the individual a sharer or partner in the associated activity so that he feels its success as his success, its failure as his failure, is the completing step."[19]

The concern some educators have with training goes beyond the points Dewey makes above.[20] There is a compelling argument to be made that a bias toward the training model leads to a bias toward certain aims of education, namely, toward those aims which are measurable. They would argue that this bias contributes to the "crowding out" of other aims that are more difficult to specify or measure, but are nonetheless important. This makes training antithetical to education. Training is always limited in ways teaching is not. It always suggests confinement. People are trained for jobs, as mechanics, in math, etc. No one can be trained in a general sort of way, and this lack of specificity is precisely what is suggested by education.[21]

We can hypothesize that training is being conducted when one or more of THE CONCEPTS OF TEACHING is being adopted:

In the standard sense, is at some points, at least to submit oneself to the understanding and independent judgement of the pupil, to his demand for reasons, to his sense of what constitutes an adequate explanation. To teach someone that such and such is the case is not merely to try to get him to believe it... Teaching involves further that we try also to get him to believe it for reasons that within the limits of his capacity to grasp, are our reasons. Teaching, in this way, requires us to reveal our reasons to the student, and, by so doing, to submit them to evaluation and criticism.

Israel Scheffler

Thomas Green provides us with an excellent example of teaching. After providing evidence, research, explanations, etc., a teacher has shown a student that Columbus discovered America. And yet, the student still refuses to acknowledge that Columbus discovered America. The student argues that since there is considerable evidence that other Europeans visited North America before Columbus, and since other people were already living in North America, it does not really make a lot of sense to use the concept of "discovery."

This response from a student would not be seen as a failure of teaching — quite the contrary. It would be a sign of success because the concept of teaching is tied inexorably to the giving of reasons and the cultivation of intelligence. It is important to recognize that while teaching involves getting someone to believe something, it is necessary that they believe it because they think they ought to, i.e., because there are good reasons. There is a certain aspect of teaching that calls for the learner to look beyond the learning, and to add to the learning.

While Green's example above stands as an example of successful teaching, it would stand as an example of unsuccessful indoctrination because the purpose of indoctrination is to transmit a belief and have it adopted. Whereas the grounds for belief are critical for teaching, they are inconsequential to indoctrination.

Israel Scheffler summarizes these points eloquently:

Teaching may be characterized as an activity aimed at the achievement of learning, and practiced in such a manner as to respect the student's intellectual integrity and capacity for independent judgement. Such a characterization is important for at least two reasons: First, it brings out the intentional nature of teaching, the fact that teaching is a distinctive goal-oriented activity, rather than a distinctively patterned sequence of behavioral steps executed by the teacher. Secondly, it differentiates the activity of teaching from such other activities as the following is evident: 1) a skill is being learned through routine or drill; 2) specified, measurable, behavioral objectives are being used as a goal of the learning process; 3) there is some concern with the underlying rationale for the learning but this is far from the primary focus.

Propaganda, conditioning, suggestion, and indoctrination, which are aimed at modifying the person but strive at all costs to avoid a genuine engagement of his judgement on underlying issues.

The term "indoctrination" originally was used to mean the implanting of doctrine, usually Christian doctrine. The term was used in a neutral way to describe how one learned the teachings of the Catholic Church. As time passed, the term took on pejorative connotations and "indoctrination" became associated with totalitarian governments and coercive educational methods. The concept of "education" is sometimes used in contrast to describe what is considered to be the humane practice of democratic states. The pejorative sense of "indoctrination" continues to exist, especially in the United States.

Analyses of indoctrination, usually focus on four areas: the method of the indoctrination, the content of the lesson, the consequences of the indoctrination, and the aims or intentions of the individual in control. I. A. Snook's classic work in this area has advanced considerably discussion on all four of these aspects of indoctrination.[22]

Indoctrination in some ways stands in opposition to conditioning, and for this reason it stands at the opposite end of Green's topology. Green's single axis of organization, though, distracts us from the similarities that conditioning has with indoctrination. These similarities include: the use of what can be characterized as the "stamping in" process, their justification on moral grounds as an expedient, and their relative lack of success in the manifestation of intelligent behavior.

Thomas Green's example of teaching above (on Columbus) shows that indoctrination, while associated with belief, and "knowing that," differs in a critical way from teaching. R.S. Peters agrees with Scheffler, acknowledging that teaching involves the learner "in such a way that the learner is brought to understand and evaluate the underlying rationale for what is presented."[23] Peters also points out that indoctrination "involves either merely the inculcation of beliefs or the addition of a rationale which discourages the evaluation of beliefs, e.g., the appeal to authority as a backing."[24]

We can hypothesize that indoctrination is taking place when one or more of the following are evident: 1) when the shaping of belief is being achieved through unjustified pronouncements; 2) when challenge to, or discussion of, the basis for the belief is discouraged; 3) where there are arguments that the ends justify the means; 4) where intentions are suspect. These four tests for indoctrination cover the critical aspects of indoctrination, and will help to assist in the evaluation of business development.

In this section we have reviewed existing analysis of these four means of development. The literature we have cited is a part of an extensive body of work that critically analyzes the nuances of education. This literature almost universally demonstrates the highest regard for the concept of teaching and the kind of learning that is a by-product of teaching. Training is generally seen to have application in some areas, though it is viewed as a limited way to educate. Indoctrination and conditioning, however, as they are seen as a way to "stamp in" behavior or belief, are almost always seen as an unsatisfactory means of development.

In the next section we will look to the models employed by business development and how they compare to the framework we have established in this section.

Section III

A Model of Development for Business[25]

We can hypothesize that teaching is taking place when one or more of the following are present: 1) there is a concern that the learner understands underlying issues; 2) the learning designated to take place is generally more difficult to specify since it is more general; 3) there is a concern for the broader development of the individual.

The Concept of Indoctrination

It is, in fact, logically impossible for a person to know that he holds his beliefs as a consequence of indoctrination, because it is something that an individual cannot say himself truthfully in the present tense... Indoctrination has taken place when people think they hold their beliefs evidentially but in fact they do not — when thy use reason as a weapon under the illusion that they are seriously inquiring. All of us live with this illusion to some extent.

Thomas Green

In this section four different contributors to business development will be investigated. This investigation will compare their strategies of development to the model established in the previous section. The four contributors include a vendor (Kepner-Tregoe), a professional organization (The American Society for Training and Development), a leading theorist in business development (Malcolm Knowles), and a best-selling author (Stephen Covey).

The Kepner-Tregoe (KT) Consulting Group

When I started my career as a corporate trainer, my first task was to learn how to instruct a course which prescribed a theory of management. This course was a product of the Kepner-Tregoe consulting group.

Kepner-Tregoe (KT) is an international management consulting firm that was founded in 1958. KT maintains its corporate headquarters in Princeton, New Jersey, USA and has offices in 10 other countries. KT reports that its consultants "conduct business in more than 40 countries and in 14 languages," providing service to "over 60 of the Fortune 100 and 400 of the world's largest companies."[26] For his efforts in the field, Ben Tregoe, one of the founders of KT, was named to the Human Resources Development "Hall of Fame," a distinction he shares with 16 other individuals.[27] KT has four major products, all training programs, in the following areas: Problem Solving and Decision Making, Analytic Trouble Shooting, Project Management, and Engineering Peak Performance.

Engineering Peak Performance[28] (EPP) is their only program offering that prescribes a theory of management and a system to support the theory. My responsibility was to enable managers to learn this system, its theories about motivation, human behavior, etc., and the attending way to manage human behavior. The cornerstone of this system is the "performance model." This model was designed by KT to "force (us) to examine the performance system in much the same way that we would analyze a machine's system." The model shows how (see the diagram below) "in a particular situation a performer is called upon to take an action (response) which produces a result (consequence). Information is then fed back to the performer concerning the adequacy or appropriateness of the result."[29]

$$S \text{------} P \text{------} R \text{------} C$$

Situation — Performer— Response— Consequences

According to the instructor's guide, the model gets away from each manager "seeing a different problem" when confronted by the same situation "depending on their assumptions about people and why they behave as they do."[30] Instead, the model encourages objective, systematic analysis, with the performer being equivalent to a part in the machine, "like the machine, the human being in the work setting is part of a system — a performance system."[31]

Based on the analysis in the previous section, it is clear that this model falls into the "conditioning" mode of development. Since part of the management of the performance system includes discussion of standards of performance and job responsibilities, we cannot say that conditioning is all that is going on here. However, what we can say is that the analysis of the situation and the resultant understanding of human behavior is driven almost entirely by the behaviorist concepts of conditioning, consequences and reinforcement.

The instructor's guide states this clearly:

> People's performance is strongly influenced by the consequences attendant upon this performance. People tend to avoid things which result in negative consequences and to do more often those things which result in positive consequences. This happens so frequently that it can be stated as a "law" — behavior is governed by its consequences.[32]

Over the years I have seen other, similar models, that formed the basis for development initiatives. The works of Robert Mager, Ferdinand Fournies[33] and others, share the biases of the consequence driven KT model.[34] We will also see this in the ASTD materials and in Covey's book which attacks the superficiality of behaviorism and conditioning.

As we saw in section two, these models are very different from the development models valued by schools. Most notably, business models leave out any notion of giving reasons as a way to bring about the desired result, or "response." Little or no attention was paid to equipping managers to learn how to explain, how to give reasons, i.e., to teach employees. Instead, the reliance upon conditioning techniques sends a message to managers that they are behavior engineers, who, as Ferdinand Fournies says, have "behavioral rental agreements" with employees.

Given my background as a graduate student in education, I was surprised by the extent the course relied on behaviorist principles. I was also surprised that my learning, as a trainer, was achieved primarily through indoctrination. That is, the behaviorist model was imposed upon me as the only sensible model, and there was little attention given to alternative models, or the reasons this model was appropriate.

In the book that I received from KT that accompanied the course, the connection and reliance upon behaviorism, and training, as opposed to teaching, was explicit.

The proper sequence of teaching has always been a subject of contention with teachers and industrial trainers. But animal trainers don't argue about the sequence of teaching their subjects. There is a right place to start in training a rat; and if we don't start there, we shall either become completely lost, or take forever to arrive at our destination. The animal trainer who carefully follows the principles of B.F. Skinner will never cease to marvel at the ease with which the subjects learn . . . these principles are perfectly general and also apply to humans — who are at least animals, whatever else they might be.[35]

We will turn next to another source that will provide verification of the use of the behaviorist model, and will also expose other differences between the two models. In particular, we will see the disdain that some critical players in the business community have for the concept of teaching.

The American Society for Training and Development

The American Society for Training and Development (ASTD) is the largest professional training organization in the world, with a membership of more than 60,000 in the USA alone. The ASTD's mission is to "provide leadership to individuals, organizations, and society to achieve work-related competence, performance, and fulfillment." This mission statement and the discussion that follow are based upon the ASTD Reference Guide to Professional Human Resource Development.[36]

In this book there is an entire chapter "Planning for Learning and Instruction," that is devoted to theories of learning and instruction. The authors identify four theories of learning: pedagogy, behaviorism, cognitivism, and developmentalism. Each of the four theories of learning has a corresponding theory of instruction.

The authors summarize their research on learning theory and instruction in the following table.[37]

	Pedagogy	Behavioral	Cognitive	Developmental
Theorist	None	John B. Watson Ivan Pavlov Edwin Guthrie Edward Thorndike Clark Hull Kenneth Spence B.F. Skinner Albert Bandura	Wolfgang Kohler Edward Tolman Kurt Lewin Jerome Bruner	Jean Piaget Clark Rogers Malcolm Knowles
Definition of Learning	General awareness of knowledge: information received	Conditioning	Development of internal classification schemes	Problem solving: influenced by stages of development
Human Nature	Passive, reluctant learners	Influenced by the environment	Influenced by individual interpretations of external events	Active, eager learners
Role of Instructor	Crucial	Model	Provides environment suitable to learning	Facilitator
Role of Learner	Unimportant	Shaped by environment	Crucial	Crucial

In the above table and in the accompanying text, the authors begin their attack on pedagogy and its theoretical and operational underpinnings. They begin by *not* identifying any "theorist" who holds this view of pedagogy, and by identifying Malcolm Knowles as the spokesperson against pedagogy.

Although there is no one spokesperson for the theory, Malcolm Knowles has summarized it while describing his own developmental theory. Advocates believe instructors should plan instruction carefully, sequencing information by the logic of the material.[38]

By not identifying anyone who holds these views, the authors conveniently avoid anyone holding them to account for their characterization. They proceed, claiming:

> They (advocates of pedagogy) . . . ignore learners' experiences, assume learners will understand that what they learn will have future uses not readily apparent to them during instruction, and assume that the learner is dependent on the instructor for guidance.[39]

The paragraph closes with an even more outrageous generalization about individuals who practice pedagogy:

> Pedagogues believe they have the right to use strong discipline to force learning when students lack motivation and that they should be expert on the subject matter rather than on instructional design. Pedagogues often reach these conclusions based on their own experience.[40]

It is easy to see why they do not wish to identify anyone who holds these views, for it is difficult to imagine that anyone would admit to them. Their diatribe against "pedagogues" does not end there. In their review of learning theory and adult learners, the authors expand their attack on "pedagogy" to include the concept of the "teacher" in the conceptual carnage. They cite Alan Tough, who along with Cyril Houle and Malcolm Knowles, is viewed as a leading theorist of adult learning.

Teachers, Tough discovered, tend to interfere with adult learning by imposing a pedagogical structure on an otherwise natural, freewheeling, and discovery oriented problem-solving process.[41]

We do not have to go very far in the literature of education to defend the good name of teaching from this kind of attack. For instance, Plato in the Meno provides the classic example of a teaching style that is a model for the facilitating style identified in the table as "developmental." Rousseau, thousands of years later, describes a thoughtful and humanistic account of the education of Emile, and, in our own time, John Dewey and others have reacted to elements of schooling that were counterproductive to the development of children.

The material from the ASTD makes explicit their preferences for development. They end their attack on pedagogy, teachers, and schools generally, with the following sweeping generalization:

Despite the best efforts of scholars, pedagogy has largely remained the dominant philosophical orientation of teachers in primary, secondary, and higher education. At the same time behaviorism still dominates HRD practices in organizations.[42]

We cannot lose sight of what we have here — a major organization claiming in its handbook that our schools are characterized by the view that the learner is not important, that learner experiences are ignored, and that motivation is achieved through punishment. It is a wonder that anything at all is learned in our schools. And, while no one in particular can be cited as a spokesperson for this theory, everyone in the schools is guilty of the practice.

All of this is done in the name of adult learners, and their "natural, freewheeling, and discovery oriented problem solving process," who they apparently are rescuing from, well, being treated like children.

It is interesting to hear what the ASTD has to say about the adult learner:

Although much has been written about teaching adults, solid knowledge of the subject is limited. What is known can be summarized in a few major points. According to various writers, adults initiate their own learning projects in response to significant life events — such as marriage, divorce, parenthood, promotion or job transfer.[43]

They go on to add two more major points that are "known" about adult learners.

Their motivation to learn increases as the number of significant events in their lives increases, and they tend to pursue learning experiences directly related to these events. Generally, they are especially open to learning, before, during, and after a significant life event, and this time is called a *teachable moment*.[44] *(Their emphasis)*

After this review of what is known about adult learners, it is easy to agree with the ASTD in their assessment that our knowledge is limited! What they claim is "known" is either contestable or outright nonsense. If we are to take the above statements at face value, the older a person is, the more motivated they are to learn. This is hard to believe. Also, the claim that adults are especially open to learning "before, during or after" significant events says nothing at all — it leaves nothing out!

The ASTD vision is to be considered "the worldwide leader in workplace learning and performance by the year 2000."[45] One can only hope that in this quest they also learn to treat fairly the views of others and establish a defensible justification for the views they hold.

In order to more fully understand their disdain of pedagogy, teachers, and schools we turn next to a source of their prejudice, the work of Malcolm Knowles. Knowles, like Ben Tregoe, is another of the elite 16 members of the Human Resources Hall of Fame.

The Work of Malcolm Knowles

Welcome to an adventure in self-directed learning. I'd like to
start off by setting a climate for our mutual inquiry. First, I'd
like to it to be a warm climate. I'd like for you to feel that I
care about you, even though I don't know you.

Malcolm Knowles

In a letter to Merriam Webster Dictionaries in 1968 Malcolm Knowles alerted the authors that he was writing a new book that (he somehow knew) "would be widely used in our field," and requested that they help ensure the correct spelling of a neologism that may "result in a new word being added to the lexicon of adult education in our country."[46] The word was "andragogy," and it was introduced in contrast to "pedagogy." Knowles introduced this concept in order to underscore the difference between adult learning and children learning, and he set about the task at the expense of a theory he calls "pedagogy."

Knowles was successful in his goals, and his story of success tells us much about the values of those who accepted, and continue to accept, his model. His views are widely accepted in the business community and he has led the assault on the "pedagogical" model and its associated concepts. In his zeal to establish the importance of the experience adults bring to learning settings, Knowles overstates his case in his early works. The table cited above from the ASTD, which identifies the role of the learner as "unimportant" to those who practice pedagogy, was taken from Knowles.

In making his case in 1973, Knowles argued forcefully that because adults enter learning situations with a great deal of experience and knowledge, that an entirely new, and comprehensive theory of adult learning ought to be constructed. Part of his theory included a rejection of pedagogy and its attending concepts.[47] However, in 1980, Knowles retreats considerably from this position. In response to questions regarding the evidence supporting his position, Knowles does an about face, and denies that he has tried to establish andragogy as superior to pedagogy. He pleads:

> People frequently ask me what research has been done vis-a-vis the andragogical model that supports the proposition that it is superior to the pedagogical model. My automatic-reflex response is, "That is not the question; nobody, — at least not I — is saying that."
>
> This kind of question arises from a curious disease that seems endemic in the world of learning theory. It might be called panacea-addiction. Philosophers call it either-or thinking. It is a compulsion for neat, simple, single solutions to complex problems.[48]

Knowles goes on to say that andragogy is:

> ...not an ideology at all, but a system of assumptions about learners that needs to be tested out for different learners in different situations. In a sense, it is a system that encompasses the pedagogical model since it makes legitimate the application of pedagogical strategies in those situations in which the pedagogical model is legitimate.[49]

But the damage was done. The ASTD book was published *after* 1980, and interestingly, Knowles continues to propagate, and market, his earlier views.

In 1987 and 1990 Malcolm Knowles, in collaboration with a vendor, Organization Design and Development, copyrighted an "HRD Style Inventory,"[50] that is still in use today. This inventory is a series of questions that identify whether an individual "may be categorized as *pedagogically* oriented or andragogically oriented."

Despite his claims that he is not forcing an either/or proposition in 1980, he is clearly doing this, and, there is more. Not only is Knowles forcing a choice, but in doing so, he clearly wishes to impugn the pedagogical model, and teaching. The tables on the following page show the earlier negative associations of "pedagogical."

Remarkably similar to the table above from the ASTD, it ties the concept of teaching to an environment characterized by low trust, aloofness, and a motivation style driven by "external rewards and punishment."

There are a number of suspicious things at work here and at least three confusing issues. First, it is odd that, given the relative lack of knowledge that exists with respect to adult learners, that Knowles and others did not pursue learning differences as they relate to gender. Recent work in this area[51] has surfaced significant, substantial, and troubling issues. It is tragic that the popularity of Knowles' ideas has crowded out other models of learning and has distracted business development from potentially more useful investigation, e.g., women's ways of knowing. It is also curious that groups like the ASTD are still carrying Knowles' torch long after its flame has been extinguished. The second confusing aspect of his work is his claim that learning is enhanced by delivery in a style that conforms to the preferred learning style of the learner. It could be argued that if one were truly interested in building the capacity to learn, consideration would be given to do precisely the opposite of what Knowles, and others, advocate. The use of alternative styles would likely increase the capacity of the individual to learn in different ways. The irony here is that Knowles falls victim to the trap of seeing the content at hand as the only concern in determining delivery style.

Assumptions		
About	**Pedagogical**	**Andragogical**
Concept of the learner	Dependent personality	Increasingly self-directing
Role of learners' experience	To be built on more than used as a resource	A rich resource for learning by self and others
Readiness to learn	Uniform by age-level and curriculum	Develops from life tasks and problems
Orientation to learning	Subject-centered	Task - or problem - centered
Motivation	By external rewards and punishment	By internal incentives, curiosity

Process Elements		
Elements	**Pedagogical**	**Andragogical**
Climate	Tense, low trust Formal, cold, aloof Authority-oriented Competitive, judgmental	Relaxed, trusting Mutually respectful Informal, warm Collaborative, supportive
Planning	Primarily by teacher	Mutually by learners and facilitator
Diagnosis of needs	Primarily by teacher	Mutually by learners and facilitator
Setting of objectives	Primarily by teacher	By mutual negotiation
Designing learning plans	Teachers' content plans Course syllabus Logical sequence	Learning contracts Learning projects Sequenced by readiness
Learning activities	Transmittal techniques Assigned readings	Inquiry projects Independent study Experiential techniques
Evaluation	By teacher Norm-reference (on a curve) With grades	By learner-collected evidence validated by peers, facilitators, experts Criterion referenced

Finally, the ultimate irony of Knowles work is that he must succumb to the tactics he disdains and finds so useless to make his point. He uses the medium of a book to construct his argument. In constructing this argument he must convince, he must teach. And, people who accept his arguments must see his reasons and accept them on their merit.

Why should any employee, adult or otherwise, deserve anything less?

The Work of Stephen Covey

In his best-selling book *The Seven Habits of Highly Effective People*, Stephen Covey summarizes "200 years of success literature" that he reviewed as a part of his doctoral research. While the book has had application across a wide spectrum of American society, his success in the business arena has been startling. As a part of this success Covey has established a leadership institute in Utah, and has marketed his "Seven Habits" program with outstanding success.

The appeal of Stephen Covey has much to do with the strength of his attack on the development models of the last 50 years. Covey begins this attack, and the book, by vilifying what he calls the "Personality Ethic," a way to success that is based upon "quick-fix influence techniques, power strategies, communication skills, and positive attitudes."[52]

The Personality Ethic is relatively new in the "success literature" emerging over the last 50 years or so. Before this, according to Covey, almost all the success literature focused on "integrity, humility, fidelity, temperance, courage, justice, patience, industry, simplicity, modesty, and the Golden Rule."[53] And, people can only experience "true" success and enduring happiness if they integrate these principles into their "basic" character. Covey calls this competing model the "Character Ethic," and his book is about getting back in touch with the principles of this ethic.

Covey portrays the Personality Ethic as focused on style and technique, not substance. Using these techniques is analogous to cramming your way through school, taking a short cut, and therefore never achieving what Covey calls "true mastery." For Covey, this is unnatural:

> Did you ever consider how ridiculous it would be to try to cram on a farm —
> to forget to plant in the spring, play all summer and then cram in the fall to
> bring in the harvest? The farm is a natural system. The price must be paid and
> the process followed. You always reap what you sow there is no shortcut.[54]

Covey relies frequently on the "natural" as a way to argue for what is proper or correct, likewise, what is not labeled as "natural" is inappropriate.

It is difficult to follow Covey in this regard. His use of what counts as "natural" is equivocal. He sees humans as a part of this natural model yet at the same time capable of unnatural acts. He sees farms as natural but schools as unnatural, ignoring the use of chemicals, machinery, the creation of hybrids, etc., in the "natural" farm system. Covey also conveniently ignores the existence of all sorts of learning models in nature. He continues:

> This principle is also true, ultimately, in human behavior, in human relationships. They, too, are natural systems based on the law of the harvest. In the short run, in an artificial social system such as school, you may be able to get by if you learn how to manipulate the man made rules, to "play the game." In most one-shot or short-lived human interactions, you can use the Personality Ethic to get by and to make favorable impressions through charm and skill and pretending to be interested in other people's hobbies.[55]

Here Covey has identified human relationships as natural in the first two sentences, then in the next sentence asserts that schools are an artificial system. Somehow, schools and the human relationships that they make possible, are artificial contrivances built on man made rules, and, inexplicably, are "one-shot" and short lived. Covey rightly mocks the insincere aspects of many management training programs that seek to condition such behaviors as interest, recognition, etc.

It is critical to note here that Covey needs to use the concept of "natural" to make his points. Covey uses the concept for its connotative power — he is not trying to rationally construct an argument, rather, his appeal is to our emotions. The strength of his appeal is that he sees the superficial aspects of the quick fix development models. He continues his attack, now directed to the business environment:

> I have seen the consequences of attempting to shortcut this natural process of growth often in the business world, where executives attempt to "buy" a new culture of improved productivity, quality, morale, and customer service with strong speeches, smile training, and external interventions . . . But they ignore the low-trust climate produced by such manipulations.[56]

Again, Covey is correct to see that when employees feel they are being manipulated they will respond hesitantly and will be wary to trust their leaders. His diagnosis of superficiality and low trust is accurate. In light of the model established earlier, and the superficiality of many business development models, Covey has come to the same conclusion for different reasons. And, because of this, his solution will be different from those offered here. In this context, it is interesting to see what he offers as an answer.

Covey asserts that what is needed is:

> We need a new level, a deeper level of thinking — a paradigm based on the principles that accurately describes the territory of effective human being and interacting — to solve these deep concerns. This new level of thinking is what *Seven Habits of Highly Effective People* is about.[57]

This "paradigm" shift that Covey is calling for is dramatic because of "the powerful impact of conditioning" and the strength of the current social paradigm of the Personality Ethic. His principle centered habits provide all the answers, and we all can achieve them, but "we need to think differently, to shift our paradigms to a new, deeper, inside-out level."[58]

What Covey suggests is that we need to be deeper to achieve his goals. He handles any opposition to his program by claiming that:

> The reality of such principles or natural laws becomes obvious to anyone who thinks deeply and examines the cycles of social history.[59]

Covey poisons the wells of discourse with claims such as these. His assertion that anyone who does not agree with him simply "has not thought deeply enough," undermines his credibility, and provides us with evidence that he too is relying on indoctrination. As established in the previous section, the characteristics of indoctrination include the shaping of belief with unjustified pronouncements, and a tendency to discourage discussion on the basis, or reason for a belief. Covey's work, however compelling for its attack on the simplicity and superficiality of many development models, becomes what it criticizes by such vatic and unsubstantiated claims.

It would be extremely cynical to claim that Covey's work is motivated by the lure of the $50 billion market of business development. It is interesting, however, that Covey employs techniques successful by the competitors he criticizes. He does use an "800 number" to offer a free, self scoring "Personal Feedback Profile" to help you evaluate your current level of effectiveness (this is done in the text of his book). He does intimate that he has the answer to our problems. He does offer training seminars across the country based on the "Seven Habits" that are not very different from their predecessors. This we can accept, for how can Covey be blamed for giving to business what it wants?

What is a problem with Covey's work is that he does not invite inquiry into critical areas of his work. For Covey, some things are simply a matter of faith. His reliance on "natural" laws to justify his position, and his predilection toward insulting those who do not agree with him (they just are not "deep" enough) is convincing evidence of Covey's prejudice. To disagree with him is, in a sense, to commit blasphemy. To his credit, he owns up to the source of his views:

> As I conclude this book I would like to share my own personal conviction concerning what I believe to be the source of correct principles. I believe that correct principles are natural laws, and that God, the Creator and Father of us all, is the source of them, and is also the source of our conscience. I believe that to the degree that people live by this inspired conscience, they will grow to fulfill their natures; to the degree that they do not, they will not rise above the animal plane.[60]

In this section I have attempted to establish that models of development valued by business lie at either end of Green's topology, that is, in indoctrinating, conditioning, and, to some extent, training. We have also seen that the practice of teaching is not valued. In the next, and final, section, I will discuss how it is that business development suffers from the biases of the models they favor, and how the concept of teaching can fit into a philosophy of business development.

Section IV

Implications for Business Development

In summary, we have argued to this point that the model valued by business development differs from the model valued by schools. The critical differences are that the business model relies heavily on conditioning, training and indoctrinating, whereas the schooling model exalts the teaching model, which is disdained by business.

This final section will discuss the implications of this kind of development bias. First, I will address the concept of teaching and reasons why businesses may seek to avoid its use. Second, I will discuss the seven reasons why I believe the model valued by business needs to be re-engineered.

The most striking result of this analysis is the disdain that can be found in the business development literature for the concept of teaching. It is interesting to speculate on the reasons why businesses tend not to value the teaching model. Indeed, one could develop reasons that would satisfy the practical and the pragmatist all the way to the revisionist and the Machiavellian. Let's entertain some of these reasons:

Reason #1 — (For the conspiracy minded.) Corporations do not want to encourage teaching and thinking because employees would see the exploitation and unfairness of corporations. The lack of societal accountability relative to the amount of power that corporations wield has been a concern of academics for decades.

Reason #2 — (For the pragmatic.) There is no need to encourage employees to think about anything except their jobs. They only need to be concerned with achieving results in their job performance. The Taylor model provides us with just about all we need to see the point here. The concept of teaching is designed, in part, to prepare citizens to contribute to a democratic society where their participation in political activities is critical to the proper functioning of government. While employees today have greater say than ever before, corporations are still decidedly totalitarian.

Reason #3 — (For a different kind of pragmatic.) The models of development that are valued by the corporation are consonant with the values of that culture, i.e., to the extent that businesses value measurable results, quick fixes, etc., there will be a corresponding bias in their preferred model of development. The behaviorist models with measurable objectives and accountability fit into this system, as does indoctrination.

Robert Jackall, in his incisive book about the world of corporate managers, suggests to us other reasons why teaching is avoided — it has to do with what will sell and the politics of development. Jackall gives the following advice to consultants looking for success:

> (1) Suppress all irony, ambiguity, and complexity and assert only the most obvious literal meanings of any phenomenon; (2) ignore all theoretical issues unless they can be encapsulated into a neat schematic form easily remembered, "operationalized," and preferably diagramed; (3) always stress the bright side of things, inflating, say, all efforts for change, whether major or minor, into "revolutionary" action; downplay the gloomy, troublesome, crass, or seamy aspects of big organizational life or, better, show managers how to exploit them for their own advantage; (4) provide a step-by step program tied, of course, to one's own path breaking research, that promises to unlock the secrets of organizations; and (5) end with a vision of the future that makes one's book, program, or consulting services indispensable.[61]

Jackall's incisive cynicism should give us pause to stop and reassess the field of business development. I am optimistic that there is hope for business development, and offer the following as reasons that progress is possible.

Seven Reasons for Change in Business Development

1.) The biases of business development are often counterproductive to achieving the strategic aims of the business. To the extent that businesses overemphasize skill development and neglect knowledge acquisition, their development models are out of balance. They also risk being reactive in their philosophy of development. This happens because most corporations hold employees accountable in their appraisal process for demonstrating skill sets that were established in the past.[62] As such, development gets out of balance. Instead of employees learning in ways that are consonant with, e.g., strategic interests of the corporation, they are often working to develop skill sets designed for success in the past.

It is worth adding that regardless of whether an employee has acquired a skill or not in a training session, the employee still needs to exercise judgement as to when to use that skill, and to what extent. No matter how "skilled" an employee becomes through training, they still require proper judgement and thinking skills to be successful.

2.) If reason #1 is not valid today, it will be soon, given the rapid expansion of knowledge and the bias against knowledge acquisition that business models exhibit. It is important for business development to embrace, not avoid, the knowledge revolution. It has been estimated that there has been more information produced in the last 30 years than in the previous 5,000 and that our information supply will likely double in the next five years.[63] This knowledge is a source of strategic opportunity for corporations, something that needs to be capitalized upon. As we have seen, the rhetoric against pedagogy spills over into related areas (e.g., teaching and knowledge acquisition). To the extent that this rhetoric inhibits development strategies that accommodate knowledge, it restrains the promise of employee development. If our models of development neglect knowledge, or see knowledge (and organizational learning), only as a way to make existing processes more efficient, they are woefully lacking.

3.) Businesses need to have productive dialogue about: the ends and means of development, the role of vendors, and the politics of business development. The influence of vendors in the area of business development cannot be overstated. While it is easy to blame these vendors and the attraction of a $50 billion market on the ills of business development, we cannot blame consultants for giving businesses what it desires. If Robert Jackall is correct, then a big part of the reason vendors are so successful is tied to politics at high levels of the organization. Jackall says:

> The results of the untiring efforts of consultants and the reciprocal anxiety of executives is the circulation at or near the top of organizations of ever changing rhetoric of innovation and exhortation. These rhetorics get disseminated throughout the corporation and become rallying cries for a time, and sometimes are instituted, until new rhetorics overtake them. Each group fuels the other's needs and self images in an occupational drama where the needs of organizations get subordinated to the maintenance of professional identities.[64]

The politics of development within corporations, and the need of managers to appear "leading edge" keeps the vendors in business. It is time to get the politics out of business development, to admit that there are no easy answers, to not be swayed by the program of the month, and to engage in productive dialogue regarding the aims and means of development. In this regard, business development has much to learn from the volume and quality of debate that is characteristic of professional schools of education. These discussions are therapeutic and help organizations understand who they are, and what they wish to become.

4.) It is important that development initiatives acknowledge the dignity of the individuals who work at the corporation and the complexity of their interactions. This is nothing more than a call for the corporation to respect the individuals they employ. Training programs that focus on skill building at the expense of thinking and understanding, (e.g., the nuances of communication, the delicate and often unnerving aspects of supervision, and the general difficulty of interaction in the business environment), will be rejected by employees. The "easy answer" models of business development are insulting and serve only to damage the reputation of those responsible for their delivery.

5.) Business development models would benefit from a closer relationship with professional schools of education. Businesses tend to "benchmark" against each other in order to improve activities. For business development, this raises a number of questions. First, it is important to ask whether copying others will cause what is wanted. This question was addressed in the beginning of this paper: is development the engine for change or an effect of something else? Businesses will not get very far by copying effects and not causes! (I am reminded of Wittgenstein's remark that it does not make sense to read another of the same newspaper to see if what you read in the first was true.) The alternative models of development that are offered by professional schools of education deserve investigation.

To the extent that business development is influenced by vendors who are not interested in educational research, businesses are failing to "cash in" on the research from professional schools of education. Of particular note is the neglect of any advances in business development in the areas of women's ways of knowing and critical thinking. These two areas have received much attention in the past decade and show much promise for application in business. It is difficult to explain why "adult" education receives so much attention while other, more worthy areas, are crowded out. A closer relationship with professional schools of education could prevent this from happening.

6.) Reliance upon conditioning and indoctrination and other forms of "stamping in" behavior and belief do not build respect for authority. As described in the second section of this paper, the "stamping in" of behavior by conditioning, and of belief by indoctrination, is morally questionable. When this is practiced by corporations, it leads to a lack of respect for authority and a low trust level among employees. For these reasons alone, any short term, or narrow, success using these methods is probably not worth the long term disadvantages. The models used for business development should avoid these methods.

7.) The time is right to address a new model of business development. Today, more than ever the needs of the corporation are in line with a model of development that encourages learning, requires workers to use sound judgement, and demands an understanding of the nuances of communication, thinking, and strategy. If this is true, individuals in corporations need precisely the kind of individual that their development models cannot deliver.

Some 25 years ago, a Yale legal professor named Charles Reich wrote a book entitled *The Greening of America*. Reich's book was about the decline of American society and, in a twist of irony, the "wasteland of the Corporate State." In his book, Reich wrote that "we have underestimated the amount and kind of education needed to make any individual able to adapt to change."[65] Reich goes on to say that what we urgently need "is not training but education, not indoctrination but the expansion of each individual."[66] Reich called for this educative process to be a lifelong process, not one that stops with graduation from college.

Reich's words, and others like them, have been debated for decades in professional schools of education. It is time that similar debates occur in the arena of business development. This paper is a calling for such a debate.

As the appeal of Reich's words testify to my values and hopes about education, so too they match up in critical ways with the needs of business. As demands for adjusting to change, for thoughtful decision making, for capitalizing on the knowledge explosion, and for matching learning with strategic advantage evolve, new models of business development are likely to emerge. A model is needed that is capable of supporting the kind of individual that Reich describes, and who could contribute and thrive in an environment like that described in the Nordstrom Company's employees' handbook which has two rules: Rule #1: Use good judgement at all times. Rule #2: There will be no further rules.

This chapter is a calling for discussion about what such a model would look like and how to address the promise that education might bring to a corporation, the promise that Reich sees, and the promise that is implicit in the words of the Nordstrom company.

It is my hope that the contribution of this chapter will inspire others, more talented than I, to investigate these issues, to help untangle the confusion, and to increase the chances for useful dialogue. I am mindful of Nietzsche's remark that "if you cannot be a saint of knowledge, at least be its warrior. They are companions and forerunners of such sainthood."[67]

Notes

1. See Thomas Green, *The Activities of Teaching*, (New York: McGraw-Hill, 1971).
2. I am indebted to David Nyberg for this learning and for his guidance, for his teaching. See his "Education as Community Expression," *Teachers College Record*, (Spring 1977).
3. See Daniel Lortie, *Schoolteacher*, (Chicago: University of Chicago Press, 1975), for an interesting discussion on this topic and its relevance to teacher training .
4. This phenomenon happens the other way too, and attacks on our school systems often invoke models of business development.
5. Gilbert Ryle, *The Concept of Mind*, (New York: Barnes and Noble, 1949).
6. I have substituted "teaching" for "instruction" in this model. Green uses Israel Scheffler's example of teaching in his analysis but prefers to use "instruction" in his model.
7. See T. Green, *The Activities of Teaching* (New York: McGraw-Hill, 1971), R.S. Peters, "What is an Educational Process," in R.S. Peters, ed. *The Concept of Education* (London: Routledge and Kegan Paul, 1967), and I.A. Snook, *The Concept of Indoctrination* (London: Routledge and Kegan Paul, 1972).
8. See Godfrey Vesey, "Conditioning and Learning" in R.S. Peters, *The Concept of Education* (London: Routledge and Kegan Paul, 1967).
9. *Ibid.*, *Vesey*, p. 65.
10. See N.L. Gage, *The Scientific Basis of the Art of Teaching* (New York: Teachers College Press, 1978), and Robert Geiser, *Behavior Modification and the Managed Society* (Boston: Beacon Press, 1976).
11. See Michael Apple, "Behaviorism and Conservatism," in Bruce Joyce and Marsha Weil, eds., *Perspectives for Teacher Reform*, (Prentice Hall: Englewood Cliffs, New Jersey, 1972), pp. 237-62.
12. See Mary Anne Raywid, "The Discovery and Rejection of Indoctrination," *Educational Theory*, (Winter 1980), vol. 30, no.1, pp. 1-10.
13. R.S. Peters, *Ethics of Education*, p. 168.
14. T. Green, *The Activities of Teaching*, p. 24.
15. See Israel Scheffler, *The Conditions of Knowledge*, (Glenview, Illinois: Scott, Foresman, 1965.), p. 95.
16. R.S. Peters "What is an Educative Process," in *The Concept of Education*, p. 15.
17. Carl Bereiter, *Must We Educate?* (Englewood Cliffs, New Jersey: Prentice Hall, 1973), p. 8.
18. John Dewey, *Democracy and Education*, (New York: The Free Press, 1916), p.13.
19. John Dewey, *Democracy and Education*, p. 14.
20. See D.A. Nyberg and K. Egan, *The Erosion of Education*, (New York: Teachers College Press, 1981), pp. 45-55.
21. See R.S. Peters, "What is an Educational Process," in R.S. Peters, *The Concept of Education*.
22. See I.A. Snook, *The Concept of Indoctrination*.
23. R.S. Peters, *Ethics and Education*, (New York: Scott Foresman, 1966), p. 168.
24. *Ibid.*, Peters, p. 168.
25. Israel Scheffler, "Philosophical Models of Teaching." *Harvard Educational Review;* vol. 35, (Spring 1965), p. 131.

26. "Kepner-Tregoe's Consulting Capabilities," (Kepner-Tregoe, Inc., 1991), p. 3.
27. See "Training Magazine" February 1995, vol. 32, no.2, p.67. The HRD of Fame was founded in 1985 by Training Magazine, and honors the foremost figures in the field of human resources development.
28. In their current redesign of this program KT is dropping the reading level in the course materials from an eighth grade level to a sixth grade level.
29. Kepner-Tregoe Program Leader Instructor Guide, "Managing the Performance System," 1980, e/twO7.005.
30. *Ibid.*, p. e/twO7.003.
31. *Ibid.*, p. e/twO7.004.
32. *Ibid.*, p. e/tw08.006.
33. See Ferd Fournies, *Coaching for Improved Work Performance*, (New York: McGraw, 1987). Fournies writes (p. 61) that the scientific approach to people management, "behavior modification," has demonstrated that "not only can people's behaviors be changed regardless of what their attitudes might be, but once the behavior is changed the attitude usually follows (if you care to know about the attitude)."
34. A good example is *Managing Behavior on the Job*, by Paul J. Brown, (New York: John Wiley and Sons), 1982. This book is a part of Wiley's self-teaching guides and includes "Five Steps to Managing Consequences" and other such chapter headings that serve to simplify.
35. Thomas F. Gilbert, *Human Competence*, (New York: McGraw Hill, 1978), p. 265.
36. William Rothwell and Henry Sredl, *The ASTD Reference Guide to Professional Human Resource Development*, (Amherst, Mass.: HRD Press, 1992).
37. While the ASTD gives no reference for this table it is similar to a table in Malcolm Knowles' work referenced later in this section.
38. *Ibid., ASTD*, p. 334.
39. *Ibid., ASTD*, p. 334.
40. *Ibid., ASTD*, p. 334.
41. *Ibid., ASTD*, p. 337.
42. *Ibid., ASTD*, p. 337.
43. *Ibid., ASTD*, p. 337.
44. *Ibid., ASTD*, p. 337.
45. *Ibid., ASTD*, p. xvii.
46. *Ibid., ASTD*, p. xvii.
47. *Ibid.*, Knowles, passim.
48. Malcolm Knowles, *The Modern Practice of Adult Education*, (Chicago: Follett Publishing Company, 1980,) p. 59.
49. *Ibid.*, Knowles, p. 59.
50. Malcolm Knowles, *Are You an Andragog?* (King of Prussia, Pennsylvania: OD&D Resources).
51. See Carol Gilligan *In a Different Voice*, (Cambridge: Harvard University Press, 1982) and Mary Belenky, et.al., *Women's Ways of Knowing* (New York. Basic Books, 1986).
52. Stephen Covey, *The Seven Habits of Highly Effective People*, (New York: Simon and Schuster, 1989), p. 19.
53. *Ibid.*, Covey, p. 18.

54. *Ibid.*, *Covey*, p. 22.
55. *Ibid.*, *Covey*, p. 22.
56. *Ibid.*, *Covey*, p. 38.
57. *Ibid.*, *Covey*, p. 42.
58. *Ibid.*, *Covey*, p. 44.
59. *Ibid.*, *Covey*, p. 34.
60. *Ibid.*, *Covey*, p. 319.
61. Robert Jackall, *Moral Mazes* (Oxford: Oxford University Press, 1988), p. 142.
62. Corporations will analyze job duties and identify "behaviors" or "competencies" for success in a job position or job family. Most often, these descriptions are not directed toward future skill requirements, let alone knowledge requirements.
63. See Richard Wurman, *Information Anxiety,* (New York: Doubleday, 1989).
64. Robert Jackall, *Moral Mazes*, (Oxford: Oxford University Press, 1988), p. 142.
65. *Ibid.*, p. 361.
66. Charles Reich, *The Greening of America,* (New York: Random House, 1970).
67. Friedreich Nietzsche, "Thus Spoke Zarathustra," *The Portable Nietzsche,* (New York: Viking Press, 1968), p. 333.

Chapter Eight

Values and Conflicts in the Training of Physiotherapists

Elizabeth M. Walker

Background

Professional education within the National Health Service involves the pre- and post-registration education of many healthcare professionals. In examining the changes in the pre-registration education of physiotherapists and the benefits and conflicts that have resulted it is first important to consider the current and future requirements of the physiotherapy profession.

Current and Future Requirements

At the Yorkshire Board Conference held in 1987, Miss Bromley, ex chairman of the Chartered Society of Physiotherapy (CSP) Council, suggested that 'physiotherapy expands with developments in technology, and with social and economic change'.

Morbid changes in the demographic structure and in the nature of morbidity have led to alterations in society's needs of the healthcare professions. There is an increasing number of elderly people in the population. The average life expectancy has increased which has resulted in an increased demand for care of the elderly services (Ham, 1985).

Resources for healthcare are finite. There is a need to contain expenditure and ensure value for money. The monopoly of a single NHS employer is diminishing due to the major changes being brought about by the Government White papers — 'Working for patients' (DHSS, 1989) and 'Caring for people' (DHSS, 1989). Self-governing hospital Trusts, local authorities, GP's, and the private hospital sector are now recognised as employers of health care professionals. The need for physiotherapists along with other professional groups to be able to justify what they do and to be able to demonstrate their ability to provide a valuable and cost effective service in a variety of clinical settings is becoming increasingly important (Richardson, 1992).

The past decade has seen a rapid growth in information technology. Increasingly, physiotherapists will be expected to be able to use information systems in hospitals and other healthcare settings. There has been a rapid development of machines on the market available to physiotherapists with little or no information as to their validity and reliability or their benefits compared with other forms of treatment.

Physiotherapists need to be trained to solve problems in patient care, management and education. Problem-solving requires the ability to delimit the problem, identify, analyse and synthesise the elements in a particular situation, develop alternative solutions, choose the one that holds the greatest prospect of success, evaluate outcomes and alter the plan accordingly (Barr, 1977). This approach is important if physiotherapists are to adapt to changes in the future.

These requirements have brought about many changes in the undergraduate curriculum, the way it has been taught (the process) and the institutions in which schools are situated. Whilst there are many benefits in these changes they have also resulted in many conflicts.

The Curriculum

Pre-registration education is very similar to medical education in that it faces the problem of curriculum overload. Due to rapid scientific and technological advances, the subject matter grows at an increasing rate whilst the length of the course remains fixed. There is pressure to add new content to the curriculum. Until recently it had been difficult to delete anything from the curriculum even if it was considered obsolete by many practitioners. However, the change from diploma to degree programmes has resulted in schools of physiotherapy becoming more autonomous. It is now largely up to the lecturers to determine the number of hours devoted to the teaching of practical skills such as massage. One of the criticisms of the diploma courses was that too much time was spent on the teaching of subjects that many practitioners felt were little used in clinical practice. The reason that so many hours were devoted to teaching massage was partly due to interpretation of the curriculum being largely in the hands of senior teaching staff, some of who were cast in the traditional mould, and to the historical background of the profession.

Originally called the Society of Trained Masseuses, the profession was established in 1894 by a small group of well born nurses and midwives dedicated to what at that time was called 'medical rubbing' and determined to protect it from massage scandals that were circulating at the time. It was with the object of protecting 'medical massage' against the slurs that the founders set out to create a society which would restore its good name as a proper treatment. It is interesting to note that when, in 1943, the title of the Chartered Society of Physiotherapy was adopted, there was much apprehension about dropping massage from the title which seemed 'almost equivalent to forfeiting our birthright' (Wicksteed, 1948).

However, despite this historical influence, there may be justification in including massage in the curriculum. 'Physiotherapy is handling' (Williams, 1986). Manual traction, chest clearance and mobilisation techniques are modalities of treatment frequently used by physiotherapists. Since these treatments are beneficial in the treatment of pain, muscle spasm, swelling and stiffness, it is important that therapists hands are 'sensitive' to the patients' tissues. Assessment of neurological and musculo-skeletal problems require therapists who are competent in differentiating between normal tissue and that which exhibits signs of underlying pathology. Massage facilitates its process. Recent technological advances have led to the introduction of machines which are able to reduce swelling. However, due to financial constraints, these machines may not be available. Removing massage from the curriculum could therefore result in therapists who are inadequately prepared for future contingencies.

It is also important to consider that there are other groups who may fill in the gaps. People who are aware that physiotherapists have not said lately that they are the society of massage have begun to claim that *they* have these skills. They are running courses and becoming the massage profession in this country. As a profession, physiotherapists ought to be fostering the use of these techniques, developing them and carrying out research in the use of touch and handling if they are its core base. If the profession is not careful it may slide off into other academic worlds that really belong to other professions and ignore their own.

The change from a diploma course to an Honour's degree course has resulted in inclusion of the teaching of research methodology and behavioural sciences, and the introduction of a student dissertation. However, due to financial constraints the regional health authorities will only fund *three* year courses.

The Process

The discipline or subject-centred curriculum is the most common model for medical education (McGahie et al, 1978). This has also been true of physiotherapy education. Subject-centred curriculum involves the separate teaching of various disciplines and frequently emphasises the acquisition of large quantities of factual information taught by a didactic approach rather than by critical assessment and appraisal of that information (Barr, 1977). This has led to a criticism of lack of correlation between theory and practice, and of a fragmentation of concepts that makes clinical practice difficult (May 1983).

Physiotherapists are expected to be able to accurately identify a patient's problems, use evaluation data to determine the nature and extent of the underlying pathological condition causing the problem, and select and justify treatment on a scientific basis. To do this, therapists must possess problem-solving skills as well as theoretical knowledge.

Despite the growing awareness that a subject-centred curriculum may not meet the current and future requirements of the profession, there has been a reluctance to change. There may be several reasons for this reluctance. Historically both physiotherapy and medical schools have been established on a subject-centred curriculum. Educational traditions which have been developed over long periods become difficult to criticise even from within. The change from subject-centred to more integrated courses has been viewed as threatening by the teachers of the individual subjects. Some teachers whose preferred teaching style consisted of a didactic approach have had difficulties in adapting to a problem-solving approach where emphasis is placed on active, student-centred learning based on small group discussion.

Clinicians who are responsible for the supervision of students whilst they are on clinical placement value the students' problem-solving skills. However, there is often criticism if they feel the students do not have the 'knowledge we had!'

The Institution

It has been argued that the development of a profession follows a well recognised continuum, and a number of clearly demonstrable steps can be identified (Wilensky 1964). One of the later steps most professions take is to better their perceived status in the eyes of their members and society at large. This usually involves the upgrading of their education process to degree level. In the past, the Department of Health and Social Security (now the Department of Health) actively blocked attempts to institute degrees in physiotherapy (Physiotherapy 1979) as, although committed to the training of many paramedical groups it had been on the basis of providing qualified staff to perform a clinical task. Despite initial setbacks, the policy of the CSP for development of an all graduate profession came to fruition in 1992 when all physiotherapy students were accepted on to degree programmes. The move from hospital-based schools to those in institutions of higher education has been based on the following:

First, that physiotherapists should be more competent and adaptable to technological change (Palastanga, 1990). The curriculum (CSP, 1984) states that students should be able to 'discuss recent technological development relevant to the assessment of patients, recording of observations, storage and analysis and retrieval of information including the use of microcomputers'. Education within HE should allow students access to resources that are enjoyed by other students in these establishments. Physiotherapy educators would not only be able to enlist specialist teachers in the area of information technology but also in other areas where physiotherapists have only basic knowledge, such as behavioural sciences.

A sound grounding in research would result in graduates able to carry out critical evaluation of treatment modalities which would lead to an improvement in physiotherapy services. This would ultimately reduce costs. Physiotherapists need to develop problem-solving skills in order to respond to social, economic and technological advances. The greater breadth and experience available in higher education would better prepare them for this (Palastanga, 1990). An all-graduate profession would also lead to the development of higher degrees in physiotherapy which would further benefit the practitioner and the patients.

One concern regarding the change has been the danger of what Warren-Piper (1984) calls 'academicisation', where the academic parts of the course are given greater priority and importance than the vocational elements. This is particularly important as completion of the degree programme provides the graduate with licence to practice.

The move into Higher Education has coincided with a time of great change for universities. Modularisation and semesterisation have become the norm within universities and physiotherapy education has had to follow the same route. It is a requirement of the CSP and The Council for Professions Supplementary to Medicine (CPSM) that all physiotherapy students must undertake a minimum of 1000 hours of supervised clinical experience. Modularisation does not lend itself easily to incorporate the profession-specific elements of such courses.

Fieldwork (clinical) education is an essential component of the undergraduate education of the healthcare professions (Crist, 1986). Fieldwork education allows the student to apply learned knowledge to clinical areas. Integration between theory and practice is considered to be vital. The transition of pre-registration courses from diploma to degree status has necessitated the inclusion of behavioural sciences and research methodology into an already overloaded curriculum. Nevertheless the importance of clinical education continues to be recognised by the profession and the CSP. Many schools have adopted an academic approach to supervision as described by Bogo and Vayda (1987). Here clinical education takes the form of a block system which follows the learning of a particular area, such as cardiology, in the university environment. Although this model has advantages, the changing pattern of healthcare has meant that many students are sent on four to six week 'block' clinical placements many miles away instead of 'half-day' placements near the school. This has resulted in clinical visits by the school lecturers occurring less frequently than when local placements were used (Walker, 1995). This is of significance as clinical supervisors may need advice regarding the students performance. This is of particular importance now that grades awarded to the students contribute towards their end-of-course assessment. It is often difficult to find sufficient placements in specific clinical areas for large numbers of students where they will be exposed to positive learning experiences.

Demands on physiotherapy lecturers have increased. Under the system of diploma courses, the main responsibility of lecturers was to teach and prepare their students for the national examinations organised by the CSP. The move to degree courses has resulted in internally assessed courses with additional work, including setting and marking examination papers and course work, preparing and submitting course documents, and implementing course evaluation (Walker, 1995). The move into higher educational establishments has resulted in the expectation of lecturers to show evidence of research activity and their research attainment in the form of publication of papers in refereed journals. Organisation of post-graduate courses is expected. Whilst this is recognised as being important for the development of the profession, it has caused a certain amount of stress for lecturers of a profession which has a small research base. The more experienced lecturers may not hold a higher degree and therefore feel concerned about their future. Lecturers may not feel that they can be as 'available' to students as they were when diploma courses existed in hospital-based schools.

Conclusion

Physiotherapists need to be able to adapt to social and economic change, and to the rapid advances in information technology. The ability to be able to justify their skills is becoming increasingly important. The move from diploma to degree courses within higher educational establishments with greater emphasis on research methodology and towards a problem-solving approach should prepare them for this. This paper has attempted to examine the benefits of these changes and the conflicts that have resulted.

References

Barr, J. S. (1977) "A problem-solving curriculum design in physical therapy," *Physical Therapy*, 57 pp. 262-270.

Bogo, M. and Vayda, E. (1987) *The practice of fieldwork instruction in social work: Theory and practice.* Toronto, Buffalo, London: University of Toronto Press.

Chartered Society of Physiotherapy Curriculum of Study (1984)

Crist Hickerson, P. A. (1986) *Contemporary issues in clinical education.* 1 (3) New Jersey: Slack Incorporated.

Department of Health and Social Security: Secretaries of State for Health, England, Wales, Northern Ireland and Scotland (1989) "Working for Patients". HMSO.

Department of Health and Social Security: Secretaries for State for Health , England, Wales, Northern Ireland and Scotland (1989) "Caring for people". HMSO.

Ham, C. (1985) *Health policy in Britain.* 2nd edition. London: MacMillan.

May, B. (1983) "Teaching : A skill in clinical practice," *Physical Therapy* 63 (10) pp.1627-1633.

McGahie, W. C. Miller, G. E. Said, A. W. Telder, T. V. (1978) *Competency-based curriculum development in medical education.* Public Health Paper 68 W.H.O.

Palastanga, N. (1990) "The case for physiotherapy degrees," *Physiotherapy,* 76 (3) pp. 124-126.

Physiotherapy, (1979) "The CSP's policy on degree courses," 65 (11) pp. 353-354.

Richardson, B. (1992) "Professional education and professional practice today-do they match? *Physiotherapy,* 78 (1) pp.23-26.

Walker, E. M. (1995) "Improving the links: fieldwork educators' conferences," *British Journal of Therapy and Rehabilitation,* 2 (7) pp.382-385.

Warren-Piper, D. (1984) "Sources and types of reform" in: Goodlad, S (ed) *Education for the professions.* Guildford: SRHE and NFER.

Wicksteed, J. H. (1948) *The growth of a profession.* London: Edward Arnold.

Wilensky, H. A. (1964) "The professionalisation of everyone," *American Journal of Sociology,* LXX (2) pp.137-158.

Williams, J. I. (1986) "Physiotherapy is handling," *Physiotherapy.* 72 (2) pp. 66-70.

Chapter Nine

The Dynamic Nature of Ethical Issues and Its Implication for Training Today's Business Students

P. Everett Fergenson
Susan G. Rozensher

Introduction

To read a newspaper today and to not see an article dealing with ethical problems of some business or business person borders on the impossible. We read about unethical and illegal conduct continually. Environmental contamination and dumping, stock manipulation, illegal payoffs are daily fare.

Business professors, in general, believe that the ethical climate today is worse than it was a decade ago (Rozensher and Fergenson, 1994). "Crisis" is a very strong word, but it would not be an exaggeration to say that, in a general sense, the ethical behavior of people involved in commerce has reached a crisis or at least a trigger point in the consciousness of the public. While we could point to the "usual suspects," i.e., the home, the family, religious institutions, childhood education etc., we must, to some extent at least, hold higher education to blame. It is here that training in business takes place. It is here that some understanding of what constitutes ethical behavior in a business context should take place.

Much, if not all, of our discussions about ethical behavior in the world of commerce involves coverage of issues that professors individually feel are important today. We believe that simply taking a snap-shot of today's issues and teaching them disregards the reality that issues of ethical behavior have a dynamic quality to them. They emerge and recede in importance; sometimes quickly, sometimes slowly.

Depending upon legal constraints, enforcement of existing laws, political philosophies, and public outlay, among other factors, these issues can and often do re-emerge.

In order to make the ethical training of business students more effective, we must consider not only those issues important today, but those issues which are likely to emerge or re-emerge.

In the United States today, a seemingly quickly changing political climate will, in all likelihood, change the landscape of ethical issues and behavior.

As the American Government becomes less regulatory, that is to say less constraining and less interfering in business conduct, it is incumbent for the business person to become more self-regulatory. It is important that self-regulation be ethical. A training model based upon the dynamic nature of ethical issues, we believe, will end in the ethical training of business professionals at a time when it is most needed.

Methodology

A cross-section of American public and private colleges and universities was generated by a simple random sample of 50 schools drawn from the population of institutions belonging to the American Assembly of Collegiate Schools of Business (AACSB, 1989).

The deans of the schools comprising the selected sample each received a packet containing 40 questionnaires. They were requested to distribute these questionnaires to faculty mailboxes. Each questionnaire came with a reply envelop addressed to the researchers to provide confidentiality to the respondents.

Completed questionnaires were received from 80 percent of the schools sampled. Of the 40 schools represented, no one school provided more than six percent of the responses. The proportion of public versus private schools in the cooperative sample was 41 percent and 59 percent respectively. This closely parallels the 42 percent to 58 percent AACSB membership.

The number of respondents totaled 337. Among the areas investigated was the importance of various issues dealing with business ethics. Faculty members were asked to select the two most important issues today and also to select the two ethical issues in business that were most important ten years ago.

To facilitate a comparison with previous research, the authors used this particular list of issues taken from a list used by the Ethics Resource Center, as reported in *Ethics Education in American Business Schools* (1988).

The frequency with which each of the ethical issues was chosen was then converted to a rank. The issue mentioned most frequently was ranked first, the next most frequent, second etc. A comparison between the ranking today and ten years ago was then computed for each issue.

Results

We have compared the rankings of a decade ago with the rankings today and developed a measure of change in importance by subtracting the rank of a decade ago from today's score. This yields a positive rank change for issues that have become more important over the last decade and a negative rank change for those issues which have become less important. The larger the score, the larger the change either in the positive or negative direction.

Table 1 lists the issues, their current rankings on importance, their decade ago ranking on the same scale and the concomitant change in ranking that has occurred over the last decade. Table 2 breaks the data from Table 1 into those issues which have become more important, those which haven't changed, and those which have become less important.

Table 1
Change in the Importance of Ethical Issues Over the Last Ten Years
Rank*

Issues	10 Yrs. Ago	Today	Change
Accuracy of Books and Records	13	11	-2
Codes of Ethics	7	9	+2
Conflict of Interest	5	8	+3
Discrimination by Age, Race, or Sex	8	1	-7
Employee Concerns (Privacy, etc.)	9	5	-4
Environmental Issues	2	5	+3
False Advertising	11	7	-4
Honesty	4	4	0
Personal Business Ethics	3	2	-1
Product Liability and Safety	6	3	-3
Proprietary Info./Intelligence Gathering	12	13	+1
Relations with Customers	10	10	0
"Wall Street Ethics" (LBO's, etc.)	1	11	+10
Other	14	14	0

*Based upon 337 responses

Table 2
A Comparison of the Change in the
Importance of Ranking of Ethical Issues

Have Become More Important

Codes of Ethics	+2
Conflict of Interest	+3
Environmental Issues	+3
Proprietary Information	+1
Wall Street	+10

No Change

Honesty
Relations with Customers
"Other"

Have Become Less Important

Accuracy of Books and Records	-2
Discrimination by Age, Race, Sex	-7
Employee Concerns	-4
False Advertising	-4
Personal Business Ethic	-1
Product Liability and Safety	-3

Issues Which Have Become More Important

Codes of ethics have increased slightly. They were not considered an important issue a decade ago and now are considered, at best, moderately important.

Conflict of interest was moderately important a decade ago and even though it has increased a bit in importance over the last decade, it is still not listed in the top one-third of the issues evaluated.

Environmental issues were moderately important a decade ago and now have emerged as the second most important ethical issue in business. We will re-visit this issue later in this paper.

Proprietary information has shown a statistical increase in importance but the significance of the increase is minimal. It is one of the last important issues even today although it has increased in importance one rank from thirteen to twelve.

Wall Street Ethics which include insider trading, bank scams, bail-outs, LBOs, Junk Bond Scandles etc. has become the "hot issue." It came out of nowhere and is now the number one issue in business ethics we will also revisit this issue later in this paper.

Issues Which Did Not Change in Importance

There were two issues which did not change in importance; honesty and relations with customers.

"Personal honesty" is relatively important and has remained so. "Relations with customers" was not considered a decade ago and remains unimportant.

Issues Which Have Become Less Important

Accuracy of books and records, while it has become slightly less important, was never a very serious issue in the first place. It slipped two ranks; from eleventh to thirteenth.

Discrimination by age, race, or sex is the issue which has receded the most. Ten years ago it was the number one ethical issue in business, today it is of moderate importance at best. It now ranks eighth out of the thirteen issues ranked. We will return to a discussion of this issue.

Employee concerns, which includes working conditions and to some degree issues of privacy has slipped in importance. A decade ago it was moderately important and today is among the least important issues. This change and its repercussions warrants further discussion.

False advertising is considered an unimportant issue today whereas ten years ago it was moderately important.

The importance of personal business ethics has changed little over the last decade. Product liability has slipped from its ranking ten years ago as the third most important ethical issue to a moderately important sixth place today. We will speak more about this presently.

Discussion

We have seen that a number of issues have become more important over the last decade while a number of others have become less so. The changes range from the insignificant to the extremely large.

Taken by themselves, the changes would make an interesting and possibly illuminating subject. When we review these changes in the light of proposed and, in some cases, enacted legislation, in the United States, the importance of ethical education becomes even more important. When we overlay the increased importance of ethical training for business professionals with the amount and type of training they receive, we have on our hands, we believe, a crisis in the training of business professionals.

To ascertain a pattern of relationship between ethical issues and legislation let us just turn our attention to some of those issues which have decreased in importance, namely:

- Discrimination by age, sex, and race
- Employee concerns over workplace conditions
- Product liability and safety

All three of these issues were important issues in business ethics a decade ago, ranking first, fifth and third, respectively. All three have dropped dramatically in importance due in large part to socially conscious, some would say social engineering, or legislation.

Affirmative action plans of various types have lowered the level of age, sex, and racial discrimination. Of this there can be little doubt. OSHA legislation has made the workplace considerably safer. High monetary awards for accidents and injuries as the result of unsafe products has, in no small way, lead to industry's largely successful attempt to more products safer.

At this point we should be able to heave a sigh of relief were it not for the reaction of various groups to the legislation and the changes it has wrought.

Affirmative action is under attack in the United States and has been for a number of years. It seems to be making a retreat (Franklin, 1995). As affirmative action plans retreat we will see, I believe, the reemergence of discrimination in the workplace as a major issue in business ethics.

OSHA, while not so heavily under attack as affirmative action, is still being threatened.

The issue under the most strenuous attack, as of this writing, is product safety and liability. Limits on payments legislation has passed both houses of Congress independently and a compromise bill is currently under discussion (Lewis, 1995).

The pattern that has emerged appears to be as follows: a problem reaches some threshold of public consciousness via any of a large number of mechanisms, i.e., catastrophic event, media hype, the "pet" issue of someone of prominence etc. When it becomes evident that the issue should or must be dealt with, legislation ensues and the issue, if solved, is seen to be trending downward — it becomes less important. Occasionally legislation does not seem to work either because of lack of enforcement or poor, weak legislation and the issue remains "hot."

If the issue, when addressed by legislation, is too costly for business either monetarily or in terms of operational efficiency, a backlash occurs and the legislation is, in many cases, either over-turned or modified and the problem returns.

If this model is reasonably accurate, we can expect "Wall Street ethics" and "Environmental Issues" to continue to be dealt with in some manner by government. Should the compliance with legislation or proposed legislation be too costly, we can expect one of two scenarios:

- The issues will remain important because business will continue to fight against their increased financial burden, or,
- successful legislation will make the issues less important. Business will mount a strong lobbying campaign in the halls of government and in the media to roll back the legislation and the issue will return to its prominent place on the list of issues.

How does this all relate to what we believe is a crisis in business ethical education? We postulate a number of ways:

1. Some believe that the best way to teach business ethics is through the use of cases (French and Granrose, 1995). This may be true, but if cases are to be used, our hypothesis implies that we must consider the dynamics of ethical issues rather than take a static "snap shot" in order to determine the issues to study via cases. We must look at three different groups of issues:

- those emerging from moderate to important
- those considered important
- those which were important but have decreased in importance and whose legislature control is under attack

2. We must inoculate students against a corporate culture which, in large measure, seems to be held in check via governmental legislation. As legislation is rolled back the consequences of eventant behavior is less predictable, i.e., uncertainty increases as to the consequences of behavior. As uncertainty increases, particularly the uncertainty that punishment will follow "bad" behavior, the need for personal ethical control increases. This relationship between uncertainty and ethics is discussed in more detail elsewhere (Dawes, 1988).

In a time when business faculty opine that business ethics have either decreased or at best, remained the same (Rozensher and Fergenson, 1994) and these same faculty spend little time on ethics: only about twenty percent of undergraduate and thirty percent of MBA faculty spend more than three to four hours a semester on ethical issues, it is important that they "get it right." Spending too little time, often on the wrong issues exacerbates a crisis in moral behavior in the market place. The crisis in moral behavior implies a crisis in the ethical training of these same individuals. We hope that the paradigm for the coverage of ethical issues that we have postulated here, and which will aid in the more effective training in ethical behavior of our future business leaders.

References

AACSB Membership Directory. (1989) American Assembly of Collegiate Schools of Business, St. Louis, MO.

Dawes, Robyn M. (1988) *Rational Choice in an Uncertain World*. Orlando, FL: Harcourt Brace Jovanovich Inc.

"The Damages Bill is Veto Bait." (1995) *New York Times* (13 May), editorial.

Ethics Education in American Business Schools. (1988) Washington: Ethics Resource Center.

Franklin, Ben A. (1995) "In the Second 100 Days will Clinton Keep His Contract?" *The Washington Spectator*, 21(10) (May), pp.1-4.

French, Warren A. and John Granrose. (1995) *Practical Business Ethics*. Englewood Cliffs: Prentice-Hall.

George, Richard J. (1987) "Teaching Business Ethics: Is There a Gap Between Rhetoric and Reality?" *Journal of Business Ethics, 6*, pp.513-518.

Hoffman, W. Michael and Jennifer M. Moore. (1982) "Results of a Business Ethics Curriculum Survey Conducted By the Center of Business Ethics." *Journal of Business Ethics,* 1, pp. 81-83.

Katz, Adolph I. (1980) "The Status of Business Ethics Education in Business School Curricula." *Information and Management*, 18, pp.123-130.

Lewis, Neil A. (1994) "Senate Agrees on Bill to Cut Civil-Court Damage Awards." *New York Times*, (10 May), pp. A1 and D20.

Rozensher, Susan G. and Everett P. Fergenson. (1994) "Business Faculty Perspectives on Ethics: A National Survey." *Business Horizons*, (July-August), pp.61-67.

Chapter Ten

If It's Not Hurting It's Not Working

Chris Gaine

The focus of this chapter is the development of an informed professional commitment towards racial equality in primary school student teachers. It deals with a group of 17 women, mostly aged between 18 and 25 during their four years of BEd training in one college. The majority — twelve — had grown up in largely white areas, had had few personal encounters with ethnic minorities, and few recalled coming to college with a particular interest in the issue of "race". The findings which emerge from interview, questionnaire and other data[1] elicited from the students can be summarised as follows:

a) during their training there was considerable conflict between students (including some of the group) and the initial teacher education (ITE) staff within specific courses focussing on "race" (on grounds such as "extremism", irrelevance, "anti-white bias" etc.) Hostility towards particular members of staff persisted long after the specific courses finished;

b) nevertheless, there was a shift in at least five of the group towards a more "anti-racist" stance (elaborated on below) by the time they graduated. In their judgement this was not true of numbers of their peers in their year group;

c) five of the group seem to have begun their studies with a less defensive attitude about white racism than the others. Four of these were the only ones later to articulate a political understanding of racism (again, this is elaborated later).

Two key questions underlie both the practice described here and the findings:

(i) how useful (or otherwise) is the concept of "racism" as a tool for students to evaluate (and re-evaluate) their own attitudes as well as educational practices and processes?

(ii) how do teacher educators promote a critical consciousness without merely destructive student/tutor hostility?

The Context

In focusing on teaching about "race" to student teachers this paper touches upon many personal, practical and political pressures. Students come to initial teacher education with a wide range of experiences, orientations and personalities, as do their tutors. The formal teaching situations in which they meet are conditioned and constrained by a host of additional factors, ranging from formal government criteria, to media agendas, to teaching styles, to timetabling exigencies.

The group of 17 women on which I concentrate most is clearly opportunistic rather than representative (though there were very few males in their cohort of 83 students). They were volunteers, in the post-exam period of their final year, responding to my request for interviewees on the subject of the "race" courses they had experienced earlier at college. By that stage none were hostile to me or the courses (though some had been at the time), indeed they presumably had some special interest to incline them to volunteer at all. Their comments on themselves may be doubted as potentially self-serving, their comments to me as subject to an obvious (though by this stage informal) power imbalance (Oakley: 1981) and their comments on their peers as only partially informed, at best. Nevertheless, these very biases reveal something about the positioning and negotiation which take place in personal and professional discourse about racism. It also needs to be said that few of us have views about "race" or anything else which are fixed and immutable, an unchanging framework which structures everything we say. An integral part of the respondents' memories and their more current observations is the process of talking about them and reflecting upon them. Memory and perspective are constantly constructed and reconstructed, elaborated and changed. This talking is a part of their sense-making, not something separate. For some it may be a crucial part: it is not often that in a non-assessed, unofficial setting we spend time with individual students and systematically talk through with them what they have learned over a four year period. Perhaps that was part of their motive for volunteering.[2]

This is a particularly interesting group in the way their own biographies coincide with some relevant events and currents in the past two decades. They graduated in 1991. Most were in the middle years of secondary school when the Swann Report was working towards its conclusion that Britain needed "Education for All" (DES: 1985). Most attended white schools in areas peripheral to multiracial cities or in much more ethnically isolated ones. They had been subject, knowingly or not, to policy initiatives in LEAS with regard to "race" by the time they finished A levels, and knowingly subjected to them during ITE. In addition, they have lived through the rise and rise of the New Right with its accompanying media and political discourse of derision about anti-racism. Generally about nine or ten years old at the time of Thatcher's accession, they had their primary schooling in the unreconstructed, sloppy seventies, began secondary school around the time of the Brixton and St. Paul's troubles, spent their teenage years in the Tories' post-Falklands heyday, and their young adulthood in the partial flowering of Thatcher's educational vision of a market of restored values (in which they now teach).

It is also important to note that during their ITE they were subject to a mismatch, a friction between changing currents in government policy. Dating from concerned HMI reports in the late 1970s (Taylor, in Graves 1990) the Committee for the Accreditation of Teacher Education required, as a minimum, that "...courses should cover ... the school in its wider social context, including issues of culture, gender and race" (CATE: 1989). As the 1980s wore on, government faced demands from the New Right to remove what they saw as a pervasive and corrosive multiculturalism in education generally and this increasingly determined the media and rhetorical agenda (see Hill: 1990; Ball: 1994; Gaine: 1995). It had significant effects on National Curriculum content and as far as ITE is concerned, culminated in the effective removal of the relevant CATE requirement in 1993.

The Students

If space permitted I would include the entire transcript of one particular student. For me as a teacher interested in anti-racism she is almost too good to be true. Her interview is a linear narrative of increasing personal awareness, critical questioning, political analysis and professional reflection. She moves from schooldays in Sussex and an emergent sensitisation to racism (through A level geography and reading To Kill a Mockingbird), to complacently truanting from a day course about racism in her first year at college, to an untraumatic acceptance of her own complicity in racism during her second year (and anger at others' resistant "smugness"), to a critique of the implicit racism in set literary texts and a sharpened perspective on the rest of the curriculum. At one point she says:

> It's an amazing change though, because it's not just working on your mind. I mean, I don't know how this happens to a person, but before... even after

reading To Kill a Mockingbird, having all that kind of thing, well I would still laugh at racist jokes. Now how I come to the position now, of not finding them funny... I don't know how... how I've come to that, but I have... It's actually finding it offensive, which, having been someone who laughs at them and told them and whatever... having gone to a position where you don't even want to smile.... And it's not as if I'm holding it in, thinking "I shouldn't laugh at this" it's inside, I'm not laughing... (Jane)

I do not think that this is too good to be true in the sense that she is misrepresenting herself, falsely constructing herself in a particular way (although, as I recognize above, the very process of talking is part of constructing oneself). It may be that from doing so she would gain esteem in my eyes, but she had little need of it: there was no compulsion to be interviewed, I had no means of influencing her results, we had barely met as individuals in four years and she was a week away from leaving college for good. Her own self-esteem did not need such a serious misrepresention in any obvious way: her relevant marks were excellent, her chosen dissertation topic was on exploring racism through literature, she spoke with passion, conviction and coherence.

Yet she was too good to be true in another sense. Having gone through a series of formal and planned educational experiences she had changed. She is the ideal imaginary student we teachers have in mind when designing courses: open minded, prepared to be self-critical, willing to accept challenges. The trouble is that she may be the only one for whom the courses we designed were really suited: they may have served many others rather less well....

Returning to the group as a whole, five grew up and went to school in areas adjacent to substantial black or Asian populations: fairly central Bristol, Crawley, Harrow, North London and Barking, Essex. Two were from areas on the peripheries of Southampton and Portsmouth. The remaining 10 came from a continuum of moderately to very ("racially") isolated towns: Caversham (Berks), Folkestone, Cheltenham, the Isle of Wight, Buckingham, three from Sussex, then Saffron Waldon (Essex) and Plymouth. One grew up with a widowed mother, another's was recently divorced, but all the others had grown up with both parents.

They mostly came to college either straight from A levels or after a short gap, though one had qualified and worked as a midwife in a multiracial area before beginning ITE at 23 and two were in their late 30s. Few had given very much thought to issues of "race" or racism, except one who had made a positive decision to avoid it in her training:

The race stuff in the Bulmershe prospectus seemed wacky to me... so I didn't apply there. It wasn't exactly something I didn't want to know, but I didn't want to come out as some idealistic teacher... you know, odd, and I thought I won't be training for London.... (Tina).

Apart from the five who grew up in "adjacent" areas, few had had any first hand contact with black or Asian people:

> I saw some at the university nearby...there was an Asian woman in the office I worked in for a while... but mostly I came across them as manual workers... (Heather).

> I had some black friends in the 6th form, one in particular, we're still in touch (Claire).

> There was a "village" at home where overseas people came to live for a while... their children came to our school, perhaps four black children in each class. We never really seemed to mix, I don't know why.... (Angela).

Of those from "adjacent" areas, only Megan, Tracey and Katie had gone to mixed primary and secondary schools and had had many inter-ethnic friendships. Another had contact of a sort with racism:

> Though the area was mixed I noticed that our grammar school had a few, maybe one or two Afro-Caribbean girls and a couple of Asians...and there was another ... school down the road for that area and a lot of the, you know the blacks and the Asians went to the one down the road. So did you notice that, at 14, 15 or whatever? Yeah, yes I did, because....I figured it wasn't fair but I didn't know if it was the actual report system from primary school that put you into the school or whether it was the culture of the different backgrounds of people.... We noticed when we were going to school...white people going this way and black people going that way, it was weird really, the schools were so close.... (Emma).

About half had had clear racist messages from their immediate families and friends:

> Alf Garnett, that's my Dad. "Don't ever bring a black boy home..." and things like that. He said he met someone at work the other day "He was a Sikh in a turban, but he was a very nice man" as if it was surprising that a Sikh could be a nice man. Our neighbour moved out last year and it was "Oh I hope we don't get Asians in next door" (Tracey).

> ...my sister's had the same experience as me yet she's incredibly racist. And members of my family wind me up, because they know my stance, so they wind me up just to see me get up on my soap box and attack them. I mean I don't know how much that is racist and how much they just want to get me going.... (Angela).

> My brother's definitely really racist, he and my sister call Asians pakis and that... and they get away with it.... (Teresa).

My Dad says things like you've got to get out of their way in the street, you don't know what they'll do.. He's quite bad, he really gets me going. He used to tell racist jokes when I was younger, and his friends, well now I can just walk out or make my feelings known.... He says he's just winding me up but you know really they are his views.... (Katie).

Though at least as many remembered comments and attitudes opposed to racism, either specifically or in ways they perceived as unambiguous:

...I was about 13, 14 ...'cos my Dad's in the same position as me, no contact or whatever with black people and I can remember him saying after watching something on television...saying he was ashamed to be white...and then he said, on meeting black people he feels that they have an absolute right to loath us and despise us...just on his colour, not knowing him as a person (Jane).

I think a lot of my attitudes have grown up with Mum and Dad...not specifically them saying you shouldn't, you know...about race, just everyone was just generally accepted...though one set of grandparents are definitely racist (Claire).

Before I was born my Dad was in America for a year, during that period when Martin Luther King was assassinated. He went into a restaurant, it was a whites only restaurant and he went in with a black friend and he was told either we can serve you and not your friend or.... And he said "We're going, not staying".... being told that from when you were very young...it's obvious what your Dad thinks about that sort of thing. I was about seven or eight when he told me that. This is the way my Dad is. He doesn't necessarily say "Oh this is how you should treat people" ...you just see it from experience (Emma).

There was one thing, when we were younger, before we knew better we used to use the name nignog and they just clamped down on that, I was about five or six. We were told off for that.... (Angela).

Megan described herself as "lucky" to have grown up in a family where very close inter-ethnic friendships were the norm. She had pre-school memories of a Hindu friend of her mother's who married a white neighbour, and of another Indian who married a cousin.

...my mother always taught us to look for the best in people, she was always tolerant to other people, that's how, I think like my brother's got this really special relationship with an Indian, they were best man for each other....

All but four came from loosely middle class families, a handful with parents who were teachers, nurses and one clergyman. The four exceptions' families had roots in the Welsh valleys (two) and East London (two). Of those who were willing to say, seven voted Labour in 1992, four Liberal Democrat, and two Conservative. Amongst the newspapers read regularly there was no clear preference — and some rarely read one — though the Star and the Sun were more often actively disliked than the others.

Christian beliefs played a significant part for seven of the group in their attitudes towards racism, though Jane states it more firmly than anyone else:

> Do you think your Christianity has anything to do with your attitudes? A lot, but definitely my Christianity... upon my understanding of the Bible, whatever their experience and upbringing, people have no excuse to be racist... Once...with my fiancee, we'd sat down to Sunday lunch and someone was saying about "all these Muslims wanting all these rights" and that kind of thing.... And his sister said "Well anyway, I don't think that black people and white people will ever get on until they get to heaven...they just can't". And, you know, we'd just come home from church where we were... Jesus and everyone is saying that the Kingdom of God is here and now.... I hate people who just sit back and wait to die for everything to be all right, you know....

The majority had grown up in churchgoing families though they had carried this into their own adulthood in varying ways. Five professed no religious beliefs at all, including the two in their thirties.

> When you say "You shouldn't be thinking in a racist way, are you saying that as a religious person, or....? Probably more moral really.... Though I suppose religion teaches you how you should treat people.... (Emma).

> I'm Church of England. I was taught in primary school "treat other people as you'd like to be treated yourself", I was taught that particular outlook and it's managed to stick in my mind.... (Angela).

> I'm a Christian, but not actively. When people talk about Christian beliefs that doesn't really feel like me... but I try to be good to other people, that kind of thing. Mum says we'll have to start going to church, but with her night shifts (in nursing) we never seem to (Cathy).

> ...I don't conform to any religion. I don't think you can be a human being and turn a blind eye to these things (Mary).

Overall, although it was clearly important to some of the group, there was no simple correspondence between religious belief and their attitudes to racism or their response to the courses.

The Courses

ITE institutions attempted to meet the CATE criterion about "race" in a variety of different ways. In my own, we went for a fourfold plan. Firstly, all BEd students would take part in an awareness-raising day about "race" and racism during their first year (RAT). These were in groups of 16 or 18 at most, each led by a black or Asian trainer, and consisted of videos, discussions, and small group work which would allow space to explore ideas and feelings (detailed in Gaine: 1987). Attendance was meant to be compulsory, there was no assessed work. In their second year they would have a compulsory ten week (15 hour) "teaching studies" course (RGC), intended to build upon RAT with factual data, theoretical analyses and educational strategies. It was taught in a fairly traditional format of lectures, videos, and seminars, assessed by coursework and exam. Thirdly, they would also learn through "permeation" of the issue through their other courses, achieved through a programme of staff training. Fourthly, there was a specialist option available late in their final year. The Swann Report (1985, p.611) had recommended placements in multiracial schools, via distant urban outposts if necessary, but this was rejected as firstly misdefining the issues as urban problems and secondly as inevitably limiting provision to a volunteer minority.

While the focus in this paper is the explicit courses in year one and two, it is worth saying at this point that no-one in the group acknowledged any significant learning from permeation. Main subjects (which occupied half their time for four years) were mentioned fleetingly three times, once critically, and for one student the final year dissertation was the crucial experience which cemented her interest into conviction. Students were able to state a preference for one of the few multiracial schools available for teaching practice. Two did, one of them observing what she described as "appalling practice". Of the others, none acknowledged any significant learning at all about multicultural or anti-racist work while in school.

Most of the planned provision was a product of its time. It was underpinned by notions of racism widely held by anti-racists in the '1980s (for example see Berkshire: 1983; ILEA: 1984) and to which I had little trouble gaining formal agreement within the college. Ten years on, it is striking how unambiguous Swann — a government report, after all — was about this:

> ...a satisfactorily permeated course would in our view be one in which... various concepts of "racism": intentional, unintentional, institutionalised would be understood, and the student equipped to combat such phenomena, as well as the manifestations of personal prejudice in him/herself, in colleagues and in pupils (p.558).

Essentially we held that racism was endemic in a society which had economically exploited and culturally dominated other peoples defined as "races", in the main and most obviously black and south Asian people. We also read the evidence of lower pay and poorer provision of jobs and housing as indicating that this continued as a defining feature of British society.

This account alone could be counted upon to antagonise many whose socialisation and home culture inclined them to think of Britain as civilised, democratic and fair, with a history to match. When asked what he thought of British civilization, Gandhi was famously supposed to have remarked "I think it would be a good idea". Many of our students would not have seen the joke:

...in the evaluation I wrote that you made me ashamed to be white, British and Christian, I felt you were saying that, I didn't feel proud of that whereas before I had... (Tina).

...the first session of RGC sticks out in my mind....because I think it was blatantly something the other way round, you know, opposite Did it feel like it was saying Britain is terrible? Yes! We're all rubbish, yes, yes (Pat).

But this account of racism did not stop there. It did not identify white racists as malignant, conscious discriminators but as ordinary people, people who took on racist cultural assumptions with their mother's milk, routinely institutionalised racist practices in their jobs, and recreated racist discourses in their interaction with friends, family and the media. In other words, the people who carry racism around are white people just like the students, their families (and their lecturers). This is especially pertinent and difficult to deal with in ITE because one is explicitly engaging with the reproduction of cultural knowledge and assumptions: that is what student teachers are preparing to do. There is, or ought to be, no hiding place.

One device we developed to illustrate this was a series of questions. One asked what were the commonest goods traded in Timbuctu in the 1500s? The answer — books — surprises almost everyone since it is not our usual image of Africa. Another asked why black footballers get bananas (not oranges) thrown at them by hostile spectators. The racist association between black people and monkeys was pointed to as part of the cultural racism most British have grown up with. A third question asked students to consider what kinds of things they heard people say about black and Asian people. The comments are always almost entirely negative, maybe abusive, so from their own pens/mouths students can demonstrate the prevalence of racist attitudes in their own experiences.

The above strategies were used in the RAT sessions. In RGC the main teaching tools in putting across our understanding of racism (or at least the ones which were remembered) were two tape/slide packages: The Enemy Within (Catholic Commission for Racial Justice, 1982) or Recognising Racism (Birmingham LEA, 1983). Their provenance would not suggest to most people that their content was radical, anti-white, or deliberately designed to antagonise, though they had that effect on many: "I was very angry...that first session was awful... that dreadful slideshow." (Barbara). The first contains a black academic saying "What I really don't know what to do with is liberal racism. I don't know where it's going to hit me..." The second, more often remembered, has the white middle aged male narrator saying "It took me a while to realise that I was something of a racist myself... and it's likely that you are too, if you're white". This rooting of racism in ordinary people's everyday consciousness and actions is profoundly threatening: we expected students to find it hard to chew though not ultimately indigestible. At a rational level one can hedge such an exercise about with assurances that racist ideas and images are taken on unconsciously (as both courses and the RAT trainers took pains to do) but it is hard for students not to feel accused by it. Most did, and most were angry about it.

> I...remember people at the time really hated you because they felt so antagonised... We all felt that you thought we were all racists.... (Heather).

> I did feel a bit wound up... well... partly because I walked in there and you felt you were being told you were a racist... and although then, well my back just got up and I didn't feel very good about it. So that wound me up a bit.... Was it actually said? I don't think it was said like that, totally out, you know, you are a racist, but it was partly implied.... I think other people... went away and they just shut off their mind totally because they just thought "Well, that's it. They're just some sort of extreme. They think we're racist so that's it" (Emma).

> I got the feeling (the black trainer) was saying we're all racist... I think a lot of people were annoyed. I remember you saying we're all racist... In the first few lectures I was angry, all I could see was how is this relevant to me? I felt threatened, angry... You gave the impression we were intentionally racist.... (Tina).

Whatever our intentions it is clear here that students picked up our implicit assumptions and read them almost as accusations of intentional, consciously chosen racism on their part. They were angry, though generally not confident enough to make a public challenge. Some wondered if it was a deliberate provocative stance on our part, some, apparently, stopped listening in self-defence:

> I would have lynched him black trainer... and I was very angry with you at first... I thought he was very offensive. I felt that in his efforts to try and prove the point he actually made everyone more hostile, instead of open. Perhaps its the way I react to things, but if someone sort of attacks me my immediate reaction would be defence.... It was quite a volatile day, I can tell you (Barbara).

You felt hostile because you felt implicitly accused? Yes, yes very much so, guilty before I opened my mouth (Linda).

...it was assumed (in RAT) that we were racist and that we needed to be... to have that taken away from us. I mean I've always been violently anti-racist. So you felt insulted? Not necessarily insulted, just felt that it was a waste of time. Some of it was interesting but... Were you told you were all racist or did you feel it was assumed? It was an assumption (Angela).

...you showed a film which more or less said that all white people are racist, just by definition. That really got people's backs up. It even got.. even I thought it was a bit... you know, I wasn't sure about this, and I'm quite liberal, compared to a lot of people here. I know it made a lot of people very angry watching that, and because that was near the start it soured the whole course for some people, they immediately felt threatened and they had to get their backs up and protect themselves.... (Tracey).

I was uncomfortable in RAT, in the RGC I just felt angry... perhaps you did it just to get people's backs up, them being told they were racist (Pat).

Indeed Pat referred to this, unprompted, in the follow-up questionnaires, seven years after the course:

I didn't like the way the way the tutors branded us as racists in our first lecture...

Some students suggested that part of the hostility was merely or largely defensive/reactive (like Barbara and Tracey above) and likely to wear off as the cognitive message sunk in:

I think that a lot of people, that if you provoke them in a way they don't see that you're challenging them to think, they think you're having a go at them.... (Cathy).

These are mostly comments about their own reactions, but without exception the students testified to a general climate of resentment, discussed and referred to well away from the timetabled teaching slots, often merging a demonisation of myself as Mr. Anti-racism with media-fuelled paranoia about what would now be called authoritarian political correctness. Rumours were rife about likely sanctions against transgressors:

There was a rumour that if you turned out to be racist you were going to be taken off the course (Mary).

Some people thought if you said the wrong thing the college would throw you out (Laura).

People said things like "If you wear a black jacket CG will complain" (Tina).

Some became less angry as time went on, moving to a partial acceptance of the idea of a pervasive, sometimes unconscious racism in white people:

> At the time in year one, I would have said I wasn't racist, but there were lots of things I hadn't considered... (Laura).

I put to some of the later interviewees, including Laura, that others had said with hindsight, that they did have racist ideas which needed challenging. She was silent for a long time at this point then simply said "I think that's very brave..... Some people don't like to admit that they actually are racist, depending on how you see yourself, I don't see myself as racist..." Others, as Laura said, were brave:

> ...at the time I thought "Load of rubbish", you know, "He doesn't know what he's talking about..." and then I thought about it, and I thought about the people I'd come in contact with for most of my life and I thought well possibly, well you know I'm as guilty of that as anybody else. The course on race was very difficult because I had to really rethink my whole... all my ideas.... I remember the turning point. I went home and I remember having an argument, well... a discussion with my parents, so I was obviously stewing things over a lot. I didn't feel discomfort by the end of the course because by that time I'd actually begun to really question... what I'm doing here (Barbara).

> ...and then I got to gradually thinking, hang on, all this racist stuff isn't as cut and dried as I think it is (Linda).

> Yes it was traumatic, because it stirs up the very feelings that you've got, your feelings might be wrong or something... The turning point was when another lecturer gave one of the lectures, cleverly, she knew we were getting angry, she gave us a talk which made us not feel bad... she said none of us want to be racist... we're on a path. So instead of feeling we're all being racist we were also trying not to be racist. It wasn't condescending because of the way she said it. I think that defused the situation, or definitely did for me anyway. I don't know, it was an eye opener... this course was actually delving into how you were as a person... it was uncomfortable because you have to re-examine yourself (Pat).

> Unless you really sort of confronted the issue then it's sort of... actually confronting it will really make it clear in your mind.... That was the kind of thing that came across in the lectures. At the beginning you know, some people may say they're not racist but it's... they do small things perhaps, and you do it unconsciously... That kind of thing.... I saw the course as being in a way provoking people to think about how they actually feel and whether they can...whether they did do little things (Cathy).

...yes there was one session when we were talking about all of us being racist in one way or the other and not actually being able to admit that to ourselves... and an awful lot of people walked out of that thinking "How dare he think I'm a racist?" How did you feel about that? Well, at that time I wouldn't have thought I was! (laughter)... but I've got some racist ideas inside the way most people have. I think it was of benefit to me and the fact that I was actually waking up to the fact that I am a racist, and I know I think I'm better equipped to deal with that myself.... (Mary).

In RGC was when I got the feeling that... of realising that there was more to it. I couldn't just sit back and say "Oh yes, equality for everyone". That's when it first hit me (Claire).

In a way it worked for me because it totally shocked me I think... so it worked quite well. Afterwards I realised how you tend to fix certain ideas about certain races, then attach that idea to everybody in that culture or in that race, regardless.... I can see that now but I didn't at the time. And I think I've got less resentful as I've gone through college really.... Yes, I suppose I was a bit resentful at the beginning. It opened my eyes a little bit because I... I don't think I was exactly patronising, that's not exactly the right word, but...almost (Emma).

Laura's phrase "how you see yourself" is apposite, since the mix of intellectual and emotional challenges clearly struck at the students' sense of themselves. What stands out in these comments is the very personal shifts they describe: "I had to rethink ...all my ideas"; "... you have to re-examine yourself"; "I was waking up to the fact that I..."; "..That's when it hit me"; "It opened my eyes." They were only able to assimilate the concept of racism which underpinned the course by modifying their own self-concept. In one sense as course leader I knew this perfectly well, though with hindsight the scale of change at which we were aiming, in individual terms let alone multiplying that by 80, was formidable.

Nevertheless, some did achieve this shift in their sense of themselves. Emma observes:

I suppose I must have felt superior in some sort of way... By the time the second year course had started I had accepted that... I was eager to learn then.

Apart from the comments above about insight and perspective, many did identify what they had learned in terms of factual details, especially in RGC. Cultural and linguistic complexities are often referred to, as are key facts about immigration:

I thought it was good experience... when they suddenly asked you how many percent of the population were actually from ethnic minorities I said... sort of... about 50%. So from that point of view it was good... (Emma).

So how long did the resentment last... four years? (...laughter...) I can actually remember... there are certain sessions that we did in RGC that I remember being very very interested in ... You did one on the Indian sub-continent didn't you? Now that I found very interesting, and the one on the Red American Indians was another one where I was actually mesmerised (Barbara).

We could see the need to be told about the different cultures and everything, we needed the information.... We had to get into pairs and discuss any time we'd come into contact with racism... and some discussion about knowing what to call, how to describe a person, whether it was black... coloured. The names are a stumbling block for a lot of people....(Angela).

As for the rest of the cohort, while all the interviewees felt the hostility had diminished — "Between then and now the feelings have died" (Angela), "The hostility had definitely lessened by the end of the course, definitely..." (Emma), most nonetheless felt it was still present, there was still a core of students who felt more irritated than informed: "I think there are some who are still hostile" (Mary).

My diary accounts, the interviews and the judgement of the staff on the course all suggest that while the courses were in progress the majority of students felt angry and accused (while we felt battered, demoralised and the targets of considerable hostility).

Some of the flavour comes over in the extracts quoted. In others, words like hostile, antagonistic, resentful and tense occur often. Yet, contrary to what many students thought, we did not set out to antagonise them. The core tutors and all the visiting RAT trainers, had substantial experience of anti-racist work. We were all steeped in accounts and experiences of pervasive overt and subtle racism, but we were also used to judging the starting points of groups we worked with (or we thought we were). We were all heavily involved professionally and personally in combatting racism, but we were all teachers too and were acutely aware that people do not learn when they feel attacked. We were consciously toning down the analysis and the passion we used elsewhere, but for some students, apparently, it was clearly too much and the idea that they were, for instance, not being blamed for racism was not effectively conveyed.

It seems we failed to convey something else, too. A further tenet of the model of racism we employed was that relative to black and Asian people white people and institutions have power. This again defined racism as more than personal prejudice, it made a point about its location in social structures (and hence not everyone is individually responsible for its creation). Though this is a somewhat crude colour/racial dualism, we wanted to make the point that there was a sense in which almost all white people were implicated in racism insofar as they participated in or benefited from personal attitudes, cultural assumptions, institutional procedures and societal structures which disadvantage, oppress or demean black and Asian people.

Most of the students thought we were saying that they were irredeemable racists while black and Asian people had no prejudices about anyone. For only four of the group an analysis of racism in terms of power either made emergent sense at the time or struck home quietly as time went on:

> The thing about power, racism being a combination of power and prejudice, I think it was the power thing that stuck in my mind, then it twigged, it really seemed to twig. I was really ignorant about racism and everything, well I still am — I still consider myself a liberal racist, though I don't want to be. Some said they felt accused of being racists when they felt they weren't But that's the whole point isn't it? I expect they do believe they don't want to be racist and therefore they're not, but you can't help it.... (Teresa).

> I think you have to accept what whites have done, the prejudice and everything. I think that's quite a big thing to do, then once you've done that you can view things... I don't think a lot of people felt like that though (Katie).

> ...to be honest I know I'm a racist in the fact of who I am, I can't help that for the fact that white people have power... if that's your definition of what racism is (Megan).

These four expressed no memory of feeling unfairly accused in the taught courses and they also volunteered greater factual recall of details of particular sessions than the rest of the group. They also all signalled annoyance, frustration or impatience with — in their view — most other students, though they felt the fissure widen at different times:

> Do you remember any reactions you had to the RGC course? Lots really. I can remember myself being very, very angry about a lot of the things which went on, but not about the course, about people's reactions to the course... especially because people got so uptight, and were, sort of talking along the lines of "How dare you stand up there and call us racists". Really, for myself I had absolutely no trouble whatsoever believing that I was racist and believing that everyone else in the room was racist...and I was angry at their ...this sounds so arrogant... what I call their naivete and their stupidness to honestly believe that they weren't.... I mean, they were all brought up like me, most of them, weren't they? They come to this college which has hardly any black students, so I just naturally assumed that they'd had the same exposure to things as I have and if I can freely admit I'm racist why can't they? And I used to get so cross with how arrogant they were, that there was nothing wrong with their views or how they behaved, such a stubbornness, you know they all, they wrote off your course.... In a sense a lot of people made up their minds not to learn or not to even go! I couldn't believe some of the things that were being said, to be honest, really... such hostility, defensiveness. I can remember being so angry with ____, at some of the rubbish... what I considered rubbish... she was talking. I can remember being so angry... (Jane).

It's difficult to say, but the more middle class they are outwardly the more hostile they seem to be to things like this.... it undermines them, I don't know. I think it caused such hostility in the second year, people were really challenged, they really had difficulty accepting they were racist liberals... A lot of the students were just downright hostile, they were ignorant about it... Their ignorance annoyed me more than anything. A lot of them went in saying we're not prepared to listen from the very start, very defensive (Teresa).

(Teresa's comment here echoes the earlier point about how students' sense of themselves was challenged.) This strong disapproval of others' attitudes was also expressed by Mary and Claire. Most of the group, whatever their initial and later reaction to the courses, did not develop this kind of analysis. Emma, while recounting her own father's positive action to get more black churchwardens, tended to describe racism (and her response to it in school) in terms of cultural difference and unfamiliarity. And no notion of racism being about differential power (rather than simply personal prejudice) reduced the resentment Angela felt or informed her reflections three years later:

I can remember a feeling... people didn't like the fact that just the white students were getting racial awareness training.... We felt that the overseas students...not because they're racist or anything, I'm not pointing any fingers, but we felt that they ought to get the day as well. The decision she refers to here was complex and certainly contestable, but she contests it here solely from an understanding of racism as reducible to personal prejudice.

Some Conclusions About ITE

Course Design and Teaching Methods

The main conclusions to be drawn from the material discussed thus far point in two different directions as regards sensitisation to racism and the engendering of a professional commitment to work against it. The interviews suggest that the attitude shift which many of the group found traumatic during the specific courses persisted at least two years to the end of the degree. The follow-up questionnaires expressed varying but continuing commitment to multicultural and or anti-racist work after three years of teaching (details are given later). Most continued to believe that what they perceived as a relatively confrontational approach was necessary to make them examine their own racism or ideas about racism (though there is a degree of ambivalence in some). What I (and they) cannot say is whether it was useful, or positively harmful, for the others' development:

If you'd asked me a year ago, what you're asking me now, I might have marched in here and said "Don't do those courses, they really create hostility because they're destructive". But they're not destructive, are they? Because if you have...a fairly open minded individual then they will think about what you're saying. They will go away, they won't go home and just dismiss it. They will actually think about it. The trouble comes when you haven't got people that are prepared to take it on board but then it doesn't matter...if they're not going to listen they're not going to listen are they? ...So I don't know what the solution is, really (Barbara).

So was it counter-productive? No I don't think so, not really, because I think it made people really sit up and think and I suppose you can turn people off by hitting them too hard or something but I think it made people more... examine their own views. It made me examine my own views.... If you hit them hard even though you're making them angry and you're making them feel threatened, at least they're starting to think about the issues... Others say if you hit people that hard the shutters go down... Yeah it could work the other way..yeah... (Tracey).

It is perhaps worth reiterating that the staff's intention was not to be confrontational or intimidating, though that is scarcely credible given some of accounts. One reading of the data is that the material is inherently threatening however it is presented and is bound to produce negative reactions, as Mary suggests:

I think the whole idea of race freaks people out anyway... you've got so many barriers before people will talk about race in any honest way.

If this were the case then arguably hostility would be only be avoided by avoiding the issue of white racism. I put this to Claire:

Some people would say, sock everybody hard, and that hurts, but that it actually shakes people out of complacency and they think about it... Actually it's not my view although people usually assume it is. There's another view that you start where your learners are, ever so gently and unthreateningly... But does that work though? Because people are often immediately threatened, or seem to be. Well, yes. I'm not sure how you raise the issue without, I mean if you raise it without any challenge at all, then you haven't raised it. Yeah, yes, that's just it.

It is hard to separate the students' response to feeling threatened and accused from their relative lack of confidence in speaking in groups, whatever the subject. The "thinking aloud" which is often necessary for people to clarify and explore new ideas is doubly difficult if teaching groups are large, the students both young and new at the college, and the subject matter controversial. The odds were against many speaking at all and this must have militated against the assimilation and acceptance of new ideas:

> I know one thing was...people were worried about what they were going to say in front of you, that was definitely a thing, you know... you can't say what you think.... (Claire).

> I think there was a lot of...people who sort of felt "Oh I'm not going to say anything because if I say anything it might be taken the wrong way" (Cathy).

> Another girl... she said "I'm just keeping my mouth shut".... I think a lot of the younger students like to think they have the right views and aren't confident enough to speak out.... (Barbara).

In practice, changes were introduced in RGC. By the following year there were far fewer large group sessions with such potential for oppositional feelings, and less analysis of racism.

The atmosphere was nothing like so fraught and hostile. On the other hand, fewer students in subsequent cohorts chose the optional "race" course in year four, giving at least tentative support to the theory that if the students were not challenged, then they were not stimulated either. I began these interviews initially because from this year group, from whom colleagues and "race" courses had taken quite a beating, 30% chose the final year "race" option (in preference to seven others).

Staffing

In practice, course design and teaching methods have a good deal to do with who is doing the teaching. Most of the hostility was remembered by the interviewees as being directed at me as course leader and as the person "fronting" most sessions, indeed, only three other college staff are even mentioned in the interviews (apart from the RAT visitors). My position as the most visible target aside, I have no way of judging the personal dimension in this hostility. I clearly intimidated many, but I do not know if this is simply because I personified the issue or whether the issue became merely personalised. For the interviewees it was the former:

> Do you remember the hostility as being mostly at me? Sitting here now I can't even remember who the other tutors were. But don't you think that being hostile to particular tutors is only an excuse for something else? Like...? Well, their own...defensiveness.... (Jane).

> We all needed someone to attack because we felt so attacked (Angela).

but they may be wrong. There may be some way of promoting perceptive critiques without provoking personal criticism. If staff are seen to care "too much" about the issue, or too easily constructed as "extreme", they may thereby provide an escape route for those who want one. On the other hand, they may care "too little" and take such steps to be "objective" and distant that such a course touches no-one in the way — by some students' own accounts — it needs to. There is no easy answer to this dilemma, it is simply one which teachers have to live with.

The issue of permanent black or Asian staff (who might well be perceived as caring "too much") was only raised directly by one interviewee, though it was often discussed with the visiting black and Asian trainers. Given the strength of feeling revealed in this study, they were usually glad to get away (though evaluations showed that while some students felt threatened, others found them very enabling). The prospect of being a permanent black member of staff fronting such work in a largely white institution, being the resident and obvious target for hostility and walking the consequent personal and professional tightrope, was not one which appealed. It may sound trite to say that white racism is a white problem, but it scarcely an anti-racist move simply to employ one or two black staff, at least not to work on this kind of course.

Patterns

In the interviews I tried to explore individual trajectories and where students' individual agendas came from, though the nature of such an exercise precludes any firm conclusions. The group fall into two distinct sub-groups. A widespread feeling of anger and outrage at the perceived accusation levelled at them all was reported by the first of these, except that for the most part they did not include themselves in it. There are good reasons to believe them. Their memories of the RAT and of RGC tended to be more specific, they remembered content, they remembered (accurately) specific things staff or the visiting trainers said and recalled specific lines of argument or analysis. Their memories were both more specific and more positive than the others'. They also used different language about themselves and about racism: they had a more political understanding of racism and owned their own racist socialisation and assumptions much more readily. The clearest example of this is Jane, but there is also Teresa "It was the power thing that stuck in my mind.... I still consider myself a liberal racist"; Megan: "I know I'm a racist.... white people have power" and Katie "you have to accept what white people have done". In the follow-up questionnaires two of these, Jane and Teresa, asserted how different their attitudes were to when they began college.

The second, larger sub-group remembered annoyance, irritation, even hurt, over three years later about feeling "accused" of racism (and seven years later in Pat's case). Many remembered little or nothing of the factual content of a course lasting weeks, but they remembered negative emotions. They also reported how widespread they felt this reaction was among their colleagues. All but two tacitly or explicitly acknowledged some shift in their own attitudes and a recognition that some of their initial anger had been defensiveness. Interestingly, in the questionnaires Pat and Laura continued to acknowledge a major shift in their own attitudes, while the others indicated that they felt "pretty much the same" as when they began college.

There may be a further sub-group to be drawn from these who could almost be called indifferent, though they are more likely to be found amongst non-interviewees in the rest of the cohort. By definition I could not interview any and can only speculate about them. They would, presumably, have been stirred into anger in the way most of the interviewed group describe, but would not perhaps have re-evaluated their own views to the same extent. There is an obvious logic in suggesting this sub-group since there is a continuum of response even amongst my relatively few volunteers, and many of the interviewees characterise themselves as more concerned about "race" than some of their friends.

I suspect there was probably yet another fourth sub-group of students who were actually hostile, who recognised much of what we were saying about white racism from the inside and were not inclined to let go of it. This again is a logical possibility and there are hints of their existence in what several of the interviewees said. It is impossible to estimate the relative sizes of these four sub-groups, and my attempts to elicit such judgements from the interviewees produced wide variations.

Predispositions?

I would very tentatively suggest that most of the interviewees and certainly the first sub-group, were not typical in their approach to "race" and perhaps inequality generally. From their families, some had had consistent or at least clear positive messages about "race" (Megan, Angela, Jane and Emma) or more generally about caring about people and treating them fairly (Claire, Cathy and Mary) sometimes with a strong moral/religious core (Claire, Megan, Jane and Emma). Two of the four who had a political analysis mentioned a strong emphasis at home of discussion and listening (Jane and Katie).

Some had kinds of minority or marginalising experiences themselves: an Italian father who spoke little English (Teresa); discovering she was adopted and possibly Jewish, as well as being one of the few working class students in the BEd (Tracey); working as a female carpenter before taking up A levels at twenty (Louise). Emma is the daughter of a poorly paid vicar in a very comfortable middle class area; Heather left grammar school at 16 tired of being labelled as less worthy of interest because she was not Oxbridge material; Linda's parents badly wanted sons so she recalls consciously following male role-models;

Megan remembers her Welsh accent being mercilessly mocked in an English school; she and Katie came from bilingual (Welsh) families. A disproportionate number were breaking female stereotypes in their main subject and felt it: seven in maths (Tina Angela, Louise, Teresa, Cathy, Laura and Emma) — there were only 12 in the whole year group — and two in science (Mary and Barbara). In various ways and to varying degrees, perhaps these women had experienced being positioned as "other", outside of the mainstream.[3]

Two others, who experienced a shift in views after the initial anger, also had biographical influences which may be significant: Heather's black boyfriend was heavily disapproved of by some of her family; Tina's sister, in a very Christian family, married a Jew. All of these things, while clearly not necessarily connected with wider social attitudes, in these cases may have facilitated a wider concern, awareness or willingness to question received wisdom — and oneself. This is speculative, I have not interviewed all their contemporaries, but years of association with students as their teacher or personal tutor suggests to me that the biographies of many of the group may have been a predisposing factor towards their greater acceptance and capability to learn from the "race" courses.

In one sense my findings confirm some very obvious truisms about teaching. Students are all individuals, with different starting points, perspectives, needs, emotional orientations to different topics, and a range of different other influences upon them. On the one hand teachers and lecturers know this, and yet many of those responsible for the curriculum, from CATE to individual course planners, specify content, hourages and the learning styles implicit in the organisation of teaching. I am not arguing that this could easily be otherwise: it takes very flexible, imaginative and well resourced teaching to treat students as individual learners. Practicalities seem to dictate that we have to employ economies of scale and consequent assumptions about students starting in approximately the same place and having similar sorts of learning trajectories to undergo.

The trouble is that they do not. I would suggest that more useful learning may have taken place had we addressed individual agendas much more sensitively. The background factors which I asked about and which were disclosed do not enable us to distinguish between the first two sub-groups identified above, but they may in theory, mark them off from many of their peers. If we were to address individual learning agendas more sensitively these might be the kinds of experiences and issues to explore in devising more individualised or targeted learning programmes. Other things being equal, this is the direction I would take. The irony of all this is that, in practice, the courses studied here exist no more. The government has prescribed hourages for other courses and time to be spent in school, so there is no room in the college timetable. Whatever challenges with regard to "race" the students may receive in future are left to permeation and school placements, though as the interviews reveal, they provided few in the past.

A Longer Term View

Whatever students do and say whilst at college, their practice as teachers will be mediated by a host of new factors. To gain some impression of how their thinking and practice had developed I contacted the group again four years after they graduated[4] with a questionnaire.

The first issue I wanted to raise was whether, with all the other demands on them, they found it hard to develop a multicultural/ anti-racist perspective in their teaching. About half were finding it fairly hard, the rest rather easier. I scored their responses on agree/disagree statements[5] and hard or not, seven stated that such a perspective came naturally into their teaching with only two who were not finding this (agreement score 32 from a possible maximum of 50). Bearing in mind that they were mostly working in isolated or peripheral white schools, the seductive effect of a climate of "no problem here" was also of interest. All disagreed that "whatever I used to think, issues of 'race' and culture don't seem relevant here" (score: 14) and strongly disagreed with "I am fairly indifferent/inactive about this issue these days" (score: 14)

An obvious test of this would be the extent to which they, despite any contrary pressures like time (mentioned by several) "really work at producing an anti-racist/multicultural environment". This statement produced an agreement score of 41.

It would be unwise to take these replies too literally. Here was the opportunity to represent oneself to a former tutor who has taken the trouble to make contact, in relation to his special interest. Given that these were not anonymous replies it is hardly likely that a teacher who has become entirely indifferent to racism would return such a questionnaire saying so — they probably would not return it at all (if they had become positively antagonistic to my concerns they would probably not put such sentiments into writing and hence would not reply either). The respondents may have exaggerated their continuing interest, either through simply being co-operative or a wish to be "loyal" to me. Sceptics might also doubt the extent to which the claimed commitment is put into practice, after all, few of us could claim to achieve all that we would like. While I can, therefore, make no unassailable claims about these teachers' practice, I nevertheless think it would be an extreme scepticism which discounted all their replies. At the very least they indicate that some interest and commitment is still present.

As regards their experiences in their schools, six reported specific incidents which "highlighted the importance of teachers thinking about 'race'" (such as examples of pupil or parental attitudes). Eight had had explicit and sometimes strong encouragement from their head teachers "to develop work to do with 'race' and culture" and no heads had been discouraging. Only two had experienced hostility and/or specific discouragement from a more experienced colleague, compared to three who had been encouraged, and five who had found support from other NQTs. On the other hand, while one or two were in schools with a climate clearly and explicitly positive about these issues, meeting interest from colleagues when they raised it, six met indifference (score: 14) and sometimes puzzlement.

They were also asked for brief reflections on their "race" courses at college. "My attitudes today about 'race' and multicultural education are pretty much the same as when I left college" scored 48 and there was a range of open-ended comments:

> ...reaffirmed my feelings on the issue and gave me the knowledge and background to produce strong arguments for multicultural education and against all forms of racism. Certain things stay with me... most importantly, the need that was emphasised so strongly to bring in multicultural education and combat racism in so-called "white" schools (Katie).

> ...it gave me valuable detail on other cultures/religions... (Emma).

> ...provided me with excellent professional advice... was a useful and practical course that gave me greater insight and understanding.... The little I have taken from the "race" course has gone a long, long way in my teaching and I feel that it has served me well... (Teresa).

> The challenge brought to my thinking has lasted. They have had a valuable input into who I am and what I do today (Jane).

> ...certainly raised my awareness and helped me distinguish between anti-racist and multi-cultural... (Angela).

> ...helped students to realise that "race" is an issue which needs to be addressed rather than ignoring it... (Megan).

> ...above all made me aware of racist attitudes in myself and others. By being aware I was able to deal with it. The courses gave me the confidence to plan work on other cultures... (Pat).

> ...an important way of addressing one's own beliefs and prejudices... (Mary).

These seem to me to give further weight to my assertion earlier that there was continuing commitment and interest. Space was also given for open-ended advice or comments to student teachers.

The one respondent in a multiracial school (Tracey) wrote a lot here, both about the positive benefits in terms of enjoyment but also the negative pressure from right-wing activity (her school is in East London). However, all the rest in their white schools were universally positive about the need for multicultural/ anti-racist work:

If your prime concern is the interests of the child... then you cannot fail to address anti-racist education (Teresa).

...vital in providing children we teach with a sound balanced education and outlook on life... (Claire).

Keep hold of your ideals... (Katie).

It is imperative for pupils that they receive input of this kind... (Jane).

Some offered tactical advice too, about effectively integrating issues throughout the curriculum, setting realisable goals, not expecting instant results and tailoring ideals to the local climate. ·

Conclusion

Despite the obvious limitations of this research and the database the material presented here raises, in my view, a number of significant and substantive issues about racism, anti-racism and the role of ITE.

At the beginning I raised two questions:

(i) how useful (or otherwise) is the concept of "racism" as a tool for students to evaluate (and re-evaluate) their own attitudes as well as educational practices and processes?
(ii) how do teacher educators promote a critical consciousness without merely destructive student/tutor hostility?

In the work described here the notion of racism employed was both personal and political, and all the more difficult to handle as a result. We were unambiguous in rooting the courses in an understanding of racism which challenged more comfortable ideas of it being distant, psychologically aberrant and "extreme". It seemed to us that this was an essential intellectual tool for students if they were effectively to examine existing and past practices and to reflect creatively on their own. If the tool is effectively passed on to students I would want to argue that it is both illuminative and dynamic: it is useful to them as reflective and critical practitioners and it can be used in many situations over a long period (it does not wear out). The testimony of a minority of the group support this.

On the other hand, this theoretical underpinning produced conflict and hostility, some of it, arguably, merely destructive. This is primarily a question of effective teaching and the answers may lie at least as much in administrative arrangements which are sensitive to students' needs as they do in teacher expertise and knowledge. The dilemma is about challenge without attack, provoking without hurting, leading without forcing, and it may be that this cannot be done in year cohorts lumped together for convenience and in disregard of their individual starting points.

The effective removal of the courses considered here by newer government stipulations about content and hourages is not something I welcome. Nevertheless, there is scope for some optimism in the findings of this study. Despite (possibly) being in a minority at college and despite entering teaching in a difficult and demanding period, these teachers have not met hostility or resistance to their anti-racist commitment, which they claim is not diminished. Perhaps the Right were right to object to such work in ITE, perhaps, for some, it worked.

References

Ball, S (1994) Education Reform, Open University

Berkshire (1983) A Policy for Racial Equality, Royal County of Berkshire

Birmingham Education Authority (1983) Recognising Racism

Catholic Commission for Racial Justice (1982) The Enemy Within

Department of Education & Science (1985) Education for All, HMSO

DES (1989) Circular 24/89, HMSO

Gaine, C (1987) No Problem Here, Hutchinson

Gaine, C (1995) Still No Problem Here, Trentham

Hill, D (1990) Something Old, Something New, Something Borrowed, Something Blue, Hillcole Group

Oakley, A (1981) Interviewing Women — a Contradiction in Terms? in Roberts, H (1981) Doing Feminist Research, Routledge

Taylor, W (1990) The Control of Teacher Education in Graves, N (1990) Initial Teacher Education — Policies and Progress, Kogan Page

Notes

1. The group were interviewed in depth towards the end of their BEd course about particular key moments in their own thinking about "race" and racism and about course structure and provision.

   They completed questionnaires three years after they had begun work as teachers in various largely white primary schools. The issues raised in the interviews were generated from some course evaluations, notes of conversations with colleagues and diaries I kept as course leader.

2. The interviews took place in my office, in informal seating and took the form of hour-long focused conversations (which were taped). There was no set order of questions, though the sequence tended to be related to the sequence of their own lives. The names used here are not their real names.

3. One might argue that as women all have had marginalising and disempowered experiences, but there are two reasons why I am not exploring this here. Firstly, almost all the cohort were women, and I am trying to identify factors which distinguish between women. Secondly (and somewhat contradicting the thesis that experiencing one inequality helps insight into another), the group showed an extraordinary range of views about the gender elements of their course.

4. Postal questionnaires and an explanatory letter were sent to the group in the Spring term three and a half years after they began teaching. Linda proved untraceable, Mary had never entered school teaching, five did not reply. In sending the questionnaires I wanted to establish both how the group's perspectives had changed and how their experience of teaching may have affected this. They had entered teaching in the full throes of changes brought about by the National Curriculum, all but one were in largely white primary schools (showing remarkable congruence with their own schooling), and I have indicated in papers 4, 7 and 8 that there is little to suggest that by 1991 there was widespread commitment in such schools to multicultural or anti-racist work. On the face of it, therefore, there were considerable pressures against them developing this kind of work, as new teachers, in addition to the upheavals already in progress.

5. The things I wanted to raise were framed as agree/disagree statements on a five point scale. Given that 10 teachers replied, complete agreement of everyone with a statement would produce a score of 50, complete disagreement a score of 10. In general their responses were too scattered to be represented in this way, but in some cases I have indicated the strength of dis/agreement numerically.

Chapter Eleven

Imparting Social Values Through Literature: A Challenge to Legal Training

Susan E. Grady

Introduction

Few legal educators on either side of the Atlantic have found a teaching method which has been judged by the majority of students as an effective answer to the age old problem of imparting social values to future attorneys. That this education is necessary is due to the fiduciary duties that lawyers undertake for their clients. That this education is necessary is also due to public perception (in the United States anyway) of attorneys as having few, if any, ethical impulses. Part of the problem is that, as in any profession, the disreputable lawyer receives the publicity while the ethical lawyer does not. The more important reason for the public perception of attorneys as unethical is the lack of understanding of the adversarial component of law. The public at large believes that an attorney will do anything to win the case, not necessarily for his/her client's sake, but in order to add to his/her record of wins, whether it be for pride's sake or for marketability's sake, or both.

Law students are taught that the adversarial system should bring out the best in each attorney, and by extension bring out the best in each side of the case. The trial is a search for the truth and the implication, if not expressly stated, is that both sides will ethically follow the rules of procedural law. Since law schools in the United States are presently undergoing scrutiny by law students, law professors, and members of the legal profession, this is an excellent opportunity to look at the need for the teaching of legal ethics, the ways that it has been taught in the past, and proposals for the future. It is the thesis of this paper that ethical behavior can best be illustrated and taught by the use of literature. Additionally this paper takes the position that raising the law student's awareness of social values through the teaching of law and literature is equally needed in both the United States and the United Kingdom.

A Short Comparison of the Study of Law in England and in the United States

(For a more comprehensive review of the materials in Sections II and III see Klein article, 1991, pp.601-641)

England

In England students who wish to study law must pass their A-level exam and in most cases undergo a personal interview. The English are more flexible than the Americans in that they place less emphasis on test scores and grades and more emphasis on a student's personal attributes.

There are three steps to becoming a lawyer in England. The first is an academic degree, most usually a three year undergraduate degree in law. As in the United States, the law curriculum is quite rigid which leaves students few opportunities for electives. Unlike the United States, the emphasis is on the rule, not the theory of law. Students learn through lectures and through study in small tutorials.

The second stage of legal training in England is vocational. At this point in the student's career, he/she must decide whether to become a solicitor or a barrister. A solicitor counsels clients in their legal affairs and may represent clients in the lower courts. A barrister is a litigation expert and handles all trial work in the upper courts. In the first part of the vocational stage a student takes a nine month to one year vocational program developed to give him/her the practical skills needed by either a solicitor or a barrister. During the latter part of the vocational stage, a student serves as an apprentice to either a solicitor or a barrister depending on the student's choice of profession. In the third stage of becoming an attorney the student must pass the Law Society exam if planning to be a solicitor or pass the Bar exam if planning to become a barrister.

The United States

In the United States in order to become an attorney a student must first possess a four year college degree. There is no pre-law curriculum of undergraduate study as there is, for example, in medicine; nor are any types of degrees disqualified. The student takes an aptitude test, and based on the results of the test and his/her college grades the student is admitted into a three year graduate program for a law degree. As previously noted the curriculum leaves room for very few electives. The present teaching method in the United States is the primarily the case method which was developed in 1870 by Dean Christopher Langdell of Harvard Law School who believed that this method made law more scientific because cases could be considered observable data. The case method differs from the lecture method through the questioning of students on the holdings of cases and then through analogy of the probable rule of law in future cases. Due to criticism about the lack of practical skills of law graduates, most law schools in the 1970s imitated, to a very limited degree, the vocational phase of the English legal education by requiring students to enroll in at least one practical skills courses. It was also at this time that due to the publicity of the unethical behavior of lawyers in the Watergate scandal, the American Bar Association required that an ethics course be taught to each student (Jerry, 1992, p. 3).

Upon graduation, the student, if he/she wishes to try cases in court, must pass the bar in the state in which he/she wishes to practice. Once a student has successfully passed the state bar he/she may, on request, be admitted to the federal bar which enables one to try cases in any federal court.

Criticisms of Legal Education in England and the United States

England

Critics of the legal educational system in England cite the findings of the Ditchley Park Conference of 1967 which recommended that the United States model of law study be followed with law school *becoming* elevated to graduate study. It was believed that the English method is too narrow and the students are taught law at too early an age. Law students ". . . have not been exposed to other disciplines, including the humanities, in the way that the American system of postgraduate legal education ensures" (Aristodemou, 1993).

One rationale for the critics' concern is their deference to the thinking of those in independent Commonwealth countries who believe that academic studies should be pursued at a university while the practical courses should be taught at a professional law school (Phillips, 1978, pp. 31-43). Another belief of those concerned with legal education is that there should be a merging between the role of barristers and solicitors in England to follow the lead of some of the Commonwealth countries (Phillips, 1978, pp. 19-26). At this point in time the choice of becoming a solicitor or a barrister must be made relatively early because each profession sets its own core requirements and it is virtually impossible to change careers without additional training. In addition a blending of the rights and duties of solicitors and barristers would create a uniformity among the Commonwealth countries which would be valuable in a shrinking world.

A second major criticism is the type and/or quality of instruction in the English system. Professors in colleges and universities must teach for the standard exam, not necessarily those materials which they feel is most important. In addition, focusing primarily on the rules of law doesn't enable students to develop analytical skills. Although the vocational phase of the English education is a strength to the American mind, critics of the English system claim that there are no common standards for apprentices. There is too much concentration on law as 'professional training', and too little concentration on the exercise of law.

The United States

Critics of the United States' legal educational system allege that even though law students are required to take a practical skills course, for all intents and purposes, they graduate with virtually no practical skills. As in the English system, these skills courses are often supervised by the newest members of the bar, and since there is little, if any, academic challenge, these courses are assigned second class status by educators as well as the students. In 1993, a task force of the American Bar Association recommended "… that law schools dramatically increase their emphasis on instruction in certain lawyerly skills and values in order to better prepare their students for the practice of law" (emphasis mine) (Stark, 1994, p.126).

A second major criticism of legal education in the United States is that there has been so much emphasis on the case method that other ways of teaching and new courses such as the theory of law is being overlooked. In the more progressive institutions new approaches to law have been successfully presented to and well received by students. In great part this has been due to

> …the intellectual tapestry of legal scholarship, teaching and curriculum is richer and more diverse than even a decade ago. The courses being taught are more complex and diverse. Law is no longer so easily and rigidly subdivided into "legal" and "social" or "moral" components, with only the "legal" issues the subject of law courses and legal analysis. (Barnhizer, 1989, p. 230)

This diversity comes from differing schools of thought about the content of law courses whether it be the critical legal studies movement, the Chicago school of law and economics, or the ever increasing strength of the law and literature movement.

Law and Literature

There are two main approaches to the law and literature movement. The first is law as literature. The principle here is that some legal documents and/ or judicial decisions can be studied as if they were literature. Although all writing is literature in the broadest sense, I do not hold with this course of study except for literature majors who wish to experience the richness of selected legal writings, much as they may wish to contemplate and appreciate any subset of well written works from Donne's essays to modern Japanese fiction.

The second approach of the law and literature movement is the use of writings recognized as literature which illustrate a topic or topics relevant to future or present attorneys. These topics could span from literature depicting an ideal lawyer (Portia in *The Merchant of Venice* or Atticus Finch in *To Kill a Mockingbird*) to the way the punishment of evil reflects the values of society in the earliest novels (Defoe's *Moll Flanders* or Hawthorne's *The Scarlet Letter*) or the thesis of this paper — the use of literature as a vehicle to impart legal ethics to law students.

Legal Ethics

Should Legal Ethics Be Taught?

Whether or not legal ethics should be taught at all is a matter of opinion and controversy. Many scholars maintain that by the time that students become law students, their ethical and social values have been set. However, traditionally ethics and morals have been taught since the time of the ancient Greeks. In England, the teaching of ethics dates back to medieval universities, while in the United States, ethics played a major part in the curriculum of colleges founded by both the clergy and the laity. In 1915 about seventy percent of the law schools in the United States offered ethical instruction but in the late 1950s only about two thirds of responding accredited law schools offered legal ethics (usually for only one hour a week) (Rhode, 1992, pp. 35-36). However, after the Watergate scandal in which the ethics of many lawyers including the President of the United States were suspect, the American Bar Association required that accredited law schools teach legal ethics including the *Code of Professional Responsibility*.

How Can Ethics Be Taught?

This is one of the basic arguments that seems never to be solved. There are two schools of thought which are equally adamant. The first position is that ethics should be a free standing course with a certain number of credits attached. Critics of this viewpoint argue that by isolating ethics into a separate course, the students' inference is that ethics is a separate issue from the materials in other courses whereas these critics believe that ethics is an integral part of one's every day existence.

The second position is that an ethics component be attached in some, most, or all other law courses. This satisfies the integration argument, but critics of this position allege that materials which are "added" to other courses are in reality not taught at all because of the belief that since everyone is teaching them, no one teaches them. Another problem with this position is that teaching ethics is an interest and a skill that not all professors possess just as not every professor is interested in and/or skilled at teaching contracts or criminal procedure.

No matter which position is followed, the basic question with the teaching of ethics is whether it can be taught? The corollary to this is if so, how? It is my belief that ethics can be taught if the professor keeps certain things in mind. First of all the professor must continually be cognizant of the fact that each student has his/her own code of ethics, much of which is fixed through family values, religious values, and/or cultural values.

The purpose of an ethics course is not to transfer the professor's own personal social values to students, but rather to emphasize the commonality of the ethical beliefs that most persons share. Secondly since this is a course in legal ethics, ethical philosophies or ethical situations should concentrate upon particular situations that lawyers may face because of the realities of the legal system in which they must, not only function, but survive. Many law students believe that ethics courses are a waste of time because they consist of either philosophical theories which seem to the students to have very little relevance to the life the student will be beginning, or consist of situational ethics where the students parrot what they "feel" to be the answer the professor is looking for, but an answer that the student wouldn't necessarily choose in real life. Many of the situational ethics are unrealistic for us as students or professors to judge because often the answer depends heavily upon one's financial circumstances and responsibilities.

Literature as the Basis for the Study of Social Values

The solution to the problems set out above, it seems to me, is to use works of literature as class material for an ethics course whether it be a free standing course or a module which is attached to a preexisting course or courses. There are many advantages to using literature for this purpose. First of all, reading good literature is enjoyable. This might at first blush appear to be a rather frivolous argument. However, if something is enjoyable it receives more than just a cursory skimming; in addition something that is well done tends to make an impression where lesser writings would not.

Secondly there is a wealth of literature from which the professor can select. Obviously literature is not written only for attorneys, but there is much that would be appropriate and useful for attorneys to appreciate. There are several types of literature that would be very valuable for a lawyer to understand so that he/she would have the potential of becoming a more socially responsible attorney and human being.

There are two major perspectives literature can illustrate which can benefit attorneys' sense of social responsibility. The first is contained in works of literature where the emphasis is on lawyers balancing their legal duties to their clients with their duties as officers of the court. These legal strategies and interactions with the legal system are good examples of situational ethics with which law students will relate. The second perspective is contained in works of literature where the focus is upon characterizations of those who are nonlawyers affected by the legal system. The situational ethics with which these characters must cope provide attorneys with a better understanding of their clients' (and others) circumstances, motivations, and emotions.

A law professor who is not trained in literature may argue that he/she would not know what materials to select. This concern has a very simple remedy for there are law review articles which give bibliographies of suggested texts that would be appropriate for courses in law and literature. That this has long been an object of discussion, for some at least, is evidenced by an 1922 revision of an 1908 law review article which provides a list of legal novels with an admonition by the author John Wigmore that each attorney has a "... special professional duty to be familiar with *those features of his profession which have been taken up into general thought and literature*" (Emphasis Wigmore's) (Wigmore, 1922, p. 28). In a later law review article, Richard Weisberg, who is one of the leading proponents of the law and literature movement, has updated Wigmore's list (Weisberg, 1976, pp. 17-28). Another legal scholar provides more specific guidance in selecting texts by presenting a bibliography of works of literature used in actual law and literature courses accompanied by the course descriptions provided by law schools throughout the United States (Gemmette, 1989, pp. 267-340). Although these articles are written primarily for those wishing to teach a course in law and literature, they contain some excellent suggestions for reading material which would give legal ethics professors suggestions for materials which might be included in a course on social responsibility for attorneys.

A second concern of a law professor who is not trained in literature could be that he/she would have no skills in teaching the material. This is a genuine concern as there is a special expertise in teaching literature. However, in this instance, the intent is the examination of the ethical issues presented in the literature. A professor who is qualified to teach ethics will find nothing novel in this change of material. For those professors who wish to somewhat immerse themselves in literary criticism, there are excellent law review articles (including those mentioned previously) which provide a bibliography of secondary works about law and literature (Papke, 1980, pp. 421-437; Suretsky, 1980, pp. 421-437).

If an ethics professor selects a classic work of literature, it is almost certain that there is at least one law review article on that specific novel, play, or short story. The *Index to Legal Periodicals* has a separate listing for law and literature and I would imagine that there is an English counterpart to this index. For the computer literate, there are on-line searches available in most, if not all, law libraries. As ethics professors gain confidence in using literature as a vehicle for teaching legal ethics, they will find many of these law review articles informative (and even fun).

In addition to law review articles which can be found in various law journals, there are law reviews which have produced at least one special issue devoted to a certain topic concerning law and literature. *Cardozo Studies in Law and Literature* and the *Yale Journal of Law and the Humanities* are law journals which are committed to solely publishing articles on law and literature. In 1992, a book entitled *Legal Fictions: Short Stories About Lawyers and the Law* was published in the United States. While not all the short stories are appropriate for a legal ethics course, this book is another excellent source of material.

A book which I consider indispensable for both the novice and the experienced professor alike is *Poethics: And Other Strategies of Law and Literature* by Richard Weisberg. This book's title utilizes the word poethics which, in the words of Weisberg, "... endeavors nothing less than to fill the ethical void in which legal thought and practice now exist" (Weisberg, 1992, p. 4).

Ways to Teach Legal Ethics Through Literature

Due to the fact that there is so much diversity in the types of literature a professor can select, it might be beneficial to move from the abstract to the specific by the use of a hypothetical syllabus. To do so it is necessary to make some decisions with not all readers may agree. This, to my mind, is the way it should be. Listening to differing opinions, for me, is another of the attractions to teaching social responsibility in this manner.

In designing my syllabus I am going to make use of my earlier premise that two main themes which can be illustrated by literature as text for legal social responsibility are concerned either with a lawyer's perception of the world or an expansion of the lawyer's world by providing sensitivity to and for a nonlawyer's world view. Both of these themes expedite the expansion and shaping of our own ethics because we, as attorneys, identify with the former and develop new understandings because of the latter.

Of these themes, each can be presented in class by using the same form of literature throughout the course, or a variety of literature throughout the course. Each can be presented in the same general time frame, or in varying time frames. Each can be presented with the same type of hero(ine) or with differing types of hero(ine)s. This is one of the major benefits of using literature to teach legal ethics; there is such a vast amount of material that a professor could vary the content of the course throughout his/her teaching career and not repeat the exact syllabus twice. Naturally a professor will develop attachments to certain works and/or discover that some materials work better than others in the classroom with his/her style of teaching. These may become perennials, but other works will be discarded and as the professor develops more confidence, he/she will begin to experiment with works not in the bibliographies.

Another advantage to using literature to teach legal ethics is that the professor can define literature in his/her own way. A classic definition of literature is "a body of written works related by subject-matter (e.g. the literature of computing), by language or place of origin (e.g. Russian literature), or prevailing culture standards of merit" (Baldick, 1990, p. 124). Purists would view literature as falling into the third section of the definition and though there may be some arguments as to what the proper standards are, all purists would agree that a basic test for literature is that it must pass the test of time. Other academics would define literature more broadly believing that contemporary literature, while not passing the test of time, speaks more to the modern person than the Greeks or Shakespeare. Some professors would combine the traditional and the modern; some would elect to use all American literature, or all English literature, or a composite of any or all of the above. It is possible for instance to take one particular action and compare it as viewed differently by time and/ or by culture. One can then ask whether we are becoming more or less ethical, or what right we have to impose our ethics upon another culture versus whether we have a duty to impose our social values upon another culture. One could also ask if any of these questions answerable outside of the particular situation we have just read about, i.e., is ethics like the case system where we are able to draw a conclusion from several situations or is it more like our ability to draw a conclusion from the vagueness of a statute? Or not?

Now that the reader has some sense of the possibilities that using literature as textual material provides, I offer a hypothetical syllabus. In order to provide the reader with more choices, I have primarily used works of literature that are not mentioned in any of the bibliographies cited previously. In order to present some type of consistency, I have limited my selections to North American twentieth century authors. Unfortunately, there are only two women in my selection; if I had used more of the "classic" works of literature, that would not be the case.

Syllabus for Social Responsibility for Attorneys

Course Objective

The ethical dilemmas faced by attorneys will be discussed as they relate to the rights and duties of attorneys as described in the *Professional Code of Ethics*. All viewpoints will be welcomed as one purpose of the course is to examine individual and cultural ethical beliefs and another is to discover the commonality and the differences of ethical beliefs among class members.

Course Criteria

In addition to a final exam scheduled by the university, each student must turn in five position papers on any five works of literature listed below. The 3-5 page typewritten paper should extract an ethical issue in the work, discuss the character's options and discuss the option it is *most realistic* to believe that character would select. You must then give your position on the ethics of both the situation and the action you believe the character would take. Please remain *realistic!* Papers are due before or on the day on which the work is to be discussed in class.

Readings

Week 1   Introduction to Course. Lectures upon Ethical Philosophies.

Unit I. *Learning to Think Like a Lawyer*

Week 2   *One-L* by Scott Turow. This is a diary of a first year law student at Harvard Law School. It portrays the ways that the author and his classmates changed during their first year of law school. One of Turow's major concerns was whether his sense of social responsibility was heightened or lessened.

Week 3   *The Alchemy of Race and Rights; Diary of a Law Professor* by Patricia J. Williams. Although this book is subtitled a diary, it is more like a journal in that it is not chronological. Turow was a white male at Harvard Law School; Williams was a black female at Harvard Law School. She relates some of her thoughts and experiences both as a student and as a professor of commercial law at the University of Wisconsin.

Week 4   *The Associates* by John Jay Osborn, Jr. Osborn worked as an associate on Wall Street and is now a law professor teaching law and literature. This is both a " coming of age" story and an inside look at a large corporate law firm.

Unit II. *Differing Career Paths of Lawyers*

Week 5   The Sole Practitioner *Death Penalty* by William J. Coughlin. This book was written by an administrative law judge and includes two very timely legal issues. The first has to do with a doctor who assists clients in suicides and the second concerns an appeal of a products liability case against a large manufacturer which has won on the trial level. It is unusual to discover a fictional version of an appellate court scene and this one is outstanding.

Week 6   The Public Prosecutor. *Fade the Heat* by Jay Brandon. This book was written by an ex-district attorney. It concerns a district attorney who has just been elected and whose son is accused of rape. The son claims that he is innocent and that he was set up. This novel deals with the father's " thinking like a lawyer" being misunderstood by his family as he tries to both support his son and uphold the law.

Week 7   The Defense Attorney. *The Dividing Line* by Richard Parrish. This book was written by an ex-county attorney who is now in private practice. This book is set in the 1940s right after World War II and concerns a New York City attorney who was nearly destroyed by the war and who must move to Arizona for health reasons. To support himself and his children, he accepts a job in the Bureau of Indian Affairs where he ultimately defends an Indian accused of murder.

Week 8   The Politician. *All the King's Men* by Robert Penn Warren. The author of this book is a nonlawyer who was an author, editor, and literary critic. This novel won a Pulitzer Prize and is loosely based on the life of the Louisiana governor Huey Long. It follows the career of a politician and the way he, and those around him, deal with power.

Unit III. *The Law's Effect Upon Nonlawyers*

Week 9   *A Time to Kill* by John Grisham. This best selling author has retired from his practice in order to write full time. This is his first novel which was rereleased after Grisham was so successful with *The Firm*. This is an excellent transitional book because although the main character is a sole practitioner, the book is really a portrait of a small southern town, and the differing factions which become involved in a murder trial.

Week 10   *A View from the Bridge* by Arthur Miller. This playwrite is not an attorney and is less interested in legal strategies than the judicial standards for proof. This play is about the Salem witch trials in Massachusetts and was written by Miller during the McCarthy "witch hunt" for communists in America.

Week 11   *Fear on Trial* by John Henry Faulk. This is the autobiography of a radio and television personality who was blacklisted by AWARE, Inc. which was an organization devoted to identifying communists. Faulk writes about his historic libel suit discussing both his problems of gathering evidence in the prevailing climate and the trial itself.

Week 12   *The Great Gatsby* by F. Scott Fitzgerald. This novel is a portrait of the lawlessness of the 1920s in the United States. Fitzgerald, a career author who was not legally trained, depicts the portrait of a man who made his money through an unspecified (but shady) means and who tries to join the upper class. However, the plot is not as important as the tone of the book.

Week 13   *The Handmaid's Tale* by Margaret Atwood. Atwood is another career author with no training in law. Her novel is the direct opposite of Fitzgerald's lawless society; it is a futuristic society that is ruled by a totalitarian government. The heroine of the book is a member of a downtrodden class and the plot centers upon at her interactions with those of her own class and with those in a higher class.

Week 14   *Make No Law: The Sullivan Case and the First Amendment* by Anthony Lewis. Although not an attorney, Anthony Lewis won a Pulitzer Prize 1963 for his reports on the Supreme Court. This book traces the reasons for the Sullivan case, the decision, and the impact of the decision on the citizens of the United States. It also presents readers with some historically enlightening situations and conversations.

Conclusion

I think it appropriate for Richard Weisberg to have the last word.

Interdisciplinary approaches come and go, but to my mind Law and Literature (already, in its modern incarnation, more than fifteen years old) deserves the tremendous influx of talent and attention it has attracted. The merging of our two most influential narrative enterprises is bringing about not just a refreshing but indeed an enduring opportunity to understand our cultural life...

Law and Literature, as it has been practiced (as it is practiced here), embraces the world to which narrative traditionally has been linked, the world of stories. Whether we read fictional law or lawful fiction, it is our imagination, our fears, and our deepest aspirations that will be touched by this effort to link our culture's two most central narrative endeavors. Changes — drastic and needed changes — are in the air. The interrelation of law and literature, freed from undisciplinary constraints, continues its struggle to understand and to lead (Weisberg, 1992, xiv).

References

Aristodemou, Maria (1993) "Studies in Law and Literature: Directions and Concerns," *Anglo-American Law Review*, 22 (May/June) pp. 157-193.

Barnhizer, David (1989) "The Revolution in American Law Schools," *Cleveland State Law Review*, 37, (2) pp. 227-269.

Gemmette, Elizabeth Villiers (1989) "Law and Literature: An Unnecessarily Suspect Class in the Liberal Arts Component of the Law School Curriculum," *Valparaiso University Law Review* 23 (2) (Winter) pp. 267-340.

Jerry, Robert H. II (1992) "The Legal Profession, Legal Education, and Change," *The University of Kansas Law Review*, 41, pp. 1-10.

Klein, Sandra R. (1991) "Legal Education in the United States and England: A Comparative Analysis," *Loyola of Los Angeles International and Comparative Law Journal*, 13, pp. 601-640.

Papke, David B. (1980) "Law and Literature: Comment and Bibliography of Secondary Works," *Law Library Journal*, 73 (Spring) pp. 421-437.

Phillips, Sir Fred (1978) *The Evolving Legal Profession in the Commonwealth*, Dobbs Ferry, NY, Oceana Publications, Inc.

Rhode, Deborah L. (1992) "Ethics by the Pervasive Method," *Journal of Legal Education*, 42 (March) pp. 31-56.

Stark, Jack (1994) "Dean Costonis on the MacCrate Report," *Journal of Legal Education*, 44 (1) (March), pp. 126-129.

Suretsky, Harold (1980) "Search for a Theory: An Annotated Bibliography of Writings on the Relation of Law to Literature and the Humanities," *Rutgers Law Review*, 32, pp. 728-738.

Weisberg, Richard H. (1992) *Poethics: And Other Strategies of Law and Literature*, New York: Columbia University Press.

Weisberg, Richard H. (1976) "Wigmore's 'Legal Novels' Revisited: New Resources for the Expansive Lawyer," *Northwestern University Law Review*, 71, pp. 17-28.

Wigmore, John H. (1922) "A List of One Hundred Legal Novels," *Illinois Law Review*, 17, pp. 26-33.

Wishingrad, Jay (ed) (1992) *Legal Fictions: Short Stories About Lawyers and the Law*, Woodstock, New York: The Overlook Press.

Chapter Twelve

Christian Social Thought and Management Education[1]

Robert G. Kennedy

In nothing has the Church lost her hold on reality as in her failure to understand and respect the secular vocation. She has allowed work and religion to become separate departments, and is astonished to find that, as a result, the secular work of the world is turned to purely selfish and destructive ends, and that the greater part of the world's intelligent workers have become irreligious, or at least, uninterested in religion. But is it astonishing? How can anyone remain interested in a religion which seems to have no concern with nine-tenths of his life? The Church's approach to an intelligent carpenter is usually confined to exhorting him not to be drunk and disorderly in his leisure hours, and to come to church on Sundays. What the Church should be telling him is this: that the very first demand this his religion makes upon him is that he should make good tables. Church by all means, and decent forms of amusement, certainly — but what use is all that if in the very center of his life and occupation he is insulting God with bad carpentry?

Dorothy Sayers
"Why Work?" (1942)

The Paradox of Management Education

In my office I have a bookcase containing most of the textbooks on business ethics currently in print in the United States. I estimate that there are about 75-100 such books now available. Every passing month sees a few new titles appear, and perhaps some old ones disappear. This collection is evidence of the interest in the topic, not only among business educators but among business managers as well. It is probably fair to say that there has never before been such attention paid to this area of applied ethics — but then this is to say nothing new.

I would, however, like to call attention to three observations. There is evidence to support these observations, some of it anecdotal and some systematic, but I will not try to prove them to be true. Instead, I think that if readers reflect on their own experiences they may find them to be accurate.

First, despite the attention given to the subject in business education, on both the graduate and undergraduate levels, there is no dramatic sign that management practices have changed greatly as a result of classroom efforts. Indeed, many companies have made heroic efforts to bring ethical considerations to the fore in their management practices, and often these efforts have been supported and facilitated by academic advisers. Nevertheless, I submit that the causes that lie behind these efforts are extracurricular. In fact, senior managers at large corporations have sometimes remarked that they are surprised and disappointed at how ethically insensitive their new young employees can be. Those of us engaged in teaching ethics in business schools might reflect on the level of confidence we have that what we do really has a decisive impact on the decisions our students will make later as managers.

Second, and related (perhaps even causally) to the first, is the observation that ethics still dances on the periphery of management education, or floats delicately on the surface. Different schools adopt different models for implementing a program of education in ethics, but I am aware of none that succeeds in weaving ethics into the very fiber of professional formation. (For that matter, professional schools of medicine and law may not be much further ahead in this regard.) The predominant attitude seems to be that education in ethics is something to be distinguished from professional training. Whether it is a patina to be applied to the finished product, or a parallel educational track, ethics does not really penetrate the study of finance and marketing. Now by saying this I certainly do not mean to imply that these two disciplines are immoral in their practices, but I do think that practitioners tend to be amoral. In fact, I think that a good measure of the success of ethics education in a business school is the degree to which the teaching of finance and marketing are transformed. For the schools with which I am familiar there is little or no change.

Third, there has been a change historically in some aspects of business education. The intense concern with ethics that I described earlier was not a characteristic of business education in most schools, say, forty years ago. It was, though, a characteristic of schools affiliated with religious denominations. In fact, if you were to survey the few texts available in this area from the 1950s, you would find that most were written by professors teaching in such schools. You would also find the authors were not too shy about borrowing from the philosophical and theological traditions of their denominations. Today, however, no such "religious" inspiration is apparent in either the origins or the content of business ethics texts. Furthermore, for the most part, courses in business ethics, especially at the graduate level, rarely appeal to these traditions even in religiously affiliated universities. One would be quite surprised, for example, to find a business ethics course taught at a Catholic university that was recognizably influenced by Christian social thought. Now the issue here is not whether such courses should have a dogmatic content — they should not. The issue really is why faith communities with a rich tradition of reflection on social issues choose to set aside that tradition when they teach professional ethics. This is the issue I wish to address today.

Why Management Education Pays So Little Attention to Religious Reflection

There are no doubt a number of reasons that may be adduced to explain why management education is so little influenced by religious reflection. I have four such reasons in mind — I will return to them in a moment — but I wish to stress from the beginning that I have rarely detected hostility toward faith or theology as a motive. On the contrary, it has been my experience that a great many managers and business professors are themselves persons with faith commitments that they take quite seriously. Indeed, those who teach at religiously affiliated universities often do so by choice, i.e., precisely because the commitment of the university is important to them. What is puzzling, then, is why these faith commitments do not translate into a more explicit application and expression in the classroom.

On some accounts these faith commitments emerge on the level of personal witness. That is, individual professors, inspired by their faith, make certain choices about how to treat materials and issues in the classroom. Perhaps they emphasize fairness or honesty, or encourage students to battle prejudice in the workplace. These are certainly laudable positions but, however well-intended, they miss the point. While it is probably true that faith provides a strong motivation to behave ethically, religious reflection has no monopoly on ethical principles. Professors who urge their students to do good and avoid evil may be provoked to do so by their beliefs, but the substance of their exhortation is not really different from popular ethical views. Religious reflection (and here I must speak from the tradition with which I am most familiar, the Christian social tradition), while not hostile to most popular ethical views, provides several additional benefits: a rationale for accepting (and committing to) these ethical principles, a rich tradition in which the implications and applications of the principles can be discussed and appreciated, and a foundation for a successful integration of these principles within a whole human life. None of these benefits can be realized if the tradition in which they are grounded disappears into the background.

There are at least four reasons — perhaps we should say factors, or even characteristics of contemporary management education — that discourage religious reflection from being an explicit element in our curricula. The first (the "Dominant Models" factor) is that certain models of business activity have come to dominate our thinking about business, and in the process these models have artificially isolated business from its larger context and crowded out other possible paradigms. A second reason (the "Diversity" factor) is that student bodies in Catholic schools have become more diverse, and faculties somewhat more reluctant to teach material that may be perceived as inaccessible to students who are not Catholic. A third reason (the "Specialization" factor) has to do with the increased specialization of most academic disciplines, not least the business disciplines. The result is that fewer and fewer business professors in Catholic institutions have some formal experience with the tradition, and few professors of theology and philosophy have an interest in applying their disciplines to business and organizational issues. Fourth, proponents of the Christian social tradition have a history of rebuking businesspeople for their misbehavior (actual and apparent) while failing to offer constructive criticism (the "Criticism" factor). Consequently, business professors and students, to say nothing of practitioners, see little value in exploring the tradition for helpful insights. Each of these four factors deserves to be explored a bit further.

The Dominant Models Factor

It is probably fair to say that the majority of business students bring a certain concept of business with them when they begin their business education. This concept might be described in terms of three elements, or paradigms:

1. The Economic Theory of the Firm — The purpose of a business is to make money, and indeed to make as much money as possible, for the owners of the business. In a publicly-held corporation the purpose is to maximize the wealth of the shareholders, usually by focusing attention on keeping the market price of the company's common stock as high as possible.

2. The Theory of the Corporation — Managers are employees (or perhaps even agents) of the owners of the business, and are therefore obligated to act and to make decisions for the benefit of the owners. Furthermore, since the owners of a publicly-held corporation are the shareholders, managers have a primary responsibility to work for the benefit of the shareholders and to follow their instructions (or the instructions they could be presumed to give).

3. The Marketing Theory of the Company — The most successful businesses will be those who attend most closely to the wants of their customers. Therefore, it is the obligation of managers to determine what customers want in the areas in which they do business and to do their best to supply these products and services, independently of any moral considerations.

Each of these theories tells us something about what a business should be, and consequently about how managers should behave. Taken together they have the effect of sharply reducing the scope of legitimate managerial activities and focusing these activities on the benefits to be produced for shareholders, often to the near exclusion of the consequences for non-shareholders. All are widely accepted by business professors, business students and practicing managers, but all are seriously misleading. Even so, they have served to crowd out theories from other quarters to the point that they are rarely questioned in management education programs. Indeed, in subtle and not-so-subtle ways, students are often instructed that focusing on other goals as of principal importance (whether in place of or along with maximizing benefits to shareholders) is inconsistent with competent management and dangerous to one's career. To raise questions about the validity of these theories from, say, the perspective of Christian social thought is to be unrealistic and perhaps even unfair to the students upon whom one imposes these alien views. On the contrary, however, I think that the extent to which ethics has penetrated a business curriculum and been taken seriously may be measured by the extent to which these three paradigms are mitigated, especially in the teaching of finance and marketing.

The Diversity Factor

In the United States the secularization of Protestant universities began in the 19th century and was completed in the 20th.[2] Over the last 30 years or so a strikingly similar process has been at work in Catholic universities, who are almost all now struggling with questions of how their Catholic identity will be exhibited in the 21st century. Though these questions are not at all unique to Catholic universities, relatively few distinctively Protestant universities remain. Nevertheless, this factor would affect them in much the same way as it now affects Catholic schools.

There are probably several explanations for this turn toward secularization — economic, demographic, and so forth.[3] There is even reason to believe that some academics began with the goal of diluting the Catholic character of these institutions and, as with the Protestant universities before them, this is what has happened.[4] In any event, as promising Catholic students were sent off to do graduate work at secular universities, and as an increasing proportion of non-

Catholic faculty were hired, it was inevitable that faculties would be less attentive to Catholic voices and Catholic perspectives in most disciplines.

Some good consequences followed from this, but some bad as well. To be fair, a good bit of Catholic scholarship earlier in the century was mediocre and insular. Our institutions were often inbred, and while this created a high degree of unity, it also resulted in a dogmatic resistance to new ideas and a detachment from the rest of the profession. This might have been tolerable for a time in, say, theology or philosophy, but in many professional areas it could be deadly.

The practical experience brought to the classroom by many instructors, and the fresh ideas and critical standards taken from the best secular schools have contributed greatly to the improvement of professional education in Catholic universities. So too have the bright students of various faiths and ethnic backgrounds who now attend almost every Catholic university. Nevertheless, something has been lost, or perhaps misplaced, and that something is the legitimate voice of Catholic thought in our graduate programs in law, business and medicine.

The Specialization Factor

A third factor that has influenced the declining role of Christian social thought in professional schools is the increasing scholarly specialization of the faculty. Professional ethics requires some interdisciplinary background on the part of the instructor or a teaching team. Few philosophers are genuinely interested in applied ethics, and as specialized education has begun earlier (reaching well into the college years), fewer business professionals have made a systematic study of ethics. The problem is compounded if we include Christian social thought because some competence in theology is required as well if someone is to teach the subject properly. These competencies are rarely found in individuals, and difficult to sustain in any event. What is really required is a cross-functional team and some real interdisciplinary collaboration.

However, even in Catholic universities, with their historical emphasis on the liberal arts, this kind of collaborative spirit has too often been unusual. In some cases, younger scholars are discouraged from collaborating at the very time in their careers when they might be most open to it on the grounds that interdisciplinary work will endanger their chances of achieving tenure. This seems especially to be true for philosophers and theologians inclined to work with colleagues in the business disciplines.

The Criticism Factor

A fourth factor to consider is the historical relationship between Christian social thought and commerce. Philosophers and theologians have always had a disdain for business, and this attitude has certainly persisted during the last century or so of the development of Christian social thought. Very little attention has been given to the possibility of constructive criticism of business, nor to the support of business people as active Christians.

The theoreticians of Christian social thought have correctly observed that businesspeople do not always function fully in accord with sound moral principles, and indeed that there are many temptations to lie, cheat and steal. Theologians have sometimes made the mistake to think that since business sometimes does not act ethically that it cannot act ethically. They have falsely moved from a descriptive observation (which would come as a surprise to no one) to a normative conclusion.

As a result, they have more often seen their task as one of limiting the damage that business does than as one of offering constructive criticism and spiritual support. It is small wonder that businesspeople, a great many of whom are serious Christians, find very little in the practical teaching of their churches to support their vocations.

What Can Christian Social Thought Offer to Management Education?

There can be no serious question about the fact that management education, to say nothing of business practice, is in considerable turmoil today. Every few months a new approach to management captures the public eye. Experienced managers have been through a long series of new frameworks that held promise not only to revolutionize managerial practice but also to stabilize it — Management by Objective, the Search for Excellence, Total Quality Management, Reengineering, the Learning Organization, and many, many others. Instead of highlighting what is universally true about management and giving practicing managers skills and tools they could use in any situation, this parade of theories and techniques has left managers and educators fatigued and frustrated. Some are intimidated by the pace of these changes, while many others, more sensibly, are skeptical of the possibility and value of management education. In addition, the demands placed on practicing managers in the face of this "permanent whitewater,"[5] many of whom are struggling to keep pace in downsized organizations, effectively discourage them from reflecting on anything other than the short-term skills they will need to handle tomorrow morning's problems. Too often, as a result, corporate training programs become little more than interruptions to be endured rather than benefits to be pursued.

To be sure, the volatility of today's business environment certainly demands flexibility from managers. New situations and new problems call for new solutions. Nevertheless, some things remain constant: businesses must still create wealth and show a profit, products and services must still be sold, work must be made productive, and so on. Most importantly, even though situations change, people remain fundamentally the same. Their goals and frustrations, their joys and suffering, their potential and their limitations, have not changed. I submit that the best managers realize that they do not merely manage processes and things, but people, and it is people they must understand most thoroughly. It is here that we may find what is most stable about management, and it is here that Christian social thought has the most to offer.

Just over one hundred years ago, in his encyclical Rerum novarum, Pope Leo XIII discussed the "social question" in terms of three parties: the State, labor, and ownership. Since then the functional role of owners has been taken over by professional managers, but Christian thinkers have scarcely noticed.[6] This tradition has paid more attention throughout its history to issues concerning the State and to the problems of labor in a developed economy. The problems of management have been largely ignored, but Christian thought has a great deal to contribute here. By way of illustration we will consider the ideas of human work and the role of the manager.

Human Work in Christian Social Thought

An industrial engineer, Howard Rosenbrock, once observed that the designer of a modern factory had made thoughtful use of robots in the facility, only using them when there was task that made good use of their capabilities. When the task involved was "beneath" the ability of the available robots, it was often given to a human worker. Rosenbrock remarked, "We may say, paradoxically, that if he had been able to consider people as though they were robots, he would have tried to provide them with less trivial and more human work."[7] We may acknowledge his insight into what appears to be a wasteful, though widespread, approach to job design, but we may also ask what "more human work" might be. Surely managers need to know if they are to improve the practice, but unfortunately neither engineering nor the management disciplines have much to offer on this issue.

Psychology and sociology may have something to contribute here, but so does the Christian community, which claims an expertise in humanity.[8] First of all, in a Christian context work is not understood as a punishment, but as an integral part of a human life. It is not to be equated with employment, but encompasses any productive activity, whether formally compensated or not. Through work persons provide a livelihood for themselves and their families, and make their marks on the world around them. While often hard and painful, work nevertheless is a kind of self-expression, and even a collaboration with the Creator. Furthermore, everyone who works is also affected and shaped by the work they do. In a critical way, the worker is always more important that the work; it is always a person who accomplishes the task, and the tasks, taken singly or together, are always for the sake of persons.

Why should any of this be of concern to managers or students of management? First of all, to the extent that this tradition is true, we must recognize that managers are persons who are affected by the work that they do. They cannot remain unchanged for the worse if they collaborate in creating and reinforcing situations in which other persons are systematically underused, misused, or abused. Furthermore, one need merely to look at the sorts of problems with which both corporate human resource departments and operations managers must commonly deal: absenteeism, careless injuries, repetitive stress injuries, alcohol and substance abuse, frustration and boredom, alienation, disinterest, sabotage, lack of initiative, careless work, disloyalty, frequent turnover, and so on and on. There is no doubt that the lazy and unreliable we will always have with us, but there is also no doubt that we can manage much better than we often have. We know this is true because some larger companies do remarkably well at addressing these problems.[9]

Generally what these companies do is acknowledge the worker as a person and devise structures and strategies that respect this fact. For example, W. Edwards Deming, one of the most prominent theorists of the Total Quality Management movement insisted on recognizing the humanity of the worker through such key principles as "Drive out fear" and "Remove barriers to pride of workmanship." Deming, who appears to have been motivated to adopt these principles as a result of his practical experience rather than religious convictions, insisted for many years that quality problems were far more likely to be the fault of mismanagement (poor job design, poor communication, abusiveness, etc.) than the fault of workers.

Successful companies have discovered, sometimes to their great surprise, that their employees want very much to make a quality product, or provide a superior service. They find that workers and managers alike can accept responsibility and make sound decisions, and that they perform much better when they participate in decision making. Indeed, there is a high degree of correspondence between the principles Christian social thought concerning work and the best management practices of successful companies. One may well wonder, then, if even greater success could be achieved if Christian insights into the human person and the principles that follow from these insights were applied more systematically to management problems.

Management as Vocation

Another area in which there seems to be a great deal of ambivalence in practice concerns the role of the manager in an organization. We have already discussed briefly a common view of managerial responsibility, but we might fruitfully approach the question by setting this view aside and considering what Christian social thought could contribute.

The Christian idea of vocation can be useful here. Now the notion has a number of connotations in Christian theology and we certainly do not need to address them all. For our purposes, suffice it to say that the idea includes the conviction that individuals are naturally parts of communities and that each person has received gifts (talents and other resources) from the Creator which it is his obligation to use for the benefit of the community. Any legitimate role in the community (that is, a playing out of a personal vocation) will aim at some benefit for that community. When we look at management, then, we might ask what benefits managers contribute and for whom?

In practice, as others have pointed out, a business firm is a complicated system of constituencies, none of which can function effectively without the others.[10] Sound management practice recognizes these constituencies and respects their interests. Very broadly it seems fair to say that managers organize work: they organize resources so that opportunities for gainful employment are provided to others, and they structure the work itself so that workers may effectively collaborate. In succeeding at their work, managers facilitate the creation of useful goods and services for the community and put productive resources to good use, often in order to create wealth. This is their vocation. Note, however, that there are several distinct but related elements and, as a result, managers must aim at achieving a balance among the benefits their work aims to provide. While some maintain that managers should focus their attention on creating wealth for shareholders, I think that it is reasonable to reject this, and the Christian concept of vocation would support this rejection.

A number of other concepts tied up with the Christian social tradition are relevant to business and management, including the ideas of the common good, of the structure human communities, of integral development, of solidarity and subsidiarity, of virtue, of having and being, and many more. While this tradition is not be self-sufficient, it surely has something worthwhile to contribute to management education. What remains is to consider how it might play this role.

Where Do We Go from Here?

In my judgment there are at least two remaining issues or obstacles that must be confronted before Christian social thought can play a meaningful role in management education. The first is that it must be legitimated, both as an intellectual discipline and in the context of our universities. The second is that it must be organized in a teachable form. In other words, the relevant elements of the Christian social tradition must be thought through and articulated in such a way as to correspond to the issues as they occur in management.

The Legitimation of Christian Social Thought

Over the past 100 years or more great changes have taken place in the theory and practice of management. We have come to recognize that many of the factors that affect organizations are external to them and almost impossible to control, or even predict. The environment in which organizations function seems chaotic, very little within or without appears stable. As a result, practicing managers are often compelled to react to circumstances and factors that affect their immediate situations and are rarely able to view what they experience in a larger context. Management theorists are also subject to this turbulence and myopia as they try to make sense out of such a complicated whole.

The essence of wisdom in social situations is not the ability to predict with accuracy what will happen if a certain course of action is followed. Instead, it is the ability to judge whether some strategies are better than others and more likely to produce genuinely satisfactory results. This depends upon the capacity to see things as a whole and not merely as an aggregate of parts. It is precisely this perspective that Christian social thought offers to management education. This perspective consists of a number of insights, but surely among them are an expansive concept of fairness and justice, a conception of organizations as real human communities, and an understanding of human work which can acknowledge its personal as well as productive dimensions. These and the other pertinent aspects of Christian social thought are not nearly so subject to the changes that affect organizations and so can be especially important to seeing stable elements in a turbulent environment.

Nevertheless, despite the contended usefulness of the Christian social tradition, there remain to be overcome the four factors discussed earlier that discourage us from teaching it in business schools. The first of these, the dominant models factor, can only be overcome by a direct criticism and discussion of the inadequacies of these models. While each of the models points to something true about business organizations, none of them is adequate as an operating theory for business. The Financial Theory of the Firm points to the primacy of shareholders in managerial decision making, but the reality is that shareholders are often not the principal constituency to be considered by well-managed firms. Similar objections could be brought against the Legal Theory of the Corporation, including the fact that the "employment" relationships understood by the prevailing legal framework may well be inadequate to describe the evolving relationships we actually see in the workplace. Moreover, the Marketing Theory of the Company in some of its common forms attempts to ignore ethical issues related to its products, which at minimum is an imprudent public relations strategy. Even taken together these three common theories are inaccurate and inadequate and we ought to tell our students so. Christian social thought, if its insights and elements are presented properly, can provide a foundation for a critique of these theories as well as the basis for the construction of a more adequate conception of business.

The diversity factor presents a different set of challenges. To the extent that our institutions have become secularized there may be some suspicion of the appropriateness of discussing the Christian social tradition in the business classroom. Indeed, for some teachers, even some of those otherwise well disposed toward the tradition, an explicit presentation will seem to be catechesis. It is important to point out that the Church's tradition is not something derived simply from Scripture. Instead it is a result of nearly 2,000 years of dealing with people in a bewildering variety of organizations and cultures. The Christian churches present their social tradition as a result of reflection on this experience in light of the Gospel and of the ethical sensitivity stimulated by the Gospel. Even so, there is very little in the tradition that is so closely tied to a set of religious beliefs or documents that it cannot be accessible to someone who does not share those beliefs or accept those documents. Furthermore, there are many commonalities with respect to business and organizational life between Christian social thought and other major religious traditions, in Judaism and Islam. Considering the relatively high number of people who report that religion is important in their lives, it should certainly be possible to identify such common elements and introduce them to the curriculum.

The specialization factor is relatively easy to address, especially in institutions that recognize the problems it causes. The key is to invite collaboration with experts in other fields such as economics, management, marketing, finance, sociology and so forth. Not only is it impossible to collaborate effectively without developing an appreciation for someone else's discipline, but collaboration enriches the application of Christian social thought to the business disciplines. Furthermore, should not be limited to academics, but can very fruitfully include practicing managers and executives, both within and without the classroom.

Finally, the issue of Christianity's unfriendly critique of business must be met with a constructive criticism. Managers know quite well that what they do is flawed; there are few professions more aware of the limitations of their practice. What they need is not further scolding but affirmation of the good they do accomplish and practical suggestions about how they might accomplish more. While some managers may be unconcerned about "doing good" in their drive to "do well," a great many would willingly benefit from creative suggestions about how they can conduct their affairs in genuine service of the common good. We might take a cue here from Pope John Paul II's encyclical Centesimus annus, which does not offer a critique of businesses and the market economy until after it has acknowledged the contributions both make to the common good of the human community.

Making Christian Social Thought Teachable

At least two related things must be done, in my judgment, to make the tradition teachable in a business context: a coherent model of what business is about must be articulated as a alternative to the dominant models discussed earlier, and the numerous correspondences between the tradition and sound, successful management practice must be pointed out.

In order to articulate an alternative model for business several underlying concepts from the tradition need to be explained and established. Among these concepts is the right to private property (and its limitations), the priority of the worker over the work done, the importance of being over having, and the distinction between genuine and apparent human goods.

I will not attempt to articulate here what this alternative model would look like, but I will offer some suggestions about what its outline might be. First, a business might be better understood not as a system for maximizing shareholder wealth, but as a collaborative community whose goal is to organize work so as to produce economic goods. These goods are enjoyed directly by customers, and the wealth created is distributed directly to employees and shareholders, and indirectly to other constituencies, such as civil communities. On this conception, a business is an integral part of a larger system (the tradition often speaks of mediating or intermediate organizations), and not merely an autonomous wealth-producing piece of property.

Furthermore, a business is justified morally by its goal, which here must be to help create and sustain the common good of the larger human community by supplying certain needed and useful economic goods. More precisely, the moral purpose of a business is to aim at enhancing human welfare by helping all persons involved to become more fully and completely human, not merely to possess more. This means, for example, that managers must attend to the work they organize so that it genuinely contributes to the human development of their workers, even if efficiency must sometimes appear to be sacrificed.[11]

While this description might seem unusual at first glance, I submit that it is not at all uncommon in actual practice. A survey of the mission statements and ethics codes of large and successful businesses (and often of small, successful businesses as well), reveals that many businesses conceive of what they do in similar terms. Indeed, few see actually themselves as mere instruments of shareholder aggrandizement. They are concerned about their customers and their employees, they are concerned about job satisfaction and the quality of life in their communities, and they sincerely attempt to address these concerns while providing an attractive return on the investment of their shareholders.

In more specific areas we can see further correspondences between the Christian social tradition and good management practice. For example, as more and more jobs involve a significant degree of "knowledge work" the nature of the job changes. Knowledge work by its very nature requires the worker to be self-directing. A frustrated and dissatisfied knowledge worker is not only inefficient, but also ineffective, and often in ways that are not immediately apparent. Consequently, prudent managers know that they must deal with the more personal (or loosely speaking, spiritual) aspects of the job, just as the tradition suggests for all workers.

Another example has to do with competition. There are any number of examples of firms whose main competitive objective has been to defeat their competitors. In recent years we have had some striking instances of companies so focused on their principal competition that they failed to notice that their markets were changing in ways that would cost them dearly.[12] A healthier focus of competition would be upon providing the best possible contribution to the common good. This is hardly a unique insight of the Christian social tradition, but it is another instance of a correspondence with sound management.

The rich tradition of Christian social thought has a great deal to contribute to business education, despite the difficulties of finding a place for it in the curriculum. We owe it to students to give them the opportunity to confront this tradition and judge it for themselves. To paraphrase the words of Pope John Paul on the occasion of his first visit to his native Poland, "Christ cannot be kept out of education in any area; the exclusion of Christ from a person's education is a sin against that person." Hopefully, in Christian universities at least we can be encouraged to find appropriate and effective ways to return Christ to the business classroom.

Notes

1. I wish to acknowledge the generous support of Msgr. Terrence J. Murphy and the Aquinas Foundation for a grant in the summer of 1993 that supported some of the early research for this paper.
2. See George Marsden, *The Soul of the American University* (New York: Oxford University Press, 1994) for a careful account of the history of this process in American Protestant universities.
3. We might remember that about 40 years ago the prominent American church historian, John Tracy Ellis, wrote a widely influential article decrying the quality of Catholic scholarship ("American Catholics and the Intellectual Life," *Thought* 30 (1955) 351-388). It is probably the case that the concern to make Catholic universities more intellectually respectable also contributed to the effort to make them more broadly accessible.
4. See Philip Gleason, "What Made Catholic Identity a Problem?" in Theodore M. Hesburgh, CSC, ed., *The Challenge and Promise of a Catholic University* (South Bend, IN: University of Notre Dame Press, 1994) 91-102.
5. Peter Vaill coined this colorful term in his book, *Management as a Performing Art* (San Francisco: Jossey-Bass, 1989).
6. Also unnoticed has been the fact that ownership of public corporations in many countries, notably the United States, has passed from a few wealthy families to the middle classes (including skilled workers) through their huge investments in pension funds. See Peter Drucker, *The Unseen Revolution: How Pension Fund Socialism Came to America*. (New York: Harper & Row, 1976) for an early account of this change.
7. Howard Rosenbrock, "Engineers and the Work that People Do," *IEEE Control Systems Magazine*, vol. 1, # 3.
8. The consideration of human work here depends a great deal on the encyclical Laborem exercens (1981) by Pope John Paul II, and the discussion that followed.
9. Often these problems are less severe in smaller companies. Perhaps this is because larger companies tend to become more impersonal and so less resistant to pressures that dehumanize the workplace.
10. See Douglas Sherwin, "The Ethical Roots of the Business System," *Harvard Business Review*, November-December 1983, pp 183-192, for a secular discussion of this theme.
11. I strongly suspect that a systematic investigation would reveal that almost all (if not all) job designs that sacrifice human dignity and development for the sake of efficiency are, in the end, also relatively inefficient. Forced labor, for instance, may appear to be efficient but I think there is ample evidence to show that the other costs involved (supervision, poor quality, sabotage, etc.) outweigh the efficiencies in any but the most dysfunctional circumstances.
12. The examples of the American auto industry in the 1970s and more recently of the competition between Coca Cola and Pepsico come to mind.

Chapter Thirteen

The Benefits of Using a Competence-Based Approach in the Education of New Teachers: Fact or Fiction?

Pat Mahony

In 1992 a Local Education Authority (LEA) in London initiated a project to develop a profile of teacher competences for use with Newly Qualified Teachers (NQTs) and their teacher-mentors. The project team consisted of one LEA Inspector and three members of staff from different Higher Education Institutions (HEIs). Our work was informed by our experiences of developing competence frameworks in initial teacher education (ITE) and by the literature identifying the complex issues raised by competence based approaches to teacher education. Each of us was responsible for different elements of the project and within our small team there existed a range of commitments to competence based approaches to teacher education — from the severely sceptical to the positively enthusiastic.

The 'Need for Something'

For some years it has been almost a cliche to claim that induction for Newly Qualified Teachers (NQTs) into their first year of teaching, forms the weakest link in the professional development of teachers. Even before September covered the probationary period for beginning teachers (DfE 1992a), research suggested that LEAs differed markedly in relation to the quantity, quality, content and principles underpinning provision:

> What an NQT receives can vary from a package of carefully-organised, structured information to a few badly-duplicated sheets. The information can have been specifically tailored to engage the interest and involvement of the newly-appointed teacher, or it can consist of maps, addresses, offices, personnel lists and bureaucratic information.... Additionally, an authority may make clear what the new teacher is "entitled to" from both school and authority, but may also specify very explicitly the "expectations" held of the NQT. The criteria, procedures and formalities of assessment and evaluation may be contained in some detail. On the other hand, in some authorities virtually none of this will be available for NQTs, schools, mentors or anyone else. This experience was echoed in a survey which we conducted last year amongst those probationers who had left our PGCE course in Summer 1991. Whereas 40 per cent of them had had approximately ten induction sessions arranged and supported by their LEA, some 15 per cent had only had one/two sessions, whilst a few had experienced 20 or more sessions. In short, what counts as induction at the moment seems to be very much a bagatelle which varies wildly from situation to situation (Sidgwick, Mahony & Hextall 1993).

Whilst acknowledging that all was far from well before its abolition, the probationary year did at least provide a statutory framework within which much good practice was to be found and potentially shared. However, the delegation of funding to schools through Local Management of Schools (LMS) further weakened the role of the LEAs as potential providers of high quality support for NQTs (Early 1992). LEAs could simply no longer afford to employ the advisory staff necessary to work with NQTs either centrally, and (as was common within best practice) in the context of the employing school.

There was however, recognition of the fact that new teachers need 'help and guidance from a nominated member of staff who has been adequately prepared for the role' (DfE 1992a) and government grants were available to support the shift from LEA provided induction to more school based provision. Teaching competences were mentioned as part of this process:

The Department's objectives in supporting expenditure by LEAs and GM schools on induction training are to:

> improve links between initial teacher training, induction of NQTs and INSET during the early years of teachers' careers, particularly through the development of profiling and competency based approaches to professional development. (DfE 1992a)

Predictably there was much concern about whether the shift to school-based induction was a sensible move. The findings of HMI did little to reassure critics that schools would be able to provide the necessary support:

Schools varied greatly in the quality of support offered to probationers. Informal support was almost invariably good, but well structured provision was much less common. Only a minority of schools had an established induction programme or a policy statement on induction. Schools under LMS are likely to be expected to assume an increasing responsibility for the induction of new teachers. It is important that LEAs provide guidance which will assist schools in formulating effective induction policies and practices (HMI 1992).

Of course it could be argued that the point of the government grant was precisely to enable LEAs to provide this guidance, however not all LEAs were successful in their bids for the grant and thus were placed in a position where they had neither the resources nor the power to translate policy into practice.

Many other concerns have been raised about the changed arrangements for induction. For example, the basis on which a school chooses mentors for NQTs, how the mentor's role is defined and monitored, are questions raised by Menter and Whitehead (1992). Yet there is no acknowledgment within the official guidance that these are important issues and underpinning the shifts in language and meaning contained in Administrative Memorandum 2/92, is a fundamental and unacknowledged tension between the use of 'profiling and competence-based assessment' for the purposes of enhancing professional development and its utilisation for the quite other purpose of providing a 'licence to teach'. In its ambiguity it also raises, but does not resolve, questions about exactly what constitute the procedures for the 'adequate' completion of the induction phase. It carries the implication that competence and profiling procedures for initial teacher education are firmly in place and that these can be unproblematically translated into procedures for induction with notions of progression built into them. In addition there is slippage between the use of competences and the notion of teacher appraisal. These have come from quite different directions and are seen as having different purposes. More importantly, from the point of view of the discussion on competences, the official documentation does little to clarify the conceptual confusions which abound in this area nor quiet the critics of competence-based approaches to teacher education.

The Problem with Competence

The fact that 'something was needed' did not make the prospect of producing a framework for use by busy teachers, any easier. Objections in principle and in practice have flowed thick and fast from critics of competence-based teacher education. First there are those who:

> reject the idea of competence-based teacher education on the grounds that it encourages an over emphasis on skills and techniques; that it ignores vital

components of teacher education; that what informs performance is as important as performance itself; and that the whole is more than the sum of its parts. (Whitty & Willmott 1991).

However, as the authors go on to point out, 'this rejection partly derived from a reading of early American checklists of teacher behaviour, which are ticked by an observer'. There is no reason in principle why skill and technique should be over emphasised, nor why vital elements of teacher education should not be included. The knowledge and understanding which inform performance can be broadly specified and indeed have been (DENI 1994, Devereux 1995) and a demand can be built into the framework of competences that teaching be seen in a holistic way and as a value-laden activity (Mahony & Harris 1996). Critics may reply by complaining that the concept of 'competence' is now not being used in its correct, strictly behavioural sense; but in this case their argument becomes one which is true by definition.

Leading on from this, a second set of concerns has centred precisely on the question of what competences are and whether they are of use in teacher education. Norris (1991) for example leads us through a maze of definitions and issues and concludes that: 'The trouble with competence is that it now has a currency way beyond its operational or conceptual reach.' In similar vein, Furlong (1992) warns:

> Writing a critique of competency based teacher education today presents considerable difficulties because of the enormous variation in interpretations of the approach. When writers as theoretically diverse as Jessup (1991) and Elliott (1990) can both claim to be writing about competences, any critic must approach the area with caution.

It is tempting to invoke Humpty Dumpty's solution to this proliferation of definition:

> When I use a word,' Humpty Dumpty said, in a rather scornful tone, 'it means just what I choose it to mean — neither more nor less.'

> 'The question is,' said Alice, 'whether you *can* make words mean so many different things.'

> 'The question is,' said Humpty Dumpty, 'which is to be master — that's all (Carroll 1872).

However, to do so would be to ignore over one hundred different accounts of teacher competence which now exist in the UK and further, to ignore that they represent deeply-held convictions about what it means to teach well or to be a 'good teacher'. Put crudely, the ground being contested in the debate over competences is in relation to the teacher's role in 'delivering' a pre-specified body of subject knowledge on the one hand and on the other, the teacher as moral agent engaged in a complex series of inter-relationships with children. What it is to teach well on the first model involves a high degree of subject knowledge, techniques of classroom management and knowledge of procedures for planning, assessment and reporting pupils' progress. At the other end of the spectrum, knowing how to communicate with children becomes crucial. What is really at issue is not whether competence frameworks can conceptually accommodate knowledge and understanding but rather what kind of knowledge and understanding 'good teachers' need. While no-one has seriously advanced the proposition that teachers should be ignorant of subject knowledge, knowledge of children and the ability to interpret their actions, vilified as the dangerous theory of the 1960s and 1980s, has come under attack from prominent politicians (Major 1992, Patten 1992). In this sense, critics of the 'competence movement', in noting that it is being developed alongside an account of teaching with which they profoundly disagree, have perhaps confused the account itself with the attempt to frame it in terms of competences (Mahony 1992).

Those who reject narrow and simplistic definitions of competence are quite right to do so. Anyone who has spent any time at all in the classroom is quickly made aware that the complexity of teaching arises in part from its status as an activity which centrally involves communication and interaction between human beings.

When we talk of 'pupils' (which much of the official guidance does), the activity of teaching pupils can be made to sound deceptively simple. When we think of Angie who was sexually abused by her father or Elavalagan who recently fled from Sri Lanka or Sophie, a middle class 'boffin' in a working class school, then what it means to teach, immediately becomes more complex. The same is true of teachers too. They do not simply have 'personal qualities' but similarly act out of, are influenced by and in turn reconstitute social and political identities. What it means to begin a teaching career in a school where there is little awareness of racism, positions teachers differently according to whether they are black or white. Quite simply, teaching involves relationships between people whose personal, social, cultural and political identities are complex. Second, teachers do not only respond to children per se but also to their actions. The quality or professionalism of these responses depend on the extent and sophistication of their understanding of children's actions. These are not abstract questions. For example, what I as a teacher do when Natasha slams her pen down and thunders round to Darren's seat to shout at him, depends on how I understand her action. As a beginning teacher I may get no further than describing and then punishing Natasha's action as a piece of disruptive behaviour — which it is — the whole class by now have lost the concentration it took me fifteen minutes to achieve. But as I learn more about the research which informs our understandings of pupils and classrooms I will know that there are a whole range of possible explanations which could account for what Natasha did. I will also know that until I have investigated the incident in order to ascertain Natasha's intentions and beliefs, those explanations are not available to me and so I am not in a position to describe her action — only the behaviour which I observed. It may be that she launched an unprovoked attack or that she rehearsed her lines in the school play or that she retaliated against Darren's continual sexual harassment. All three descriptions are consistent with the behaviour which I observed but will require a very different response from me, depending on what she and Darren say. In the first and second case I might remonstrate with her, in the second, given the knowledge I have of the effects of harassment in the classroom, both of them.

Understanding teacher's actions is equally important. Much of the time we interpret or read actions unproblematically, embedded as they are in our routines and the shared meanings of social life. Only rarely do we need to ask 'what on earth are you doing?' and at that point it is usually because we cannot fit the observable behaviour into the background of intelligibility which we take for granted. Much of the time teachers do not make explicit the knowledge or theories which inform their actions. When we describe ourselves as 'marking' for example, we take it for granted that our colleagues know that we are not scribbling on pupils' work but rather that we are engaging in the kind of professional activity which we believe will provide the kind of feedback necessary to support their improvement. However, when we come to induct beginning teachers into this professional activity we have to be able to describe teacher action in a much less theoretically condensed way. This is necessary not only to introduce them to the kind of knowledge they need to acquire but also what it means to utilise it in their professional judgements. In this way, theories (beliefs, knowledge, intentions and purposes) which inform the activity of teaching are made explicit and the professional conversations concerned with the 'why' questions of teaching made possible. It is the answers to these 'why' questions which provide important evidence for judging that someone is a competent teacher rather than a teacher competent in a particular school. Similar arguments can be advanced in relation to those (student) teachers judged incompetent. It is truly remarkable that those who object to competences on the grounds that the complexity of teaching cannot be adequately represented, apparently find no difficulty in examination boards, of providing clear accounts of this complexity and of how failing students have not grasped it.

So far I have argued that the criticisms of the competence movement fail to demonstrate that teaching, viewed as a complex, social, value laden activity cannot be adequately represented by competences (broadly conceived). However, given the enormously difficult task of framing an adequate account, the further, equally difficult task of operationalising it within a tension between the dual purposes of supporting professional development and assessment, the question has to be asked 'Why bother'?

The Benefit of Competence

It was against a background of policy confusion that the project to develop an account of teaching competence appropriate for NQTs began. The sense of chaos produced by 2/92 was real and all parties in the project clearly had a major interest in producing a workable account. The LEA, in receipt of the government grant awarded for this purpose, wanted to develop a competence framework for NQTs, along the lines suggested by 2/92. The three HEIs were already engaged in developing accounts of teaching competence which pre-dated 9/92 and shared a concern that the complexity of what is involved in teaching well, should not be lost. In addition, it did seem that a profile of competence could have enormous potential for empowering NQTs by involving them both in framing and using explicit criteria through which they would be able to monitor with others, their own development as beginning teachers. It was also accepted that competences, could provide a rational basis for planning the educational needs of NQTs. That this need exists arose from two sets of concerns; the first of these raises questions about the role of teachers in a democratic society of the twenty-first century:

> We must be able to articulate what kind of teachers we want and why, what professional characteristics and qualities teachers must possess, what learning experiences are needed for their development and how school based and centralised provision can be integrated to provide for these in a coherent framework. Only if the profession adopts a collective stance on these issues can it plan for a preparation for teaching which is informed by reason rather than the ad hoc contingencies of policy motivated both by ideological antipathy and a market place driven by price rather than principle (Inman, Mahony, Sidgwick 1994).

The second concern related to the way in which competences were thought to provide two kinds of bridges; a bridge between school-based and central provision and a bridge between the period of initial teacher education and the first year of teaching. The Chief HMI had commented in his Annual Report for 1989/90:

> Often ... there is no mesh between LEA and school programmes; the needs of new teachers are inadequately identified, and induction fails as a bridge between initial teacher training (ITT) and teaching itself.

A profile of teacher competence did not only potentially benefit the NQTs. Teacher mentors too could be supported by having a document which would provide a shared language in which professional issues could be discussed, focus attention on the degree to which opportunities really were available for the NQT's development and could help clarify what realistically could be achieved in the first year of teaching and what should be a matter for continuing professional development. Thus with varying degrees of reservation, the project team embarked on the process of developing a profile of competence for NQTs and their teacher mentors.

The Project

One of our concerns within the project was to begin to develop an account of NQT competence generated by the NQTs and mentors themselves. Previously the LEA had used a framework based on Circular 9/92 (DfE 1992b) (the official version of the competences to be achieved by new secondary teachers) and was dissatisfied by the way in which it seemed to provoke a 'dry' and bureaucratic response from mentors (Carter et al 1994). Therefore we believed it was important, in order to maximise ownership of the profiling scheme by those who would be using it, not to impose the competence descriptors from 'on high' but rather to invest some time in eliciting from both groups, their views on desirable developments in the first year of teaching.

Eleven mentors and sixteen NQTs attended meetings on different occasions at the LEA's Professional Development Centre. They were asked to identify what ought to be the characteristics of NQTs by the end of their first year of teaching. Personal constructs were elicited from both groups and sent back for comment and amendment. The final data was used to form the framework for the LEA's new profile of NQT competence.

The project neared completion at the point when Circular 14/93 (DfE 1993) was published (the official version of the competences to be achieved by new primary teachers). Our impressions were that the elements identified by mentors and NQTs and the language in which they expressed them were very different from those set out in 14/93. This might be thought to be unremarkable; there is after all no definitive 'truth' about the nature of teaching contained in the official documentation and nor is one claimed. It was however somewhat surprising given that the mentors were already working with 9/92, a framework not dissimilar to 14/93 and they were well used to commenting on the progress of NQTs according to its categories and in its language, albeit in a way which was perceived as 'distant' (Carter et al 1994). In order to explore the matter further and using all the data which had been generated by the project, the teachers' statements were compared with the competences as laid out in 14/93. This it was felt would provide another voice on the subject of teacher competence. First the mentors' and then the NQTs' statements were mapped where possible on to the relevant DfE competences. This exercise did not of course yield any firm conclusions about what experienced or new teachers 'really' believe is important in teaching but it did provide insight into the priorities of busy teachers as expressed after a day in the classroom. Notwithstanding the potential for misinterpretation of the mentors' or NQTs' comments and given the possibility of variously interpreting 14/93, some interesting results emerged.

DfE Competences not Mentioned by the Mentors

A significant number of the 14/93 competences were not mentioned. There was relatively little comment which fitted within **'Curriculum Content, Planning and Assessment'** or **'Further Professional Development'** and in relation to **'Teaching Strategies'**, mentors simply did not express themselves in a way which indicated even a remote match with the DfE's way of describing practice.

In seeking to explain these results, it cannot be that mentors were unaware of the statutory obligations of teachers, many of which are implied or directly stated by the DfE competences. These formed a routine, every-day part of their professional lives and were for some time high on the political agenda. We know too, from the evidence of their assessments of NQTs' progress, articulated against an earlier draft of the LEA profile based on Circular 9/92, that they were well able to work within a DfE model of what constitutes competent teaching and to understand and interpret its discourse. It could be that the mentors interpreted the question which we asked them as an opportunity to set their own priorities and in this respect what they produced could be seen as deliberately oppositional to the official version of the competent teacher. Or it could simply be that what was omitted was regarded as so self evident that they viewed it as not requiring mention. Finally, it could simply be that they needed longer to complete the task given that, in common with many experienced teachers, their knowledge about what teachers need to know and understand in order to develop competence, has over time become an implicit part of their professional practice. The comments from this mentor when she returned the first draft of the results provide some evidence for this view:

> I found several of the sections disappointing and even embarrassing! I do hope this is only a first draft. So much of it needs more careful thought and rephrasing and I haven't time or confidence to do it alone. I think the nature and timing of the meeting was not conducive to the serious consideration which I think such a document needs.

The implication of her comments about 'time' become particularly relevant later.

DfE Competences not Mentioned by the NQTs

In comparing the data from the NQTs with the competences as listed in 14/ 93 a rather different picture emerges. Difficulties in where to place their comments in relation to the DfE competences were much reduced by virtue of the fact that the language in which they expressed themselves was much more akin to the official descriptors. They may not have **meant** what officials at the DfE mean but what they said was in many cases virtually identical. This could suggest that the government's vision of a competent teacher is currently being successfully achieved within existing, HEI provided courses of initial teacher education. Alternatively, as new teachers it could be that they had not yet reached the point where their knowledge had become tacit but rather were still self-consciously trying to come to terms with their responsibilities. Very few of the 14/93 competences were left unmatched by the NQTs. These were:

Assessment and Recording of Pupils' Progress

2.4   Newly qualified teachers should be able to:
2.4.4 provide oral and written feedback to pupils on the processes
       and outcomes of their learning
2.4.5 prepare and present reports on pupils' progress to parents

Further Professional Development

2.7   Newly qualified teachers should have acquired in initial training
       the necessary foundation to develop:
2.7.3 the ability to recognise diversity of talent including that of
       gifted pupils
2.7.8 vision, imagination and critical awareness in educating their
       pupils.

As with the mentors we could speculate about the reasons for these omissions. It could be that these competences, in the NQTs minds are incorporated in more generalised comments about practice. Or it could be that in some cases they form part of the routine of professional life and in others that they are perceived as marginal to the main task of teaching thirty children day after day. The fact that no NQT ever mentioned 'vision, imagination or critical awareness' (aspects which often figure in professional conversations with student teachers) does perhaps signal that successful induction has occurred into the relentless and exhausting 'hard graft' of the first year of teaching.

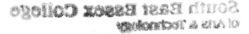

Mentors and NQTs Agree to Differ with the DfE Personal and Professional Qualities

A large number of the statements from both mentors and NQTs could not easily be mapped on to the DfE competences. These fell into a number of categories the largest of which by far for both groups was what might be called **'Personal and Professional Qualities'**. Mentors expressed these as the 'ability to be adaptable and flexible', 'the ability to accept constructive criticism', 'humility' and 'willingness to learn'. 'Stamina' 'hard work', 'effort' and 'energy' and the responsibility to maintain these while 'maintaining a sense of perspective and realism', 'self management' and 'self esteem' were all deemed to be significant. Personal qualities such as 'tact', 'humour', 'open-mindedness', compassion' and 'lack of self importance' all give clues about what for these mentors, was an ideal NQT. While it could be dangerous and open to much abuse to debar new entrants to the teaching profession on the grounds of personal qualities, it does seem that for these mentors this was by far their greatest priority and preoccupation.

Similarly, NQTs put a high priority on being flexible and adaptable with a number of their statements apparently coming from the heart: 'good at thinking on your feet, e.g., when the video blows up'; 'coping with sudden changes of routine' and 'flexibility — to exchange ideas and negotiate resources'. 'The ability to seek and use advice' was also viewed as important; 'discussing problems rather than bottling it up', the 'need to be receptive and adaptable to feedback' and the 'ability to evaluate advice' were all phrases which recurred. The 'ability to work alone' was significant for a number of NQTs and presumably marked a shift from their experience as students, where they would have had more opportunity to work alongside other adults in the classroom. 'Being open to ideas', 'being methodical', 'being resourceful, sensitive and receptive' were all personal or professional characteristics deemed to be important as was 'the ability to cope with the workload'. The 'need to be able to step back from situations', the 'ability to justify classroom practice', 'having a rationale for classroom practice' and the 'ability to evaluate own practice' all seemed to mark the fact that the NQTs attached importance to reflecting on, reviewing and being able to articulate their beliefs about practice.

Relationships with Children

The other large group of cards from both groups which could not be readily mapped on to the DfE competences concerned teachers' **'attitudes to and relationships with children'**. Mentors rated 'empathy with children', 'ability to set up a dialogue with pupils', 'ability to reassure individuals', 'refusing to dislike individual pupils' and 'open-mindedness towards pupils' potentials' very highly and these may all have been expressions for what one mentor called 'child centredness'. An interesting issue emerges at this point as to whether it would be possible for a teacher to develop the DfE competences to an acceptable level and yet thoroughly dislike children? It may also be that the current official preoccupation with teachers' subject knowledge has little impact on those actually doing the job. It could even be on this evidence that the increased time in school for student teachers, is likely to operate against the former Secretary of State's objective of eliminating child-centred ideology from the initial education of teachers.

Similarly, NQTs produced a large number of statements though this category was not as proportionately large as the mentors'. NQTs spoke in terms of 'being prepared to spend time building relationships with children', 'encouraging independence in children', 'building children's self-worth' and 'valuing children's opinions', though they framed their expressions in much more formal language than the mentors whose warmth towards and identification with children was much more strongly expressed.

Planning, Organising and Managing

In the area of planning, mentors seemed to be working with a more complex model than the DfE. According to the Circular 14/93, NQTs should be able to use knowledge of the curriculum to plan lessons. It was evident that according to the mentors, knowledge of children, of classroom management and of teaching strategies were all needed to inform planning for children's learning. Thus terms such as 'planning for special needs', 'planning for differentiation', 'planning for flexibility', 'reflection in planning' and 'planning for individual match' were used frequently. Mentors also understood what has to be managed by teachers in much broader terms than is expressed by 14/93. According to mentors everything about teaching and teachers (including stress) has to be 'managed', while DfE talks in more limited terms of managing 'time'.

For the NQTs, as with the mentors, 'planning', 'organising' and 'managing' covered a much wider range of activities than suggested by DfE. Everything had to be planned; short term and long term, work for individuals, groups and whole classes, as a team member and as an independent individual teacher, for the everyday routines and for crises. Everything had to be managed too whether this be time, classrooms, childrens' learning, resources for learning or the movement of children round the school. Similarly everything and everybody had to be organised, demonstrating a sharp awareness that teaching and learning require minute attention to detail.

One other area of discrepancy between the mentors' and the DfE's accounts emerged. First, mentors did overtly mention 'awareness of equal opportunities' whereas it could be argued that the DfE competences have to be interpreted by those who already possess such awareness in order to be made explicit. This omission is somewhat surprising since for a number of years, the British government has remained a signatory to a European declaration which commits member states to including Equal Opportunities in teacher education.

On the other hand NQTs mentioned 'equal opportunities' surprisingly little given the alleged obsessions of their ITE college tutors. 'Teaching children with English as a second language' and 'knowing the expectations of the community' may well reflect the fact that the NQTs had not yet absorbed resolutions to the complex issues of teaching in a multicultural environment, into that body of knowledge which for experienced teachers, becomes implicit.

Other smaller though significant groups of NQT statements which could not straightforwardly be mapped on to the DfE competences, as these are expressed, were 'having aims and objectives', 'to know, implement and **critique** the National Curriculum'. Finally a common thread running through all their statements was the need to be able to reconsider and justify the decisions taken or the strategies being adopted. This may be because these NQTs were trained within an ideology of teacher education in which 'reflective practice' was emphasised or it may be that their relative lack of experience and confidence generated the need for explicit review and self monitoring.

Mentors, NQTs and DfE Agree

Some of the mentors comments did easily map on to the DfE competences. By far the largest categories where this occurred were:

2.6.2   create and maintain a purposeful, orderly and supportive environment for their pupils' learning

2.6.1   establish clear expectations of pupil behaviour and secure appropriate standards of discipline.

This was also the case for the NQTs and many clues were given in their responses, as to **how** 'discipline' might be achieved and maintained. 'Ability to organise and manage the learning environment to maintain control', 'ability to gain and keep attention', 'ability to formulate and maintain classroom routines over the year for an atmosphere conducive to work' and 'ability to establish a safe, secure framework to show the boundaries of acceptable behaviour' were all comments which showed the NQTs as having grasped that 'discipline' is not something isolated from other aspects of teaching. Sometimes, more specific strategies were revealed; 'highlighting positive behaviour where possible' and 'ability to use school discipline codes to establish class rules'. Within all of it perhaps their anxieties occasionally peeped through; 'gaining a variety of strategies for managing disruptive behaviour', 'ability to keep disruptive children calm', 'ability to deal with arguments so the children are not aggrieved', 'what to do with a child who is constantly wanting attention and exhibiting challenging behaviour?' and 'interrogation skills for dealing with fights, to be just and for children to know it will be so.' Finally, NQTs apparently felt it was a legitimate to expect them to be able to provide 'evidence of criteria for discipline' and a 'rationale for discipline strategies'.

A notable feature of both mentors' and NQTs comments which mapped on to the competence referring to the development of:

> 2.7.2   effective working relationships with professional colleagues (including support staff) and parents was the breadth of understanding about what this involved. Beyond general comments such as 'can form good relationships with colleagues' and 'puts effort into relationships with colleagues', there were pointers from both groups as to the kinds of qualities needed, such as 'demonstrates friendliness and flexibility with colleagues'. NQTs made many more comments than did the mentors about classroom support and the way this had to be planned for, organised and managed.

NQTs seemed particularly preoccupied with relationships with parents and again, beyond the general comments referring to building positive relationships with parents, particular references seemed to be made to their own experiences. Comments such as 'ability to sort out problems between parent/child', 'ability to negotiate with parents honestly but tactfully', 'ability to act rationally with parents' and 'ability to calm down parents' hinted at a host of stories waiting to be told.

Conclusions

Three different discourses were found to exist within the material described above; how the mentors describe competence is very different from the account given by the DfE. How the NQTs describe it is superficially closer to the DfE's account but on closer analysis it seems that for them the whole business of teaching is more challenging and requires more thought, self-examination and review than anybody seems to appreciate. Both mentors' and NQTs' statements implied a view of teaching as complex, as centrally involving children and relationships with others. They would undoubtedly argue that the DfE account could be improved by the additional recognition that teaching centrally involves building positive, professional relationships with children and that the opportunity to acquire the relevant knowledge about children is made available to teachers early on in their education.

There was no evidence that either group was inclined to reduce their accounts of teaching to simple, discrete checklists of behaviour, quite the contrary. When asked to group the statements under more general headings they found it difficult because 'everything links up with everything else'.

The project did reveal how easy it is for NQTs to become swamped in their first year of teaching by the nuance and particularity of the sheer volume of what they have to deal with. It would seem that a competence framework could support them to move beyond the immediate priorities set by life in the classroom by reminding them of the broader dimensions of the teacher's role and of the need for further professional development is important. What should be the focus of this further study is of course the proper subject of debate.

There were a number of substantial differences between the mentors' and the NQTs' priorities and the language in which these were expressed. It cannot therefore be assumed that a profile framework could merely be picked off the shelf and interpreted uniformly. It would seem then, that school-based induction programmes should begin with a number of professional conversations between mentor and NQT about what a profile of competence means to the parties involved — how they understand the particular document being used, to what extent they agree with it as an account of teaching and what they want to amend or emphasise. The profile can support these conversations but cannot replace them and thus it would seem that competences cannot, on their own, fulfil the early promise of functioning as 'a bridge'.

As with any learning, the profile will depend for much of its success on the rapport which develops between NQT and mentor (a point emphasised by the mentors). This rests as much on the competence of the mentor to mentor (rather than teach) as it does on the receptiveness of the NQT. In addition, a process for using it has to be developed and this in turn is not without its problems (Mahony & Harris 1996). All of it requires a considerable investment of time if the professional needs of mentors as well as NQTs are to be properly recognised. It is at this point that a healthy dose of scepticism is in order.

The Problem with the Context of Competence

The point that for profiles to really support the development of learning to teach, **time** needs to be available for proper professional conversations to occur, is obvious. It is equally obvious that time is what no-one has. We live in a world shaped by market relations in which schools now routinely cost teacher time in the effort to work within their budgets. If we suppress our excitement at the potential of profiles to empower beginning teachers, to make explicit the standards which they are expected to achieve and to insist that the criteria by which they are judged must be open to scrutiny, it is possible to understand the current official enthusiasm for competence-based teacher education as representing a more cynical move.

Markets (even quasi-markets) need products (Le Grand & Bartlett 1993) and it is possible to conceptualise teacher competences as the specification of the product 'teacher' (Sidgwick, Mahony & Hextall 1994) The advantage for the market is that the more explicit and detailed this product specification becomes in relation to competences, the more flexible and transferable they are to new contexts. In addition, the simpler the product specification, the more cheaply it can be produced; it does after all take more for teachers to know **why** than **how**. Furthermore, if teaching is defined according to discrete component parts, then training or education as we know them, could completely disappear — it would be very easy to move financial responsibility from the state to the individual or employer with competences being incrementally consumed.

Even if we are not yet far along this path, competences can already be seen to fit well into the new managerialist agenda with its emphasis on constant self improvement (to enable schools to remain competitive and 'up to the wire'), increased control over teachers work by more sophisticated methods of surveillance (to ensure cost effective ways of working) and initiatives encouraging individualistic rather than collective action. It may only be a matter of time before the competences outlined for new headteachers in the Headlamp scheme (TTA 1994) become the basis for performance-related pay.

The issues which face us for the future are considerable. We need to maximise the opportunities to develop adequate profiling systems. This means clarifying what is involved in good practice and what is involved in developing it. It means being prepared to assert collectively that quality cannot be achieved individually or 'on the cheap' and that the question should not be 'Can we afford to educate our teachers well'? but rather 'Can we afford not to'? Above all it means keeping a watchful eye on the purposes to which competences are put, empowerment or social control.

References

Carroll, L. (1872) *Alice Through the Looking Glass* The Nonsuch Press: London

Carter, J., Johnson, G. & Mahony, P. (1994) *Competence-based Approaches to Professional Development: Newly Qualified Teacher and Mentor Perspectives*, Wandsworth LEA

Department of Education Northern Ireland, (1993) *Review of Initial Teacher Training (ITT) in Northern Ireland: report of the development group*

Devereux, C. (1995) 'Competences for Initial and Continuing Teacher Education', unpublished paper

DfE (1992a) 'The Induction of Newly Qualified Teachers' *Administrative Memorandum 2/92*

DfE (1992b) 'Initial Teacher Training (Secondary Phase)', *Circular 9/92*, Department for Education

DfE (1993) 'The Initial Training of Primary School Teachers: New Criteria for Courses', *Circular 14/93*, Department for Education

Early, P. (1992) *Beyond Initial Teacher Training: Induction and the Role of the LEA*, NFER: London

Furlong, J. (1992) 'The Limits of Competence: A Cautionary Note on Circular 9/92', UCET Annual Conference, Oxford

HMI (1992) *The Induction and Probation of New Teachers*, 1988-'91

Inman, S., Mahony, P. & Sidgwick, S. (1994) 'Partnership in Practice: The Goldsmiths Model' in (ed) Williams, A. *Issues in Teacher Education*, Falmer Press: Lewes

Johnson, G. (1994) 'The Project Design' in Carter, J., Johnson, G. & Mahony, P. *Competence-based Approaches to Professional Development: Newly Qualified Teacher and Mentor Perspectives*, Wandsworth LEA

Le Grand, J. & Bartlett, W. (eds.) (1993) *Quasi-Markets and Social Policy,* MacMillan: London

Mahony, P. (1992) 'The Development of Competences in Initial Teacher Education at Goldsmiths: Issues and Concerns', ESRC seminar paper, Manchester

Mahony, P. & Harris, V. (1996) 'Competences and the First Year of Teaching' in (eds) Hustler D. & McIntyre D., *Developing Competent Teachers,* David Fulton Publishers: London forthcoming

Major, J. (1992) Extract from Speech to the 109th Conservative Party Conference at Brighton, Oct. 1992 reprinted in Chitty, C. & Simonds, B. (eds) (1993) *Education Answers Back: critical responses to government policy*, Lawrence & Wishart: London

Menter, I. and Whitehead, J. (1992) 'Response to Request for Information on Mentoring', seminar paper, Bristol

Norris, N. (1991) 'The Trouble with Competence' *Cambridge Journal of Education*, Vol, 21 No. 23, pp 331-341

Patten, J. (1992) Extract from Speech to the 109th Conservative Party Conference at Brighton, Oct. 1992 reprinted in Chitty C. & Simonds, B. (eds) (1993) *Education Answers Back: critical responses to government policy*, Lawrence & Wishart: London

Sidgwick, S., Mahony, P. & Hextall, I. (1993) 'Policy and Practice in the Professional Development of Teachers' *International Studies in the Sociology of Education*, 3 (1) pp. 91-107

Sidgwick, S., Mahony, P. & Hextall, I. (1994) 'A Gap in the Market?' in *British Journal of Sociology of Education*, Vol. 15. No. 4 pp. 467-479

TTA (1994) 'The Headlamp Scheme' Teacher Training Agency

Whitty, G and Willmott, E, (1991) 'Competence-based Teacher Education: Approaches and Issues', *Cambridge Journal of Education*, 21 (3) pp. 309-317

Chapter Fourteen

Some Value Conflicts Experienced by Women in the Workplace

Rita A. Knutsen
Marlene K. Malenda

"What else do women do but work? We were married at the height of the Depression and I had to work because there were few jobs and little money. When our first child was born my husband had lost his job and hadn't found a new one. He stayed home and cared for our daughter and even dusted! I was lucky there! Years later when he had a business and we had two children I continued to work sewing dresses. I also helped him in the store and did the housework. Women never have time to relax . . . there's always something to do. We wanted our children to have what we didn't — an education — and that takes money. I always worried that the kids would get sick . . . it would have been easier on me if I didn't have to work, but what about my husband? We were a team."

Connie, 82-year-old woman,
former seamstress

If you believe what you read in history books, the prosperity of the United States is absolutely man made. Very few female names appear in the index of any standard economic history of the United States. Prior to the 1980's, "if the word 'women' occurred in the index at all, it referred to the remarks on the growing trend of women employed outside the home or the impact of their 'emancipation' on the birthrate."[1]

Economic historians concede women's work has always been a part of the economy and essential to it, but they did not think it necessary to pay special attention to it. In this paper we will attempt to give a voice to some of the value conflicts experienced by women in the workplace. These value conflicts, as well as personal interests, clearly influenced and motivated one woman to found a successful family business. This experience will be noted.

*****

It is no secret that the majority of American women work because they have to. Over the past decade studies have repeatedly shown that without two incomes, many families would not make it from one paycheck to the next. Today, working to indulge an ego need alone is as antiquated as love beads. According to a new study *Women: The New Providers* released in early May 1995 by the Families and Work Institute, a New York non-profit research group, in 45 percent of dual-earner households, women earn about half or more of the income. When you take into consideration the women in single-parent households, the numbers become even more striking: 55 percent of all working women make about half or more of the household income.

Reflecting upon this information, it remains startling to see what University of Washington sociologist Julie Brines found in a 1995 study of income and housework — wives do the overwhelming amount of chores no matter what percentage of the income they bring home. Not surprisingly, in traditional families women's work is greatest and it decreases as the family income increases. However, Brines goes on to say that "when women's earnings skyrocket past their mates', the husbands retreat to their La-Z-Boy lounge chairs."[2]

The truth remains that working women experience a variety of opposing messages and with these messages value conflicts vis-a-vis their roles in society. Some of these value conflicts seem to be trans-cultural, while others appear to be peculiar to the United States. Historically women have been expected to be responsible for child care and household supervision — two areas in which working women appear to experience significant amounts of stress and tension.

In her well-researched book *The Second Shift*, Arlie Hochschild declares, "One reason women take a deeper interest than men in the problems of juggling work with family life is that even when husbands happily shared the hours of work, their wives felt more responsible for home and children. More women kept track of doctor's appointments and arranged for playmates to come over.

"Partly because of this, more women than men felt torn between one sense of urgency and another, between the need to soothe a child's fear of being left at day care, and the need to show the boss she is 'serious' at work. More women than men questioned how good they were as parents, or if they did not, they questioned why they were not questioning it. More often than men, women alternated between living in their ambition and standing apart from it."[3]

After work I have little energy or patience to spend playing with my daughter and even less time for household chores. I am always concerned about earning enough money and worry about keeping my daughter in day care . . . sometimes I think that she thinks she only must do what her teachers tell her to do and not me!

> Laurie, 26-year-old single parent,
> inbound freight coordinator for a major toy chain

This conflict is alluded to in an article on women's employment which appeared in the *U. S. Department of Labor Statistics Journal* for April 1995. The piece stated that often women choose to leave full-time employment for part-time positions or total unemployment "because of unequal distribution of responsibilities at home including responsibilities for housekeeping, cooking and child care."[4] Women are the ones who most often take on the obligations of managing relationships within the family and outside it as well. Women are often penalized for appearing too intelligent, too assertive and/or too attractive. In order to fully accept these roles, women have often given up their economic opportunities and their independence. They often opt out of participation in civic activities (a networking opportunity from which more men benefit), to say nothing of putting their obligation for personal well-being at the very end of the "things to do" list.

Someone has said that men apologize for their weaknesses; women apologize for their strengths. It does not take an excessive amount of reflection on the conversations you have had with both males and females to affirm that observation at least 95 percent of the time.

In their book, *Members of the Club, the Coming of Age of Executive Women*, authors Dawn-Marie Driscoll and Carol Goldberg report, "Striking differences between men and women at the top of the corporate or professional ladder should not be minimized. The higher a woman's education, the more likely she is to be employed and the less likely is she to have children. Two-thirds of women under the age of 40 who have reached the upper echelons in companies are childless. This fact alone suggests that they are quite different from their male peers, virtually all of whom are fathers, many whose wives do not work outside the home."[5]

Obviously successful women executives flourish because of the choices they make. Some choose career over parenthood while others focus on their career because of the inability to bear a child. More often than not, these women become successful in a way known to men — long hours of work and the possession of the appropriate credentials.

"In 1989 *The Harvard Business Review* published an article by Felice N. Schwartz, president and founder of Catalyst, an organization that had been working with corporations since 1962 on issues concerning women. Schwartz proposed that corporations distinguish between two types of women, those who were career-primary and the career-and-family sort."[6] It became apparent that a "Mommy track" was being encouraged in businesses. This track was peopled by those women who would interrupt their careers to care for their children, returning to work after their children were established in school and no longer needed as much attention. This hiatus has been accepted as a fact of life since corporate structures were unable to accommodate them.

"Feminists leapt to attention, because clearly Felice Schwartz was suggesting that corporations institutionalize the so-called 'Mommy track.' Though she never used the term, a few months before her article was published, *The New York Times* had reported that some law firms had informally established a special 'track' for mothers, assigning them less demanding work. The catch was that they would never make partner. Many feminists were sure that top businesses would use the concept of a' Mommy track' as an excuse to keep women out of top positions. Why couldn't Schwartz have spoken of a 'parent track' they demanded — of the need to offer concessions to fathers as well as mothers?

"Once again, equality feminists felt the best, and most practical, approach was gender-neutral. Lynn Hecht Schafran, for example, noted that lawyers notoriously worked long hours and had a high divorce rate. The men, too, were concerned about the toll on their families, and many hoped that, as more women entered the profession, its demands would lessen. So far that hadn't been true."[7]

Not all women with families have reduced their work commitments. An increasing number of women have managed to handle both a demanding job and an active home life. The description of this working-woman's life appeared in a woman's magazine in the late 1970's and was praised and presented as a model of sorts. Listen to her story and imagine her life:

"She rushes from home to work in the morning, eating yogurt in the car for breakfast; has lunch at the spa where she works out; leaves child care to her husband, who also has a managerial position forty miles from home; pilots a small plane in her leisure time for pleasure; teaches a class on the side at a local junior college leaving the children with grandma or with sitters." [8]

This lifestyle could be called "keeping up with the hamsters." Today a much larger number of women appear to be more interested in developing additional family time and, thankfully, have begun to take another look at the world inhabited by "Supermom."

Those who seem best able to handle a demanding career and an active family life are those women who are very organized and whose attitude is positive and happy. They are women who, for the most part, have rejected the traditional notion of their being the primary caretaker. The men in these relationships take an active part in parenting and a responsibility for the household. With the couple's combined incomes, people are hired to perform various tasks or family members assume these roles. Here the family functions as a cooperative unit. Other families choose a team approach, hiring full-time household help with the housekeeper and/or the nanny sharing in the day-to-day responsibilities.

However, this applies to a very small percentage of working couples. Know that in the United States only 5.5 to 6 percent of women operate at this level with the ability to make these life choices. The vast majority of working women are not involved in exciting careers. Like most men they are not getting rich at their jobs. According to the U. S. Department of Labor, the overwhelming majority of working women make less than $25,000.00 a year.

The May 22, 1995, issue of *Newsweek* reports, "Jobs in the growing service sector have gone primarily to women. And that . . . coupled with the facts that more women are entering the job market with college educations and more are refusing to drop out to rear children . . . has helped narrow the gap between men's and women's wages. In 1965, women earned 59.9 cents for every dollar men earned; by 1990, the gap had shrunk to 71.6."[9]

What happens with the money that is earned? "A 1992 study found that in upper-income, two-earner families, 68 percent of the second paycheck goes to child care, household help, clothing, transportation, and other work-related costs."[10] This reality is one of the primary reasons why a woman struggling with the pressure to leave her child in another's care seriously considers leaving the workplace. "Yet for every woman unhappy in a job who has taken advantage of the opportunity her husband's income affords her to leave, probably fifty to a hundred others have not even allowed themselves to contemplate such a possibility . . . It is not simply their own fears they must contend with; they must also confront a chorus of other voices warning them not to leave their careers behind. 'Our fathers and mothers who underwrote higher education remind us that our careers won't wait forever and we didn't go to college for nothing,' Kim Triedman, a twenty-nine-year-old video producer, wrote in a *Ms. Magazine* article about her decision to stay home with her daughter. 'Our employers give us explicit policy on maternity leave . . . and subtler shows of our bosses' displeasure. Our husbands let us know that the mortgage is due and our bank balances are dropping.' "[11]

> "My mother always told me to study hard, get into a good college and marry a nice Jewish cardiologist. I guess I didn't study hard enough. Mom was very disappointed after I received my Master's degree in chemical engineering and decided to stay home with my children. After all, having a daughter who is an engineer is more prestigious than having a daughter who is just a mom . . . . Anyway, life is long and I have lots of years ahead to work. Right now my children are young and no one can do a better job raising them than I can."
>
> Donna, a thirty-six-year-old mother of two,
> chemical engineer on hiatus

"Throughout the 1980's, a woman with a college education and good job prospects whose principal occupation was that of a homemaker could expect to be viewed like a leper. In a 1985 survey of the alumni of Harvard and Stanford, nearly half of the people questioned said that women who stayed at home were less respected than women who worked . . . By the 1990's, however, women in certain circles who decided to stay home were no longer so much shunned as they were used as sounding boards." [12]

Perhaps this opinion, along with the feelings experienced by women themselves regarding their varied roles of employee, mother, wife, homemaker led to more and more women starting up their own businesses. This is a notable trend.

In a national study recently released by the National Foundation for Women Business Owners and Dun & Bradstreet Information Services, it was discovered that women-owned businesses now employ 35 percent more people in the United States than the Fortune 500 companies employ worldwide.

"The study, *Women-Owned Businesses: Breaking the Boundaries . . . The Progress and Achievement of Women-Owned Enterprises*, reports that women-owned businesses now number 7.7 million, provide jobs for 15.5 million people and generate nearly $1.4 trillion in sales.

"Women-owned firms, while expanding in numbers and employment levels, have also remained viable over the long term. Nearly three-quarters of the commercially active women-owned firms in existence in 1991 are still around today, compared to only two-thirds of all commercially active firms." [13]

Let us now take a closer look at the experience of Rita A. Knutsen, one woman who began carving out a place for herself and her family in the world of business. Here are some of the circumstances and decisions she made which led to her success.

A Focus on One Woman's Experience Which Led to Founding a Family Business

"When I went to school in Italy, they gave me an examination to see which one of us would be able to go on for more schooling. I got the best grade — higher than the mayor's son! But we were just peasants, and my mother didn't realize how important it would be for me. I wasn't allowed to go. Several years later, I came to the United States with just my mother and my sister — three women alone. I was 16 so I had to work. My sister was too young to work. She was only 13. My mother was too old. She was 40."

Words Spoken to Rita by her Grandmother

Founding a successful business which employs all the members of my nuclear family and 230 others is a challenge I readily accepted somewhat inadvertently. The force which drove me was one for security, in addition to one well known to working women with children — the stress of caring for a family.

I am currently the C.E.O. of Quest I, a multi-purpose health and tennis club, as well as The Fountain, a European-style day spa. Together these businesses grossed $5,500,000 in 1994 and are expected to top $6,500,000 in 1995.

I was born to a mother who had the good fortune to be educated during the 1920's to become a teacher. Not long after I was born my parents were divorced and my mother was left with the daunting task of raising a daughter on her own. To do this she had two full-time jobs. Materially I wanted for nothing, even though I was born during the Depression and my childhood was darkened by World War II.

When I was ten years old, I was sent away to boarding school. The value system I learned from this experience was that money equaled security. I thought that I had rebelled against that notion, for all I ever wanted was a family.

After graduating from high school, I attended college for a year and received an Associate's degree in secretarial work. At the end of that year, when I was eighteen years of age, I married. My dream was to be a wife and mother who stayed at home and raised her children, or so I thought. Sealing the pact to work together as a family unit, my husband and I moved to a dairy farm in New York State where he had worked each summer as a teenager.

Our first child, a daughter Karen, was born to us when I was nineteen and our second child, a son Harold, Jr., was born two years later. During that time we had rented a farm and began our own dairy. In the midst of having children and struggling to maintain our dream of being an intact working family — to say nothing of keeping the farm afloat — I discovered that I had a knack for sales.

I began selling home cleaning products to area housewives. I could do this in the evenings when Harold was home to care for the children. He provided the appropriate parental supervision, saving us the expense of a babysitter. From this business I went on to work for another company selling china and crystal to young women who were engaged to be married. It wasn't long before I was offered a job as unit manager. I turned it down because I knew I didn't want to depend on anyone but myself to be successful — and successful I was! By working only four evenings out of seven, I was earning $200 a week which was a considerable sum of money in 1953. With that money we were able to not only feed our family, but the cows as well.

Dairy farming requires considerable hard work. To support the farm an additional income was imperative from the very beginning in order for our business as well as our family to survive. It wasn't long before we realized that we were in financial distress. Remaining dairy farmers would prevent us from getting out from under the debt which we were incurring. We had to give up our dream of living quietly and simply on a farm. After paying our creditors, we moved back to New Jersey, living temporarily with family.

Our first successful business venture was a flower shop. Here I had some experience as my stepfather owned a florist shop where I had helped after school as a teen. My mother inherited this business when he died. Upon our arrival we were encouraged to open a branch flower shop in a nearby community which had a store available for rent. The location was ideal — next door to a funeral home and near several churches. It also had a small apartment where our family could live. Harold and I had an agreement — I would provide the brains and he the brawn. Together we would be successful. To learn the creative side of being a florist, Harold went to design school. On the other hand, I was responsible for the business management of the flower shop, an interesting inversion of roles that only occurred to me later.

The shop was flourishing and once again I discovered that I was pregnant. There was no way that the five of us were going to be able to live comfortably in a three-room apartment, so we purchased a house within walking distance of the shop and the children's school. The location of our home was crucially important to us as we wanted our children to be with us after school hours so that we could supervise their activities properly and they would have an opportunity to experience some responsibility for the family business.

I gave birth to our third child, a son Jeff, when I was twenty-five. He was born prematurely and was diagnosed with multiple handicaps. Needless to say, this was a devastating blow to Harold and to me. This was also another pivotal point which gave me incentive to found a successful family business. We resolved that this child was going to have the best medical and educational opportunities available. Indeed, this desire would demand significant financial and emotional resources. We decided to hire a housekeeper for a short time and this freed me to create a larger and more prosperous business. Three years later, Harold wanted to purchase a second store. When I expressed my concern that we did not have the necessary funding to proceed and that I didn't know how I could operate two stores, Harold told me, "Don't worry. You will figure it out." Harold's faith in me had not wavered.

My life became increasingly absorbed in developing various systems for our flower business — purchasing flowers, keeping samples ready in the stores, managing finances — all the various tasks which consume people involved in operating a small business. However, I was also very much aware of my responsibility to care for our children, especially our youngest son whose cerebral palsy left him with small and large motor coordination problems and with speech and hearing difficulties as well.

While maintaining my work schedule, I had to include a one-hour round trip three times a week to a special nursery school for children afflicted with cerebral palsy. Every Saturday I drove Jeff to the New York League for the Hard of Hearing where he learned lip reading and received speech therapy. One summer I transported him five days a week for six weeks to a special program. Our hope was for Jeff to have a life that was as normal and as unencumbered as his older siblings. This was, perhaps, an unrealistic expectation, but we worked hard to achieve that goal.

In an attempt to be fair to our other children, Karen received dance lessons and I became a den mother for Harold, Jr.'s Cub Scout pack. I didn't want to neglect our children in any way. My belief was that my children were extremely fortunate in having both of their parents available and accessible to them. Everything in their lives would receive the attention of at least one, if not both, of their parents. Again, I fed my fantasies of being the PERFECT mother! I cooked nutritious meals — roast beef, mashed potatoes, only *fresh* vegetables, homemade soups and pasta sauces. My experience growing up in an Italian household was that the mother was expected to cook, and to cook well and at all times. That was the message I absorbed as a child and reinforced by my mother who would often call to ask what I had prepared for the family's dinner.

Frequently personal needs prompted my civic and business pursuits. This is most evident in my decision to become involved in the exercise and fitness market which is very much a part of the culture of the United States. For example, the children, particularly Jeff, were in need of a place to swim regularly in the summer and to have a place for supervised recreation when school was not in session. Consequently, I became part of a town board of directors which decided to build a swim club. This effort was so important to me that I was willing to personally sign for the loan at the bank that would finance the project.

Simultaneously we began a side business called Creative Foliage. We actually built large artificial plants for office buildings and provided a service to clean them as well. It began as an experiment. Harold had become quite talented as a floral designer. When artificial flowers and plants became fashionable, we were asked by a local bank to do several very large arrangements for their offices and the public areas of the bank. Since we really had no idea what to charge them for our services, we sent them what we thought was an enormous bill. After clarifying a few items, the bank paid the bill in full and rewarded us with additional business!

This windfall led us to set our sights even higher! We paid off our home mortgage and expanded Creative Foliage which became a more commercially competitive venture. By the time we decided to phase out the business, our older son was involved in the company and we were already in the process of building a tennis club (but I'm getting ahead of myself).

When our children were fourteen, twelve and nine years of age, we moved to a more suburban community. After a summer of driving back and forth to our former community where the children could participate in the swim club's programs, I decided to interest the residents of our new community in a similar club. It was at that time that I spearheaded a private, non-profit cooperative swim and tennis club — all of this while we had two flower shops, Creative Foliage and were involved in directing the swim club!

Our life was crowded with activity, but life was more than just work. We enjoyed a wide circle of friends and always took the time to relax and enjoy living. Tennis was becoming a very popular sport, especially among the growing upper-middle class. Since I had been involved in the building of two not-for-profit civic tennis and swim clubs, I was convinced that I had the experience to build one for our family. I began referring to this undertaking as the "Two for Love, One for Money" phase of our lives.

I sought out three successful business men to become my partners in this endeavor, Ramsey Racquet Club, an indoor tennis facility built in 1975. Three years later after lengthy negotiations, we bought out the partners since I sensed that this tennis club would be our best opportunity for a family-run business. We sold the flower shops, phased out Creative Foliage and were on our way once again.

The tennis club was so successful that we decided to take it one step further and expand it into a health and fitness center. This was the beginning of the big dream — Quest I — the possible dream! We assumed an even heavier financial burden. The new physical layout was designed, a fresh business plan was drawn up and an additional 15,000 square feet of space was added to our building — a building that already occupied 40,000 square feet. This current multi-purpose facility includes an indoor track and a swimming pool, whirlpool baths, steam rooms, saunas, cardiovascular and weight training equipment, a snack bar, a sports attire boutique and a large physical therapy/sports medicine center. Quest I is a place that is good for promoting physical health, to say nothing of one's appearance. In addition to providing work and income for the family, I found myself with a host of other employees — receptionists, personal trainers, physical therapists, aerobic exercise instructors, coaches, lifeguards, secretaries, managers, bookkeepers, accountants, attorneys — all occupations necessary for this type of business. Strangely enough, the majority of them are women!

A good idea is something that I find irresistible, and so I decided to add another feature to the club — a European-style day spa. Since Quest I is located in an affluent part of New Jersey, The Fountain was born to serve the needs of the "Baby Boom" population. As a group, "Baby Boomers" are stressed, accustomed to indulging themselves and they are committed to fighting the aging process. Although The Fountain has an identity all its own, it is capitalizing on the reputation and the membership base of Quest I.

Over the past ten years, there has been a marked increase in the number of resort spas across the United States. As a result, a large segment of the affluent population has come to appreciate the benefits of regular massages, facials and various body treatments offered at these resorts. Our clientele express a desire to avail themselves of these offerings on a regular basis. This phase of our business, begun eighteen months ago, is flourishing.

I take great pride in the large number of women employees — a significant majority of our staff. I am also proud of the fact that our company serves our employees' needs in many ways. We offer flex-time scheduling and after-school care. Part-time employees may take school vacations off to be with their children and, for those who wish, our employees have the option of having their children participate in our summer camp programs at greatly reduced rates. I am presently looking into the feasibility of expanding our child care facility.

My employees know that my door is always open to them and that I am a willing listener to their personal concerns. I find it easy to empathize with the harried and hectic pace of their lives and I have frequently assisted them in adjusting their work schedules to help make their parenting less burdensome. I have offered counsel where I could and have even participated in a training program for counselors.

At this point in my life, I see myself as a person who has gained an enormous amount of wisdom and life experience — not only as an adept entrepreneur, but, more importantly, as a married woman who has most often viewed herself as a working mother.

The conflict I have yet to resolve is the tension created by my dual roles of mother and employer to my children. In my attempt to give them economic independence, I seem to have made them dependent on me for their livelihood. It is my hope that I will work out that conflict before I enter the next phase of my life.

Some Encouraging Signs of Support for Women in the Workplace

"What women have brought and will continue to bring to the workplace is a break with the past. They have made things visibly different and in doing so have called into question the ways that things have been done until now."[14]

There are still significant voices in our society who would like things as they were and wish that the "toothpaste could be pushed back into the tube." However, this is not possible. Some time in the mid to late sixties, women began to have their consciousness raised by the budding feminist movement. Although it was not embraced heartily by all, portions of the feminist agenda were, particularly that part that encouraged equal pay for equal work.

At that time, more women began to look around their split-level houses and ask themselves that age old and serious question, "Is that all there is?" The answer to that query appears to have been a resounding "No!" Women started to pursue higher education toward avenues of employment which were most likely not traditionally female. This was often done by a part-time student who managed to juggle her course load along with her laundry load, reading textbooks while rocking the baby. Frequently these "supermoms," as they were to be known for a time, had at least an additional part-time job as well as a marriage.

Women such as these who sought fulfillment in many areas of their lives are today physicians and professors, attorneys and financial analysts, engineers and small business owners. Their presence in the work place has challenged the status quo and differences are beginning to be noticed.

> Knowing that I could take my baby to work with me was a relief! He wasn't in the office with me, but in the day care facility provided by the company for which I work. It made getting there on time easier since I didn't have an extra stop. Besides, I'm able to spend lunchtime with him if I like so that I can feed him.
>
> Peggy, 32 years of age,
> human resources manager for pharmaceutical firm

There are many more companies in the nineties that can be considered family friendly. "The number of employers in the United States offering child care assistance rose from 110 in 1978 to 7,000 in 1990, says research analyst Daniel Dreyer of Work Force Program. The increase from 1989 to 1990 was remarkable: from 4,200 to 7,000."[15]

The Voucher Corporation's Lend-A-Hand Child Care Assistance Program offers support to working parents in a creative manner. Parents with children too sick to attend school or day care often have to miss work, but not if their company is enrolled in this program. "The plan provides participating employers with the names of qualified sick-child care providers in their area and advises parents to preregister with any three. The employer pays at least half or all of the cost of the care. Parents then have the services of a trained care giver sent to the home or can leave the child at a hospital or day care center with a drop-in facility for sick children."[16]

The value of flex time is mentioned by many women who work for companies which provide the option. Beginning work earlier than usual is a boon for those parents who have a problem with after-school care. Most people would rather begin work at 7:00 a.m. than at 10:00 a.m. since they can avoid the worst of the commuter traffic and can be home by the time the children return on the school bus.

Jobs with flexible schedules are also necessary for people involved in caring for the elderly. "Company surveys show that, typically, 7 percent to 12 percent of workers report having some responsibility of an older relative now, but by 2020 an estimated one in three will have elder-care responsibilities, says Andrew Scharlach, professor of aging at the University of California at Berkeley. Three demographic trends are predicted behind the surge: The population is aging rapidly, people with chronic illnesses are living longer, and more women . . . who make up three-quarters of those who care for the elderly . . . are in the work force than ever before."[17]

I help care for my husband's father and both my parents all of whom live in New York City. This means that I travel in every other day to clean, cook, and take them to doctors' appointments. Fortunately, my job allows for great flexibility and I can often rearrange my schedule to serve their needs. Without my husband's help and the aid of my teenaged children, I do not think I could manage.

Lidia, 45 years of age,
married mother of three,
administrative assistant

"In a 1992 study by the Families and Work Institute of 305 workers caring for elderly relatives, 25 percent had changed jobs because of their responsibilities, 39 percent reported being distracted at work, 22 percent had considered quitting and 14 percent had dropped out of the work force altogether. Elder-care responsibilities end up costing companies $17 billion a year, or 2,500 per care giver per year, including time missed from work and the cost of replacing employees who quit to care for relatives . . . In fact, managers and executives, arguably the employees companies can least afford to lose, are often those hardest hit by elder-care problems. That's because they are generally in the forty to sixty age range, when responsibilities for an aging relative are most common. Partly because the issue has affected so many high level executives personally, the number of elder-care programs has grown rapidly in a short time."[18]

*****

In conclusion, there is an obvious abundance of material on the issues of working women and their concerns and needs which will continue to surface. It is evident that many corporations (both large and small) are grappling with these problems. Some businesses presently offer programs that are helpful to women in their dual roles of homemaker and wage earner. Some efforts, while small, are notable and their number and scope will continue to grow as the number of women in the workplace increases.

Freud commented on two ingredients for the good life — work and love. In 1995 women, and most likely men as well, would add — and the time to enjoy both. One can only hope that the business community will reach beyond producing a sizable profit for its shareholders and realize that the inclusion of family well-being could be a boon to "the bottom line."

Notes

1. Caroline Bird, *Enterprising Women* (New York: W. W. Norton & Co., 1976), p. 18.
2. Michele Ingrassia and Pat Wingert, "The New Providers," *Newsweek* (May 22,1995), p. 36.
3. Arlie Hochschild, *The Second Shift* (New York: Viking Press, 1989), pp. 7-8.
4. *U. S. Department of Labor Statistics Journal* (April 1995), p. 43.
5. Dawn Marie Driscoll and Carol Goldberg, *Members of the Club, the Coming of Age of Executive Women* (New York: The Free Press, 1992), p. 102.
6. Flora Davis, *Moving the Mountain* (New York: Simon & Schuster, 1991), p. 304.
7. *Ibid.*, p. 304.
8. *Woman's Day* (February 1978).
9. Ingrassia and Wingert, "The New Providers," pp. 36-38.
10. Barry Glassner, Career Crash (New York: Simon & Schuster, 1994), pp. 78-79.
11. *Ibid.*, p. 80.
12. Barry Glassner, *Career Crash*, p. 78.
13. *Suburban News* (May 24, 1995), p. 25.
14. Susan Easton, Joan Mills and Diane Winokur, *Equal to the Task* (New York: Seaview Books, 1982), p. 168.
15. Patricia Aburdene and John Naisbett, *Megatrends for Women* (New York: Vallard Books, 1992), p. 235.
16. *Working Woman* (March 1995), p. 10.
17. Julia Lawler, "Why Companies Should Care," *Working Woman* (June 1995), p. 38.
18. *Ibid.*, p. 41.

Chapter Fifteen

Professional Attitudes, Judgment and Confidentiality: Tensions in School-Linked Services*

Michael E. Manley-Casimir
Mary T. Hall

Introduction

The proposal that the neighborhood school should assume a pivotal role in linking health and social services to education so that children (and their families) receive the most complete array of services available to support their educational development, presents a singularly daunting challenge for schools and for those teachers and administrators (inter alia) who work there. The idea and practice of schools providing a variety of non-educational services to students is well-established. In the United States schools have historically acted as the locus for a variety of health services, food programs and other social services (Tyack, 1992). So the movement to establish the school as the pivot of "integrated" or "coordinated" services is a logical extension of existing practice.

*   Previously published in R. Levin (Ed.) (1994), *Greater than the Sum: Professionals in a Comprehensive Services Model* (pp. 63-77). Washington: American Association of Colleges for Teacher Education. Reprinted with permission.

Other jurisdictions are moving in similar directions. In Britain, for example, the recently enacted Children's Act (1989) effectively replaces a patchwork quilt of older legislation with a comprehensive and coherent legislative framework for the care and nurture of children—a framework that incorporates both private and public law. In Canada, extensive examinations of childrens' services have provoked new legislative initiatives and policy consolidation in the provinces of Quebec (1985), Ontario (1987), and Nova Scotia (1990). In British Columbia the recent Sullivan Royal Commission on Education acknowledged "the school [as] the only public agency required, by law, to deliver services to all children in a given age range," and so argued that the school was "...the natural site where integrated services might be planned and, indeed, delivered" by other agencies (Royal Commission on Education, 1989). The movement towards some form of integrated children's services with the public school as the hub of such services is clearly powerful and eliciting considerable support.

What, however, is distinctive about these various proposals is the explicit affirmation of the school as *the* central social agency responsible for inclusive social welfare directed towards children, youth and their families. Such an affirmation, while fully understandable and perhaps desirable, presents a 'thicket' of administrative tensions and difficulties affecting the possibility of successful implementation.

Among the many tensions and difficulties inherent in these proposals—difficulties that are well-documented elsewhere (Morrill, 1992; Kirst, & McLaughlin & Massell, 1990), the tasks of achieving effective coordination and collaboration between the school and other service providing agencies seem particularly problematic because they require the development of new modes of working between and among professionals from a variety of disciplines, occupations, ideologies and practices—professionals whose roles in the past have not necessarily required the extent or kind of close cooperation and collaboration essential to effective implementation of school-linked services.

The purpose of this chapter, then, is to explore these "across-professions interactions" (Crowson, Smylie & Hare, 1993, p. 2) in terms of three dimensions of administrative practice—the tensions flowing from distinctive professional ideologies, norms and attitudes, from distinctive views of the use of judgment in administrative decision-making, and from conflicting approaches to the need for confidentiality in special relationships involving students and their families. The chapter begins with an argument in favor of the proposition that schools should become the pivot of service linkage on the grounds that each child is entitled to the best available array of services to maximize his or her potential; it then proceeds to examine the related tensions in across-professions interactions and concludes by identifying the pre-conditions and strategies necessary for successful resolution of these tensions.

The Case for the Child

David Tyack (1992, pp. 28-39) attributes current reform proposals to two visions that serve as political imperatives: one is that of *the nation at risk*—a vision predicated on the need to ensure the maximum educational and social development of each child/student to enable the United States to maintain its international competitive advantage; the other is that of *children at risk*—a vision predicated on the extreme and unacceptable differences in service provision to children whose lives are blighted by familial dysfunctions: poverty, abuse, homelessness, poor nutrition, *inter alia*. These imperatives drive the current proposals to establish a coordinated approach to school-linked services. While the power of these visions is clear, we start here from a conception undergirding both these visions: a conception of the child as a person uniquely entitled to these services, not to satisfy political imperatives nor to overcome the ravages of poverty, though both are important, but rather to affirm the idiosyncratic value of each child as a person in community.

Such a view implies a re-definition of the relationship of child and family to school—what elsewhere I have referred to as a new social compact (Manley-Casimir, 1988). The choice of the word 'compact' was made to convey the idea of an agreement characterized by common consent—one that is normative in conception and design but not primarily nor even necessarily legally enforceable or constitutionally compatible, though both might become true through processes of constitutional and legislative change or judicial affirmation.

The definition of a new social compact involving the child in the society or the student in the school inevitably derives from a conception of childhood on the one hand and a conception of society's interest in and responsibility towards children on the other. Such a conception of the role of the child and the responsibility of society to the child itself rests on implicit or explicit assumptions about the value of the child *qua* child, of the child as a young member of the community and of the child as a future adult member of the society; such a conception also rests on assumptions about the best interest of children and young people, about the standards of care necessary for physical, emotional and spiritual health and development, about the needs and stages of maturation of the young, about the tension between dependency and independence, about the limits of childhood and beginning of adulthood (Skolnick, 1975). These assumptions all imply normative judgments about the child in the culture, the value placed on the child and childhood, and consequently implicate policy decisions flowing from such judgments.

Defining Principles and Elements of New Social Compact

Articulating a new social compact addressing the relationship of child or youth to society, and of student to school requires a perspective, a framework that allows us to think systematically about the issue of 'rights' in a coherent way. Such talk of rights flows from a general conception of relationships and entitlements of persons in a community. Martin Golding (1968) suggests that the social ideal governing the community determines the system of rights enjoyed by the members of that community. The rights are derived from the social ideal. So, for example, in the United States the U.S. Constitution, interpreted and extended by judicial interpretations, embodies the social ideal to which Americans commit themselves and to which U.S. society aspires. Golding's schema includes two types of rights—option-rights and welfare-rights. The heart of option-rights is the idea that individuals possess a limited sovereignty over property, things, and themselves. The individual's personal sovereignty is limited by the sovereignty others can claim, by duties to others, and by duty to self. Otherwise individuals may act at their *option* or discretion.

Welfare-rights complement option-rights. Just as freedom is central to option-rights, so equality is central to welfare-rights. Welfare-rights are essentially the rights of community members to an equitable share of the material goods and services of the community. As Golding notes:

> These are welfare-rights, and are rights to the goods of life or are derived from such rights. The great expansion of rights in modern times has taken place in respect of welfare rights. Treitschke, I believe, has been credited with the statement that the greatest modern innovation is the idea that every person has a right to an education, and this would fall into the category of welfare rights. (Golding, 1968, p. 543)

Clearly the problematic issue concerns full membership status in the community. Full members (usually defined as 'legal adults') claim all the option-rights and welfare-rights to which they are entitled by the terms of the ideal. The question at issue is to what extent do those who are less than full members enjoy the rights which the ideal imports? Traditionally, children and teenagers are considered minors, that is, not full community members and consequently not entitled to the rights enjoyed by a full member. This is a misleading and mistaken view. It is clearly difficult to argue persuasively that children should be free to exercise as a child the option-rights they will exercise as an adult. Arguments can be made that the exercise of such rights in the community and school should be 'developmental'; that is, that children and youth should be given the opportunity to learn about such rights, the nature of rights, the duties and obligations of such rights and to practice the exercise of these in school. When they show the capacity to exercise these rights responsibly then, the developmental view holds (Magsino, 1977-78), they should be granted the freedom to do so. Such a proposal is educationally defensible but practically difficult, because students will evince the maturity to exercise rights responsibly at different stages and ages. Further, as I have argued elsewhere, such a view of rights in the context of schools implies a radical re-structuring of schools as organizations away from the definition of traditional, authoritarian bureaucracies and towards constitutional, i.e. rule and rights governed bureaucracies (Manley-Casimir, 1980).

The issue of welfare rights is, however, an entirely different matter. There is no reason in principle why the full array of welfare-rights should not be conferred on each and every individual child and student. In that welfare-rights imply an equitable share of the essential goods and services of the society, and in that education is one of these essential services, there is a compelling reason to extend the welfare right of education to every student. The claim of the young to welfare rights, however, goes beyond education; just as children and youth need quality schooling and education, so too they need quality shelter, food, clothing, medical care, love and emotional support, *inter alia*. Just as hungry school children cannot concentrate on lessons and learning when their stomachs are growling, so too emotionally or physically abused youngsters cannot attend to school or homework when their homes are cells of despair and oppression.

The entitlement to the welfare right of education is a **substantive** statement that involves not just issues of quantity, i.e., number of years of formal schooling, but issues of curricular choice, access to opportunity, compensatory education, quality of instruction, to mention only some of the most obvious. The entitlement also implies, however, that the material, psychological, and medical conditions necessary to benefit from educational services are also present and available; hence access to and provision of appropriate services is an essential pre-condition for educational success.

What, then, does such a view imply about the properties of a social compact? If we agree that children and youth are entitled to education as a welfare right, then we are saying that the community has a responsibility to ensure that the necessary and sufficient conditions for the realization of that welfare right are in place for each and every child. The affirmation of education as a welfare right also carries with it the principle that the realization of the right must attend to the needs of the individual child or student; this in turn implies not "uniform" or "same" treatment but treatment that is "fitting" to the special needs and circumstances of the particular child.

The acceptance by the community at large of the responsibility to provide the necessary and sufficient conditions for the educational benefit of each child and that the necessary and sufficient conditions are predicated on "fittingness" reflects the three dominant elements in the social compact: responsibility, caring and community. Such a view may be construed as collectivist and may as a result be anathema for some. Such is not the intent. It proceeds from the recognition that the primary responsibility for the welfare of children lies with the family; it proceeds also from the recognition that as children grow to young adulthood they have a responsibility to develop their own faculties and capacities; but it also acknowledges that for some people life is hard, unbearably hard, and under these conditions the community at large has a responsibility to care for and help those disadvantaged "families" and children.

At root this view holds high the value of the child in the culture. Trite though it may be, it must be so because the child is the future. And, quite aside from motives of self-interest, the child *qua* child is entitled to the affirmation of self, in all ways that will foster the development of autonomy, rational action and emotional health requisite to adulthood.

The social compact proposed here acknowledges the importance of socialization but does not permit this to be either the only or even the primary goal of public education: the primary goal of public education must be to develop in children and youth the capacity for autonomy and a sense of personal responsibility, the capacity for rational action following critical reflection and ethical deliberation, the capacity for productive and fulfilling labour, and the capacity for emotional health, caring and compassion for those less fortunate.

For the social compact to be achieved, for children and youth to maximize their educational development, it is practically necessary for school-linked services to be available. Several models of service delivery are possible but all imply a central role for the school.

The Central Role of the School

The need to provide youth and their families with school-linked services is compelling. Thornburg, Hoffman and Remeika (1991) recognize the key role of schools in addressing the needs of children and families:

> Schools must adapt to the changes in family structure, values and attitudes, and the economy. They must work with the conditions and outcomes these changes have created in ways that will undoubtedly be very different than in the past and even today. Change is never easy and always takes time—time that is running out. Schools, however, must take time to make the crucial changes necessary. Collaborating with other community service programs to alter the conditions that place children, youth, families, and society at risk is a must! (Thornburg et al., 1991, p. 207)

"School leaders have increasingly realized that the education system alone has neither the ability nor political clout to address the full range of children's problems" (Jehl & Kirst, 1992, p. 97).

The current demand for school-linked, integrated services emerges from present economic and social imperatives.   "As the economy falters and competition with other countries intensifies, there is a great concern about the decline in children's economic and social conditions, as well as dissatisfaction with school outcomes" (Jehl & Kirst, 1992, p. 97).   Previous attempts in the 1960's and 1970's to integrate children's services revealed that the extensive needs of children could only be met by recognizing the central role of the school and by encouraging the involvement of other agencies.   The effective provision of school-linked services, therefore, imply collaboration of professionals from a variety of agencies and traditions.   Effecting such collaboration requires recognition and resolution of the tensions that may arise in across-professions interactions.

Tensions in Across-Professions Interactions

The collaborative approach, while commendable, must resolve tensions between: interdependency and professional autonomy, joint ownership of decisions and professional discretion, collective responsibility and professional mandate, power dispersion and control of power, and confidentiality and information sharing.   Fundamental distrust may be at their core.   Finklehor, et al. (1984) note "…collaborations are not always easy to initiate.   They often require the surmounting of institutional mistrust that has grown up over many years" (p. 214).   An examination of the potential tensions in a collaborative approach may reveal clues to overcoming this mistrust.

Interdependency and Professional Autonomy

A central premise of the collaborative approach is the belief that an exchange of ideas produces solutions that agencies working independently are unable to achieve.   Professionals from a range of disciplines are likely to be both encouraged and threatened by this observation.   They may be encouraged to the extent that recognition of limitations is often a first step towards solutions.   At the same time, their professional autonomy may be threatened by the suggestion of cooperative problem solving.   Bayles (1988) notes a common feature of professionals is the autonomous nature of their work.   He argues that the monopolistic view of a professional often contributes to conflict with other professions over domains.   Is it possible to plan and implement a collaborative approach, while allowing professionals to maintain a degree of autonomy?   The initial stages of collaboration often include drawing attention to stakeholders' mutual concerns.   This exercise serves to heighten stakeholders awareness of their interdependence and potential for mutual problem solving (Gray, 1989).

Joint Ownership of Decisions and Professional Discretion

Responsibility for identifying and solving problems rests on the participants in a collaborative approach. The competition between value systems and professional perspectives require debate, analysis and accommodation through negotiations, allowing for a more complete understanding of the problem. ". . . the outcome of collaboration is a weaving together of multiple and diverse viewpoints into a mosaic replete with new insights and directions for action agreed on by all the stakeholders" (Gray, 1989, p. 14). The role played by the school principal is crucial to the creation of effective collaborative decision-making (Jehl & Kirst, 1992); so much will rest on the capacity of the principal to recognize and value the discretion professionals bring to their definitions of self and to the task at hand.

Manley-Casimir (1990), following Davis (1969), argues that the exercise of discretion is central to administrative decision making, and Bayles (1988) argues that professional autonomy is dependent to some extent on the exercise of discretion. Adler and Asquith's (1981) paper on discretion and power reveals the inherent tension between professional discretion and shared decision making.

> Although the professions have extremely wide discretion, the power and status of the professional groups concerned and the esoteric nature of their professional knowledge have, on the whole, ensured that professional prerogatives have gone unquestioned. (Adler & Asquith, 1981, p. 15)

A collaborative approach does not imply that professionals forfeit their exercise of discretion. The challenge involves achieving a balance of professional discretion and shared decision making. Professionals from a range of school-linked, integrated services need to meet this challenge in their pursuit of a common goal—to address the needs of children and their families. Successful collaboration requires mutual respect for individual values and professional ideologies.

The influence of individual values and professional ideologies is central to both joint decision-making and discretionary decision-making. The collaborative approach attempts to reconcile individual values and professional ideologies in pursuit of a common purpose—to clarify the problem and offer direction for solutions.

> When stakeholders hold conflicting values and widely differing perspectives on the problem, initial interactions must be designed to promote valid exchange of information and to search for common ways of framing the problem. (Gray, 1985, p. 925)

This view is consistent with Trute, Adkins and MacDonald's (1992) observation that a shared ideology among key professionals is critical to coordinated services.

In a similar vein, a growing body of research recognizes the influence of values on the use of discretion in administrative decision-making. Vickers (1985), for example, notes "...the dominance of governing human values must be taken for granted in any study of the process; and it is these values which select and in part create the 'facts' which are to be observed and regulated" (p. 96). Begley and Leithwood (1989) identify the significant influence of personal values on administrative decision-making. Greenfield (1986) and Hodgkinson (1988) are strong proponents for further research focusing on the value aspects of administrative behaviour. A closer examination of the influence of values in both joint and discretionary decision-making will provide a key to relieving the tensions between these two approaches.

Collective Responsibility and Professional Mandate

...ownership of the collaboration must be shared within the group. If the process of developing school-linked services is seen as an effort to fulfill a particular agency's agenda at the expense of another's, the process will fail. (Jehl & Kirst, 1992, p. 100)

Heath and McLaughlin (1987) note successful collaborative efforts must overcome "entrenched notions of 'turf' and entitlements" (p. 580) by bureaucratic and professional groups. Collaboration involves negotiation of a new set of relationships among the stakeholders (Gray, 1989). Shared responsibility is central to these relationships according to Jehl and Kirst (1992). They suggest collegiality as a possible resolution of the tension between professionals accustomed to fulfilling their own mandates and shared responsibility. The development of a common philosophy will contribute to collegiality.

Trute, Adkins, and MacDonald (1992) examine the differences in philosophy between police, child welfare and community mental health in regards to child sexual abuse. Their concluding remarks offer a possible resolution to this third tension. "The challenge is to create an interdisciplinary atmosphere where these differences in approach can be resolved, and where each professional group can fulfill its professional mandate, while finding a course of intervention that serves in the best interest of the victimized child and his or her family" (Trute et al., 1992, p. 367).

Power Dispersion and Control of Power

At the outset, it is critical for a school-linked coordinated service program to consider the power balance among stakeholders. Gray and Hay (1986) caution:

Powerful stakeholders who perceive they have little or no interdependence with others will undoubtedly try to preserve their individual control over the domain and will resist collaborative interventions that aim to balance power among the stakeholders. (p. 99)

Gardener (1992) identifies equal partnerships between 'stakeholders' as a key issue in the development of school-linked integrated services. "...increasingly, management will be about horizontal partnerships among agencies and firms that do not control, but depend upon, each other" (p. 91). Power dispersion allows stakeholders greater control over the problem (Gray, 1985). Gray argues, however, that equal power distribution is neither necessary nor desirable, as it can lead to inaction. Gray and Hay (1986) identify expertise, control of the public policy process, and resources as possible sources of power to support or oppose the project; in addition, participants in collaboration gain a degree of power.

Confidentiality and Information Sharing

A fifth tension present in across-professions interactions concerns the issue of confidentiality in dealing with children, youth and their families in the context of school-linked services. The tension arises because human service professional are usually bound both by legal duties and professional norms of confidentiality in their relationships with clients. The sharing of secrets between client and professional lies at the heart of the confidential relationship. As Bok notes

> Confidentiality refers to the boundaries surrounding shared secrets and to the process of guarding these boundaries. While confidentiality protects much that is not in fact secret, personal secrets lie at its core. The innermost, the vulnerable, often the shameful: these aspects of self-disclosure help explain why one name for professional confidentiality has been "the professional secret." (Bok, 1988, p 231)

Without knowledge of secrets shared, professionals are unable to discharge their roles effectively. So, in the context of school-linked services, where a number of different agencies and associated professional individuals are involved, the problem of information sharing becomes acute and necessarily implicates the issue of confidential information.

A joint report of Joining Forces, the Center for Law and Social Policy and the Education Commission of the States, "Confidentiality and Collaboration: Information Sharing in Interagency Efforts" provides an excellent discussion of these issues, identifies the various dimensions of the problem and the tensions at work, yet concludes that "...it is possible to develop means of exchanging information that are effective and practical on a wide scale, while still respecting legitimate rights to privacy" (Joining Forces, et al., 1992, p. 2).

The central principle permitting interagency information sharing and collaboration is that of "informed consent." Providing the individual about whom confidential information is held gives informed consent for the release of that information to specific people, for specific purposes, the duty of confidentiality can be legitimately breached. Such a practice must satisfy federal and state law but is workable. "Some of the most promising interagency approaches are ones that affirmatively embrace the idea that informed consent for the release of information is part of empowering the individual as an active participant in resolving personal and family issues" (Joining Forces, et al., 1992, p. 2).

The provision of medical services to students through school based clinics raises more complex issues of confidentiality and personal privacy. Since many students are legal minors, it is usual for informed consent to come from parents or legal guardians. Courts and legislatures have, however, recognized the need to treat adolescents differently so they can receive essential medical services on an independent and confidential basis (English and Tereszkiewicz, 1988, p. 7). States permit minors to consent to medical care in a variety of situations; provisions extend both to the emancipated minor (one who is essentially independent) and to the mature minor (one who is capable of making an informed decision). In these cases informed consent can be given by the minor. English and Tereszkiewicz advise practitioners to take the minor's age, intellectual or cognitive maturity and ability to understand the information to be disclosed into consideration in evaluating his or her capacity to give informed consent.

The Challenge of Effective Inter-Agency Collaboration

An increasing body of literature documents the need for a collaborative approach in the provision of comprehensive support for youth and their families. "The problems faced by children and families are simply too large and too complex to be taken on alone by any one system" (Levy & Shepardson, 1992, p. 46). Collaborative planning and subsequent collaborative action is necessary to address the diverse needs of children (Thornburg, et al., 1991). A high level of communication and cooperation is critical to a successful collaborative relationship (Dryfoos, 1991). Jehl and Kirst (1992) point out that schools play a pivotal role in addressing the multiplicity of children's issues evident in our society. Schools, however, are unable to address these issues alone—they must collaborate with other community agencies.

> For school-linked service efforts to be effective, the participating agencies will have to change how they deliver services to children and families and how they work with each other. (Larson et al., 1992, p. 9)

The possibility of school-linked services being successful in focusing the variety of health and social services on the needs of children, youth and their families will clearly depend on effective interagency collaboration. Central to the success of this collaboration is the leadership of the individuals representing the various organizations involved but particularly crucial is the leadership role of the principal of the school in effecting a culture fostering genuine collaboration (Rallis, 1990, pp. 198-205).

'Collaboration', as Barbara Gray advances, requires as a pre-condition the recognition by the stakeholders in the situation that they have a shared interest in advancing their joint vision (Gray, 1989, p. 6). In the case of school-linked services, such interest must involve the marshalling and coordination of the best available services to support and enhance the general welfare of the child and family and the particular educational progress of the student in school. Such a joint vision, or something very similar, must form the joint purpose of collaborating agencies. Furthermore, the agency representatives must not only agree to the joint vision in principle, but must also develop and sustain a clear and abiding commitment to this sense of purpose. Without this sustained and dedicated sense of purpose the collaboration will not last. Possible key stakeholders in a collaborative approach to school-linked services include representatives from education, parent groups, business, religious groups, health and social agencies, the criminal justice system and youth. Opportunities for collaboration involve two categories: resolving conflicts and sharing a vision. Gray identifies the following key elements as essential to successful collaboration:

1. the stakeholders are interdependent,
2. solutions emerge by dealing constructively with differences,
3. joint ownership of decisions is involved,
4. stakeholders assume collective responsibility for the future direction of the domain, and
5. collaboration is an emergent process. (Gray, 1989, p. 11)

The weaving together of different viewpoints and perspectives in the sense of a joint vision is essential to effective collaboration. Such mind-meeting and perspective-acceptance generates a sustaining ethic of legitimacy to the joint enterprise prerequisite to the next step—the marshalling of resources from diverse sources in support of the common sense of purpose—the best possible social support for the educational development of the youth of today, the citizens of tomorrow.

References

Adler, M., & Asquith, S. (1981). "Discretion and Power." In Michael Adler & Stewart Asquith (Eds.), *Discretion and Welfare* (pp. 9-32). London: Heinemann Educational Books.

Bayles, M.D. (1988). "The Professions." In Joan C. Callahan (Ed.), *Ethical Issues in Professional Life* (pp. 27-35). Oxford: Oxford University Press.

Begley, P.T., & Leithwood, K.A. (1989). "The Influence of Values on the Practices of School Administrators," *Journal of Educational Administration and Foundations,* 4(2), pp. 26-39.

Bok, S. (1988). "The Limits of Confidentiality." In J.C. Callahan (Ed.), *Ethical Issues in Professional Life* (pp. 230-239). New York: Oxford University Press.

British Columbia. (1989). *Royal Commission on Education: A Legacy for Learners.* Victoria: Queens Printer.

Crowson, R.L., Smylie, M.A., & Chou, V.J. (1994). Administrative Issues in Coordinated Children's Services: A Chicago Case Study. In R. Levin (Ed.), *Greater than the Sum: Professionals in a Comprehensive Services Model* (pp. 115-126). Washington: American Association of Colleges for Teacher Education.

Davis, K.C. (1969). *Discretionary Justice.* Baton Rouge: Louisiana State University Press.

Dryfoos, J.G. (1991). "School-Based Social and Health services for At-Risk Students," *Urban Education,* 26(1) (April), pp. 118-137.

English, A., & Tereszkiewicz, L. (1988). *School-Based Health Clinics: Legal Issues.* San Francisco: National Centre for Youth Law.

Finklehor, D., Gomez-Schwartz, B., & Horowitz, J. (1984). "Professional's Responses." In D. Finklehor (Ed.), *Child Sexual Abuse: New Theory and Research* (pp. 200-215). New York: Free Press.

Gardener, S.L. (1992). "Key Issues in Developing School-Linked, Integrated Services," *The Future of Children: School Linked Services,* 2(1) (Spring), pp. 85-94.

Golding, M.P. (1968). "Towards a Theory of Human Rights," *The Monist,* 52(4) (October), pp. 521-49.

Gray, B. (1985). "Conditions Facilitating Interorganizational Collaboration," *Human Relations,* 38(10), pp. 911-936.

Gray, B. (1989). *Collaborating.* San Francisco: Jossey-Bass.

Gray, B., & Hay, T.M. (1986). "Political Limits to Interorganizational Consensus and Change," *The Journal of Applied Behavioral Science,* 22(2), pp. 95-112.

Greenfield, T.B. (1986). "The Decline and Fall of Science in Educational Administration," *Interchange,* 17(2) (Summer), pp. 57-80.

Heath, S.B., & McLaughlin, M.W. (1987). "A Child Resource Policy: Moving Beyond Dependence on School and Family," *Phi Delta Kappan,* (April), pp. 576-580.

Hodgkinson, C. (1986). *The Value Bases of Administrative Action.* Paper presented at the American Educational Research Association, San Francisco.

Jehl, J., & Kirst, M. (1992). "Getting Ready to Provide School-Linked Services: What Schools Must Do," *The Future of Children: School Linked Services,* 2(1) (Spring), pp. 95-106.

Joining Forces, Center for Law and Social Policy, Education Commission of the States. (1992). *Confidentiality and Collaboration: Information Sharing in Interagency Efforts*. Denver: ECS.

Kirst, M.W., McLaughlin, M., and Massell, D. (1990). "Rethinking Policy for Children: Implications for Educational Administration." In B. Mitchell & L.L. Cunningham (Eds.), *Educational Leadership and Changing Contexts of Families, Communities and Schools* (pp. 69-90). Eighty-Ninth Yearbook of N.S.S.E., Chicago.

Larson, C.S., Gomby, D.S., Shiono, P.H., Lewit, E.M., & Behrman, R.E. (1992). "Analysis," *The Future of Children: School Linked Services*, 2(1) (Spring), pp. 6-16.

Levy, J.E., & Shepardson, W. (1992). A Look at School-Linked Service Efforts. *The Future of Children: School Linked Services*, 2(1) (Spring), pp. 44-55.

Magsino, R. (1977-78). "Students Rights in Canada: Nonsense Upon Stilts?", *Interchange*, 8(1-2), pp. 52-70.

Manley-Casimir, M.E. (1980). "The School as a Constitutional Bureaucracy." In Don B. Cochrane and M. Manley-Casimir (Eds.), *The Development of Moral Reasoning* (pp. 69-81). New York: Praeger.

Manley-Casimir, M.E. (1988). *Responsibility and Caring in Community*. Unpublished report submitted to the Royal Commission on Education, Simon Fraser University.

Manley-Casimir, M.E. (1991). Taking the Road not Taken: Reframing Educational Administration for Another Day. In P. Ribbins, R. Glatter, T. Simkins, & L. Watson (Eds.), *Developing Educational Leaders* (pp. 115-132). Harlow, UK: Longmans.

Morill, W.A. (1992). "Overview of Service Delivery to Children," *The Future of Children: School Linked Services*, 2(1) (Spring), pp. 32-43.

Nova Scotia. (1990). *Services to Children and Their Families Act*, Chapter 5.

Ontario. (1987). *Child and Family Services Act*. Statutes of Ontario, Chapter 55.

Quebec. (1985). *Youth Protection Act*. RSQ Chapter (p. 34.1).

Rallis, S.F. (1990). "Professional Teachers and Restructured Schools: Leadership Challenges." In B. Mitchell & L.L. Cunningham (Eds.), *Educational Leadership and Changing Contexts of Families, Communities and Schools* (pp. 184-209). Eighty-Ninth Yearbook of N.S.S.E., Chicago.

Skolnick, A. (1975). "The Limits of Childhood," *Law and Contemporary Problems*, 39, pp. 38-43.

Thornburg, K.R., Hoffman, S., & Remeika, C. (1991). "Youth at Risk; Society at Risk," *The Elementary School Journal*, 91(3), pp. 199-207.

Trute, B., Adkins, E., & MacDonald, G. (1992). "Professional Attitudes Regarding the Sexual Abuse of Children: Comparing Police, Child Welfare and Community Health," *Child Abuse and Neglect*, 16, pp. 359-368.

Tyack, D. (1992, Spring). "Health and Social Services in Public Schools: Historical Perspectives," *The Future of Children: School Linked Services*, 2(1), pp. 19-31.

Vickers, S.G. (1965). *The Art of Judgment*. London: Chapman and Hall.

Chapter Sixteen

First Year Transitions from the Law School to the Courtroom: A Paradigm of Value and Ethical Conflicts Faced by New Professionals and Their Educators

James Clark
Edward Monahan

Law: The Maligned, Troubled Profession

America is experiencing the dark flowering of what some scholars have called the "crisis of the professions." As Donald Schon has observed:

> Professionals claim to contribute to social well-being, putting their clients' needs ahead of their own, and holding themselves accountable to standards of competence and morality. But both popular and scholarly critics accuse the professions of serving themselves at the expense of their clients, ignoring their obligations to public service, and failing to police themselves effectively.... The crisis of confidence in the professions, and perhaps also the decline in professional effectiveness in the larger sense, seems to be rooted in a skeptical reassessment of the professions' actual contribution to society's well-being through the delivery of competent services based on special knowledge. (Schon, 1983, pp. 11-13)

Instilling Values in the Educational Process

The October 1994 *Gallup Poll Monthly* reported that 46% of a randomized sample of Americans responded that they considered the "honesty and ethical standards" of lawyers as "low or very low;" while 36% ranked attorneys as "average," 14% as "high," and only 3% as "very high." Pharmacists, clergy, dentists, and college teachers ranked at the top four positions of the list of twenty-five professions, indicating a high level of public trust in these professionals; U.S. senators, insurance salesmen, U.S. congressmen, and car salesmen ranked at the bottom of the list. In the area of honesty and ethical standards, the public ranked lawyers at 17 among 25 professional groups— eight slots from the bottom (McAneny and Moore, 1994). This ranking might be confounded by the fact that the majority of politicians are also attorneys.

There are few social institutions more denigrated in contemporary America than the profession of law. Such public hatred is not a new phenomenon. There was probably tremendous audience response to Shakespeare's "The first thing we do, let's kill all the lawyers" (*Henry IV*, Act 3, Scene, 4). But it is paradoxical for Americans to despise those professionals on whom they must rely for protection and advocacy in any major business or legal endeavor they pursue. Not only that, America is a democracy founded on a written constitution and those rights and protections contained in that foundational document of values. In the face of any government action against a citizen, the criminal defense lawyer is the first and virtually only line of defense. Furthermore, despite their attitude, Americans are watching criminal trials on television in numbers that have justified the founding of a special cable channel devoted to televising trials, *Court T.V.*

How can we explain this state of affairs? If we focus for purposes of this paper on the criminal defense bar, the most available conclusion is that Americans have grown weary of the machinations of defense attorneys, especially in pursuit of "special excuses" like insanity and extreme emotional disturbance. Many social scientists and legal scholars mark the watershed year as 1982 when John Hinckley was found "not guilty by reason of insanity" of attempting to assassinate President Ronald Reagan (Low, Jeffries, and Bonnie, 1986). Public opinion polls indicated that 85% of the American public thought justice was not done; while 75% stated that they did not favor the use of the insanity as legitimate defense. After a twenty-five year judicial trend of bringing mental health explanations into the courtroom and thereby expanding potential criminal defenses, government officials (spurred on by citizen outrage) began the nationwide reform of the insanity defense which has resulted in far more narrow acceptance of mental health evidence in American state and federal courts. What is probably most interesting about the *Hinckley* case is that it was a statistical aberration of utmost symbolic importance. The insanity defense is employed in only 1% of all felony cases, but it continues to be seen by the public as representative of the corruption of the American legal system (Perlin, 1989, p. 390).

It is critical to note that the anger has come not only from outside the legal profession; the self-criticism has also been harsh. For example, in his Sonnett lecture at Fordham Law School in 1973, United States Supreme Court Chief Justice Warren E. Burger despaired over the inadequacy of representation of trial attorneys: "To say that we have a 'crisis' in the availability of adequate legal services may go too far, but sober, careful and responsible observers of the legal profession have posed the need in precisely those terms" (Burger, 1973, p. 227). In fact, Burger presented the British legal profession as probably superior with its specialized litigators, fewer lawyers (only one-tenth specializing in trial work), a viable system of apprenticeship, and a unique professional community of barristers. Furthermore, Burger noted that "The focus of the inadequacies of [American] advocates has tended to center on the criminal process, and it is plainly correct that this be given close attention and high priority" (1973, p. 236).

A 1978 survey of federal judges found that 41.3% believed that there was a serious problem with the adequacy of attorney's trial performance (Devitt et al., 1979, p. 219). A much more recent survey of appellate judges found that they considered 14% of legal counsel in the American appellate system to be ineffective (Rapp, 1992, p. 296). And in an American Bar Association monograph entitled *Criminal Justice in Crisis*, a blue-ribbon panel reported that resources for attorneys representing poor people were profoundly inadequate and that this often resulted in "inferior representation" (American Bar Association, 1988, p. 43). As Supreme Court Justice William Brennan argued, "We cannot accept the notion that lawyers are one of the punishments a person receives merely for being accused of a crime" (*Jones v. Barnes*, 1973, p. 3319).

One eminent trial lawyer recently assessed the state-of-affairs in America's felony courts as so deleterious that the "judgements of the criminal courts cannot be seen as legitimate and entitled to respect so long as such poor quality of representation is tolerated " (Bright, 1994, p. 1880). Such inadequacy is even more troubling because it is in the context of increasing public demands in the United States for stiffer criminal penalties, mandatory sentencing, and widespread support for death sentences.

Providing the best quality representation to persons facing loss of life or imprisonment should be the highest priority of legislatures, the judiciary, and the bar. However, the reality is that it is not. So long as the substandard representation that is seen today is tolerated in the criminal courts, at the very least, this lack of commitment to equal justice should be acknowledged and the power of courts should be limited. So long as juries and judges are deprived of critical information and the Bill of Rights is ignored in the most emotionally and politically charged cases due to deficient legal representation, the courts should not be authorized to impose the extreme and irrevocable penalty of death. Otherwise, the death penalty will continue to be imposed, not upon those who commit the worst crimes, but upon those who have the misfortune to be assigned the worst lawyers. (Bright, 1994, p. 1883)

Critics lament the inadequacies of law school education in preparing aspiring lawyers for practice, especially regarding the practical skills of interviewing and counseling clients, interviewing witnesses, and negotiating. Even those who dispute the scope of this so-called "competence crisis" have acknowledged the need for reasonable and thoughtful incremental change in legal education and recognize that there is a significant level of incompetent performance (Crampton and Jensen, 1979, p. 269; Maddi, 1978, p. 144).

What are the implications of such inadequate professional performance for the law school? Recognizing the continued need to ensure the competence of lawyers, the American Bar Association (ABA) launched an extensive study of the systems of legal education and professional development of practicing attorneys in the United States. This 1989 study, called the *ABA Task Force on Law Schools and the Profession: Narrowing the Gap* (widely known as the "McCrate Report") found no "gap" yawned between the professional school and courtroom. Rather, the study proclaimed that legal educators and practicing attorneys were, in fact, "engaged in a common enterprise— the education and professional development of the members of a great profession" (ABA Task Force on Law Schools and the Profession, 1992, p. 3). Nonetheless, the report recommended that law schools promote the infusion of practical skills coursework in order to better prepare students for the realities of post-graduate practice.

While praising the spirit of the recommendations, law school deans and faculties nonetheless have argued that such changes in the professional curriculum as radical and impractical. Certainly it would be optimal to ensure that law schools would have "law students so well trained experientially in craft and values that shortly after graduation they will render 'competent' service to their clients." While noble in intention, the McCrate Report's "vision cannot be achieved absent a society, a profession, and universities' central administrations that are willing to pay a price for such training. None has chosen to do so, and the law schools and their students cannot possibly do so by themselves. The problem, in short, is predominantly economic, not pedagogical. Exhortation alone will not solve it" (Costonis, 1993, p. 197).

Law schools were only part of the McCrate Report's scheme. It conceptualized legal education as involving law school as a significant but only initial step to be followed by careful preparation for the bar exam, intensive "in house" training and mentoring in the new attorney's place of employment, and finally, life-long continuing legal education. An important, counterintuitive finding was that "American programs of transition education suffer from a surfeit of substantive law and a concomitant lack of skills instruction" (ABA Task Force on Law Schools and the Profession, 1992, p. 293). This is in great contrast to legal training in the Commonwealth jurisdictions which focus on the development of practice skills in the context of learn-by-doing/feedback formats.

Therefore, one important remedy for the crisis in the legal profession is to recognize the importance of continuing education programs, especially through increasing the sophistication and intensity of their curricula. The Task Force recommended that such programs should focus on *fundamental lawyering skills* (problem solving; legal analysis and reasoning; legal research; factual investigation; communication, counseling, and negotiation; litigation and alternative dispute-resolution; organization and management of legal work, and recognizing and resolving ethical dilemmas), and on the *fundamental values of the profession* (provision of competent representation; promoting justice, fairness, and morality; improving the profession; and professional self-development. Such program curricula must become "an integral part of the lawyer's continuum of professional development" (ABA Task Force on Law Schools and the Profession, 1992, p. 304).

The ABA Task Force recommendations appear rational and hopeful. But do they sufficiently address the pressing needs of attorneys who embark on particularly challenging endeavors, for example, those entering the public defense bar? Additionally, are there non-rational problems that remain unidentified and therefore unresolved in this powerful profession's self-scrutiny? For example, recent psychological investigations of attorneys suggest other possible reasons for inadequate performance. Attorneys suffer depressive disorders at rates two to four times higher than the general population. Alcoholism and drug abuse plague as many as 25% of attorneys who have practiced twenty years or more. The common burden of work overload is an extremely serious problem, and although "the deteriorating work environment has not led to a mass exodus from the profession, it has affected the lawyers' quality of work and productivity, their firms, their clients, their satisfaction with the profession, and their families" (Benjamin and Sales, 1992, p. 288). These studies also indicate that the inability to successfully balance work and healthy personal functioning may result from earlier law school socialization to the notion that "the firm" and "the career" deserve complete loyalty regardless of the personal cost. The ultimate irony is that not only is personal happiness compromised, but in the long run, the possibility of successful and ethical professional practice is as well (Monahan and Clark, 1995, p. 318).

Finally, what if Schon and his like-minded colleagues are correct in their argument that professions as effective social institutions are failing? Then, it would seem that the crises in ethics, values, performance, and reputation that plague the profession of law are very likely a paradigm of what other professions are experiencing in America and probably not easily remedied by traditional continuing education programs or any other single response. If this is true, then the newly graduated lawyer who enters this complex arena not only faces the challenge of mastering his craft in the service of his clients, but must contend with a more profound struggle which threatens all he hopes to do and become.

Kentucky Public Defenders: An Exploratory Study

More immediately than in any other branch of the American legal system, the novice public defender is thrust into the formalized warfare of the American courtroom. Public defenders are lawyers hired by local, state and federal governments for the express purpose of providing criminal defense representation to defendants who are unable to pay for private counsel. While colleagues from his law school cohort are clerking for judges, researching tax problems, or otherwise fulfilling the often humdrum duties of a junior associate in a law firm, the new public defender—quite soon after licensing—is trying misdemeanor and felony cases. Private law firms assume many months of apprenticeship must pass before a novice can begin to taste courtroom action and then only as "second chair." Such incremental career movement in the private sector is the time-honored way the young attorney "pays his dues," and learns his craft. Unlike private firms, the public defender agencies lack the financial resources to maintain this tradition.

In contrast, as one observer has noted, "the presumption of competency appears to apply to public defenders from the moment they are appointed to the office—even if they have never before set foot in a courtroom" (McIntyre, 1987, p. 102). In a nutshell, their experience is "trial by fire." Clearly, this group of practitioners provides us with an interesting window into the problems that we have discussed above, because there exists no other group of young attorneys who more desperately need to leave law school with a battery of practical skills.

In order to empirically explore the problems in professional education and development we have thus far discussed, the authors employed focus group, interview, and survey methodologies to better identify, analyze, and understand the problems and experiences of novice public defenders, their supervisors, and their clients. The research was designed to evaluate one of the training programs sponsored by the Commonwealth of Kentucky's Department of Public Advocacy's (DPA) Research and Training Section. The Kentucky legislature established DPA in 1972 upon the recommendation of the governor. There are presently over 100 full-time public defenders in 16 offices across the state serving 43 counties. Another 250 attorneys do part-time public defender work in 74 of Kentucky's 120 counties. DPA is an independent agency, headed by the Public Advocate, overseen by the Public Advocacy Commission, and located in the state's Protection and Regulation Cabinet. Every year DPA represents over 80,000 citizens charged with crimes ranging from drunk driving to capital murder.

The program discussed in this paper was designed to orient and train newly hired attorneys in the areas of the criminal justice system, district court process, plea bargaining, preliminary hearings, juvenile law, expert testimony, post-conviction work, appellate procedure, drafting arguments, oral argumentation, parole hearings, extradition, mental health issues, circuit court procedures, drug cases, child sexual abuse cases, various felony cases, capital punishment cases, sentencing, and probation. Discussion and analysis of ethical dimensions of these skill areas are also confronted throughout the training.

We will first describe some of the major themes raised by a ninety-minute focus group of ten newly-hired public defender attorneys who were finishing this six-week course that spanned nine months. Nine worked as trial litigators, while one was an appellate litigator. Their ages ranged from 24 to 43 years; there were six females and four males in the group. While we cannot claim representativeness since this is a small, nonrandom sample, we present their concerns to illustrate major issues facing new legal professionals.

Although the ABA Task Force found no "gap" between the classroom and the courtroom, several participants indicated their frustration with the anti-practice stance they found in law school:

> I don't want to, I'm dogging the law school process, I know I sound like it, but it's so abstract, it's theory. I heard for three years, "It's not a trade school, we don't teach you to be lawyers, we teach you theory, how to think logically, you want to be an attorney, you do that when you clerk, you do that when you get out." Evidence, when it's a theory and abstract, is so cold and it's hard to ever pick up the situations where you would apply those rules. If you had some hands on experience with that it would make so much more sense and it would be so much easier to learn, and understand the law., But no, the professors say "It's theory, you know, it's law school, we're not teaching you to be a lawyer here...."

Another participant discussed how the isolation of law school reinforced class and cross-cultural barriers that hurt all new graduates, even those colleagues who were not working as public defenders:

> My law school was geared toward private practice business law. Only one criminal course is required and you didn't have time to take other ones if you had to meet the requirements for the school. I just don't think they're geared towards any type of public interest law at all. They don't address that interest in the student body at all and they don't teach you how to deal with clients. You know, I knew people in law school who wanted to be public defenders who had never ever, I mean they couldn't believe that their clients used the word "ain't.". They'd get upset and correct the client's grammar! And I talk to these people now who are doing this type of work who can't communicate with their client and who say that they don't even like being in the same room with their clients, they're afraid to be alone with their clients. Law school just doesn't prepare them for what they're going to be dealing with. Even people who went into private practice get divorce clients who come in with problems and they respond by thinking that "I didn't think my clients were going to come in to cry and you know, why do they do this?" These attorneys just don't know how to deal with clients. Unless you have some kind of other experience than the classroom, you're not going to be effective until after you get into practice and had a lot of experience after law school.

While there were a range of recommendations for law school curricula revisions, this response seemed to indicate the typical desire for some incremental change in professional legal education:

> I think it wouldn't be a bad idea if the law schools would sculpture into their dynamic some method where they would make their professors—who, you know, make all of us toe the line as to their way of doing things—make their professors spend a little bit of time coming out in the field working with trial lawyers every year, maybe two years, make them spend a week or two going around with a trial lawyer. I had fellows teaching me at the law school that I know hadn't walked in a courtroom in five or ten years and so they were brilliant with regard to the particular narrow category that they were dealing with but as far as preparing us to come out and go in the courtroom, they could use a little bit of time going around. I think they would have been better for us because they'd have an idea what it is like to go in that courtroom, address a jury, address the court. Because I think most of them didn't, they don't want to admit it, so they just avoid the subject. I think they were losing the dynamics that they could have helped us with.

Law schools, according to one participant, are less interested in serving the public interest than in maintaining institutional power. This is achieved by "producing" graduates who validate the ambitions of professors who see themselves as launching a new generation of high status professionals.

> I think they need to try to move their curriculum more to help the students that are in the bulk of the middle of the class and who are going to be out there working with the public. They need to emphasize less their motivating or pushing the very top of the class so that they can get students placed in these big law firms. A lot of the professors get a lot of personal satisfaction from bragging how they got a student to go to work for some "Big Ten Firm," and this young person got this huge salary. This is not serving the public as well as trying to do the best job possible for all these students that are going out dealing with the client that needs a public defender, or the person that's getting a divorce and is middle class and needs help, or the poor person that needs to file something. I mean, that's what 80% of us are working with but sometimes the law schools tend to emphasize too much that 5-10% of the "A students" that are getting those big jobs because that's what sort of gives the professors the "at-a-boy." But it doesn't help the state of Kentucky.

Another attorney expressed the overwhelming transition from law school as she entered the courtroom for the first time. Note the speaker's dichotomy between the loftiness of law school methods and the concrete social skills needed to survive in court:

> I think the issue is less whether the Socratic method works, I think the issue is more whether they need to teach people something about how to walk into a

courtroom, where to stand, what to say, and how to make objections, things like that. In law school there was only one course that they had there at the time that taught you like how to prepare an opening statement, how to prepare a closing argument. I didn't get into that course, so when I got out of law school, I knew how to write a brief but I had no idea where to stand. I didn't know how to properly make an objection or anything like that. And the only way I learned it was standing around watching other lawyers do it and the thing is, if they were doing it wrong, then I learned it wrong.

Doing the correct thing, "fitting in," and avoiding humiliation are desirable goals for any person attempting to master an unfamiliar situation. One novice described her experience and surprise when things went well:

All through law school everything we talked about was so theoretical and important, and I just always never felt like I was smart. I really doubted myself a lot. But then getting in there and believing in the client and getting him off, it just made me feel like "I can do this!" I was so excited because then I knew I could do this and I was just really glad I was doing what I was doing. It just made it all worth it.

This yearning for the concrete skills that lead to cognitive and technical mastery is typical of new attorneys. While DPA's training program, in concert with the ABA Task Force's recommendations, stresses the concepts of ethical and principle-centered decision-making, as well as the concepts of self-management and self-development, practitioners see these as more esoteric concerns, secondary to the more important projects of learning rules of evidence, litigation techniques, and, in short, developing ways to win the case. Zero percent of a sample of attorney-supervisors responding to a recent survey listed professional development skills as important (these concern psychological and ethical issues), while eighty-three percent listed practical courtroom skills as the training priority.

Juxtaposing how felony court clients view their young public defenders is revealing. Rather than focussing on lack of technique or their inexperience, one participant in this focus group of prison inmates described what he saw as more significant to the outcome of his trial:

You got a young attorney in the public defender's office. You got a 15 to 20 years experienced judge. He wins election every time he runs for it. You got a seasoned prosecuting attorney standing there. You got this clique, especially in a small town. The young attorney is naturally looking for a future. He's gonna settle down in that town and marry a young lady. He's gonna live in that town for the rest of his life. He knows he's gonna practice in that town as public defender for four years and then move on to private practice. He's got those old judges and prosecutors— they could make life pretty hard on him! If that old clique wants to, they can run him out of town. I think a young public defender is intimidated by all of that. He's thinking too much about his future to offend any of them—he wants us to go along to get along. That's why I worry how much that comes into play when he is making recommendations to me—especially how many years I should take instead of going to trial.

While the novice attorneys and supervisors in our study saw technique as the key to competence, this client—who was supported in his assessment by most inmate participants—identified the critical issues of courage, personal integrity, and the legal professional's ethical imperative to vigorously defend the client. In fact, a content analysis of the inmate focus group reveals the clients' great frustration with public defenders who were all too eager to recommend a guilty plea without thorough investigation of the case.

The development of a relationship with legal counsel was important to the inmate focus group. One participant observed:

> Before the hearing, you would feel better if you talked to the attorney before you went up. That type of reassurance is not a guarantee you're gonna get off, but just the fact that we talked about it and we got some idea of what we are going to court with. But its a time versus money thing. If you don't have money, you don't get much time... Even if he's got a big caseload and hasn't spent the time, he can talk eye to eye to me and don't put me off, and give me a line of bullshit. I've been around. Sit down and be honest, be for-real with me. Just say he was wrong and now let's get to your case. Let's make a wrong a right.

A review of DPA's training programs reveals that courses focussing on the attorney-client relationship and interviewing skills are the least popular of all at trial practice institutes, overshadowed by courses dealing with trial skills like cross-examination. Most novice attorneys, as well as experienced colleagues, see the former as "soft" courses, and far less valuable than the latter, "hard" evidence and trial skills courses. On the other hand, clients see the attorney's ethical commitment and relationship with the client, empathic listening, and respect for client involvement in decision-making as *essential* skills which lay the groundwork for what is actually presented at trial.

Indeed, our new attorney focus group strongly identified the most significant and formative experiences as involving the dynamics and meaning of the attorney-client relationship:

> A gentlemen came in, he was 67 years old, a perfect driving record til that point, got a DUI, took down a telephone pole, since he didn't have any insurance, he had to pay for the telephone pole and for the damage to the corner of some guy's garage. He pled guilty to the DUI, but he was up for a show cause why he hadn't paid for the telephone pole, damage to the garage. He didn't have a car anymore, he and his wife together drew $350 a month social security, that was all they had and they had a house payment and he had medication expenses. He was scared to death he was going to jail and he said

I can't pay it, there's no way I can pay it. I said well, how much money do you make and he told me what they brought in and I said do you have a house payment, the house payment's $200 a month and I said, I'll just enter a motion to the judge to dismiss the fine because you're indigent. And he said, you can do that? I went off, got the file, the form, typed it up, had him sign off on it. I'd only been there about 3 weeks, and we filed it and his wife sent me some construction paper drawing that she made with crayon, little flower with a thank you. I guess he went home and told her what I had done and she sent me these little colors. I thought maybe they were from his grandchild, then he said no it's from his wife, she had been sick and he said he was taking care of her now. That was pretty cool for me because this guy, he was, he had no other course, he didn't know what he was going to do. And the power to help someone like that, you don't know, I never really thought as an attorney we had that much power until you get into criminal law. We have a tremendous amount of power, we really do. It's the power is to hold some life in your hand and you have the power. It's amazing, it really is, I never really thought we could command that much power in the terms that we do, we have the power to set the law, it's tremendous. That guy was my first shot at really out of the door, you know, I had been only working for 2-1/2 weeks.

This attorney was inspired by the validation of her idealism through an emotionally powerful experience. She continues to draw inspiration from this formative experience, even when subsequent cases have been disappointing and disconfirming of her idealism. Ninety percent of the attorney focus group identified similar experiences of serving clients well as their most powerful and meaningful experiences as a lawyer. On the other hand, it is critical to note that some attorneys identify their most powerful formative experiences as being primarily negative. The following example is illustrative:

It was my first arraignment; he robbed somebody and I was to make an argument of why he should have a lower bond and that he should be released on his own recognizance. I was only able to talk with him for two minutes. The client told me that he had never been to court, he had never defaulted. I did great argument. Then the judge stopped me and pulled out a big rap sheet. Then I looked over at the guy, the client, and he didn't give a shit because he had just lied to me and we went back into the jail. I just went off on him, I just swore, I had never been that mad in my life, I just lost it. Well he was so disrespectful. He said we don't understand where people like him are coming from. Well *he* doesn't understand where *I'm* coming from! I grew up in a poor home and I'm doing this shit, you know, public defense, with no money, doing this for free the summer after finishing law school and I'm getting out from him. He gives me that attitude, I can give him attitude!

In this case, the attorney did *not* experience a validation of his aspirations to fight for justice for the deserving poor. This breakdown of intersubjective understanding and identification—the fruits of being humiliated by the client and the judge—is troubling, especially because it suggests that the lesson learned was to avoid believing in and developing relationships with clients. In fact, MacIntyre (1987, p. 161) suggests that some attorneys prefer defending guilty clients because losing such cases is less painful than seeing an innocent client found guilty. While such psychological strategies might be briefly successful in providing self-protection, is it not fair to ask what ramifications such practices have for ethical and high-quality services for clients?

Finally, the attorney focus group was asked to discuss the most significant person they had encountered since law school. Forty percent identified supervisors who had taught them important skills; twenty percent identified a trainer who they had met briefly at a trial practice institute; ten percent identified a peer; ten percent identified a "collage" of people who had helped; ten percent identified a mentor who had invested a great deal in assisting the attorney's development; and ten percent made a "don't know" response.

Implications

Our review and analysis is from the perspective of the novice attorney's struggles during the first year. Rather than having any definitive answers to this complex set of problems, we suggest several lines of reflection and inquiry that our beginning efforts have raised.

First, we consider the two worlds of law school and practice. The heart of being a practitioner of the law in the United States is to vigorously engage the role one plays in the adversary system. The prosecutor is to ensure that justice is done and the community is protected; the judge is to ensure the rules of due process as guaranteed by the Constitution and legislative statutes are respected. The defense attorney's mandate is to do everything possible to defend the life and liberty of the client. In law school this seems reasonable and self-evident. The first years of practice, however, reveal a much more complex and taxing reality. And while public defenders have been schooled in the so-called ways of "legal reasoning," such logarithms offer little to the novice professional struggling with moral, ethical, and personal issues. Even when such concerns are raised, the response is often superficial. Norval Morris has rightfully lamented that answers are "immediately and dogmatically given, based on knee-jerk political, religious, or social attitudes. Answers are given before questions are completed" (Morris, 1992, p. vii).

This state of affairs is not unique to the profession of law, but the loss of vigorous and creative dialogue might be more dangerous for this profession — ancient in origin, profoundly symbolic, and powerfully positioned to influence American society. Is the crisis of performance simply the failure of individual professionals? Some members of the attorney focus group complained that law professors were at fault for not teaching practical skills and for promoting the social rewards of "being a lawyer for the rich." Others were angry at practitioners and even with the DPA for not providing more opportunities for internships. The real crisis is not that law students do not learn enough technique. Most professional schools experience the problem of appearing irrelevant to their students (Rein and White, 1981, p. 37). The real crisis for the first-year professional is that in the rush for technical mastery, the ability to reflect on the philosophical and ethical contexts of practice is too readily forsaken. While law school education is not totally responsible for this, it is possible that the blanket devaluation of practical skills in many law schools creates an unintended "backlash" effect. Instead of being able to actively and thoughtfully integrate principle-centered reflection into their daily practice, novices tend to reject such analysis in favor of the "real" and the "pragmatic." In other words, it becomes more attractive to learn the ways to master, succeed, stand out, and win; philosophical analysis is a distraction better suited to the life of the academic. Now the practitioner hears from the other side, "This is the real world, not law school."

These two worlds seem consistent with the well-known dichotomy proposed by Donald Schon. On one side is the notion of "technical rationality," which is the embrace of systematic knowledge—theory driven and empirically validated. The professional school posits this as the superior approach to education rather than training students in specific skills—or as one of our respondents heard from her law professor—"this isn't a trade school." Professional school, according to such a vision, should be about the business of transmitting this corpus of knowledge and the corresponding epistemological stance to its students who shall emerge ready to apply them in their professional practice (Schon, 1984, p. 33).

On the other side, Schon posits the notion of "knowing-in-action," which emphasizes the process of *in-vivo* responding to the complex realities of daily practice. In other words, what most people consider the "art" of professional practice is included here—all that positivist epistemology considers as unmeasurable, and therefore, insignificant. As one scholar has observed, this creates a problematic split between the educators and the practitioners:

> The lion's share of problems that practitioners confront are situational; when practitioners talk among themselves of knowing, they frequently speak of experience, muddling through, serendipity, tacit knowing, intuition, flashes of insight, or 'just knowing.' It is difficult for professionals to combine knowing and doing. Instead the profession is split between those who take the high ground and those who slog around in the morass, or to put it another way, the profession is split between those who know and those who do.... this phenomenon is manifested in the growing rift between academicians and practitioners—their differences in language, in commitments, and sense of the profession. (Saleeby, 1989, p. 557)

Goethe, the poet *and* scientist, once wrote, "All theory, dear friend, is grey, but the golden tree of actual life springs ever green." Yet the dichotomy between the grey academics and the golden (or green) practitioners is simplistic. There are too many academicians who insist on the complexity of professional contexts—especially the philosophical, existential, and moral dimensions—to dismiss them all as blind, one-dimensional logical positivists. And there are too many practitioners all too ready to embrace technical rationality without thought for the complex contexts of practice. Witness the proliferation of "fads," knowledge delivered in workshop formats and embraced by the busy professional without sufficient analysis. In this dynamic, the professional is also guilty (if that is the correct word) of "committing" a technical rationality, because it allows him to share in the status of doing the scientific or "cutting-edge" thing without examining the validity of the approach for his particular practice context.

Some philosophers have dubbed this the "abuse of casuistry," not because they advocate that the conditions of a specific case must preclude the careful application of ethical principles, but because the rich dialogue between the particular dimensions of a case and the longstanding ethical, legal, and philosophical traditions has been lost (Jones and Toulmin, 1988, p. 342). Ironically, the new lawyer might be in the best position to take up such a dialogue, but is prevented from doing so because he has learned, all too well, that between two alien worlds such communication is impossible.

Canadian and American medical schools have adopted "problem-based learning" curricula to address an analogous problem that many medical students experienced—the gap between pre-med and medical school coursework and the unimaginably demanding work of internship and residency in the hospital. Such curricula push students to build bridges between the important contributions of technical rationality and the artistry of knowledge-in-practice early in their careers. This kind of professional education gives the student a passport and map to navigate among many worlds, enabling him to be rigorous *and* creative in his work. Early reactions to the McCrate Report from legal educators suggest this might be a difficult model to adopt. It would require more than a begrudging allowance for off-campus internships and on-campus legal clinics: it would require a pro-active spirit of experimentation with, and integration of, what has been often devalued.

A second line of analysis suggests that in the pursuit of technical mastery, the novice can forsake the human, intersubjective, and ethical dimensions of practice. The more unprepared the novice is for practice, the greater the likelihood he will be vulnerable to such errors. And, unfortunately, some novices are reinforced in this stance by supervisors who do not recognize the importance of interpersonal and intersubjective experiences. These supervisors insist that technical mastery is the most important dimension of continuing education. However, our exploratory study suggests that novices' experiences which are truly powerful have less to do with the solipsistic "high" of technical mastery and far more to do with the successful enactment of professional tasks in the context of a meaningful attorney-client relationship. The novice attorneys reported that their most powerful events involved positive experiences of intersubjectivity and communion with poor clients. Unfortunately, a review of DPA trial practice institute needs assessment and evaluation studies reveals that courses in the "professional-client relationship" and "client interviewing" are the least popular and most denigrated of continuing education courses.

In an earlier, empirical study of the defendant's perspective of the criminal court process, John Casper found that persons represented by public defenders received sentences comparable to those persons who were represented by retained counsel. Nonetheless, defendants had a significantly lower opinion of the service provided by public defenders. Casper found that public defenders spent significantly less time with clients than retained defense attorneys, and concluded that the public defender's poor ratings was associated with their failure to spend adequate time interviewing and consulting with clients (Casper, 1978, p. 50). The client focus group discussed in this study replicates this finding. Clearly, public defenders neglect this area of practice and training at the peril of developing poor relationships with individual clients and calling down disrepute as a profession.

The third and final line of inquiry that we suggest here addresses the problem of long-term personal and professional development for public defenders. We suggest that the novice public defenders have themselves pointed to the importance of reflecting on their most important experiences. Charles Ogletree has observed that such experiences of empathy and heroism powerfully serve as "motivations to sustain public defenders through trying times" (Ogletree, 1993, p. 1239). Unfortunately, these potential motivations are rarely analyzed by the attorney or his supervisors. Novice attorneys and their supervisors typically do not have the long-range perspective to request or pursue such activities which might help develop a battery of psychological and philosophical skills for long-range survival in a demanding career. In fact, our survey found that supervisors did not consider personal or professional development issues as important domains for continuing education.

If early professional experiences are so powerful, it seems reasonable to argue that they influence the development of "mental models"—cognitive and affective processes through which young attorneys build their life-long schemas of clients. Contemporary cognitive theory would suggest that influencing these person or client schemas is as important an endeavor as teaching specific techniques (Horowitz, 1991, p. 29). In other words, if mentors would guide novices to examine such experiences, they could help influence the quality of the attorney's future work with clients, colleagues, and even opponents. These include experiences of favorable outcomes and disappointing losses and even experiences of humiliation and degradation. There is something important to be learned from every significant experience, but the lesson is fully grasped only if it is explicitly explored. As social activist Myles Horton once opined, "You only learn from the experiences you learn from."

Transcending the role of supervisor, trainer, or coach, the mentor could be a critical figure for novices. In such a relationship, the novice would have the experience of observing and learning from a mentor who enacts complex professional roles with thoughtfulness and skill. In an argument that is reminiscent of Schon's critique of "technical rationality," ethicist Leon Kass asserts that mentors help overcome the gap between moral theory and moral action (Kass, 1990, p. 9).

Such a figure also integrates what might otherwise remain stereotyped and fragmented. Philosopher Michael Oakeshott argues that this is, indeed, the most effective way for any novice to learn to be an ethical and effective person:

> We acquire habits of conduct, not by constructing a way of living upon rules or precepts learned by heart and subsequently practiced, but by living with people who habitually behave in a certain manner; we acquire habits of conduct in the same way we acquire our native language. (Oakeshott, 1962, p. 62)

This philosophical insight has been empirically corroborated by numerous studies which have found that significant learning and personal change in adulthood occur most frequently in the shadow of a powerful, emotional experience (Mahoney, 1991, p. 191). Also critical is the available presence of a "role model," to emotionally support and provide the necessary guidance and structure for the pursuit of high-risk journeys into unknown professional territory (Druckman and Bjork, 1994, p. 198).

The difficulty here is that the role of mentor is tied to an organizational commitment to *invest in novices*, rather than the contemporary approach which only *trains employees* (White, 1995). The high rate of dissatisfied attorneys and the so-called crisis in performance might be less a problem of a "gap" between law school and practice, than the result of the profession's neglect to design organizational contexts for longitudinal professional development. While such an investment might be most heavily weighted at the beginning of the career, organizations also need to invest in the professional development of attorneys in mid-career and near the end of their active careers—especially because they are leading the next generation of professionals

Professional development means more than accumulating continuing legal education credits—it pertains to the maturation and enhancement of the person-in-the-professional. Continuing education in the areas of adult development and personal growth, stress management, dealing with workload dilemmas, advanced work in ethical analysis, and the relationship of personal and professional behavior could be important additions to the traditional fare of continuing education programs. Some programs, including the Kentucky DPA, have begun such efforts. Whether the legal profession as a whole will foot the ideological and financial bills for widespread reform is questionable. But such nontraditional concerns might prove an important counterpoint to the existing discussion.

The perplexities of post-modern society demand that the contemporary criminal defense attorney be even more sophisticated than his illustrious ancestors in analyzing and addressing the ethical and humanistic dimensions of practice. Paraphrasing Norval Morris' wonderful counsel: "Inquire, probe, and think through moral issues. Avoid automatic, swift, self-centered reactions. Let your decisions and actions wait until you see them in their complexity. Make war on simple solutions to subtle human problems." (Morris, 1992, p. 338).

References

American Bar Association Task Force on Law Schools and the Profession (1992) *Legal Education and Professional Development: An Educational Continuum.* Washington, DC: ABA Press.

American Bar Association (1988) *Criminal Justice In Crisis.* Washington, DC: ABA Press.

Benjamin, G.A.H. and Sales, B. (1992) "Lawyer Psychopathology: Development, Prevalence, and Intervention." In J.R.P. Olgoff, *Law and Psychology: The Broadening of the Discipline.* Durham, N.C.: Carolina Academic Press, pp. 281-301.

Bright, Stephen B. (1994) "Counsel for the Poor: The Death Sentence Not for the Worst Crime but for the Worst Lawyer." *Yale Law Journal,* 103 (7) (May), pp. 1835-1883.

Burger, Warren E. (1973) "The Special Skills of Advocacy: Are Specialized Training and Certification of Advocates Essential to Our System of Justice?" *Fordham Law Review,* 42, pp. 227-242.

Casper, John (1978) *Criminal Courts: The Defendant's Perspective.* Englewood Cliffs, N.J.: Prentice Hall.

Costonis, John J. (1993) "The McCrate Report: Of Loaves, Fishes, and the Future of the American Legal Education." *Journal of Legal Education,* 43 (2) (June), pp. 157-197.

Crampton, R.C. and Jensen, E.M. (1979) "The State of Trial Advocacy and Legal Education." *Journal of Legal Education,* 30, pp. 253-269.

Devitt, Edward (1979) "Report on the Standards for Admission to Practice in Federal Courts." *Federal Rules Decisions,* 83, pp. 215-245.

Druckman D. and Bjork, R.A. (1994) *Learning, Remembering, Believing: Enhancing Human Performance.* Washington, DC: National Academy Press.

Horowitz, Mardi (1991) *Person Schemas and Maladaptive Interpersonal Patterns.* Chicago: University of Chicago Press.

Jones, Albert R. and Toulmin, Stephen (1988) *The Abuse of Casuistry: A History of Moral Reasoning.* Berkeley, CA: University of California Press.

Jones v. Barnes. (1983) 463 U.S. 745, 103 S.Ct. 3308, 77 L.Ed.2d 987.

Kass, Leon (1990) "Practicing Ethics: Where's the Action?" *Hastings Center Report,* (January/February), pp. 5-12.

Low, P., Jeffries, J.F., and Bonnie, R. (1986) *The Trial of John W. Hinckley, Jr.: A Case Study in the Insanity Defense.* Mineola, NY: The Foundation Press.

MacIntyre, Lisa J. (1987) *The Public Defender: The Practice of Law in the Shadows of Repute.* Chicago: University of Chicago Press.

Maddi, D.L. (1978) Trial Advocacy Competence: The Judicial Perspective. *American Bar Foundation Research Journal,* 83, pp. 105-151.

Mahoney, M. (1991) *Human Change Processes.* NY: Basic Books.

McAneny, Leslie and Moore, D.W. (1994). "Annual Honesty and Ethics Poll." *The Gallup Poll Monthly,* (October), pp. 2-4.

Monahan, E.C. and Clark, J. (1995) "Coping with Excessive Workload." In R.J. Uphoff, *Ethical Problems Facing the Criminal Defense Lawyer.* Chicago, IL: ABA Press, pp. 318-346.

Morris, Norval (1992) *The Brothel Boy and Other Parables of the Law.* NY: Oxford University Press.

Oakeshott, Michael (1962) *Rationalism in Politics.* NY: Basic Books.

Ogletree, Charles J. (1993) "Beyond Justifications: Seeking Motivations to Sustain Public Defenders." *Harvard Law Review,* 106 (6), pp 1239-1294.

Perlin, Michael (1989) *Mental Disability Law.* Charlottesville, VA: The Michie Company.

Rapp, W.K. (1992) "The Unknowing Appellate Gideon: An Examination of the 'Burger Problem' Within State Appellate Structures." *Oklahoma City University Law Review,* 17, pp. 257-310.

Rein, Martin and White, S.H. (1981) "Knowledge for Practice." *Social Service Review,* 55 (1) (March), pp. 1-41.

Saleeby, Dennis (1989) "The Estrangement of Knowing and Doing: Professions in Crisis." *Social Casework,* (November), pp. 556-563.

Schon, Donald. (1984) *The Reflective Practitioner: How Professionals Think In Action.* NY: Basic Books.

White, C. (1995) "Developing New Associates: Mentoring or Coaching?" *Lawyer Hiring and Training Report,* 15 (2) (September), pp. 2-3.

Chapter Seventeen

Ancient Sources of Conflicting Values in Professional Education: Plato

Patricia Murphy

In this paper, I will illuminate three different points in Plato's writing from which we can discern a system of consistent belief regarding his attitude towards the conflict of values espoused or practiced within one's generic life, as opposed to the values practiced within one's professional life. It is my contention that a consideration of this analysis finds Plato clearly adhering to a position favoring what in modern parlance might be considered as "weak bifurcation" as opposed to "strong bifurcation". In other words, we are what we are regarding both our generic and professional lives. While we may hope to overcome our generic lives as persons in the limited domain of our professions, the likelihood of success in that endeavor is quite small. Similarly, a danger exists in extending unto our generic lives whatever excellence or virtue that may obtain in our professional lives. The implication is clear. Education for the professional cannot be restricted to mere technological information. Dimensions of considerations that span compartmentalization of our lives are essential for producing the individuals who can equate, axiologically, their generic and professional lives. No profession can be considered apart from all of general society and hence the education, while necessarily specialized for the particular skills and techniques required of a particular profession, must be imposed over a generic and liberal education of the person. We must increase the sensitivity that we bring to the fact that we cannot focus merely on what we do, but rather we must emphasize strongly what we are. In this respect, Plato's thoughts bespeak, as we might have anticipated, a priority of place for a virtue ethic as foundational in education.

The first textual reference that I would like to examine is from *Euthyphro*.[1] In this dialogue, Euthyphro considers himself a "professional" in matters of piety, and hence is taken aback by Socrates' surprise that he is engaging in a court case against his own father. The exposition of the details of the case might cause one to question the action taken by Euthyphro. That is, there is some room for interpreting the clear intentionality for murder with which Euthyphro has charged his father. Obviously those who are "experts" in piety need not concern themselves with "mens res". Euthyphro remains unfazed by the particular features of the case. He is sure and certain of the action he is taking, bolstered by his confidence in his exact knowledge of piety which borders on the arrogant. Through the process of the elenchus, in which Socrates places himself under the tutelage of Euthyphro and more than a few times gives reference to his veiled skepticism regarding Euthyphro's clear knowledge, Socrates presents an abbreviated image of the larger problem of bifurcation. The very first query into what piety is (5d5-e5) finds Euthyphro referring to the example of his own actions. Hence, the definition is rejected as an incomplete (at best) response to the question posed. Socrates reframes the question in his objection to the response he has been given to show that he is seeking a different kind of information than that which Euthyphro has provided. And so the examination is entered into in earnest. Euthyphro provides several more definitions. Each is critically examined by Socrates and found unacceptable. Often in these rejections, the confusion and perplexity that Euthyphro experiences are palpable. He reacts with exasperation, frustration, and an occasional attack on Socrates, all to veil his own threatened "expertise".

In this brief passage, the same incompleteness is cited as that which will later be discerned in the artisans, the poets and the politicians who Socrates investigates in the Apology. The feeble supposition (not necessarily correct) that one's particular action in a particular situation suffice to validate one's general knowledge at the level of the forms is rejected. It is difficult to know where the error begins: does Euthyphro feel overly confident of his action because he believes he is an expert in general knowledge, or does he believe he has expertise in general knowledge because he is quickly able to evaluate a particular situation and action? In fact, one false idea feeds on the other, so that there is a double delusion created which fosters further delusion. Euthyphro seems to be sinking, slowly, in quicksand. His efforts to free himself in fact involve him further. Finally, at the end of the dialogue he flees, stating other things to do. It is unlikely that his will be a success story, wherein upon reflection he shall finally realize the insufficiency of his own knowledge. Rather, one imagines Euthyphro as being quite careful in the future to select companions who shall not quest deeply into his allegations of exact knowledge about matters of piety. He has undergone a long process of learning, wherein the insufficiency of his alleged professional knowledge is laid bare, and this causes great pain. Given Euthyphro's personality, it is unlikely that he shall be truly transformed by this experience, but shall more probably, forget it rather quickly.

The second textual reference to which I would like to direct our attention occurs in *Apology*. There we see Socrates describing his confusion at the Oracle's pronouncement that there is no man in Athens wiser than he. Socrates recounts his attempts to disprove the pronouncement by investigating three various groups or professions in an effort to present a counter instance. The professions he chooses are the artisans, the poets and the politicians. He is, of course, unable to find that longed for counter instance despite his efforts. His explanations for the failed attempts speak volumes about the difficulties from which the various members of these professions suffered. Roughly put, each of the three investigations finds the same tendency among the examinees. From the belief (or even fact) that one possesses an excellence directly related to his profession, the professional attributes general excellence to his character.[2] Socrates is quite sensitive to this error, a sort of hasty generalization or attribution fallacy which apparently is common enough to infect each and every group that he investigates. Indeed, he is confronted in court with a representative of each of these three professions, Anytus, Meletus and Lycon. During the course of the dialogue, each of the opponents reveals the abiding quality of that flaw which so distressed Socrates during the original investigation. The desire on the part of each of the opponents, and indeed, on the part of each of the persons Socrates investigates, is to simplify or reduce both themselves and others. Their ill-chosen though opportunistic formula becomes: an excellence or particular skill or professional practice equals an excellence of person in general. Their desire to so reduce Socrates (at the expense of truth which may be the product of his conversations with the Athenian youth) takes the form of superficial predication and incomplete analysis. One instance of Socrates' recognition of this tendency, and his attempt to reveal its myopic legacy can be seen in Socrates' famous disjunctive argument against the charge of his corruption of the youth. Either his behavior was unintentional, in which case he ought not be in court, or it was self-destructive, as to do so would ultimately harm himself by association with corrupted persons, which is absurd.[3]

Finally, a somewhat more complex articulation of Plato's concern on the topic of strong bifurcation can be found (in more clearly his own voice) in the Seventh Letter. I will point to a few passages of this text, but I believe that a concern for precisely this problem of bifurcation of values between professional and private life informs the entire letter.

Perhaps no where else in all of Plato do we see so clearly portrayed the tragedy of an individual desiring quick professional training for the sake of some value external to that profession. Indeed, it is perhaps Plato's protracted relationship with this tendency on the part of Dionysius that invites the skepticism that he maintains about the authors of the letter to which he responds in the

Seventh Letter. The letter to Plato has requested advice, and it is signed by "Friends of Dion". Fearful that in fact it may be the friends of *Dionysius* who have sought his advice, merely for a political purpose, Plato begins his letter of response with the enigmatic sentence, "My reply is that I will aid your cause if your views and your aims really are the same as Dion's; if they differ from his, I will take time to think about it."[4] This is significant because throughout the text that follows, what is included is a full and articulate theory of friendship as it is authenticated only by virtue of true commitment to the practice over many year's time of philosophy. The friends of Dion, or at least those alleging to be, have requested advice of a political nature from Plato. Plato fears this may be a request not for true advice (which must entail true philosophy) but rather a desire for a quick political fix, or a recipe of sorts. In short, the alleged friends of Dion may be seeking information about what to *do*, whereas Plato, as always, wishes to discuss what one should *be*. By virtue of the curious structure and content of the letter, one is more inclined to think that Plato, doubting the unity of virtue which would truly mark the alleged "friends" as those of Dion, has indeed engaged in a high degree of "thinking about it."

The portraits drawn throughout the lengthy text of both Dionysius and Dion are extensive and contrasting. The meandering that Plato engages in, as if possibly trying to discourage any readers who are not true disciples of philosophy, is legend. We learn more about the characters of Dion and Dionysius than most would care to study. Additionally, we are presented with travelogues of Plato's two trips to Sicily and his attempts to instruct Dionysius, his loyalty in friendship with Dion, his theories on when to give advice and when not to give advice, the tests for true friendship as opposed to false friendship, the laboring in his own soul which occasioned his brief desire to enter political life, and the much lengthier commitment to a-political enterprises. We learn a great deal, through a number of narratives, about persons, psychologies, meta-philosophy, friendship, and certainly, the most comprehensive anatomy of knowledge, presented in the famous "epistemological digression" of 340d6 — roughly, 345a6. Intertwined with these teachings are several cautionary notes about written doctrine and the danger of the written word, as it is static rather than dynamic. This reference is perhaps a veiled reprimand to the advice seekers: truth cannot be capture in a written prescription (as true friends of Dion would well understand.)

The length and breadth of the letter are remarkable in and of itself, and when compared to any of the other letters. Indeed if one imagines oneself as a friend of Dionyius, posing as a friend of Dion, for the sake of pragmatic political silver bullets from the mouth of Plato, one might well imagine oneself giving up and despairing of every getting to that part of the letter. This is significant, for it reveals the degree to which Plato—once again—asserts his commitment to the ideal of the unity of virtue. Dionysius is revealed to be an archetype of the "professional" in a negative sense. What this means is that again and again we learn of his use of knowledge of a limited and focused sort in an instrumental fashion. Repeatedly his motives are informed by a desire for power, recognition from others, and acclaim. Never does he appear to be willing to develop his own character with any sense of inherent worth. His objective is always narrowly defined and self-serving.

In short, Dionysius represents the same limited focus that is opposed in the earlier mentioned passages. His desire to be a "professional" thinker and a "professional" politician are directed towards very practical goals. As evidence of this, we learn that after but a few meetings with Plato, Dionysius alleges to have learned a sufficient amount of philosophy to write articles on a variety of topics. This activity is one that Plato names as a sure sign of failed true education.[5] As further confirmation of his failure of true education, Plato provides various bits of information about Dionysius's character which are far from flattering. These criticisms include a final betrayal in the form of refusing to keep an agreement, an apparent desire for economic gain to which he was not entitled[6], reference to the instrumental value that Dionysius assigned to Plato's knowledge[7], and finally, his lack of true friends.[8]

In the last paragraph of his letter, Plato claims that his advice, "has mainly been given, so no more."[9] Yet if the readers of the letter are in fact the followers of Dionysius, they shall wonder exactly where that political strategy was presented. We can imagine them, confused and perplexed, searching the letter a second and third time to find what they had missed. If on the other hand, the readers of the letter are the friends of Dion, much advice, immediately applicable to their journey towards knowledge, virtue and the development of character which can only enhance their professional lives has been gratefully received. We can imagine these friends reflecting long and hard on the many teachings presented by Plato.

Notes

1. There are actually several references within this dialogue. I shall draw special attention to 4a-5a that shows the attitude I am examining.
2. The specific passage is 21b7-22e3.
3. This particular argument, mirroring the structure of the argument he provides for the charge of impiety, can be found in 25c5-26a10.
4. 324a2-4, L.A. Post translation.
5. 341b5-341c
6. 349c7-350b7
7. 338e5-339a3 and 345e8-346a2
8. 332c2-6
9. 351e10-352a1

Chapter Eighteen

The Common Good and the Purpose of the Firm: A Critique of the Shareholder and Stockholder Models from the Catholic School Tradition[1]

Michael Naughton
Helen Alford
Bernard Brady

One of the habits that Stephen Covey describes in his book *The 7 Habits of Highly Effective People* is the habit of "having the end in mind." All our activities have a purpose, but the habit of having the end in mind makes us take into account how all these purposes work towards a unified end or purpose for the whole of our lives. For managers to develop this habit in their work, they must ask two simple but profound questions: 1) "What kind of person should I as a manager strive to become (individual character)?" 2) "What kind of organizational community should I as a manager strive to build and maintain (organizational character)?"[2] The two questions are intrinsically related, but for purposes of time and space, we focus on the second question.

In defining what kind of organizational community or character managers want, they must draw on some underlying idea of life and commerce in which they understand the purpose of human work and action. Many managers and their organizations have adopted one of two models in defining the purpose of their organizational community, both of which are rooted in philosophical liberalism.[3] 1) Shareholder Purpose: Managerial decision making is assessed on whether it maximizes shareholder wealth. 2) Stakeholder Purpose: The company exists to benefit the primary stakeholders, namely, customers, employees, communities, and shareholders. We believe that both these models fail to serve as an adequate basis for explaining the purpose of an organization. While both express important insights into running an organization, they fail to capture a fuller meaning of living in an organizational community.

We want to bring back into the mainstream of discussion a third model, based on the idea of the common good. It is a model that leaves the liberal tradition that has formed the purpose question for organizations since the Enlightenment, and draws on a much older, communitarian and Catholic tradition that has been largely untapped.[4] We are not unaware that the common good tradition brings with it some dangers which we will discuss in the second part of this article. This is why a retrieval of the common good tradition, as David Hollenbach states, "calls not simply for retrieval of past traditions, but also for an attitude of suspicion toward the oppressive power these traditions have certainly exhibited in the past."[5] We believe that an engagement between Catholic social thought and management theory and practice contributes to the pluralistic debate in understanding the purpose of an organization as well as to a better unity between faith and work for Catholic and Christian managers.

The first part of this article sketches out the common good as it relates to organizations. The second part of the article engages the common good tradition with the shareholder and stakeholder models. This engagement highlights two competing visions for the organization: liberalism (shareholder or stakeholder) and communitarianism (common good). We argue for a more communitarian grounding for organizational purpose. This communitarian approach has a particular Catholic perspective; however, it has much in common with other religious perspectives as well as with other secular communitarians. We are hopeful that the contents of this article, while inspired by the Catholic social tradition, are not sectarian but ecumenical in its fullest sense.[6]

The Common Good and the Organization

In speaking to Argentinean managers, John Paul II challenges managers to see all their organizational activity within the framework of the common good. He defines the common good for the organization as *the creation of those organizational conditions ordered toward human development.*[7] While managers cannot develop human persons, they can either create conditions in which people have a better possibility to develop, or create conditions in which people have a better possibility to struggle and fail. The common good demands the "disciplined sensitivity" on the part of managers to those conditions of an organization that cause people to develop or suffer.[8] The common good provides a framework in which such questions are always on the horizon rather than relegated to the private domain. The idea of the common good does not provide a micro-blueprint for managers, but rather an *orientation* or moral compass that directs organizational activity toward human development.

Within the Catholic natural law tradition, the common good is founded on the notion that we desire what is good. Our desires range from the most fundamental desire for survival to the most excellent desire for human and divine community.[9] These desires get expressed in particular goods attained through particular techniques and virtues. By integrating these desires and properly ordering the goods, human development can take place within an organizational context where the good of the person is recognized to be intrinsically connected to the good of the community.[10] We describe the common good within the organization through three propositions which we explain further in the following section.

- *Fundamentality:* Human beings have a fundamental *desire* for survival expressed through *organizational goods* of profitability, efficiency, and productivity attained through management *techniques.*

- *Excellence:* As social beings, human beings have an excellent *desire* for community expressed through *organizational goods* of just distribution of benefits and burdens, participation, contribution to society and so forth, attained through *moral virtues.*

- *Integration:* The successfully managed organization creates the conditions in which the fundamental and excellent desires are integrated, and the variety of organizational goods are ordered toward human development attained through the intellectual virtue of *practical wisdom.*

Fundamental Desire and Its Goods and Techniques

Many of our students who are concerned about financial success often tell of an experience of financial instability such as parents who were laid off. They do not want to experience economic instability again. Like all of us, they desire stability and security. They realize that material needs are attained through work organizations. In order to attain these material needs on a long term basis, organizations must create certain conditions that can attract capital, use it efficiently and productively and generate more capital for further continuation and growth. To attain these fundamental goods of survival, people need a certain degree of competence in management techniques. Finance provides the skills to raise capital, production provides the skills to operate efficiently and productively, marketing provides the skills to make the product or service marketable, and so forth. If management does not generate optimal profits and efficiency, no matter how noble or personally satisfying, the organization will not be viable.[11]

Fundamentality

Desire Techniques	Organizational Goods	Management
Survival	Profitability, Efficiency, Productivity	Marketing, Finance, Production, Human Resources

Neoclassical economists make much of the fundamental desire for survival which serves as the basis of a financial theory of the firm to maximize shareholder wealth. They argue that since capital plays such a decisive role in the existence of the firm, shareholder interests must be maximized. While the shareholder version of a firm describes what is fundamental and necessary, it is not sufficient in describing what is excellent about a human organization. This point is developed in the second part of the article where we critique the shareholder model.

Excellent Desire and Its Goods and Virtues

To write only of a fundamental desire to meet material needs ignores the *social* nature and desire of people.[12] We are not simply animals seeking preservation, but we are social beings seeking community in which we develop and help others to develop. Gary Atkinson points out that people do not cease to be social beings when they enter the organizational setting. "Indeed, their social character is enhanced or intensified in sometimes dramatic ways."[13] People desire a community of work where they can develop skills and talents that contribute both to the organization as well as to society. For such a community to exist, managers must create conditions that provide broad base participation, distribute burdens and benefits, contribute to the larger community and so forth. To create such conditions successfully, managers must be virtuous; otherwise, employees will not trust managers and will find their appearance of virtue manipulative.[14]

Excellence

Human Desire	Organizational Goods	Moral Virtues
Community	Distribution, Participation, Contribution	Justice, Solidarity, Courage, Moderation

This desire for social living can be disordered from either personal vice or structural oppression, but that it exists in the human heart seems certain. Many entrepreneurs and managers do not go to work each day to maximize economic gain. They would be insulted by such a characterization. Yet, even for those who are motivated only by economic goods, we should not assume that is a normal state of affairs. For example, most people would agree that self-preservation is a universal desire; yet, when people commit suicide we do not call into question the desire of self-preservation, but rather look for the extraordinary reasons why such a person would commit suicide. We should do the same for social desires. When people no longer desire human community within organizations, we should not assume that this is a normal state of affairs.

Integrating Desires and Ordering Goods

The Virtue of Practical Wisdom: The crucial dimension in the moral life is not choosing between one's fundamental desire for survival and one's excellent desire for community. Setting the idea of the moral life within an organization in this way is, for the most part, a false dichotomy. Rather, the key to the moral life is ordering these two desires toward human development in a way that both can be achieved. With practical wisdom, management needs to order the fundamental desire, goods and techniques toward a work community where people can develop in a virtuous community.

The fundamental desire and goods of an organization do not describe fully what it means to be a human organization, since they fail to describe what is most excellent about an organization in terms of developing human community where people flourish. In general, the pursuit of fundamental goods is subordinated to the more excellent pursuit of community. But at the same time there is an order of fundamentality that prevents profitability, efficiency, and productivity from being destroyed (most of the time) by the order of excellence, since it is on the basis of fundamental goods that communities are built. By providing a dual direction as well as a dual control, the order of goods is inclusive because those goods participate in each other in a way that one is needed for the other to flourish. The fundamental goods of profitability, efficiency, productivity, and so forth control the excellent goods of distribution, participation, and contribution in that there are limits to what can and cannot be done; yet, the goods of community direct the fundamental goods to human development and not some isolated private interest.

The key to this ordering is the intellectual virtue of practical wisdom or what some may call professional competence. Practical wisdom is the capacity to discern the best means for attaining one's morally good ends. It is where ends and means meet. Practical wisdom is the ability to "do" the good correctly in particular cases. It is a key managerial virtue since it both does the good and does well simultaneously.

Practical wisdom should not be confused with slyness, trickery, and craftiness. Nor should it be seen as a utilitarian calculation whether for society or as Joseph Pieper points out for the "timorous, small-minded self-preservation" of the self.[15] The practically wise manager is not the calculator, productivity technician, or manipulator; rather, she is the person who has a grasp of the various disciplines of management, perceives the complexity of the situation, and instantiates the various moral virtues in the particular situation. Practical wisdom is the central virtue for management since it is able to order the various organizational goods together in one concrete act.

The Integration of Fundamentality and Excellence

Order of Fundamentality (means)	Order of Excellence (ends)

Practical Wisdom
Proper Order of Ends and Means

The ordering of the desires and goods will be affected by the various factors of competitive environment, market conditions, stage of development, and so forth. Consequently, different emphasis will be given to the different desires and goods at different times. For example, a start up company may find itself focusing more on the fundamental goods than the excellent goods. Start up companies tend to fold in their initial stages because of cash flows drying up and poor marketing. It is quite legitimate for them, therefore, to focus on developing fundamental goods, just as a person in need of income will also do so for the sake of preserving his or her life. However, the danger here is that the legitimate focus on productivity and profitability in the early start-up phase may habituate the entrepreneur to focus only on these goods even when that phase is past. What can prevent this? If entrepreneurs keep in view that their organization is ordered towards higher ends, then the focus on gaining profits and productivity can only be seen as a means.

A Theological Caution[16] : Within the Catholic social tradition, the common good is incomplete without a fuller theological grounding. Human development and fulfillment comes ultimately and completely through union with God. Consequently, friendship with God is the ultimate end, and most excellent desire, of the common good. As Hollenbach points out, "Everything human beings are to do, in both personal and social life, is directed to one end: union with the God who is their maker and redeemer."[17] We are not meant simply to live virtuously in an organization "but through virtuous living to attain the possession of God.'" Therefore, while the organization should display the signs of the City of God, it is not the City of God. The full theological vision of the common good cannot be manifested in the organization, since the organization is not our ultimate end. One must be careful of expecting more out an organization than it can give. A real danger exists of those who identify their lives totally in terms of their work, even when they think their work socially useful.[18] Yet, at the same time, it is through the organization, *in part*, that our ultimate end, namely union with God, is reached.

Critique of the Shareholder and Stakeholder Models of Organizational Purpose: The Primacy of the Common Good[19]

Thus far, we have sketched a broad outline of the common good model. By critically engaging this model with the prevailing shareholder and stakeholder models, we articulate some of the implications of the common good for organizational purpose and provide a fuller explanation of the model itself.

Shareholder Model

The shareholder model, both in practice and theory, has largely been influenced by the discipline of finance (which has been influenced by classical economics which has been influenced by classical liberal philosophy). In theory,[20] finance has allocated to itself *a theory of the firm* that explains the firm's reason for being, its purpose, its *ratio*, its ultimate end which is to *maximize shareholder wealth* (MSW).[21] Typifying this approach, Brigham and Gapenski's textbook on financial management define the financial philosophy of the firm in the following way:

> management's primary goal is stockholder wealth maximization. . . . This translates into maximizing the price of the firm's common stock. Firms do, of course, have other objectives; managers, who make the actual decision, are interested in their own personal satisfaction, in their employees' welfare, and in the good of the community and of society at large. Still . . . stock price maximization is the most important goal of most corporations, *and it is a reasonable operating objective on which to build decision rules.*[22] [italics ours]

There are two important things to note about this paragraph: *Two types of goods are mentioned:* fundamental or economic goods of shareholders (increase in stock price); excellent or communitarian goods (employee welfare and community welfare). More importantly for our purposes is the second point, *the order and relationship between these goods:* economic goods of shareholders are the most important among the goods. Community goods are instrumental and at best secondary to shareholders' economic good.

Why are shareholders of primary importance in organizational purpose contrasted to all the other stakeholders? Why does the attraction of capital trump the role of labor or community? Defenders of this financial philosophy justify shareholder primacy on various levels, such as property rights, economic efficiency, agency, and contract, but ultimately they attempt to justify shareholder primacy on a social ground—MSW is best for society—and consequently, they reveal what they believe is "good" for an organization to pursue.[23] They argue that a corporation does not exist unless it attracts capital which serves as the reason why MSW is so crucial to a corporation's existence. A company's ability to raise capital today depends upon its cash-generating ability in the future. The cash-generating ability determines capital investment which determines shareholder wealth. The financial relationship between the firm and employees (wages), suppliers (payments), customers (affordable products), and government (taxes) is founded on the basis of generating shareholder wealth.[24] Consequently, what's good for shareholders is good for everyone else. MSW serves the so-called common good, that is, a utilitarian notion of the common good, by allowing the most efficient and productive avenue of wealth to be generated which in the end will provide the greatest amount of utility (read: wealth) for the greatest amount of people.[25]

Critique of the Shareholder Model: In light of the common good, the shareholder model suffers on two major accounts: purpose and order. To say that the *purpose* of an organization is to MSW is to say that the highest value in an organization is material wealth. No matter how one slices it this is materialism.[26] The shareholder deifies the fundamental desire for survival, and marginalizes the excellent desire for community. An analogy is helpful here. Aquinas points out three inclinations within human nature: 1) self-preservation, 2) the passing on and nurturing of life, and 3) social living and to know and love God. If we do not preserve our lives and maintain openness to future life, the social inclination has no foundation on which to flourish; however, if all we do is preserve and procreate we would say that something is radically missing to what it means to be a human person. Similarly, without profits and other economic goods, community goods have little relevance, since they cannot exist without economic sustenance; however, if an organization is only concerned about economic goods, we should say that something is radically missing to what it means to be a *humane* organization. The founders of Reell Precision Manufacturing (RPM) express this point well in a welcoming message to new employees:

We do not define profits as the purpose of the company, but we do recognize that reasonable profitability is necessary to continue in business and to reach our full potential. We see profits in much the same way that you could view food in your personal life. You probably do not define food or eating as the purpose of your life, but recognize that it is essential to maintain your health and strength so you can realize your real purpose.[27]

When profits become the end of an organization, an inordinate attachment to the more fundamental goods prevents an organization from considering or pursuing the more excellent goods of community.[28]

The second problem with the shareholder model is the instrumental *ordering* of organizational goods in contrast to the subsidiary ordering of the common good model. The shareholder model places MSW as the highest end of the organization in which all other aspects are simply means. The model inverts the relationship of means and ends. Wealth within the Christian social tradition as well as other religious and humanistic traditions has always been understood as a means to serve other ends. That the shareholder theory is so adamant on *maximizing* shareholder wealth, all other goods are instrumental in the attainment of shareholder wealth. As the director of one company stated "'All of our businesses are for sale all of the time. If anyone is prepared to pay us more than we think they are worth, we will sell. We have no attachment to any individual businesses.'"[29] The business is for sale so long as the sale maximizes shareholder wealth. It does not matter whether employees are depersonalized, or communities suffer. Everything is instrumentalized to shareholder wealth within the boundaries of the law.

Managers face constant pressure to instrumentalize the order of desires and goods. Managers can use the excellent desire of community to maximize shareholder wealth, maximize enlightened self-interest, maximize market share and so forth. Some may argue that desire for community and virtue can be instrumental in achieving the fundamental desire for survival. Consequently, survival expressed in maximizing wealth becomes the end, and community and virtue become means. Within the common good tradition, this is a drastic mistake. As T.S. Eliot points out, "to do the right deed for the wrong reason" is the greatest treason.[30] It is the greatest treason because we not only instrumentalize others but ourselves as well by inverting the relationship between means and ends. Organizational purpose imprints a particular character on the organization that in the long-run will have significant implications. If managers order all activity toward MSW, they begin to form an organizational character as well as their own individual characters that is manipulative at its core.[31]

Most people do not want to spend a half to a third of their waking hours devoted to such a narrowly economic good as shareholder maximization. Fundamental goods of an organization must be pursued, but they also must be ordered toward the more excellent goods of community that lead to a richer notion of human development. Yet, economic goods cannot be annihilated or squeezed out in achieving community goods. Human development cannot be attained without a sound economic basis. A unity of the goods must exist in subsidiary relationship, that is, with each serving the other to attain full human development. This subsidiary ordering stands in contrast to the instrumental ordering that is found in the shareholder model. A subsidiary ordering is not oppressive nor exclusionary because the ordering does not marginalize one set of goods over another, unlike the instrumental ordering of the shareholder model. By providing a dual direction as well as a dual control, this ordering of goods is inclusive, since the goods participate in each other in a way that one is needed for the other to flourish.

At its very core, then, a common good model is teleologically ordered toward human development through the proper ordering of organizational goods. A shareholder model is teleologically ordered toward the economic prosperity of shareholders. At the very heart of both theories are moral statements of the purpose of an organization and the role of managers in an organization. The question for both theories is: which model can maintain an order of goods so that all the goods are met and people become "more human,"—where one does well and good at the same time? From the common good model, the final gain of shareholders is not the common good, although it participates as an essential element in its fulfillment, though not the defining element of an organization.[32]

Model	*Purpose*	*Order*
Shareholder	Maximize Shareholder Wealth	Instrumental
Common Good	Human Development	Subsidiary

The shareholder model does highlight a weakness of the common good model. In pursuit of such a lofty goal as the common good, an organization can pursue its excellence at the cost of its economic foundation. Organizations with a common good purpose run the danger of going beyond their financial means and competency. Consequently, they fail to contribute to the common good in the long run. The common good also runs the risk of being vague and difficult for an organization to articulate effectively. In particular, it does not lend itself to a simple formula that can easily define the purpose of the organization such as "maximize shareholder wealth." MSW is relatively clear, precise and measurable. Contributing to full human development, as the purpose of the organization, is a goal about which managers will always have more questions than answers. Yet, if managers see themselves as professionals[33] and not technicians, such ambiguity is inescapable. Human decision making, even in corporations, cannot be reduced to one simple formula.[34]

Stakeholder Model: The Multi-Fiduciary Approach

Unlike the shareholder model, the stakeholder model is more difficult to define, since its proponents are not as unified as to *why* stakeholders should be identified, and *"for what purpose."*[35] Within the stakeholder model there are multiple purposes for an organization, and this makes the stakeholder model difficult to capture in a single description. Consequently, our discussion of the stakeholder model cannot capture all its dimensions nor all its proponents. Because of space we examine what Kenneth Goodpaster calls the multi-fiduciary approach.

The multi-fiduciary approach places stakeholders on the level of "quasi-shareholders." This approach challenges the priority of shareholders in the maximization of their economic interests by interjecting an egalitarian criterion where all stakeholders interests are maximized. Where in the shareholder model management had a fiduciary (to hold in trust or to act on behalf of another) relationship to shareholders, in the multi-fiduciary approach management's trust relationship is to multiple stakeholders. Much of this approach has been influenced by rights theory where employees, shareholders, creditors, and consumers are seen to have rights that must be respected by the organization. The multi-fiduciary approach to the stakeholder model attempts to professionalize management by widening its responsibilities beyond the agent/principal relationship with shareholders. Proponents of the model argue that today's large organizations yield power to such an extent that one constituent, such as the shareholder, cannot dominate its purpose. Rather, the manager must take seriously a multiplicity of constituencies. As stated in the Council for Economic Development (CED) document that represents the stakeholder perspective, the manager is a "trustee balancing the interests of the many diverse participants and constituents in the enterprise."[36]

Recent state constituent statutes seem to vindicate the multi-fiduciary approach by broadening a board's legal authority to consider the interests of stakeholders other than shareholders in its decision making. For some U.S. states, corporate law has evolved into a multi-fiduciary approach where corporations exist for communities, employees, creditors, and customers as well as for the returns of shareholders. As Steiner and Steiner explain, "this legal position, in contrast to the stark doctrine of stockholders supremacy, focuses the accountability of directors on the overriding role of the corporation in society."[37] These statutes loosen the hold of shareholder dominance on boards and managers.[38] In discharging their duties, boards can now consider, within the law, various stakeholder interests, which include: "the interests of the corporation's employees, customers, suppliers and creditors, the economy of the state and nation, community and societal considerations, and the long-term as well as short-term interests of the corporation and its shareholders including the possibility that these interests may be best served by the continued independence of the corporation."[39]   These laws circumscribe shareholder property rights by taking seriously the rights of employees, customers, creditors, and communities.[40]

Critique of the Multi-fiduciary Approach: The multi-fiduciary approach is clearly preferable to the shareholder model from a common good perspective, since it expands the notion of organizational purpose; yet, we argue, its expansion still inadequately describes organizational purpose, and its ordering of organizational goods suffers from an egalitarian impracticality.

In terms of its *purpose*, the multi-fiduciary approach (influenced by a revised liberalism) sees the common good as a collection of individual goods for private possession.   Because this approach focuses on individual stakeholders as its starting point, it has tremendous difficulty pursuing a collective notion of a common life in which goods are shared to enhance human development.   This largely stems from its notion of rights which are viewed in the context of individual and private interests rather than communal living.   While the Catholic social tradition owes much insight to the liberal notion of rights, its own notion of rights is less individualistic and more communitarian.   The US bishops, for example, define rights as the "minimal conditions for communal living."   In commenting on this definition, Hollenbach recalls the Exodus story where the people are liberated *from* bondage *into* community, "a community of persons who are both free and co-responsible for one another's fates."[41]   The liberation into community points to a good in common that "is a good perfective of members of society which is not the private good of any of them."[42]

The multi-fiduciary approach also attempts to get more out of the notion of rights than rights can provide by dispensing with any normative theory of the good on which a community can rest.   By depending only upon rights language to describe stakeholder relations, they reduce the organization to an historical accident which at best preserves a maximum of individual freedom "according to one's private conception of the good."[43]   Yet, without some sort of communitarian perspective of a shared idea of the good, the multi-fiduciary approach eventually erodes any sense of cohesiveness necessary for an organization's identity.

This contrasting understanding of rights stems from a contrasting understanding of community.   The multi-fiduciary approach restricts its idea of community to a group of stakeholders who affect or are affected by the organization.   An organizational community results in a social contract of stakes, claims, and rights by particular stakeholders.   At best the stakeholders are bounded by contracts that enable them to pursue their individual interests.   What results is a strategic calculus in which managers attempt to maximize the sum total of particular goods.   This approach fails to take seriously the desire for community as the basis for defining what one's interests are.   Once individuals are isolated from their community of work as well as their other communities of family, church, and state, it becomes difficult to see what their good is in common. The multi-fiduciary model suffers from an individualism that presupposes that an individual is, as Alasdair MacIntyre states, "isolated from and deprived of any community within which it could systematically enquire what its good was and achieve that good."[44] While various stakeholders may benefit from the various contracts, "their contracts will not relieve their lonesomeness" because they are not asking what kind of organizational community they want to be. What fails to occur with the multi-fiduciary approach is an idea of a "community of work" where employees within the organization inspire "*a common life of desire and action*" directed toward human development.[45]

Within the Catholic social tradition as well as the Aristotelian tradition, the object of the common good is not simply human development individually understood, but rather human development within a community. The common good within the Catholic tradition can only be understood in relation to a work community where a) at least some members of the organization are able to act for the whole (leadership and authority); b) all members of the organization desire overall goals that enhance human development (purpose or mission); c) members cooperate with each other in the process of attaining those overall goals (participation); and d) members exchange between themselves "'communications' or signs aimed at producing 'communions'" (virtues such as loyalty, trust, justice, patience, and so forth).[46] A community, whether an organization, family, school, or city, cannot be sustained in a fully human way unless it collectively directs itself toward goods in common that promote human development.

To every organization, this poses two serious questions that will not be easy to determine: Are we a real community or an apparent one? Are we, in the words of Robert Bellah, an enclave of individuals brought together to pursue our individual interests and lifestyles while tolerating others in the process? Or are we a "community of work" brought together to serve a common good that includes, yet goes beyond our own particular goods? When an organizational philosophy such as the multi-fiduciary approach begins with rights individually understood, its preoccupation with rights clouds what is necessary to enhance human development with an organization.

Another difficulty with the multi-fiduciary approach is its egalitarian *ordering* of stakeholder rights which leads to the inability to order the various stakeholders to a common purpose.[47] How does a manager resolve the conflict of rights when there is no other good besides one's own right? There is nothing in the multi-fiduciary approach that adjudicates the conflicts that occur among the various stakeholders. When Dist. Corp. states that it "will exercise responsibility in our dealings with all our stakeholders and in the case of conflict balance the interests of employees and shareholders on an equal basis over time," we should ask, "what is the fulcrum that provides the balance?"[48] The key to the multi-fiduciary approach rests not with the fact that various constituents are taken into consideration but that their interests are balanced and weighed in equal return to shareholders. The critical term here is "balanced and weighed." The multi-fiduciary approach, in contrast to the shareholder model, wants to claim that there will be times that decisions will not *result* in wealth maximization for shareholders because of this balance. However, it is unclear exactly what criteria will be used to go beyond the economic interests of shareholders.[49] The multi-fiduciary approach offers a plurality of indefinite individual interests undifferentiated in their importance and unconnected to the community. Such a plurality can only lead to growing disagreement and fragmentation.

Without a notion of human development within an organizational context, and with each person constituting his/her own individual rights, conflicting claims among various stakeholders seem irresolvable. Their conflictual claims seem irresolvable because they are divorced from a theory of the good, and are reduced to personal claims. Yet, to run an organization on attempts at mediating or balancing various rights eliminates what organizations need: a common good which all employees can focus on, work toward, and if need be, sacrifice for.[50]

Model	*Purpose*	*Order*
Multi-Fiduciary	Stakeholder Rights	Egalitarian
Common Good	Human Development within Community	Hierarchical

In contrast to the multi-fiduciary model, a key weakness of the common good model is the possible over-emphasis on unity. The common good has an organic image that can be used to abuse individual rights in ordering goods hierarchically. At different times, the common good and the defense of community have been used by people to justify all sorts of inhuman practices, such as slavery, religious oppression, and the subordination of women. A danger exists within the common good tradition of seeking unity at the expense of diversity, solidarity at the expense of opposition, and community at the expense of individuality, all of which eventually undermine the common good.[51] If the common good model is to flourish as a possible alternative within today's organization, it cannot do so without the insights and developments of the stakeholder model with its emphasis on human rights and freedom. Nonetheless, while rights, freedom and autonomy are essential factors in the common good, they cannot serve as substitutes for the common good.[52]

Conclusion

What is the common good for the manager? We have argued that this question does not lend itself to immediately measurable objectives such as maximizing shareholder wealth, or a balancing act of stakeholder rights. The common good provides a new horizon for managers, a horizon that broadens their "criteria of judgment" beyond the shareholder and stakeholder models. In asking the question "What kind of organizational community should I as a manager strive to build and maintain?" within the framework of the common good model, managers can develop the habit of "having the end in mind" that is consistent with the social and communitarian nature of both themselves and their employees.[53]

Notes

1. A special thanks goes to Fr. William McDonough whose comments were especially helpful. We would also like to thank the following people for their comments and insights: Dr. Gary Atkinson, Dr. Daniel Rush Finn, Dr. Robert Kennedy, Mr. Robert Wahlstedt and the Reell Precision Manufacturing Cabinet Group.
2. John Murray informed us of these two questions, and he received these questions from Oliver Williams.
3. See Danley, J. R. *The Role of the Modern Corporation in a Free Society*, Notre Dame, IN, Notre Dame University Press, 1994. See also Campbell, A. and Nash, L. L. *A Sense of Mission*, Great Britain, Hutchinson Business Books Limited, 1990.
4. Casanova states that " without normative traditions neither rational public debate nor discourse is likely to take place. It seems self-evident that religious normative traditions should have the same rights as any other normative tradition to enter the public sphere as long as they play by the rules of open public debate" (see Casanova, J. *Public Religions in the Modern World*, Chicago, University of Chicago Press, 1994). See also Hollenbach, D. *Catholicism and Liberalism*, Cambridge, University of Cambridge Press, 1994, p. 143, on the debate between MacIntyre, who argues that we should bring the fullness of our traditions to bear on public argument, and Rawls, who argues for a "method of avoidance."
5. Hollenbach, D., "The Common Good Revisited." *Theological Studies*, v. 50, 1989, pp. 70-94.
6. The Catholic social tradition offers several advantages: a) An attempt at a normative good for the organization that includes but goes beyond simply economic goods. b) A dialogue that can integrate two important areas of many managers' lives: work and faith. Management theory and practice often takes no account of a manager's religious faith, and religious literature often takes no account of a believer's work. c) Offers a language that has a specific religious tradition, yet offers a participation beyond members of its own faith.
7. See Pope John Paul II *The Dignity of Work* Lanham, University Press of America, 1995, editors Gary Atkinson, Robert Kennedy, and Michael Naughton. Since an organization has a limited influence over human development, the pursuit of the common good for each work organization is limited in scope. Nonetheless, organizations still play an important part in creating those conditions that can favor the development of the human person, particularly in light of the products and services they produce as well as the work community they create.
8. See Buckley, M. *Redeeming the Promise: Some Jesuit Specifications in Higher Education*. Unpublished manuscript, Chapt. 6 "The Search for a New Humanism: The University and the Concern for Justice."
9. Aquinas, T. *Summa Theologiae*, I II 94. 2. Our desires indicate the incompleteness of the human condition that motivate our actions.
10. According to Virgil Michel as well as Aquinas the common good and the individual good are intrinsically connected in "that one's own good cannot exist without the common good of the family, or of the state, or of the realm." (Michel V. *The Social Question* St. Cloud, MN, Parker Printing Company, 1987, p. 25).
11. Drucker, P. *The Frontiers of Management*, New York, Harper and Row Publishers, 1986, pp. 220-227.

12. Simon points out that the common good has a powerful hold on the consciences of people, even when it is radically misunderstood. "People of debased conduct and skeptical judgment still find it natural to die for their country or for such substitute for a country as a gang. And during the golden age of individualism the conscience of men, in spite of what the theorists had to say, often recognized the common good and served it with devotion under such improper names as 'general interest' or 'greatest good of the greatest number'" (See Simon, Y. *Philosophy of Democratic Government*, Chicago, The University of Chicago Press, 1951, p. 50).

13. Gary Atkinson, unpublished paper. Also much can be made of the connection between our social nature and the word "company," which comes from companions, a group sharing bread.

14. See Aquinas I II 92, 1 and 90, 2.

15. Pieper, J. *Prudence*, New York, Pantheon Books, 1959, pp. 15.

16. There is a danger in separating too clearly and distinctly on one hand means, techniques and fundamentality and on the other hand ends, virtues and excellence. Aquinas points out that "In all honest things, utility coincides with honesty except in the last thing which is the end of all ends which alone is to be desired for its own sake" (*Second Sentences* 21. 1. 3c). Fr. William McDonough, in paraphrasing Aquinas states it this way: "only one end, God, is to be loved for itself; all other ends are to be loved in as much as they are useful in our movement to God" (unpublished manuscript).

17. Hollenbach, D. "The Common Good Revisited." *Theological Studies*, v. 50, 1989, p. 81.

18. See Pieper, J. *Leisure as the Basis of Culture*, New York, New American Library, 1963, and Aquinas, *Summa Theologiae*, I-II, q. 21, 4, ad 3.

19. While the shareholder and stakeholder models have important insights in providing the purpose of an organization, they fall short precisely in their inability to order the goods toward the common good in which all stakeholders can participate. This disordering of organizational goods stems from what Ken Goodpaster calls *teleopathy*. By combining the Greek roots for goal and purpose, "telos," and disease or sickness, "pathos," Goodpaster defines the term teleopathy as an over emphasis or "unbalanced pursuit" of limited purposes by individuals and groups (Unpublished manuscript).

20. In practice, at least in the US, financial practitioners tend to control business organizations. Where once the majority of CEOs were engineers and production people, today the majority of CEOs come from the finance department. The second most important person behind the CEO is the vice president of finance; whereas in Japan the second most important person is the vice president of human resources. It is interesting to note that in the US there is a higher payout in dividends and lower investment rates in employee training and modernization; whereas in Japan there is a lower dividend payment and higher investment rate in employee training and modernization (see Tarascio, V. J., "Towards a Unified Theory of the Firm: An Historical Approach," *Atlantic Economic Journal*, September 1993, pp. 13, and also Thurow, L. *Head to Head*, New York, William Morrow and Company, Inc., 1992, p. 54, on the multiple dimensions of the theory of the firm).

21. It is this principle of MSW that drives all the financial techniques within the book. It is interesting that finance, which attempts to be the most quantitative and so-called value free discipline in business, would see itself as the area of management which defines the philosophical question of the "purpose" of the firm.

22. Brigham, E. and Gapenski, L., *Financial Management: Theory and Practice.* Orlando, The Dryden Press, 1991, pp. 10-11.

23. See Danley, J. R. *The Role of the Modern Corporation in a Free Society,* Notre Dame, IN, Notre Dame University Press, 1994, pp. 189-190. From the property rights perspective, shareholders are the property owners, and they have rights over the company. Consequently, a manager's role is to direct the company in a way which is in accord to shareholder wishes, namely, increase shareholder wealth. This serves as the basis of agency theory. Yet, the modern corporation eliminated agency theory by defining the corporation as a legal person, not as an embodiment of shareholders. The fiduciary is related to the company, not to one particular stakeholder.

24. Rappaport, A. *Creating Shareholder Value,* New York, The Free Press, 1986, p. 12.

25. Finance borrows from economics the invisible hand principle. Once the MSW principle is put into motion *the actions that maximize stock price also benefit society.* By maximizing shareholder wealth as their direct purpose, managers also maximize the welfare of society (Brigham, E.F. and Gapenski, L.C. *Financial Management: Theory and Practice.* Orlando, The Dryden Press, 1991, p. 17).

26. It is materialistic because it reduces all organizational activity to market exchanges. See Reynolds L. and Skoro C., "Authority, Reciprocity, and Exchange In U.S. Management Thought," given at the Allied Social Science conference in Washington D.C., January 7, 1995.

27. Unpublished case study on RPM written by Kenneth Goodpaster. See also John Paul II *Sollicitudo Rei Socialis,* 38 on the desire for profit in relationship to the common good. Legal scholar James Boyd White states: "'To say that a corporation's only goal is to make money would be to define the business corporation—for the first time in American or English law as I understand it—as a kind of shark that lives off the community rather than as an important agency in the construction, maintenance, and transformation of our shared lives.'" (see Bellah, *et al. The Good Society.* New York, Alfred A. Knopf, Inc., 1991, p. 102, quoted from White J. "How Should We Talk About Corporations: The Languages of Economics and Citizenship," *Yale Law Journal* 94 (1985) p. 1416).

28. John Murray has pointed out that the shareholder model blurs together "the concept of 'jurisdiction' (namely, who should select and designate the directors who will govern . . . modern corporations) with the concept of what social philosophy criteria/norms should be utilized by those in the management professions who are in fact the designated to exercise management decision making prerogatives for given corporations within the legitimate parameters of applicable governing commercial law" (unpublished talk).

29. Campbell, A. and Nash, L. L. *A Sense of Mission,* Great Britain, Hutchinson Business Books Limited, 1990, pp. 19-20.

30. Eliot, T.S. *Murder in the Cathedral,* San Diego, Harcourt Brace Jovanovich, Inc., 1935, p. 44.

31. See MacIntyre, A. *After Virtue.* Notre Dame, University of Notre Dame Press, 1984, pp. 25ff, 68, 74.

32. Profits and cash flows serve as *regulators* or referees to the physical continuation of a corporation. But profits do not provide the *human quality* of its existence. Economic goods cannot sustain themselves over the long run since without a larger

integration of other human goods, management tends to destroy organizations either through the inside with poor worker morale, or through the outside with government regulation or consumer distrust (there are of course exceptions to this rule). This is why management is not only a science governed by economic standards and measurements. Management is also an art that must take into consideration not only quantitative standards, data, and measurements, but also qualitative standards, judgment, and appraisal (*The Practice of Management*, New York, Harper & Row, 1954, p. 81).

33. See May, W.F., "The Beleaguered Rulers: The Public Obligation of the Professional." *Kennedy Institute of Ethics Journal*, Vol. 2, No. 1, 1992, p. 28. "The word 'profession' etymologically means 'to testify on behalf of' or 'to stand for' something, to profess something that defines one's fundamental commitment. In the medieval world, the term chiefly applied not to lawyers, physicians, priests, or academics who professed and applied their respective bodies of knowledge to serve human need, but to monks who professed their faith in God as they took up the contemplative life. However, even the monk, in withdrawing from the active to the contemplative life, did not thereby withdraw from a public to a merely private existence. On the ritual occasion in which he renounced the world, the monk made a *public* profession of his faith; and his subsequent prayer life carried with it no less a public charge than to sustain, in Thomas Merton's telling phrase, 'the friendship of God for the human race.'"

34. See Tiemstra J. "Varieties of Institutional Economics: The Theory of the Firm." *Forum For Social Economics*, Fall 1991/Spring 1992, pp. 43-50.

35. Goodpaster, K. "Business Ethics and Stakeholder Analysis." *Business Ethics Quarterly*, vol. 1, no. 1, January 1991, p. 57.

36. Danley, J. R. *The Role of the Modern Corporation in a Free Society*, Notre Dame, IN, Notre Dame University Press, 1994, p. 222. See also Soderquist and Vecchio R. "Reconciling Shareholders' Rights and Corporate Responsibility: New Guidelines for Management," *Duke Law Review* 1978 pp 819-845.

37. Steiner, G. A. and Steiner, J. F. *Business, Government, and Society*, McGraw-Hill, Inc., 1994, p. 636. Along with recent state constituency laws, there are a hoard of consumer product liability laws, employee protection laws and other regulatory restrictions which place stakeholders in a status similar to shareholders in consideration of the organization (see Evan, W.M. and Freeman, R.E. "A Stakeholder Theory of the Modern Corporation: Kantian Capitalism." in Beauchamp, T.L. and Bowie, N.E., *Ethical Theory and Business*, 3rd Ed., Englewood Cliffs, Prentice Hall, 1988, pp. 97).

38. Although see Hansen C. "Other Constituency Statutes: A Search for Perspective," *The Business Lawyer*, vol 46 1991, pp. 1355-75 for the differences among the various states. Also see Karmel, R. "The Duty of Directors to Non-Shareholder Constituencies in Control Transactions—A Comparison of U.S. and U.K. Law," *Wake Forest Law Review* vol. 25. 1990 pp. 61-83.

39. Sec. 18. Minnesota Statutes 1986, section 302A.251 Subd. 5. See Tavis, unpublished paper. One rationale in support of the new constituency laws is that owners of corporations are not the same as owners of partnerships or sole proprietorships. A key distinction is that shareholders have limited liability. This limited liability grants firms to take the necessary risks for expansion and modernization without committing everything they own (Handy, C. *The Age of Paradox*. Boston, Harvard

Business School Press, 1994, p. 173). Since shareholders have been given a privilege of limited liability, they also have limited ownership which is beginning to be reflected in the law through constituency clauses. Is this unfair to shareholders? No, for two reasons: 1) Because of limited liability there should be limited ownership. 2) Corporations, especially public corporations are power agents for social change. Their power carries with it certain social responsibilities that goes beyond the principle of MSW.

40. Also, from an international perspective, Germany's codetermination laws reflect a co-fiduciary approach that ensure in corporate governance that labor has control rights in the firm (Furubotn, E.G., "Codetermination and the Modern Theory of the Firm: A Property-Rights Analysis", *Journal of Business*, Vol. 61. No. 2 1988, v.61, p. 165).

41. Hollenbach, D., "The Common Good Revisited." *Theological Studies*, v. 50, 1989, pp. 70-94.

42. McInerny, R. "The Primacy of the Common Good," in *The Common Good and U.S. Capitalism*, eds. Williams, O.F. and Houck, J.W., New York, University Press of America, 1987, p. 79. Of course the common good cannot be attained at the expense of human rights (see John XXIII, *Pacem in Terris* 60); yet, a singular focus on individual rights will most likely not inspire sacrifice necessary for common living.

43. Dupré, L. "The Common Good and the Open Society." in *Catholicism and Liberalism*, ed. by Douglass, R.B. and Hollenbach, D., Cambridge, Cambridge University Press, 1994, p. 183. See also Preamble of "The Responsive Communitarian Platform."

44. MacIntyre, A., *Three Rival Versions of Moral Enquiry*, Notre Dame, University of Notre Dame Press, 1990, p. 193.

45. Simon, Y. *Philosophy of Democratic Government*, Chicago, The University of Chicago Press, 1951, pp. 65, 49. See also Boswell, J. *Community and the Economy*, New York, Routledge, 1990, p. 25.

46. See Simon, Y. *Philosophy of Democratic Government*, Chicago, The University of Chicago Press, 1951, pp. 64-66; Boswell, J. *Community and the Economy*, New York, Routledge, 1990, p. 25; see also Soloman, R., "The Corporation as Community: A Reply to Ed Hartman," *Business Ethics Quarterly*, Vol. 4. July 1994, p. 276ff.

47. Goodpaster argues that the multi-fiduciary approach is "simply incompatible with widely-held moral convictions about the special fiduciary obligations owed by management to stockholders" which threatens the basis of private enterprise and property (Goodpaster, K. "Business Ethics and Stakeholder Analysis." *Business Ethics Quarterly*, vol. 1, no. 1, January 1991, p. 57). One has to wonder whether this critique is overstated. Germany's codetermination laws provide, in a sense, a co-fiduciary for employees and shareholders and it would seem unfair to say that Germany's economic system threatens free enterprise and property; rather, one could say that it respects it more by involving employees as co-fiduciaries.

48. Campbell, A. and Nash, L. L. *A Sense of Mission*, Great Britain, Hutchinson Business Books Limited, 1990, p. 21. As Danley points out "From the fact that different interests [stakeholders] are involved one would expect reference to another premise, some kind of moral premise, which would license an inference to the conclusion that social responsibility requires taking into consideration the well-

being and interests of each constituency (stakeholder group) and 'doing the right thing'" (Danley, J. R. *The Role of the Modern Corporation in a Free Society*, Notre Dame, IN, Notre Dame University Press, 1994, p. 189).

49. See Danley, p. 190. In order to overcome this impracticality, some proponents of the multi-fiduciary approach "balance" various stakeholder rights on the utilitarian principle of the "greatest good for the greatest number of people." This is best achieved it seems through the long-term profitability of the firm. If this is the case, then the multi-fiduciary approach is more like the shareholder model except there are technical or tactical differences over how best to attain long-term profitability (Danley, p. 191).

50. It goes without saying that rights cannot be collectively protected when they are individually pursued. An organization where labor, management, and shareholders pursue their rights individually cannot develop a community in which people can develop.

51. See Simon, Y. *Philosophy of Democratic Government*, Chicago, The University of Chicago Press, 1951, p. 50. "Although unity is an absolute perfection, there can be too much of it, inasmuch as, beyond a certain measure, the inappropriate kind forcibly displaces the proper one and destruction results."

52. See Dupré, L. "The Common Good and the Open Society." in *Catholicism and Liberalism*, ed. by Douglass, R.B. and Hollenbach, D., Cambridge, Cambridge University Press, 1994, p. 188.

53. As far as we know, this is the first time that the idea of the common good within the Catholic social tradition has been engaged with the purpose of the organization. Consequently, we do not have the advantage of a long tradition of how and how not to make the engagement between these two areas. Because of this lack of experience, we are at the beginning of the learning curve. We hope, however, that it will be the beginning of an interesting conversation. In the future, we will develop what the common good implies in compensation, job design, participation, product development, and so forth. On such specifics, points of convergence will occur with both the shareholder and stakeholder model. What will differ, however, is the philosophy of how managers come to view such practical issues.

Chapter Nineteen

Why Philosophize About Conduct? or What Became of Unjust Discourse?

William G. O'Neill

The title of this chapter, and its subtitle, are evidence of an interest during recent months stirred by an engaging issue encountered adventitiously in perusing new literature on ethics. It led to my posing a question which is not usually posed in this way by philosophers: where does being a philosopher belong as a professional activity? Where does the philosopher fit as a professional among professionals?

The profundity and enormous historical antiquity of philosophy guarantee that there is always some sort of suitable answer to the question of what may be the role of philosophy as a study or discipline. The same is true about questions concerning the general value or relevance of philosophy itself to specific problems or concerns. But what is the value of being a philosopher when one considers it from a point of view such as the thematic focus of this conference: professional ethics or values and professional training?

Philosophers do not usually think or talk about "profession" in this way. They usually think in terms of philosophy itself. Philosophers teach philosophy, which includes teaching ethics and values. Also, ethical problems are, by definition and custom, subject to philosophical analysis in numerous ways. Philosophy is about the good and the true, etc., etc. But a certain distinct anti-ethical cynicism is often to be found in discussions with "professionals" and, sometimes, in print. This is likely to be regarded by many philosophers as an "anti-philosophy" reaction. Perhaps the reaction is more accurately to be characterized as "anti-philosopher".

A recent textbook on business ethics contained a strongly supportive reference to the statement of a Vice President for Ethics of General Dynamics Corporation that ethics is about conduct, *not* philosophy. (Trevino, 1995, pp.13-15.) This textbook further emphasizes that it is not a book about philosophy but about management. Ethics are a matter of human behavior, which is best understood in an organizational context and, in any case, is manageable in such a context. This is ethics in a managerial vein.

It is not a question of what is right to do, but of why people do what they do in organizations and, therefore, of how to manage people's ethical behavior. (Trevino, 1995, pp. 143-145.) Ethical judgements depend, not on internal principles or qualities of character (although these are presented as important), but upon the external factors influencing behavior—the expectations, standards, practices, etc., of the relevant organization, group or society.

A great deal of advice, indisputably sound and sensible, is contained in the book. The book is an advocate of integrity. It strongly promotes the importance of training in ethics for managers and of teaching ethical practice for the whole corporation. The book does not create an occasion calling for refutation or dispute or criticism in a special way.

There remains, however, the disavowal of philosophy for the central purposes of the book. The disavowal is repeated during the text. (Trevino, 1995, pp. 66-70.) The disavowal raises a particular issue for a philosopher, one with deep roots and one posing a classical challenge: what is the genuine and meaningful role of philosophy in human affairs? More pointedly, is there a role for a philosopher as a mundane professional?

A variety of spontaneous replies occurs to the philosophical mind upon encountering any disavowal of philosophy in ethics: What about conscience? Are not ethics most appropriately about conscience and not simply about conduct? What about eternal principles? What about universal values? Is not such disavowal the clear road to tendentious relativism?

But one may allow that, for many reasonable and highly important purposes, ethics might simply be regarded as manageable behavior and as reflective of the norms, values, and standards of organizations or relevant groups. One might assent to this in general terms and *get on with it*. Many people will thus assent and proceed productively and usefully. Thus, as a philosopher standing before the judgment of the world of human affairs, one can perceive oneself to be vanquished. (This is said tongue-in-cheek, but with a certain genuine poignancy.)

At the point of admitting defeat, there can be seen a sort of irony, an intriguing note, which may be too precious, as well as too poignant, to pass over without comment. What is needed is a contemporary update on the progress of Unjust Discourse (Pearson, 1962, p. 166). What has become of him in two and a half millennia?

Aristophanes in the play *The Clouds* has given us a wonderful literary image and a comical treatment of something at least partially similar to what comes forth in the discussion of being ethical while disavowing philosophy. (Aristophanes, 1948, pp. 117-170.) Philosophers are represented in *The Clouds* by Socrates, who is at the head of an institution of thinkers, a polemical think tank. They have discovered the wonders of weak reasoning which, though it be weak, is nevertheless the victor over truer reasoning.

Philosophers make the worse to seem the better way. They exult in a hypertrophy of clever wit and rational hairsplitting in defense of a point. In so far as an issue is made about justice, the philosophers present the argument which, though it plead no justice, still defeats the better argument (Pearson, 1962, pp. 167-169).

Unjust Discourse and Just Discourse appear personified as characters in the play. Just Discourse represents the traditions of the best in literary paideia, from the poets, Pericles, etc. Unjust Discourse represents sophistical reasonings and argumentation. They engage in a winner-take-all competitive debate. Unjust Discourse brings to bear the weapons of "new maxims" or principles of contemporary practical thinking very artfully contrived to be relevant to what people actually do in their affairs. Unjust Discourse employs all those devices which people will readily understand or identify with and which they will be most likely to interpret as brilliant.

It is important to assert that one's behavior, even if it was not ideally perfect or absolutely pure, was acceptable (Pearson, 1962, pp. 161-167). Anyone would have done the same under the circumstances and it is unreasonable and unrealistic to assess blame. Just Discourse retreats in the face of this argument as if stung in the face by attacking bees. He sits with the audience and is silent, having been defeated by the weaker, less noble reasoner and forced to join his ranks.

Of course Aristophanes confuses Socrates with his avowed opponents, the Sophists. He also takes sophistry as identical globally with philosophy as an application of reasoning to self-serving ends. The principles emerging from the Socratic method in Socrates' discussions, such as those with Plato and other followers, are not noticed. But then, dramatic or comedic license is too grand a thing to be restricted by these considerations.

The Greeks generally, and the Athenians in particular, are aware of the need for making practical judgments in life and for not proceeding on the purest principles alone (Pearson, 1962, pp. 161-165). Before the rise of the Sophists and of high philosophy, poets were the teachers of principles. The Greek *paideia* or popular education in values had been largely literary. In this context, immediate results such as life, pleasure, and riches did not always win out over long term principles such as honor, integrity, or justice. Apart from the poets, consider also Pericles.

Each age must answer for itself in suitable ways the challenge presented by Aristophanes in the debate between Unjust Discourse and Just Discourse. Will strong, unyielding reasoning from pure principles prevail, or will weak reasoning prevail as it easily can. And if weak reasoning prevail, how does this victory came to be assimilated into justification? In the end, true reason and pure principles indeed yield to compromise and to hedging about the truth.

The professional philosopher today faces an interesting dilemma in the face of exhortations to proceed with ethics without philosophy. He will see that weak reasoning prevails repeatedly in making the worse appear to be the better. One can manage conduct without philosophy. The comic character Unjust Discourse may seem to have been dressed up anew and marched onto the stage in our own day. This is his challenge, the dilemma he poses: If the philosopher, as regards ethics, continues to do what he as done traditionally and seems most properly fit to do, he may thus appear to be useless as an abstruse figure in an ivory tower. But, on the other hand, suppose he capitulates, as it were. If he immerses himself in what is happening in the world of affairs in which ethics are practiced, or violated, and if he is drawn into the sophisticated, technical, and concrete elements of dealing with ethical conduct, he may thus appear to be useless since there may seem to be no need for philosophers in such discussions. Put another way, the question of what philosophy is good for may be answerable in a variety of ways. The question of what philosophers are good for is difficult.

Today's instruction in some of the best texts in business ethics, for example, prompts the learner to appreciate that, sadly, there is no clear or unequivocal answer to those questions which arise concerning the conflicts between loyalty to the corporation or business and concern for the protection of third parties. This is especially keen in the cases in which self-interest raises itself as a worry: whistle blowing and the like. Prudential reasoning here is clearly distinguished from moral reasoning. The maxim is to follow one's self-interest when prudential reasons outweigh moral reasons. When the opposite—moral reasons outweighing prudential ones—is the case, then follow one's obligations to others. (Shaw, 1995, p. 373.) It is a fascinating caracole of the mind thus to pit prudence over against morality. This provides the remarkable opportunity of weighing both in a logical neutrality distinct from either.

How does a philosopher intervene in defense of "the Good"? His concern is irrelevant, evidently. Whistle blowing or, even more simply, reporting wrongdoing is not even governed today by a set of principles applicable *per se*. This would be a lack of prudence. The advice of the business ethician (Shaw, 1995, pp. 369-370.) in the finest manuals is clarion: sort through the ideals involved and the obligations and anticipated consequences, and then try to make a decision as to what elements should have *the greatest emphasis*. (Shaw, 1995, pp. 79-80.) Bring on *The Clouds*.

In urging students to attainment of proficiency in understanding health care ethics, current textbooks exhort that laws, court decisions, social customs, standards of professional associations and the like are precious resources. These sources help us to reduce ambiguity on many complicated issues regarding confidentiality, informed consent, surrogates, status of fetal life, micro- and macroallocation of medical resources, approving patients for transplants, etc.

These sources, however, do not provide what is definitive. It is not even to be understood that one ought necessarily to agree with such sources of standards or principles. (Garrett, 1993, pp. 12-13.) The special value of the individual patient on the one hand, and of those things *suggested* by the individual provider's experiences on the other hand, are the supervening elements in critical ethical evaluations. Somewhat supposititious as a foundation for organized and systematically justified management of conduct.

In laying groundwork for instilling a sense of military ethics in those personnel training for leadership, the current textbook advice includes the inspiring declaration that, unrelativistically, ethics is a search for those universals by which we can judge what should and should not be done. Exemplars, generally from literary works of significant merit, are adduced to clarify many points. Ethics, however, are further declared to be fourfold in source: customs, goals, outcomes anticipated, and circumstances. A wise *blending* of these will lead us away from and beyond trouble. (Toner, 1995, pp. 16-19.) The trouble that is avoided is the moral decay and confusion which already plagues many sectors of contemporary society. Somewhat proleptic thinking.

What is or can be the expertise of the philosopher? Is the expertise of a philosopher, as applied to the matter of conduct, either genuine or useful? (Kaplan, 1992, pp. 18-42.) If we regard the philosopher's expertise to consist, to any significant degree, in the knowledge of moral or ethical theory or in metaethical reflections, it is difficult to see how this expertise is useful for dealing with conduct at the level of the corporation or of professional activities. Not since the high days of the manual tradition of natural law philosophy has there been a canonical set of direct philosophical applications of moral theory to varieties of conduct. And these canons were far from having unanimous support.

Apart from a general understanding of a few principal theories as archetypes of deciding good conduct, ethical theories in their niceties and fine points are really not necessary for practitioners in the sphere of real events. Furthermore, expertise concerning these theories, knowledge of close philosophical argumentation, is not even possible as a requirement for dealing ethically with conduct. The principles of a virtue-directed ethics may be inspiring and useful, but one need not be able to justify beyond counterarguments that this theory prevails over others. The same can be said about an utilitarian understanding of the greatest happiness principle or of the common good. Foundational discussions of moral theory are really not necessary nor possible as a requirement for a practitioner's making ethical decisions about conduct.

Consider the comparable fact that a theoretical understanding of foundations of mathematics or of philosophy of mathematics is not required for complicated mathematical applications in engineering, etc. The current status of the ongoing arguments about theories actually give rise, in textbooks about business or professional ethics, to the curious impression that moral theory is a matter of eclecticism depending on the case to be decided or even of personal attitudinal preference and nothing more. De La Rochefoucauld said that hypocrisy is the homage that vice pays to virtue. We may say that eclecticism and relativism are the homage of Unjust Discourse to philosophy.

Might the expertise of a philosopher consist in the application of theories to concrete cases and circumstances? Something like an "engineering" model of ethics in application, for example, to health care is frequently envisioned. Another way of seeing this is to think of a model of application under something like the nomological-deductive model of scientific explanation in the philosophy of science. Such a model has had a difficult history in philosophy of science and, in the thinking of some, in applied ethics as well. This model is that ethical problems or cases are "explained" and therefore solved in applying the appropriate theory to the problem or case or situation. Logic, knowledge of theory, and some bridge principles are regnant here.

The reality, however, very often is that ethicians do not involve themselves too successfully in active cooperation on the scene. Consider heath care practice. (Kaplan, 1992, pp. 3-17.) Philosophers are not really suited to "parachute" into a situation and clarify things. The results are often frustrating and unhelpfully nondirective. By sheer force of practice, many policies of high ethical concern (allocation of medical resources, neonatal practice, etc.) are settled by senior medical staff in discussions not typically involving philosophers. Even specialized ethics courses for personnel are too frequently perceived as irrelevant or missing the crucial needs of these learners. Similarly, corporate decisions of significant ethical concern on matters of daily policy are likely to be made by high level operational managers working apart from those philosophers who are employed in corporate ethics departments.

One sees in numerous instances today the presence of philosophers or philosophically trained practitioners serving on ethics committees or working in on-the-scene consultative capacities in hospitals, prisons, etc. The presence of ethicists on the scene and on the floor in hospitals has given us the term "beeper ethics" in current usage. Applications of philosophical expertise may be helpful at the level of discussion of certain institutional policies and in committee meetings, but less so, as it is reported, in the concrete highly pressured instances in which medical personnel are feeling most in need of ethical determination.

The actual making of decisions is often exceedingly complicated and is much more relevant to the medical expertise of staff and to their knowledge of technically expressed policies than to their ability to apply moral theory per se. Ethical questions in many professional areas have more to do with standards set by professional organizations, common practice accepted in organizations and the surrounding society, court decisions, and legal principles than with moral theory as such. Furthermore, moral theories are generally obscure in the matter of their principles of application, if not downright opaque, and disagreement among philosophers is to be expected.

The giving of workshops and classes as part of professional ethical training may indeed be of use, but this should be considered in conjunction with the caveat than such courses and workshops have been going on for some time and their impact generally on professional and business behavior or on the attitudes of professionals or businessmen is far from being demonstrated as very great.

Does the philosophical expertise relevant to the ethics of managing conduct consist in having the vision of the good which philosophers have or in the scope of their considerations or in their reasoning skills? On these points we must observe that a great and profound vision of the good is not inherent to being a philosopher nor is it exclusively found within the ranks of philosophers. Along with a broad scope of consideration in deciding issues and expertise in reasoning, logic, and decision making, vision is part of a set of cognitive attributes or skills which, we might argue, ought to be the attainment of educated persons in professional capacities or in responsible positions in business. These should generally be the attributes of any enlightened citizen participating in a democracy. Such mental attributes are, in fact, found quite frequently exercised outside the ranks of philosophers. Philosophers are not even the only teachers of these skills.

If the expertise were to be understood as related to something like character, suffice it to say that greatness of character is not the special province of philosophers nor even especially a characteristic of them. They cannot, as a class, boast even piety like theologians.

We must, nevertheless, be able to determine that there is truly something which is the expertise of the philosopher. And it may be thought to be a matter of having a particular perspective, of standing outside of things in a particularly helpful way. This will not be the exclusive domain of the philosopher, nor will it be agreed by everyone to be the special role of the philosopher. But it can be highly important.

What, then, should philosophers as professionals do? How can they avoid the fate of joining the ranks of Unjust Discourse? If we explore the possibilities for what professional philosophers may choose to do, or for how they may choose to react, a number of things suggest themselves.

One possibility would be, in effect, to do nothing. That is to say, to continue in the traditional manner functioning internally to philosophy as the pure thinker on moral philosophy and ethics and making excursions externally into the world of human affairs by way of discussing applications of their thought. In spite of one of the horns of the dilemma mentioned before—seeming abstruse and useless—this position can be adopted and, to a degree, defended within our context about managing conduct. Who can say prescriptively and in advance that this activity is not going to be fruitful, even highly so, for the future of the enterprise of understanding and managing conduct, particularly conduct in organizations?

New philosophical insights at the theoretical level may ultimately be interpreted in a way useful for the managing of persistent ethical problems. New fundamental forms of moral theory are possible and could create new archetypes for thinking generally about human conduct. Kant's deontology had such an effect in the late eighteenth and early nineteenth century and up to the present day.

The situation is in some respects similar to the considerations which become involved in determining policies for governmental funding of scientific research. If research is supported too narrowly on the principle of that which most closely addresses current societal needs and in the manner apparently most promising for achieving results, truly revolutionary projects of unimagined value and application become less likely to be supported. They may not succeed or even be undertaken at all.

At the end of the last century, much emphasis was placed in some advanced countries on the mechanical technology involved in music boxes. This technology was growing progressively more complex and remarkable. Predictions a hundred years ago spoke of people someday having wondrous music at their fingertips any time of day and in any home or place of business. One wonders what might have been achieved if there had been funding on an enormous scale for development of such machinery. In any case, the reality of the prediction in our own times far outstrips the prediction but in ways that have nothing to do with the mechanical technology which gave rise to the prediction. People in mid-twentieth century working with an unrelated set of interests—electronics, semi-conductive materials, miniaturization of electrical circuits—produced the fundamental requirements for the omnipresence and high quality of broadcast and variously recorded music of great fidelity—even of symphonic performances.

Doing nothing, in the sense of following through with the traditional activities of philosophy, also includes the usual teaching of philosophy. This has for centuries included teaching not only those who are to be philosophers themselves (in fact proportionally comparatively less of that is done today), but also those for whom instruction in philosophy is important for their training. This would include, presumably, those for whom the management of conduct is a concern, as well as those whose conduct is to be managed. There are some caveats here. On the matter of abstruseness and abstractness, philosophers as teachers must be careful that what they teach does not constitute simply a burden to be borne briefly for acquiring a credential. The example of the deplorable attitude of students toward studying the classics of literature (Shakespeare for example) must not be duplicated here. Not just any exposure to philosophy is worthwhile for the managers of conduct, but an exposure which is capable of truly inspiring. This may be a very difficult and thankless endeavor.

Generally speaking, the traditional position is not likely to be accepted with sympathy by those who need to manage conduct in the world of human affairs. A stronger and much more public program is needed for the profession of philosophy. This program must be aggressively and somewhat noisily promoted, in a way which philosophers are not accustomed to doing. Philosophers must find ways, in organized endeavors, to enter the realm of the journalistic press and other mass media and to connect better with the noticeable profile of public events. The program might include:

Involvement in Governmental, Professional and Industrial Policy Nationwide

Philosophers can be useful in entering the debate over public policy issues from the point of view of the broader scope of their professional concern for moral philosophy. This includes influencing policies in the direction of a fuller realization of justice or equity, of more humane treatment of persons and other creatures. It includes influencing the balancing of harms and risks of harm to the environment and to the quality of life in our society with the purposes of public policy or with standards set by professional organizations or industries. This would involve, again, an aggressive—and, therefore, uncharacteristic—storming of avenues of public notice, becoming public-relations oriented, and inducing friendly interest by the media. This is a daunting task, but one well served by genius, acute argumentation, and accomplished rhetoric.

Dedication to the Restoration of the Quality of Conscience

To the degree that the concept of conscience is made trivial or emotional, anti-intellectual or anti-technical, to that degree there will be considerable moral problems in any society or profession or corporation or industry. There is, therefore, a serious need for the philosopher's perspective and assistance. The philosopher is like Socrates: a professional life examiner. But he can do this without the presuppositions inherent in the professions or corporate life or public policy. The philosopher is inherently opposed to the excessive focus upon business or professional goals which comes with alarming tunnel vision about values and distressing rationalizations about judgments and conduct.

A conscience functioning properly, percipient and perspicuous, keeps the sense of some meaning of life alive in our decisions and works. Philosophers, by their understanding of reasoning and argumentation as well as of moral philosophy, are well situated to rehabilitate the notion of conscience as a rational skill, a learned excellence or expertise, a defensible and assessable power. In many instances one hears conscience spoken of as a kind of miasma of emotional and psychologically turbid factors, or as a kind of soft intuitive sensitivity to some sort of goodness. As such, conscience can seem to be a nuisance or annoyance getting in the way of real-world, hardnosed decision and action.

Conscience is spoken of, even in reputable textbooks, as something which can "bother" a person, which almost seems to need to be surmounted if one is to be truly fit for a particular organization or corporation. Conscience needs to be tempered with cultural awareness, etc. Philosophers can be expected to do much to rehabilitate the concept of the rational skills involved in the fundamental judgment of conscience: that *I* should (or should not) do *this now*.

Provision of an "External Eyes" Scrutiny of Professionals, Government, and Business in a Publicly Discernible Way

The external critiques of judgments, standards, rules, practices, etc., can be a most useful and appropriate occupation of philosophers in the world of human affairs. It is, among other things, a question of avoiding artifacts of the conversation or discussion from becoming normative or conceptually overwhelming. Put in other terms, the philosopher must be a kind of external watchdog warning when what is expedient becomes the standard or, still worse, the justification or the mark of excellence. He may help to avoid having the worse case seeming to be the better once again.

Avoidance of artifacts of the conversation or discussion ranges from a kind of real language analysis to confronting the situation in which the expedient becomes the standard, even if abusive, or in which the familiar becomes principle, even if unexamined.

Consider the taking of responsibility for one's actions and mistakes and also being able to comprehend their gravity. Consider being able to weigh them in the balance in assessing outcomes. In a simple example a technical categorial term, a bureaucratic term, became a sort of moral principle. The term "human error" indicates most simply a cause of some malfunction or undesired outcome which is not due to malfunctioning equipment, nor inaccurate data, but to a human being, a person, failing to do what was supposed to have been done. The term "machine error" indicated a mechanical or technological disorder in the process and called for a repair or retuning or redesigning. Human error simply puts the problem outside that category.

As time passed and the term became a kind of jargon, it gained a certain quasi-ethical weight. One may adduce human error now as an excuse. The indignant assertion of human error somehow throws criticism back upon the complainer. "I am human, therefore I am subject to human error, therefore: How dare you blame me?" The original meaning of the term is more like the statement made by the thirty-seventh President of the United States at this University after his resignation from office due to the Watergate scandal: said Richard Nixon: "I screwed up." Human error generally means that someone has screwed up and probably culpably.

While this example may not be heavy with ethical import, it is illustrative of the means whereby the familiar and repeated gains a certain weight from assumptions. In the health care profession and industry, for example, some commentators have come to see a type of abuse of power in some of the very mundane things which physicians and others do routinely: the scheduling of simultaneous appointments causing patients arriving on time to be kept waiting at length; cancellation of appointments with advance, but very short notice, for reasons which are not urgent; etc. Similar abuses can be found in the scheduling of hours by governmental or municipal departments and offices, the scheduling of work hours in highly unionized service and repair industries, etc.

These examples are of comparatively small abuses, sometimes, but the dynamics involved can lead to much more serious occurrences. The judgment of what is reasonable convenience or profit or salary, of what is fair in situations of advantage or disadvantage or compensation, of what is pardonable discrimination or harm, of what are sufficient testing or preventative measures— considering not only potential liability but effects upon end users, of what is truly a conflict of interest, etc., are subject to the same artificiality from the internal conversation or discussion.

Many largely wrong ideas, or only partially true concepts, go unchallenged in ethical discussions of this sort: the surpassing importance of being a team player, the great value of slavish dedication of time and energy to one's job or career, the often unquestioned value of getting to the top, the ineluctability of certain undesirable conduct because "everybody does it" and it would be impossible to eradicate anyway, the notion of environmental damage as an absolute and unqualified concept, and many others.

Notions in health care discussions such as dignity and autonomy, while undoubtedly of profound importance, are often introduced quite uncritically into arguments or discussions. When is the condition of a suffering patient a violation of human dignity? Is coma inherently undignified? Is informed consent a matter always and everywhere of autonomy, or is it really indemnity?

Patently and potently unjustified conclusions can result in many areas of consideration. The external-eyes reflective critique is important and constantly needed. The Socratic gadfly is needed.

Maintenance of the Perspective Referring to a Broader and Profounder Scope in a Publicly Noticeable Way

Ethical management of conduct, if it is to be of a very worthy quality, requires not only consistency as related to cases and decisions, but also consistency between decisions and principles. But which principles? Some sense of a meaning or purpose of life as a background setting for many judgements by professional people and those in business is important.

Consider that in advanced societies, even among those who are successful achievers and accomplishers for themselves and their organizations, many people's lives are miserable whether they find their jobs miserable or not. Success in life is often not truly success. The grand principles of "the Good" or the good life become precisely less relevant as the scope of reference in the discussion or conversation becomes narrowed. The prospect of real happiness must be at least suspected to become somewhat narrowed also. The managers of conduct, of course, cannot manage this dimension on the principles of contextual behavior, nor even ask the necessary questions. Just Discourse might in this way resume the stage in a contemporary sequel to Aristophanes.

Conclusion

Aristophanes presented what may well be considered a timeless conflict, a timeless fascinating mystery: weaker reasoning and Unjust discourse do indeed seem to win out in contemporary society. The Periclean or true Socratic stance cannot be maintained without sacrificing one's place as a respected member of society—respected, that is, for being sensible, for finding a way to get along, for getting on with it. The program adumbrated here is not really an answer to the challenge in the sense of arming the philosopher—or his representative, Just Discourse—with the weapons to vanquish weak reasoning or Unjust Discourse. Neither does it lay forth something inherent to philosophy itself, or to the primary philosophical impulses or vocation. It does not suggest some truth or insight previously hidden and now revealed. It proposes a set of considerations, out of numerous possibilities for philosophers, of getting into the world of affairs without engaging in the forlorn debate with Unjust Discourse. It is input from the sidelines, but relevant, sincere, and of estimable worth to society.

In this connection, it should be noted that preparation or training of philosophers, of course, is not significantly geared toward participation in such a project or program. The societies of philosophers do not give it great status. Neither is this very often a significant part of the reasons for which philosophers are hired, evaluated, promoted, or rewarded professionally.

It may be correctly assumed that philosophers who do not ignore these possibilities, who enter into the scene, are likely, as are any philosophers, to become entangled in numerous and endless debates, chronic pettifogging, among themselves over advice given publicly from the sidelines. To the extent that this is true, Aristophanes is vindicated in his strange caricature of Socrates and his fellow thinkers in their sophistical academy. Unjust Discourse is poised to win again.

Perhaps the perennial and disquieting reality overarching this conflict reflects the wisdom embedded in the humorist's maxim: a half-truth is like half a brick: a very useful thing; it can fit in where the whole thing will not go, and it is much easier to throw in a fight.

References

Aristophanes. (1948) *The Clouds*. In *Five Comedies*. The Living Cleveland: Library, World Publishing Company.

Caplan, Arthur L. (1994) *If I Were a Rich Man, Could I Buy a Pancreas?* Bloomington, Indiana: Indiana University Press.

Garrett, Thomas M., and Harold W. Baillie and Rosellen M. Garrett. (1993) *Health Care Ethics. Principles & Problems*. Second edition. Englewood Cliffs, New Jersey: Prentice-Hall.

Pearson, Lionel. (1962) *Popular Ethics in Ancient Greece*. Stanford, California: Stanford University Press.

Shaw, William H., and Vincent Barry. (1995) *Moral Issues in Business*. Sixth edition. Belmont, California: Wadsworth Publishing Company.

Toner, James H. (1995) *True Faith and Allegiance. The Burden of Military Ethics*. Lexington, Kentucky: The University Press of Kentucky, 1995.

Trevino, Linda K. and Katherine A. Nelson. (1995) *Managing Business Ethics. Straight Talk about How to Do It Right*. New York: John Wiley & Sons, Inc.

Chapter Twenty

Social Markets and Language Games: The Evolution of Vocational Training in England and Wales

Richard Pring
Geoff Hayward

Context

Let me start with several examples.

The First

Fanta Schools Art Competition National
Presentation with TV Star Sarah Greene

Invitation

The Fanta Schools Art Competition was open to 26,000 primary, middle and junior schools and attracted entries from all over the country. Children aged eight to eleven were asked to depict 'My Fantastic Friend' and to produce a piece of original writing to describe their picture.

"MAKE FRIENDS WITH FANTA"

The Second

The London Coffee Information Centre provides an educational programme.

'Although the emphasis ... is on coffee *concepts,* all educational material has been produced with the aim of contributing to the curriculum development of schools and colleges.'

Hence

'Coffee in the Curriculum' is an entirely new concept in educational communication ... Since coffee occupies a vital role in world trade and is a major source of income for many developing countries, it is considered to have a legitimate claim to normal curriculum time ... However, it is also a very interesting and adaptable commodity which relates easily to cross-curriculum application by directly integrating into science, environmental science, geography, history, home economics, economics and humanities subject areas and also because it has greatly influenced art, craft, religion and general culture.

The Third

Project SPAM

The 'British Trades Alphabet' study cards this year contain a 'SPAM Project'. What is SPAM? Why is it good for you? What is it made from? How does it get in the can?

To support the project the makers of SPAM, Liverpool based Newforge Foods, have produced an education pack containing an 8-page booklet all about SPAM and the history of canning, examples of SPAM advertisements and a SPAM Gang Badge, all packed in a special SPAM project folder.

Also available is a SPAM recipe wall chart showing 10 new ways of enjoying the great taste of SPAM ...

... competition where the first prize is a rafting holiday in the American Rockies.

The Fourth

Burger King have now sponsored a school in the East End of London. It is called, inevitably, the Burger King School. Similarly sponsored schools in the US have a very efficient way of motivating pupils. Good behaviour merits vouchers which can be cashed out at the local fast food store.

The Fifth

Unipart U is the education and training centre (physically) of Unipart — the third 'university' of Oxford with its own professor (a 'business philosopher') and faculty structure each with its own Dean. For a library it has a 'learning curve centre' and for its Information Technology a 'leading edge centre'. It integrates economic success with education and training opportunities for all, and it provides a context for ideas (from whatever source) to be nurtured and developed. Learning is its business; learning is accessible to all; but the learning that Unipart U is interested in is contrasted with that of older universities (such as its neighbour in Oxford).

The Sixth

At a recent conference I addressed in Perth, Scotland, the list of school teachers present contained several new style designations such as director of human resources and chief executive.

*****

These are random examples of how the ethos and the language of education is changing because of the involvement of business or because business is seen as an organisational model within which education might be seen to fit. It has been given a stimulus on various accounts.

First, sponsorship: the City Technology Colleges are a recent example of where employers were encouraged to set up their own independent schools, albeit heavily subsidised by government. Furthermore, schools, short of cash, seek sponsorship from local employers.

Second, employer input to education and training is encouraged — *individually,* as through schemes for engineer involvement or through participation in the governing bodies of schools, and *company-based* as through compact schemes.

Third, employers may offer *Institutional models* for the most efficient way of running schools- management structures, for instance, such as TQM.

Fourth, with regard to *Teaming models,* employers, with a background of industrial training and critical of the standards of Teaming found in those who have recently graduated from school, may feel that their training model provides insight into Teaming in general. For example, in motivating people to learn, a simple system of rewards and sanctions might be instituted — performance related pay at work becomes performance related rewards at school; assessment lies in the observation of competent behaviour; vague educational aims become precise mission statements; a rational, business-like model of Teaming takes over.

One could provide many illustrations and reasons for the growing interconnection between business and education. Many of these are healthy. Schools need the support of their community, and employers are a key element in that community. Schools must prepare young people for adult life and an important part of adult life lies in earning a living. The specific training required of industry needs an appropriate general education in schools appropriate in terms of capacities, literacy and numeracy, attitudes, social skills, personal qualities.

But this coming together raises sharply the question, too, of differences — differences of purpose, of accountability, of values and of the language through which these purposes and values are expressed.

Education and Business

Let me sharpen the discussion by drawing a contrast between an education liberally conceived and business.

First, the aims of the two seem to be very different. The aims of education concern learning and not any kind of learning. Peters (1965) describes it as initiation into worthwhile activities, that is, into those activities which, in providing a broad intellectual formation, require no justification beyond the recognition of their own intrinsic value. The aims of business concern selling a product, normally for a profit, for which particular sorts of learning are deemed necessary, not as worthwhile in themselves, but as a means to the purposes of the business. Value is derived from the market, not from the intrinsic worth of that which is to be sold. Possibly the schers of SPAM hate it.

Second, with regard to education, people are valuable in so far as they have minds to be developed and personalities to be formed; with regard to business, they are valuable either as potential purchasers or consumers of the product or as the employees devoted to creating it.

Third, the content of education is derived from selective traditions of enquiry endorsed by those who are regarded as experts or authorities within those different traditions. The content of the business, by contrast, is derived from an analysis of what is required by the market analysis of consumer demand.

Fourth, the relation between teacher and learner is essentially that between initiated and neophyte, in which the one tries to undermine his or her authority by introducing the young learner to the content and mode of enquiry through which they might explore together the uncertainties of history or literature or science. Hence, ideally the teaching faculty stresses collegiality — a collection of educated persons — in which the head is a primus inter pares, exercising authority through academic leadership as much as through executive fiat. That at least is an ideal which once prevailed in universities. The relation between business executive and staff, on the other hand, is one of 'line management' in which the person above is **in** authority rather than an authority.

Fifth, the success of an educational activity cannot be easily measured because (a) it is sowing seeds which may mature many years later, (b) that success may not be what the educator predicted or wished it to be — the educated person develops an independence of mind; whereas the success of a business activity can be quantitatively measured by criteria logically related to the purposes of the business — in particular, quantity of sales, customer satisfaction, and profit.

There are no doubt other ways of contrasting two different sorts of activity — education and business. But these suffice to bring out differences in value which seem to be inherent within different kinds of activity.

I must, however, immediately make distinctions and state reservations. Business might well be conducted within a wider moral framework in which there is a belief in the importance of the product — Smith might have gone into business with a strong moral desire to make organic food more widely available. Furthermore, there might be a strong sense of responsibility and respect for consumer and employee, reflected in all sorts of social and welfare arrangements. Again, firms such as Unipart U would see themselves to be modelled much more in the style of an educational establishment than the stereotypical authoritarian business.

Similarly, education has to have resources so that it can concentrate on its main task, and the obtaining of those resources might require selling what it is doing to ensure there will be enough fee-paying learners. Furthermore, when resources are short, educational institutions may have to be more efficient and assume the management structure which creates that efficiency in industry — hence, the turning of headteachers into chief executives and their deputies into directors of human resources. And the collegiality of a learning institution is more often a myth than a reality.

The contrast, therefore, is messy, and it is precisely that kind of messiness which needs to be sorted out. In sorting it out, we need to bear in mind the respective aims and values of each and of the danger of those values being undermined, particularly the values which are inherent within the educational enterprise. On the other hand, we must be careful. First, it may be the case that some businesses have a more enlightened view of learning than many educational institutions, and that some educational institutions are taking on broad business models of management which successful businesses themselves have rejected.

I want to illustrate this, first, in relation to the use of managerial models which educational institutions have adopted and, second, in relation to the use of a particular metaphor.

The Changing Models of Management within Education

Two things have affected the way in which management is thought about in schools and colleges. The first is the recent extraction of them from a *system* of education and the subsequent creation of quasi autonomous business units in competition with each other. The second is a more theoretical one — namely, the belief that there is a way of conceiving management which, although developed within the world of business, transcends that and is universally applicable to all management systems, including education.

The most obvious aspect of the context in which schools and colleges find themselves is that of the quasi-market, albeit within the regulations laid down by the funding councils. The *incorporation* of colleges means that each is responsible for its own financial affairs, including employment and maintenance, insurance and legal costs, strategic planning and quality control. In that respect each has to assume certain financial and administrative approaches typical of businesses. Income depends on 'customers' and so these have to be attracted to the college. And that entails a competitive approach vis-a-vis other institutions (including private training agencies) as far as the limited number of possible students. It entails a 'marketing' of courses and services. It encourages, too, the creation of new services and courses — if you like, a new market.

However, this takes place within very strict financial rules dictated by the funding councils which in turn responds to government policy concerning public expenditure. Thus, at the moment colleges are having to expand at roughly 7% per year for three years in order to retain the same funding in real terms. Or, again, what counts as a full-time student for funding purposes is defined by funding councils, not by the college (for example, taking 3 rather than 2 A Levels). Moreover, the rules change as government, in regulating student numbers, curbs the franchising arrangements of higher education. Hence, it is only a quasimarket.

This contrasts with a situation in which financial controls and strategic planning lay with local government, and the colleges were seen to provide a public service within a locally planned system of education and training. There the local government determined the distribution of numbers (for example, according to catchment areas), the courses to be run according to local training requirements, and the distribution of funds according to the perceived needs of the college. The college could concentrate upon the quality of education and training, freed from the need to compete or to market itself or to make the books balance. Furthermore, employed by the local government, teachers and lecturers were not dependent upon the welfare of their respective institutions — they could be found work elsewhere as strategic and local planning changed.

Within this quasi-market, colleges and schools have to adopt different sorts of management practice for two reasons. The first is that, within the constraints of the funding arrangements, they need to cost their different services to ensure these remain within budget and to estimate what practices are tot) expensive to run or what practices might profitably be introduced. The second is that the funds will be provided on certain conditions of quality control. That is taken to mean the adoption of 'performance indicators' whereby those outside the institution might judge the quality of education and training.

How far does this changed context affect what happens educationally? Can the educational aims of the college or school remain unaffected by these management changes? At one level it would seem so, as though there can be a separation of educational values, which inform teaching and which shape what goes on in classrooms, from management arrangements.

However, the changed management is reflected in a language which does not seem to be indifferent to educational values. In other words, management, as it is now conceived, transforms our understanding of the aims and values normally associated with education (see Pring, 1995).

The language of management would seem to require statements of objectives which will be sufficiently precise and clear as to provide 'performance indicators'. That is, the objectives will provide the measures against which performance will be judged. Management, to be efficient, must know exactly what the institution is trying to achieve. Having assessed in an unambiguous way whether the institution has achieved the objectives, then either it needs to reassess the appropriateness of those objectives or it needs to question the appropriateness of the means to their achievement (e.g., the quality of teaching). Furthermore, those objectives will be formulated according to 'fitness for purpose', namely, the satisfaction of the purposes established by the customers, upon whose business the college or school is dependent for its income. These are the employers, the students, and their parents.

Market Metaphor

What lies behind the different understanding of education and training is the shift in metaphors through which it is described — those, such as audits and performance indicators, derived from business. I want, however, in this section to dwell upon one metaphor in particular, namely that of markets.

The market is said to depict the relations between teacher and learner in a particular way namely, as a relation between provider and consumer. It represents a shift in language about education, and about the relation between teacher and learner within education.

I shall, therefore, explore how far the market is an accurate way of describing the new relations which I have described and which the government is promoting. First, it is argued that the market is a useful metaphor because it reflects a set of relationships which have not always prevailed in education but which might and should prevail if educational goals are to be reached. Thus, the school, and the teachers in that school, provide a service to a set of individuals. As with any service, the recipients are the best judges of whether that service meets their needs or wants. There is always the chance that the service might be sloppy or off target. There is a need, therefore, to provide a way in which the recipients can demonstrate dissatisfaction, mainly by taking their custom elsewhere. The argument, underlying the Educational Reform Act of 1988, is that in the past the recipients of the educational service have not had the opportunity to protest in the most appropriate manner, unless they were rich enough to pay for private education. The teachers got what they were given — the teachers and their employers were 'in the driving seat'. Under the new arrangements the recipients can object through availing themselves of the new opportunities to choose. The providers must meet the wishes of the clients, otherwise they will lose the income necessary to stay open. 'Market' is contrasted with top down planning; it represents consumer, as against bureaucratic, power.

Second, the metaphor of the market emphasises the importance of choice and the conditions for the exercise of rational choice. Imagine the archetypal market, a set of fruit and vegetable stalls. The customer is able to examine the different fruits, their quality and their prices.

They can decide whether they want several cheap apples or one excellent one — or, indeed, given the prices, whether to buy oranges instead. Paces are kept down because otherwise the customer will purchase elsewhere; but quality is kept up because otherwise the customer will not purchase at all. Fashions change for all sorts of reasons; the interest in bananas gives way to the interest in kiwi. Thus, since the customer knows best, the merchant has to be sensitive to changes in taste and fashion. Choice requires different items to choose from, but to choose rationally the chooser needs basic information about those items: the cost and the quality.

Third, 'the market' assumes the importance of competition in obtaining maximum benefit. Thus, in order to sell the product to the choosy purchaser, providers will strive to out-do the other providers in establishing lower prices or higher quality products. Furthermore, given the 'positional good' granted by a good education (by that I mean the credits obtained by education which can be swapped for good jobs and social position), then the recipient will compete with other potential recipients for the limited number of high quality products. In the fruit market they come early in the morning; in education they study late at night or pay higher fees for attendance at the most prestigious schools or universities.

Fourth, the 'perfect market' assumes that people will look after their own self-interest, indeed pursue their own self interest. If they choose not to go to the market in time to get the best fruit, then that is because they prefer to stay in bed. Early rising is a price not worth paying. Students similarly may choose immediate pleasure to the postponement of pleasure necessary for winning the educational competition — that is their choice. The market enables them to take that kind of responsibility.

These then seem to be the characteristics of educational processes and the ideal educational framework picked out by the market metaphor. Education is a commodity which can be bought or sold like any other commodity. It is much in demand because of the 'positional good' it can purchase. Since people are motivated by pursuing their own interest, there will always be a demand for the commodity. Teachers are there simply to provide it and thus to provide a service that people, in the light of their understanding of their own interests, ask for. What is needed for people to be able to choose wisely or rationally is simply the right kind of information about the quality of the commodity and about the price one has to pay for it. The government's responsibility is to ensure the framework for these market forces to operate fairly: namely, (i) schools, so that no one will be prevented from receiving an education, (ii) choice of schools, so that they can act on their judgement about relative values of the services provided, (iii) accurate information about the schools, so that, in the light of their values and desires, parents or students can be rational in their choices

Furthermore, beneath this way of conceiving the relationship between teacher and learner are certain assumptions of a philosophical kind about society and the nature of individuals within that society, about what is worthwhile and how we decide what is of most worth, about expert knowledge and access to that knowledge, about the processes of Teaming and how those processes might be evaluated. Thus, the world is the aggregate of individuals who are motivated chiefly by the pursuit of their own self-interest. Only they, in the final analysis, know what is good for them — there are no experts in educational ends. But, in the light of that self-knowledge, each individual needs accurate information about the public services which lead to that personal fulfilment. Such knowledge relates to quality of the service and to its cost, both of which can be objectively measured and clearly stated. Does it provide a product at a cost or sacrifice that makes it worthwhile? The teachers simply provide those services; their knowledge is essentially technical, an expertise in delivering the means not in determining the ends. The common good is essentially the aggregate of the individual goods, and is achieved by everyone pursuing his own self-interest. Not all can succeed as well as the others. But in trying to beat the others, all will gain more of what is wanted.

Criticisms of the Market Metaphor

There are three criticisms I want to make of the 'market' as a suitable metaphor for the educational system or of educational relationships, although it is important also to bear in mind the weaknesses of the educational system to which the introduction of the market metaphor has served to draw our attention. Educational discourse is necessarily permeated with metaphor. But the problem with any metaphor is that, whilst being appropriate to the situation in some respects, it none the less distorts it in others. In this case there is more distortion than appropriateness.

Decrease in the Benefits for All

An assumption behind creating market conditions for the distribution of educational opportunities is, not that it is worthwhile in itself, but that it is the most suitable mechanism for delivering an improved distribution of education for everyone. There are links here to the laissez-faire economic theory which argues that if all seek to maximise their wealth, all will benefit from the trickle down effect — richer people demand more services or have to invest their money. Similarly, the selfish pursuit of one's own positional good by some will benefit everyone in so far as the schools will improve their performance for everyone to attract an increasing number of potential purchasers. The total is more than the sum of the parts.

There is a limited justification for saying this. Thus, in the absence of certain market features, namely, a range of provision from which parents might choose, the dissatisfied parent cannot demonstrate dissatisfaction in the most significant way — namely, by removing the child to another school. Schools should be responsive to parental concerns and there is a danger of bureaucratic planning which simply gets it wrong. Thus, talk about the market is often a reaction to insensitive top-down planning and the assertion that parents should be partners in the education of their children — with a penalty clause attached to those schools that resist.

Nonetheless, the market is severely limited as a model for delivering education even within a social context in which all individually seek the best positional good for their children and in which schools, acting autonomously within this market economy of schooling, seek their best advantage vis-a-vis the other schools. Separate parents seeking the optimal positional good for their respective children will seek a system of schooling which puts them at an advantage over other children — let us say, a selective system in which the majority fails. The child of parent A (in, say, going to the selective grammar school) will gain more than if the children of the two families remain together (in, say, the non-selective comprehensive) but the child of parents B may lose disproportionately, losing interest and self-confidence and possibly turning in his or her disappointment to crime. As improved positional good might be more than overshadowed by a decrease in overall good of A and B put together, which indirectly will then affect A (more money has to be spent on crime prevention, for example). Thus, in opting out of local government control, certain schools gain financially but others lose out and the overall good amongst the schools is less. Indeed, this is empirically the case. Opted out schools are now in a position to select parents, and thus exclude those who normally would have gone to that school. The pursuit of positional good by one leads to the denial of positional good to others, and the schools, having to respond to the individual's pursuit of positional good, is not able to assess what the overall good is for all potential participants. In other words, cooperation might lead to the greatest good of the greatest number, but the pursuit of the individual good in a competitive system will likely lead to a position which benefits some without reference to the effect on others — and thus to a deteriorated situation from the point of view of both the loser and the dispassionate bystander. These considerations are clearly relevant to a society which is increasingly divided between the materially successful and the failures who, in their alienation and disillusionment, threaten that material success.

Misconception of Education

A more fundamental criticism must be directed against the underlying concept of education, which is reflected in the use of language. Thus, to conceive of education as a commodity to be bought and sold, as a positional good which can be swapped for social and economic advantage, ignores what might be regarded as the intrinsic value which is attributed to the activities and to the processes which the word 'education' picks out. Education refers to those activities concerning the development of the mind — the capacity to think intelligently, to engage imaginatively with problems, to behave sensitively and with empathy towards other people. It is essentially concerned with the life of the mind, and thus with how each person learns to participate actively in the traditions of intellect, imagination and behaviour that we have inherited. A policy of *educational* provision would reflect what these different traditions are, what public forms of understanding we need to master to make sense of the world both physical and social, and what we need to do to enter into these forms of understanding — how best we might acquire them through Teaming.

Therefore, a more appropriate metaphor than 'the market' is that of Oakeshott (1972) who likens education to the initiation into the conversation which takes place between the generations of mankind in which the new generation hears and is introduced to the voice of poetry and of philosophy, of science and of history, of art and of religion. These are the voices through which we have come to understand what it means to be human — one might say the conversation, always continuing, through which that humanity has been defined. The role of the teacher in such initiation is one of mediating particular stages of that conversation and of helping the young learner to participate in it. To that extent the teacher is an authority, and education, at least at the beginning, is not a democratic affair. The philosophy of choice for those who are in a state of ignorance, and whose tastes remain unformed, is empty.

Distorted View of Human Nature and the Relation of the Individual to Society

Perhaps, however, the most important defect in the market metaphor and the underlying educational philosophy is the assumption they make about human nature and the relation of the individual to others and to the state. The kind of educational arrangements one makes and the content of that education presuppose a view, a theoretical position, about what makes people tick and what is worthwhile pursuing. Behind all education is an idea of human nature, and that idea can be, and often is, an impoverished one.

Education is the initiation into worthwhile activities — into those kinds of knowing, understanding, appreciating, imagining and doing, which have value. For that reason, educational arguments are ethical, arguments about the life worth living, the personal qualities and virtues worth acquiring, the knowledge and understanding which will help the teacher to find what is valuable. But answers to those questions must lie in a view of what it is to be human. People with different views about human nature will arrive at different educational philosophies. For example, those who, within a particular religious tradition, are convinced that human nature is corrupt, will not espouse the child-centred ideas of Froebel or Pestalozzi. Those who believe that people are but complicated machines will see no wrong in reprogramming them to function more effectively within the overall social system. Those who think that people act only from self-interest will welcome a market system which regulates that pursuit of self-interest. Those who argue that the intellect is a fixture we are born with, largely unaffected by Teaming, will want a system which differentiates between those who are intelligent and those who are not. And those who, sceptical of any objective arguments for deciding what is humanly desirable, will leave questions of what is worthwhile to the customer, not to the experts within an educational tradition.

Of course, our understanding of human nature changes as insights are gained through advances in science or developments in the arts or arguments in philosophy and in theology. But that does not mean that at we can be freed from our commitment in practice, whether intelligently engaged in or not, to a philosophical position. Both the aims of education and the processes of teaching and Teaming, through which those aims are achieved, involve a set of ideas which can be articulated, criticised, improved or rejected. And, in so doing, one comes back to those ethical considerations which reflect what it means to be human.

Similarly at stake is the relation of the state to individual improvement through education. If there is no such thing as society, only an aggregate of individuals, then the pursuit of positional good is more significant than the apprenticeship to the values and activities of one's wider community. Enterprise becomes an important virtue. Competition rather than co-operation provides the social and economic background to the formulation of educational aims and programmes. And the state becomes the regulator of the ensuing competition.

Certainly, the application of the market metaphor to education reflects a distinctive view of human nature and of how the individual relates to the regulator of that market, the state. Taken to its logical conclusion, the source of what is worthwhile lies in the tastes of the consumers, not in a tradition of educational thinking. The authority of the teacher over what is worth learning gives way to the authority of consumer choice or of those who, empowered by the state, can impose what they think should be taught. The search for meaning, the engagement in argument, the enjoyment of discovery, the struggle to gain insight, which characterise the transaction between teacher and learner, give way to the attainment of measurable outcomes and behaviours. The 'useful' replaces the 'intrinsically worthwhile', performance indicators replace judgement of educated persons. The attempt to understand, which is exercised by each in different ways, with different degrees of success and at different speeds, is scored high or low on a standardised measure which makes a mockery of that attempt. Indeed, those who have to struggle are no longer welcome — not selected by schools which have power to select or excluded by schools which want to be attractive to the consumer — because they will not perform well against the public indicators of success.

Conclusion

There are various ways in which business and education interconnect. I have started with several examples. But this interconnection gives rise to a series of questions which need to be addressed.

(i) How might we give a comprehensive account (a typology) of the different ways in which they interconnect, as a basis for examining more closely the ethical questions which arise?

(ii) Are there differences in aims between education and business which set limits to how an understanding of the one might shed light on the understanding of the other?

(iii) Are the aims and values sufficiently different that the aims of the one might be distorted by too close a partnership?

(iv) More fundamentally, is there a danger that the partnerships (of many different kinds) are achieved through a shift in language which impoverishes our understanding?

References

Oakeshott, M. (1972) 'Education: the Engagement and the Frustration', in Fuller, T. (Ed.) *Michael Oakeshott and Education*, Yale University Press.

Peters, R.S. (1965) *Ethics and Education, Allen* & Unwin.

Pring, R. (1995) *Closing the Gap: Liberal Education and Vocational Preparation*, London: Hodder & Stoughton.

Chapter Twenty One

An Analysis of Education Needs Among Sales Professionals in a Multi-National Nutrition Company

R. A. Richardson
K. Morss
C. Russell
A. E. de Looy

Introduction

"The more dynamic organisations also take a different approach to encouraging training provision which contributes to lifetime learning: they concentrate on developing a strategic approach to business in organisations, rather than encouraging training per se" (Department of Employment, 1994).

This case study illustrates the type of partnership which can be formed between Higher Education (HE) and industry. The formative stage, discussed here enabled both partners to clarify expectations and meet head on apprehensions. Setting educational strategies in the market place has resulted in a deeper analysis of our product, our motivations and our working practices. It has also allowed a greater understanding of how knowledge and understanding of academic subjects needs to be packaged in a directly applicable, market and sales orientated way. What initially seemed like academic compromise of a proportion unmentionable became a challenging and rewarding lesson.

An international nutrition company with a history of providing nutrition education to its sales executives in the belief that subject knowledge is essential to establish credibility of its staff with well-informed clients such as clinicians, dietitians, pharmacists, nurses and other healthcare professionals

The Company became concerned about their approach to the training of new sales employees. There were two major reasons for their concern. First was the financial cost of their existing four-week residential training course which was held in comfortable surroundings at centrally-located venues. Employees were required to travel considerable distances from all parts of the United Kingdom to the appointed venue, returning home each weekend at the Company's expense.

The second area of concern was the appropriateness of the amount, level and complexity of the nutritional materials and issues delivered to employees with respect to their ability to market and sell Company products. The broad aims of the course were to bring a uniform level of nutritional knowledge to the sales force and to focus on areas of basic, clinical and infant nutrition as well as marketing. Course evaluation was unstructured, but a common criticism was that too much theoretical information was delivered in a didactic fashion. Other weaknesses highlighted were that the programme was too intensive and there was a lack of integration of nutritional content with sales issues. The mode of course delivery was predominantly didactic. A summative assessment of knowledge was by closed-book examination given ten weeks after the training course. This assessment primarily tested information recall rather than understanding or deep learning.

The Department of Dietetics and Nutrition, Queen Margaret College (QMC) and Cow and Gate Nutricia entered into a partnership and carried out a 'Needs Analysis' to:

- develop a method whereby the minimal level of nutritional knowledge required by employees could be identified;
- establish the level of knowledge and understanding necessary to effectively promote and sell company products;
- consider the teaching and learning skills required by company employees;
- make recommendations on how the need for nutritional knowledge may be most efficiently and effectively met and maintained.

Needs Analysis — Methodology and Results

The methodology chosen comprised 4 elements:

- a questionnaire to Company staff.
- case study analysis to Company staff to provide information on level of nutritional awareness and understanding.
- thirty second theatre to illicit needs of sales executives in simulated encounters.
- work observation/shadowing.

Questionnaire

A structured questionnaire was circulated to as many company personnel as possible. The return rate of 75% included 18 out of 18 from Sales Executives, 6 out of 7 from Regional Sales Managers, 9 out of 9 from Company Nutritionists, 5 out of 13 from Administrative Staff and 14 out of 20 from Head Office Managers. The questionnaire was designed to:

- obtain information on length of service and educational background of each employee;
- identify the importance of nutrition education as perceived by company personnel;
- evaluate the strengths and weaknesses of the current nutritional education programme;
- assess the amount of subject knowledge expected of company employees by clients;
- register staff comments on how, when and where further nutrition education programmes should be developed.

This paper will focus on the needs and the programme developed for sales executives. A summary of results from 18 Sales Executives shows the length of service ranged from 3 months to 19 years (mean 4.6 years). A third of sales executives had been with the Company for 5 years or more.

The educational background and employment history of this group was varied. Some individuals joined the company following a secondary education and early employment in sales (n=7,39%); others had a non-science degree and a sales background (n=3,17%). Almost half came with a strong science/nursing or dietetic/nutrition background which included work experience (n=8,44%). The diversity of education and experience is important to consider in the development of a nutrition education programme which should be sensitive and flexible to meet the learning needs and abilities of all individuals.

Sales executives unanimously considered nutrition education to be an important component of staff development. The company's provision and level of commitment to education was regarded as a strength. However, the weaknesses which emerged were that too much content was delivered too quickly, and that there was no assessment of understanding and its relationship with selling skills. A variety of learning strategies were suggested by respondents including workshops, practicals and group work which could take place at regional level.

Replies from the other groups of Company personnel concurred with the responses of sales executives, stressing the importance of nutrition education, and highlighting the strong company commitment to education. However, they stressed the need for a more appropriate programme with particular emphasis on the inter-relationship between sales and understanding of nutritional concepts.

The results of this questionnaire suggests that learning programmes should become more flexible and use a wider range of learning strategies in order to meet individual needs. Also that the materials should be highly focused on nutrition knowledge which participant learners could use immediately to boost sales. This was echoed at the executive board level for obvious reasons.

Case Studies

Case studies were used as a tool to evaluate understanding of nutrition amongst sales executives. In order to simulate problems sales executives will encounter in their 'world of work' case studies were developed by Company Nutritionists. Following a description of the case, questions were asked which required a justified true/false response. The questions were designed to test understanding of nutritional concepts and answers were given an 'understanding' score. When selecting the correct answer all individuals scored above 50% with a mean of 77% (range 63-94%). However, a consideration of the understanding score gave quite a different picture. Four individuals scored over 80% but 64% of the group (n=9) scored less than 50%. These results indicate that while the group are able to retain and recall information from training courses, they are lacking in their ability to understand basic concepts and to explain and move outside those areas which are not directly covered in the training course.

Thirty-second Theatre

The thirty-second theatre technique was used to address work-based problems. This method of exploring issues in a focused way allowed the role play to throw up areas of 'need'. As it simulates real life problems in a very active way the method also identifies needs which may or may not be nutritionally related. The '30-second theatre' exercise involved workshops with two autonomous groups, the Sales Executives and the Regional Nutritionists.

Prior to the workshop all participants were circulated with information explaining the exercise and the importance of their participation.

A blank pro-forma was sent to each individual who was asked to write a brief scenario based on a common problem encountered during work. The scenarios were then selected and acted out by carrying forward the dialogue, i.e., 'what came next'. Lively discussions of common problems ensued.

The key outcomes of this exercise were:

- sales executives felt confident and secure in their product knowledge;
- that weaknesses in nutritional knowledge could often and were be compensated by selling skills;
- some thought a greater depth of subject knowledge might increase the nutritional awareness of clients;
- confirmation that there was a need for good inter-personal skills;
- there should be more integration of nutrition education and selling skills in future training programmes;
- sales executives felt a need to know about recent product development, clinical trials and research, and especially about the rationale of research programmes;
- sales executives identified a need to know about the general running and infrastructure of hospitals and about the remits of the healthcare professionals they encountered.

Shadowing

During the needs analysis a number of shadowing exercises were carried out, which permitted some insight into the client encounters experienced by sales executives. During this exercise, a specific remit was to identify nutritional questions/issues arising in the 'field'.

The first sales executives shadowed was from a clinical background and was manning an exhibition stand at a study day where most of the delegates were nurses. A great deal of interest was shown in Company products, and delegates asked penetrating nutritional questions related to energy levels, taste and acceptance.

The second individual shadowed was from a background in infant nutrition. This person interacted with senior nursing staff at a children's hospital in discussing ready-to-use infant formulae. There was also a visit to a Health Board Supplies Unit. The shadowing exercise illustrated that questions of nutrition are addressed to sales personnel who are expected to act in an advisory capacity.

Outcome

The results were presented to the Company together with a plan for meeting needs as identified. A student led approach seemed to best suit this group of busy mature learners. After a series of meetings during which Company members expressed apprehension over their perceived loss of control over training a pilot was agreed.

As a result of the of information obtained through the needs analysis, a new programme of delivery has been designed, implemented and is undergoing long term evaluation. The programme includes the following key elements: Interactive independent learning packs (paper-based) have been designed around problem-solving activities, many of which are case-based. New sales staff (the students') are given explicit instructions in the use of the packs, and are asked to work through them in their own time. The content of each pack focuses on a basic concept in nutrition and interrelates closely with Company and competitor products. The packs are supported by key texts, Company literature and by Company Nutritionists (mentors). This material is designed to facilitate understanding of nutritional concepts, to relate that understanding to Company products, to develop problem-solving skills and to relate these to the workplace. It is also important to bear in mind that a critical end point for both sales and Company executives is the maximisation of sales.

After the 'students' have completed their assigned packs, they come together for workshops led by Company Nutritionists and an external advisor. The workshops are group led and present additional case-based problem solving activities which expand upon the ideas in the packs.

These workshops thus provide a forum for group discussion of issues arising from independent study or of new issues brought forward on the day. Because participants are pre-informed, workshops make effective and efficient use of contact time with nutritional experts. Time is not consumed by mere dissemination of facts.

Additionally, workshops provide a valuable experiential atmosphere for re-inforcing learning by application. They facilitate development of transferable skills such as group work, leadership, co-operation, communication and organisation, within the context of work. In addition, they provide an opportunity for informal exchanges of ideas and formation of working relationships.

In order to consolidate and extend areas explored in the learning packs, workshops and tutorials are held at quarterly regional meetings. Additionally, more focused areas of clinical nutrition relating to the promotion or launch of Company products are studied at bi-annual Company conferences.

Following completion of each learning pack (6 in series), the student is required to undertake a summative assessment. These assessments are designed not only to test the students understanding of pack materials but also to build on experiential learning. The workplace is often used as the focus of the assessment theme. Each assessment is fully explained to 'students' and marked using a standard pro-forma. Results are subsequently discussed with student and the final mark agreed. This method of assessment is a significant improvement on knowledge recall in that it seeks to draw upon and reinforce embedding the understanding of nutrition in daily practice.

Evaluation of the Programme

On completion of each module 'students' are required to complete an evaluation form. This form seeks to evaluate the learning material in terms of pack presentation, content and the relevance and importance of supporting workshops and tutorials. During one of the workshop sessions time was allocated for completion of an evaluation form and 'students' were assured that these forms would remain confidential. All participants completed an evaluation form.

Two cohorts (total n = 17) of new sales executives have now completed and evaluated two packs in the series of six (Pack 1 = Malnutrition; the identified nutritional concept is basic digestion and absorption, carbohydrate metabolism; Pack 2 = Elderly and Cancer; the identified nutritional concept is energy). Overall, the presentation and style of pack materials was well received by 'students'. They found pack materials logical and easy to understand (82%) and had no difficulty in reading the text (82%). In terms of pack content (malnutrition pack) 13 'students' and 14 'students' (elderly/cancer pack) found the materials were pitched at a level 'appropriate to their needs'. Also worthy of note is that almost all 'students' found the pack activities varied and interesting (88%) and 'students' considered these activities reinforced the nutritional concepts highlighted in the standard textbook (n = 16 out of 17). Finally, all 'students' felt that the workshops used to support packs built on and complemented learning materials.

The results from the evaluation form were also reflected in the 'students' performance in workshops. These workshops were designed to assess level of understanding of pack materials. During the early stages of a workshop session 'Students" tended to underrate their own level of nutritional knowledge and understanding. However, as the workshop sessions progressed they clearly became more confident when talking with their peers and colleagues about nutrition. Indeed, they were able to use their theoretical knowledge to solve practice based problems thereby demonstrating an understanding of pack materials.

In order to illustrate the level of understanding and confidence achieved by the group, two examples of the learner's experiences are cited:

i) At the beginning of the course one individual felt that whilst she had spent time working through the learning pack she still 'knew nothing'. Yet this individual actively participated and answered well throughout workshop sessions. Through problem solving she clearly demonstrated an understanding of basic gastro-intestinal physiology, an area she had previously highlighted as an area of particular weakness.

The above example shows how learners tend to undervalue their achievements when using the 'Open and Flexible' approach. Thus highlighting the importance of adequate and appropriate support for 'students'.

The second example focus on group activity:

ii) In order to bring together materials from two packs 'students were asked to work in groups and develop a nutritional strategy that would improve patient care. The quality of work produced was outstanding not only in terms of nutritional information but also with regard to the insight as to what practical limitations there may be in implementing their strategy.

In summary, the level of understanding, maturity and confidence exhibited by 'students' far exceeded the expectations of both trainers and members of the Company management team.

Discussion

The production of these learning packs is expensive and required initial investment. It therefore essential that there were significant efficiency gains in terms of finances and human resources. Less time is now spent by Company personnel in course administration, preparation and delivery of lecturers and workshops. This permits reinvestment of time by Company personal in areas more closely related to generating business.

Apart from the positive educational evaluation other benefits of this programme are that sales executives are no longer required to spend long periods away from their region and customers. Such extended periods of absence may have a detrimental effect on the profile of the sales executive, the Company's profile as well as diminishing the volume of business. Additionally, the sales executive is now in a position to use the 'workplace' as a focus for learning allowing them to embed their theoretical knowledge into daily practice. These learning packs are the sales executives own property and they may refer to or insert additional materials at any time.

This educational product has been well received by Company management and employees. The evaluation is ongoing and future plans include the further development of 'in-house' materials. Additionally, it is planned to adapt materials for use in post graduate education programmes of other healthcare professionals. Thus the educational; programme can be used as a marketing tool by the Company in its own right.

This partnership has benefited both parties. It has been a significant learning exercise for HE staff both in terms of "selling education' and demonstrating that the benefits of learning arranged around problem solving and case study material can be used effectively.

Index

Samuel M. Natale
Arend J. Sandbulte Professor
in Management and Ethics
College of St. Scholastica
Duluth, Minnesota
&
Visiting Fellow
Kellogg College
University of Oxford
England